THE

COMMUNITY

AND

RACIAL CRISES

edited by
DAVID STAHL
FREDERICK B. SUSSMANN
NEIL J. BLOOMFIELD

PRACTISING LAW INSTITUTE
NEW YORK, N. Y.

FOREWORD

Protest demonstrations, civil disobedience and riots are presenting a new challenge to many cities and communities across the nation. Heightened racial tensions have created a pressing need for wise leadership and for willingness to listen and to learn new techniques in public administration.

To help develop listening, learning, and decision-making skills, the Practising Law Institute applied its experience in conducting programs on the practical application of the law to the development of a special three-day forum devoted to The Community and Racial Crises. The forum was held in New York City in December, 1964. It was attended by a distinguished panel and participating audience which included municipal, state, and federal officials and attorneys, police chiefs, public prosecutors, and other law enforcement officers, professors of law, and representatives of community relations agencies and of civil rights groups.

This book grows out of that forum. Both were made possible by the generous assistance of the New World Foundation and the Rockefeller Brothers Fund.

Highly qualified specialists discuss the causes and legal framework of protest, the constitutional and statutory protection against discrimination, the Federal, State and local agencies active in civil rights matters, and the resources available to aid communities in dealing with racial problems.

The basic method of presentation is a dialogue between professors of law and Federal, State and local officials, police officers, and representatives of civil rights groups, clarified and brought up to date by editorial comment and detailed statements by the participants on the underlying issues. The value of the book lies not in any final resolution of the problem of integrating the Negro community into the mainstream of American life, but in its lessons for those in positions of responsibility on dealing more effectively with highly charged, local racial problems.

To those who presented our forum, to the authors and publishers who graciously permitted us to reprint their material, and to the New World Foundation and the Rockefeller Brothers Fund, the Institute expresses its profound appreciation.

HAROLD P. SELIGSON,
Director

EDITORS' PREFACE

The Community and Racial Crises has been written to aid public officials and civic leaders in dealing with the complex and everchanging problems of race relations in the latter half of the 1960's.

With the civil rights struggle being waged and argued in and around streets, schools, and municipal councils, the choice between peaceful progress on the one hand and needless violence on the other is usually at the local level. Many communities have been unprepared for "sudden" demands for local action. By presenting here the experiences of those who have dealt with these problems, we hope to prepare others to meet racial crises more effectively.

The Community and Racial Crises illustrates the ways in which community and civic leaders have made difficult decisions in critical situations. The emphasis is on techniques for achieving peaceful and orderly change.

Experience teaches that effective communication with the protesting groups is indispensable. However, the practical problems community leaders face in establishing and re-establishing interracial cooperation can be resolved only when meaningful communication is accompanied by meaningful programs. For this reason, one section of this book details the Federal, State and local resources available to remedy the underlying causes of racial problems.

Yet, crises may develop despite the presence of relatively good interracial communications and seemingly effective long-range plans. The kind of racial violence that erupted in several cities during the summers of 1964 and 1965 dramatizes the growing set of problems facing urban communities.

The book opens with "A Tale of Three Cities," in which the fast-moving events of racial crises in Savannah, Ga., New York City, and Chester, Pa. are described and then analyzed and discussed by the mayors and other responsible officials and community leaders concerned, as well as by the forum participants.

v

The three crises illustrate many different types of problems and attempted solutions. These are then treated more systematically in the remainder of the book. The symptomatic manifestations and their handling are the subject of Parts II and III, "Laws Governing Demonstrations and Other Forms of Protest" and "Racial Tensions and the Police"; the attack upon the deeper-rooted causes, of Parts IV and V, on Federal, State and local resources for resolving racial crises and eliminating discrimination. Finally, the Chairman's summary and the discussion of continuing problems in Part VI attempt to highlight the lessons for the future of the reviewed experiences and attendant dialogue, in the light of even more recent events.

Unless otherwise indicated, the statements and discussion come from the December, 1964 forum, and the descriptions of speakers give their positions at that time.

At the core of this book is the message that to avoid crisis situations, community leaders must make every possible effort to convince the Negro community, by word and deed, that fruitful steps to improve their situation are being taken.

None of these problems will be resolved quickly. The kaleidoscopic patterns of racial crisis will force community leaders in the late 1960's to spend more time and energy than ever before in devising and implementing solutions to our interracial problems. *The Community and Racial Crises* offers no foolproof formula for resolving these problems, but its detailed analyses should help speed the implementation of programs and policies which will benefit both the Negro population and the larger urban community.

DAVID STAHL
FREDERICK B. SUSSMANN
NEIL J. BLOOMFIELD

vi

TABLE OF CONTENTS

vii

CONTENTS

PART II

LAWS GOVERNING DEMONSTRATIONS AND OTHER FORMS OF PROTEST

PART IV

LAWS AGAINST DISCRIMINATION, FEDERAL, STATE, AND LOCAL; ENFORCEMENT PROBLEMS

PART V

FEDERAL, STATE AND LOCAL RESOURCES IN RESOLVING RACIAL CRISES

PART VI

SUMMARY

APPENDICES

ABOUT THE CONTRIBUTORS

The Practising Law Institute acknowledges its deep gratitude to the following distinguished panel members and other participants whose work contributed to this volume*:

Chairman: DAVID STAHL, City Solicitor, Pittsburgh, Pennsylvania**; Professor of Law, University of Pittsburgh School of Law; former Executive Director, Lawyers' Committee for Civil Rights Under Law; former Attorney General, Commonwealth of Pennsylvania; Chairman, PLI Special Forum; co-editor.

JOSEPH M. BAIL, Chief of Police, Chester, Pennsylvania.

BERL I. BERNHARD, Executive Director, Lawyers' Committee for Civil Rights Under Law; former Staff Director, United States Commission on Civil Rights.

DAVID W. CRAIG, City Solicitor, Pittsburgh, Pennsylvania**; former President, American Society of Planning Officials.

ROBERT G. DIXON, JR., Professor of Law, George Washington University.

JOHN H. DOYLE III, Patterson, Belknap & Webb, New York City (on leave); Assistant Director, Lawyers' Committee for Civil Rights Under Law.

JOHN G. FEILD, Director, Community Relations Service, United States Conference of Mayors; former Executive Director, The President's Committee on Equal Employment Opportunity; former Executive Director, Michigan Fair Employment Practices Commission.

HAROLD C. FLEMING, Acting Deputy Director, Community Relations Service, United States Department of Commerce; Executive Vice-President, Potomac Institute.

---

* Unless otherwise indicated, the descriptions give the contributors' positions at the time of the PLI Forum.

** Mr. David Stahl was City Solicitor of Pittsburgh during the time of his co-editorship and at publication, but not in December, 1964, when he presided as Forum Chairman; at that time Mr. David Craig was Pittsburgh City Solicitor.

xiii

GEORGE H. FOWLER, Chairman, New York State Commission for Human Rights.

JAMES H. GORBEY, Mayor, Chester, Pennsylvania.

JACK GREENBERG, Director-Counsel, National Association for the Advancement of Colored People Legal Defense and Educational Fund.

HAROLD H. GREENE, Chief, Appeals and Research Section, Civil Rights Division, United States Department of Justice.

DR. JOHN GRIFFIN, Director of Conciliation Services, Community Relations Service, United States Department of Commerce.

LAWRENCE JACOBSON, Assistant City Solicitor, Chester, Pennsylvania.

JOHN C. LANKENAU, Attorney, New York City; former Assistant United States Attorney, Southern District of New York.

STANLEY H. LOWELL, Chairman, N. Y. City Commission on Human Rights.

J. ROBERT LUNNEY, Attorney, Shearman & Sterling, New York City; member, Lawyers' Committee for Civil Rights Under Law.

MALCOLM MacLEAN, Mayor, Savannah, Georgia.

H. A. MacNEILLY, Administrative Assistant to Mayor, Chester, Pennsylvania.

JAMES A. MADISON, United States Office of Economic Opportunity.

LAWRENCE C. MALICK, Staff member, Community Relations Service, United States Conference of Mayors.

JULIUS MANGER, JR., Executive Vice-Chairman, National Citizens' Committee for Community Relations; Chairman, Manger Hotels, Inc.

ERIC M. MANN, Field Secretary, Congress of Racial Equality.

GALEN MARTIN, Executive Director, Kentucky Commission on Human Rights.

ROBERT B. McKAY, Professor of Law, Associate Dean, New York University School of Law.

PHILIP MCMUNIGAL, City Solicitor, Chester, Pennsylvania.

MELVIN MISTER, Staff member, Community Relations Service, United States Conference of Mayors.

DR. JOHN A. MORSELL, Assistant Executive Director, National Association for the Advancement of Colored People*.

GLEN R. MURPHY, Research Consultant, International Association of Chiefs of Police.

ROBERT J. O'CONNELL, Assistant Professor of Law, Marquette University School of Law.

JOHN M. PRATT, Counsel, Commission on Religion and Race, National Council of Churches.

SOL RABKIN, Director, Legal Department, Anti-Defamation League, B'nai B'rith.

GEORGE SCHERMER, Human Relations Consultant, Former Executive Director, Philadelphia Human Relations Commission; Former Executive Director, Mayor's Interracial Committee, Detroit.

SHIRLEY A. SIEGEL, Assistant New York State Attorney General, in charge, Civil Rights Bureau.

WILLIAM L. TAYLOR, General Counsel, United States Commission on Civil Rights.

RT. REV. MONSIGNOR JOHN D. TOOMEY, Pastor, St. James Church, Savannah, Georgia.

GERALD DAVID WHITE, General Counsel, Michigan Civil Rights Commission.

JOHN R. WING, Attorney, Shearman & Sterling, New York City.

JOSEPH P. WITHERSPOON, Professor of Law, University of Texas School of Law.

LOUIS M. ZIMMERMAN, Chief, Conciliation Services, N. Y. City Commission on Human Rights.

---

* Dr. Morsell's paper was prepared subsequent to the Forum, especially for this publication.

ABOUT THE EDITORS

Assisting David Stahl, Pittsburgh City Solicitor and Chairman of the PLI Special Forum, as co-editors, were Frederick B. Sussmann and Neil J. Bloomfield.

Mr. Stahl, also a Professor of Law at the University of Pittsburgh, is former Executive Director of the Lawyers' Committee for Civil Rights Under Law and former Attorney General of Pennsylvania. Mr. Sussmann, a member of the New York bar and Editor-in-Chief, Practising Law Institute, has written briefs for the American Civil Liberties Union in civil rights cases before the United States Supreme Court and other courts, and supervised, for the Institute, the PLI Special Forum. Mr. Bloomfield, a graduate of the Woodrow Wilson School of Public and International Affairs, Princeton University, has conducted a special study of segregation in the Philadelphia School District.

PART I

A TALE OF THREE CITIES

The material here presented illustrates a wide range of problems and attempted solutions. The crisis in Savannah, a city of the deep South, centered around public accommodations. The Mayor played a major role, supported by civic, business, and religious leaders. The crisis in New York involved employment policies. The municipal Commission on Human Rights played a central role. The crisis in Chester, Pennsylvania, a small northern city, involved alleged *de facto* school segregation. The Mayor and other public officials played the key roles.

The materials do not include everyone's reactions to these several disputes. Those who played major roles in shaping official reaction sketch the factual background and describe the alternatives that were considered as the crisis developed, and the factors which influenced the crucial decisions.

1.1 COMMUNITY CRISIS IN SAVANNAH

1.11 STATEMENT OF CRISIS

JOHN G. FEILD*

Savannah, Georgia, had a population of 149,200 in 1960. Located in Chatham County, with a total population of 188,000, the city has approximately 34% non-white citizens, as does the county.

The demonstrations of 1963 occurred within a context of rapid social change in this historic southern coastal city.

---

* Director, Community Relations Service, United States Conference of Mayors.

Savannah was the first city in Georgia to employ Negro policemen and firemen. Negroes have been actively registering and voting in Savannah for many years, and most public facilities were desegregated by 1960. The public schools began integration with the 12th grade in 1963-64 under a U.S. Circuit Court of Appeals order, and are continuing with the 11th grade this year. The NAACP is appealing the decision in the hope of getting a more sweeping court order.

Although some sit-ins during 1960 and 1961 had been accompanied by a prolonged 15-month boycott of local stores, as 1963 began Savannah's restaurants, hotels and motels were almost completely segregated. In June of 1963, desegregation of public accommodations became the central target of a series of demonstrations and sit-ins sponsored by the local NAACP and a local group known as the Crusade for Voters. Both groups had been involved in earlier protests.

During the first ten days of June, over 100 Negroes were arrested for trespassing in sit-ins at several major downtown restaurants. These arrests, personally ordered by the City Manager and the City Attorney, who were on the scene, were followed by a series of demonstrations and protests. The chronology of these events is briefly set down below:

June 11, 1963: Several hundred Negroes marched into city hall and crowded into council chambers for a conference with Mayor MacLean. The Crusade for Voters issued a 24-hour ultimatum to the Mayor "to get our freedom for us." At the same time, the Young Adult Council of the NAACP announced it would continue sit-ins.

That evening over 3,000 Negroes marched into the central business district. Forty-nine adults and many teen-agers were arrested. Peaceful marchers were not arrested. Arrests were for trespass in restaurants and disturbing the peace.

June 12, 1963: Three hundred Negroes marched into downtown Savannah.

June 13, 1963: The home of a Negro couple, Mr. and Mrs. Arnett Waters, was hit by rifle shots.

June 13, 1963: The Chamber of Commerce offered to negotiate. Hosea Williams, head of Crusade for Voters, publicly stated that he would not halt demonstrations unless talks with the Chamber of Commerce showed promise. A scheduled meeting between the Restaurant Association and the NAACP fell through.

2

June 14, 1963: The demonstrations were suspended following a Chamber of Commerce statement calling on operators of private businesses to integrate.

June 16, 1963: The press reported rumors that public accommodations would be integrated, and demonstrations were suspended for the weekend.

June 17, 1963: When negotiations broke down mass racial demonstrations were resumed. Mayor MacLean requested state aid. Governor Sanders dispatched 52 state patrolmen. Mayor MacLean indicated he might request martial law. No one was arrested but the papers reported that 600 had been arrested to date.

June 18, 1963: In local court actions Crusade for Voters and NAACP were enjoined from demonstrating at specific eating places.

June 19 and 20, 1963: Negroes demonstrated again, and the first violence occurred. Negroes threw bricks and bottles. Leaders of the Crusade for Voters were arrested along with 300 others.

Mayor MacLean publicly asked for an end to demonstrations. Hosea Williams, jailed leader of the demonstrations, was quoted in the press: "We are going to demonstrate until they accede to our demands or until we die."

June 21, 1963: New negotiations were arranged through civic and religious leaders, and once again demonstrations were suspended pending outcome of negotiations with restaurant operators.

June 24, 1963: Bishop Thomas J. McDonough announced that Catholic schools of the Savannah Diocese would be integrated in September.

June 27, 1963: Leaders of Crusade for Voters threatened to renew demonstrations which had been curtailed since June 23rd.

June 28, 1963: "Savannahians for Peaceful Progress," a new civic group, placed an advertisement in the Savannah *News* calling upon citizens to support store owners and businessmen if "they lead the way."

June 30 and July 1, 1963: The Board of Education approved a one-grade-a-year plan for school integration starting with the 12th grade.

July 5, 1963: Four hundred Negroes marched on the Chatham County jail to support Benjamin Clark, Crusade for Voters leader, who had been sentenced to 20 months or $1,500 fine.

July 6, 1963: A boycott of white merchants was announced following a mass meeting of 1,000 persons. On the same day thirty whites picketed to protest integration.

July 11, 1963: Racial violence erupted again when police and Negroes fought at several downtown intersections during a parade demonstration. Two Negroes were wounded by gunfire. Seventy-one persons were arrested. Some Negro leaders joined the City Manager in attempts to curb violence. Hosea Williams, leader of Crusade for Voters, was in jail under a peace warrant. His assistant, Benjamin Clark, led new demonstrations demanding Williams' release.

July 12, 1963: White segregationists undertook a march to "find out if white people have the same rights as Negroes."

July 13, 1963: Press reported "Savannah calm" after the disorder of July 11. Leon Cox, Georgia State Field Secretary for the NAACP, criticized the Savannah demonstrations as pointless.

July 15, 1963: Hosea Williams issued a plea from his jail cell to remain "nonviolent" and to cease massive street marches.

Savannah Negroes held a mass meeting, and threatened to resume marches if peace talks failed.

July 16, 1963: Negroes marched, but retired peacefully when stopped by City Manager and police.

A group of 100 white businessmen formed a working committee to settle local racial problems and announced they would negotiate with "responsible Negro leadership."

July 21, 1963: An estimated 2,000 whites attended a rally staged by the KKK.

August 2 and 3, 1963: White and Negro leaders announced that "an accord is near."

August 8, 1963: Press reported that over 50 Negroes had been convicted of trespass and fined $100 each for each offense. Over 100 remained in jail.

August 22, 1963: Hosea Williams announced that demonstrations were over.

4

Business leaders announced a plan to desegregate hotels, motels, and theaters by October 1st. Restaurant operators did not agree, but restaurants in hotels and motels would be open.

October 3, 1963: Integration of hotels and other public accommodations began without incident.

October 29, 1963: The KKK picketed the Savannah Theater and a tear gas bomb was exploded inside as theater integration began.

December 4, 1963: Eighteen Negroes sought court test of constitutionality of Georgia trespass law.

April 1, 1964: Savannah Chamber of Commerce membership voted to admit Negroes to membership by a substantial margin.

July 2, 1964: Congress passed the Civil Rights Act. Restaurants announced compliance with the law.

1.12 "WE THOUGHT THINGS WERE GETTING ALONG REASONABLY WELL"
MALCOLM MACLEAN*

In 1964, Savannah, the second largest city in Georgia, had desegregated many public facilities without any court actions. We thought things were getting along reasonably well. We had started in 1948 as the first city in Georgia to hire Negro policemen. We had desegregated the golf course and our parks. The auditorium, the library, the stadium, and the lunchroom at the airport were all desegregated, and we were proud of doing all this without lawsuits. In contrast, Atlanta fought desegregation of its airport lunchroom and its golf course through lawsuits. When the Freedom Rides started, we held conferences with the two bus stations in town, and without any publicity they desegregated their facilities. The desegregation of lunch counters presented a more difficult problem in Savannah. We met with the chain stores (mostly ten-cent stores and nationwide outfits) which had lunch counters. For a considerable length of time, we met with both the people who ran the stores and the Negro groups who were interested in desegregating the stores. After many meetings, the store operators said that they just were not going to do anything until Atlanta moved.

* Mayor of Savannah, Ga.

5

One man from a chain store said that he would not let the tail wag the dog, that they had fifteen stores in Atlanta and only four in Savannah, and they were not going to do a single thing until the Atlanta situation was resolved. That statement helped us to the extent, at least, that the Negro community knew that we had done everything possible and there was no way that we could get the management of the chain stores to change their minds.

We tried other avenues of approach which did not work out, and there was a cessation of hostilities until Atlanta desegregated. When the Atlanta desegregation announcement was made, we just went ahead. One of our difficulties was that the stores would not desegregate without a committee.

One of the conditions imposed by the stores was that they would not desegregate until a prominent group issued a favoring statement. After much thought, we turned to the clergy. The Episcopal Bishop formed a committee which in the face of many letters and calls that opposed it, issued a statement approving the move. These stores caused us a great deal more trouble than was necessary.

During this time the second of our bi-racial committees was established. The first one was established shortly after the bus desegregation. It was supposed to work in the area of public facilities, which was the only issue at that time, but it proved ineffective and was dissolved. We never formed another committee, because as long as the public was opposed to further desegregation the city administration could do nothing, even if it wished.

Negroes have always had the right to vote in Savannah. Four years ago there were 52,000 registered voters, and the Negro vote was 13,000. Now we have 72,000 registered voters, and between 18,000 and 20,000 are Negroes. Savannah's Negro leadership is not happy about the fact that voting records are no longer kept separately, because they cannot accurately tell the number registered.

Things seemed to be going along pretty well. Then in the spring of 1963, trouble began. We had a few small demonstrations by the NAACP in front of some movie houses. The head of one movie chain said he would not oppose desegregation; it depended on the other chain. The head of the other chain was asked to come to Savannah from his headquarters in Atlanta. He said that even though he personally objected to desegregating the movie houses, he would not officially fight it.

6

We proceeded to desegregate them. Unfortunately, some news media were uncooperative, and publicized the news. Publicity is often harmful to the accomplishment of transition in our society. The publicity built up a crowd. But we avoided dispersing people on the theory that if you cannot disperse Negroes, you cannot disperse whites. We have long since given up that theory. Now we disperse everybody, regardless of who they are. Not dispersing them right from the beginning was a mistake, because the first movie operator was intimidated.

In southern communities desegregating a place of business takes a lot of nerve. In Savannah, by the time we had desegregated the library, we had begun to worry about three or four other facilities, each with its attendant problems, and then we would have to start all over again. This is not an easy task. The movie operator backed out. He had never experienced such trouble before and he panicked.

There is a group in Savannah called the Crusade for Voters which is allied with the Southern Christian Leadership Conference. The leader of the Crusade for Voters told me, "We are going to start demonstrating". I answered, "What are you going to do that for? If you just take it easy, we'll have these problems worked out". He said, "The trouble with you is you're dealing with the wrong crowd of people". This conversation illustrates the power struggle that was going on within the Negro community. The question was whether the Southern Christian Leadership Conference or the NAACP would lead the desegregation in Savannah. We were in the middle as far as everyone was concerned.

Then the excitement really began. For the next five weeks we had two demonstrations a day, seven days a week, except for sporadic truces.

Actually, the demonstrations were quite peaceful, but we were unhappy about all this excitement. Finally we got the Chamber of Commerce to issue a statement saying they were in favor of both desegregation and the halting of demonstrations.

As far as the demonstrations were concerned, we had only two riots. The Reverend Andrew Young spoke to a group that had started marching down to the Holiday Inn, located in a primarily Negro district. The initial group picked up a lot of followers along the street, until they numbered about 2,000 or 3,000 people.

Some 274 of them went into the motel parking lot. The manager came out and asked them to move, but they refused.

We put a State Patrol cordon across the street so no more demonstrators could get in.

We had one more such incident when the demonstrators began to march on the jail. Some people had been arrested, so the same thing started again. Rocks and bottles began to fly. The night this incident occurred, there were little groups all over town. They held up traffic by lying in intersections. They would get up as soon as the police went to pick them up. They would run to another intersection and lie down there.

We were fortunate to have only two nights of rioting considering that we had five weeks of marching twice a day. The police did a fine job under trying circumstances.

We arrested people for trespassing and failing to obey traffic laws. But generally speaking the arrests were kept to a minimum and everything was reasonably well handled. While we were managing demonstrations with the police, negotiations were being conducted.

The objectives of the demonstrations were very simple—to desegregate the hotels, motels, bowling alleys, movie theaters, and restaurants—places over which the city officials felt they had no control. There is strong feeling in the South and in Georgia that people have a right to do what they want with their own property.

The object of these demonstrations was to bring the city to its economic knees. During the demonstrations, many people kept calling for stronger and stronger action. If the dispute had not been settled when it was, we would have had martial law the next day.

1.13 "This Could Never Happen Here"
Rt. Rev. Msgr. John D. Toomey*

When we look back a year or so to the events in Savannah, we begin to wonder why and how we got into that situation.

I was out of the city when the first riot occurred. We read in the papers about Birmingham, Montgomery, Jackson, Mississippi and other places, and we all said, "These things will never happen in Savannah. Things are too peaceful and there is too good a relationship

---

* Pastor, St. James Church, Savannah, Ga.

between the races." But they did happen, and when I read about the riot, I hurried back to town.

The Bishop, three other priests, and I had a meeting in the Bishop's office. It was suggested that we offer our services to the Mayor.

Two of us went to see the Mayor, and I think he was glad to have help. Things were not going well, and the Chamber of Commerce had just failed in their desegregation motion.

A few days later the Chancellor and I were invited to a meeting at City Hall. This was a general meeting, including restaurant and hotel people, the Negro leadership, and anybody else involved in the situation.

Despite the sentiments voiced by the speakers, we all went home and did nothing. One week later, when the demonstrations began again, we decided it was time to go underground, holding private meetings at the Manger Hotel.

At that time, the hotel and motel people were the only ones really interested in solving the problem. They were most sympathetic.

We met with some group practically every day. The Bishop played an important part; he offered his office for meetings, and on at least three occasions the Negro leadership came to these meetings. Everybody with whom we dealt during these negotiations and discussions was most anxious to arrive at a solution.

Lack of communication never entered into the problem. People started calling me as soon as I showed interest. Neither the Negro leadership nor the people who owned the public accommodations ever refused to attend a meeting.

For a time we had no more meetings between the Negro leadership and the public accommodations people, with the exception of the hotel people. The restaurant people came to the Chancery office one Sunday afternoon. The Bishop emphasized that we were not telling them what to do, that they were running their own business, and that we were simply pointing out the great danger that existed.

That was one of the reasons I got involved. For a long time I had felt that segregation was wrong, and yet I had done little about it. When the riots occurred, I felt that as a priest I had little chance of bringing worthwhile spiritual thoughts to people if their minds and their hearts were aroused.

9

Antagonisms that arise from racial prejudice are terrible and tragic. They defeat the spiritual progress of a soul. As pastor of a large suburban parish I felt that my own congregation probably had a lot of personal thoughts on this subject. Perhaps there were prejudices, but for the most part they kept open minds. We were desegregating our school at the same time. The announcement was made during the course of the racial turmoil, although I felt that we were unlikely to be heard in any responsive way while antagonisms were being stirred up. I became involved in order to bring peace and, of course, to increase justice and charity.

Meetings were held quite often. Some of the leaders who demonstrated were arrested. One City Court Judge put Hosea Williams in jail for two or three months by setting his bail at $30,000 so that he could not get out. Hosea was the leader of the SCLC and the Crusade for Voters.

Someone had to contact Hosea Williams, and therefore I began making daily visits to the jail, and became a sort of mediator. Whatever Hosea said was transmitted back to his leadership, and his representatives attended our meetings.

This went on for several weeks. We held meetings first with the hotel people alone. Then the Mayor organized what was called the Committee of One Hundred. The Mayor and I and a few others met with a Steering Committee about the first of July. I had never met most of these men, as I had not actively participated in civic activities.

I did not know what the economic interests were. I was not familiar with terms like a power structure, but I could explain what the Negro leadership wanted or at least what they would settle for temporarily, as well as the dangers of continued turmoil in the community.

Although I represented a moral entity, the Church, and although I felt the problem to be one of morality, I felt at this particular time that it was best not to emphasize the moral aspect but rather to get into the economics of the situation. When we met with the hundred businessmen at a meeting after the Steering Committee was formed, I tried to be as practical as possible, as did the Mayor. There were economic factors on both sides. The hotel and restaurant people were afraid of losing customers if they desegregated, and everybody else was afraid that if no settlement was made, the business of Savannah would deteriorate, as it had in places like Birmingham.

10

We emphasized practicalities, and the businessmen were wise enough to see the economic factors. That is not to say that they ignored the moral factor. They knew that segregation was basically wrong, yet they had to deal with economics. Subsequent meetings were held with various businesses, with the theater people, the bowling alley people, the restaurant people, and others.

We could not move the local restaurants who were afraid to do anything at this particular moment. But the hotel people did agree to desegregate their restaurants, as well as their other facilities.

We finally arrived at a solution on August 1, 1963, and presented it to the Negro leadership, which consisted at that time of the NAACP and the more militant faction, the Crusade for Voters. They accepted our package deal.

We felt things were under control about two days prior to the conclusion of our deal. Then I got word that Reverend Martin Luther King had been invited to come to Savannah for a rally on the night before these negotiations ended. I have the greatest respect for Dr. King and I applaud his receiving the Nobel Prize, but if Dr. King had come into Savannah at that particular moment, it might have ruined everything. Therefore, when I discovered that the Negro ministers with whom I had worked during the fight for desegregation were having a meeting to discuss the plans to bring in Dr. King, I decided to attend the meeting. I was received graciously, and I told them what we had in the offing, and asked them if they would ask Dr. King to put off his visit for perhaps a few months. They agreed. We went ahead with the negotiations and the agreement was completed for the hotels, motels, theaters and bowling alleys. It went into effect on October 1.

1.14 "WE KEPT IN CONSTANT TOUCH"
JULIUS MANGER, JR.*

By June of 1963 I had learned a good deal about desegregation, and the arguments for and against it in public accommodations. This knowledge proved most helpful in Savannah and other cities that I visited.

---

* Chairman, Manger Hotels, Inc., Executive Vice-Chairman of the National Citizens' Committee for Community Relations.

11

At this time I had just come from Charlotte, North Carolina, where we successfully spearheaded the drive to desegregate the downtown hotels and motels there.

I had already told our manager in Savannah to lead the drive in Savannah to desegregate hotels and motels.

During May and June of 1963 racial discord developed at an alarming rate in Savannah, where we owned a downtown hotel and a motel approximately five miles south of the city on Route 17.

In late June the Negro community was offered what was then known as the Dallas Plan, a much watered-down version of complete desegregation. The Negro leadership turned it down.

Mayor MacLean had appointed a Committee of One Hundred to study the situation and to make recommendations. By the first part of July, however, race relations had reached a point where no one would make private space available for a meeting between the races.

For nights on end there had been demonstrations which heightened the feelings between the white population and the Negro community. In that atmosphere I decided to allow our hotel to be used for secret meetings between the Negro leadership and the Executive Committee of One Hundred.

Meetings proved to be very satisfactory and there were a series of helpful discussions.

Unfortunately, one of the top Negro leaders was in jail at the time, and feelings ran so high among the Negro population that things got out of hand. That night there was rioting and the State Police were called in in large numbers in order to maintain order.

Our meeting, however, was the forerunner of others, and an agreement was reached with the leading hotels, motels and downtown theaters that desegregation would take place on October 2, 1963.

On the first day of desegregation, we virtually set up a command post to keep in touch with developments and watch for trouble. Mayor MacLean cooperated with our efforts and we knew how and where many special police were stationed around the hotels, motels and theaters. The Negro leadership also cooperated in furnishing us with the names of all the Negroes who were to be used in the first-day test. Furthermore, we knew how many Negroes would arrive in each establishment, the time of their arrival, and how long they would stay.

We kept in constant touch with all the facilities that were being desegregated, and by late evening we were sure that everything had gone smoothly and that there would be no trouble. It was a great day for Savannah, for it gave hope to the Negro community and prevented trouble in the months ahead.

In May of this year I again went to Savannah and met with Mayor MacLean and the Executive Committee of the Committee of One Hundred. At this meeting I pointed out that although Savannah was a leader in race relations among southern cities, there was a great deal more to be done in the near future if it were to remain free of trouble. I said that the Civil Rights Bill would almost certainly be enacted and that the Negroes would immediately test all public accommodation facilities for compliance.

At this meeting, it was mutually agreed that efforts should be initiated at once to get assurances of full compliance by all public accommodation facilities that were not yet desegregated. This was done subsequently. The rest is history.

In August 1964, Dr. Martin Luther King stated, "Savannah is the most desegregated city in the South". In October of this year, the National Convention of the Southern Christian Leadership Conference met there.

There were arguments for and against desegregation in public accommodations. The primary fear was loss of business. Owners feared that white customers would leave their facilities if Negroes came in. Experience has shown that where facilities were desegregated jointly, this did not happen because there was no segregated place for the white people to go. They had to stay somewhere and they generally stayed where they were before desegregation.

Another argument was that fights between the races would erupt. People would say, "We never had Negroes in our establishment before and if they come in, I'm sure we are going to have physical violence". Again experience has shown that if facilities are desegregated together, no physical violence will erupt. We knew, in fact, that in most cases the Negroes would be on their best behavior and desirous of making a good impression on the white community. As

13

it worked out, they were on their best behavior and there was no trouble.

Another fear was that large groups of Negroes would arrive at previously all-white facilities and alienate the white customers by sheer force of numbers. Again, experience told us that Negroes did not come into these facilities in large numbers except possibly in test cases. On the whole Negroes simply cannot afford to patronize public accommodation facilities in large numbers.

Another expressed fear was that Negroes would enter facilities poorly dressed or dirty and that this would cause white customers to leave. To counter this fear, I was able to point out immediately that the law allows you to set your own standards, provided they apply to everyone regardless of race, color or creed. Every state in the Union allows this.

Southern public accommodation owners told me again and again that desegregation should come on a voluntary basis rather than by law. I certainly could not agree more with that view if it were possible. However, statistics and our own checking showed that only 10 or 15 per cent of all public accommodations in the South had been desegregated by the spring of 1964. Obviously a law was necessary. In fact, many owners told me they were waiting for a law to give desegregation respectability in the eyes of their neighbors. They said they needed a law because they did not want to desegregate and anger some of their friends and business associates, or even in some cases, their city administration.

Another fear was that Negroes would bring unjust court cases and create nuisances. Some owners said, "If our hotel is full and we turn down a white man, he will look somewhere else for accommodations. However, a Negro under the same conditions may say that he is being turned down simply because he is a Negro, and bring a court action". We knew that this would not occur, since most court cases brought by Negroes usually have the backing of one of the leading Negro organizations, such as NAACP, CORE, or the Urban League. If one of these groups was to back a court action, they would make sure that discrimination actually did exist before using their time and money.

As to the morality of desegregation, I must have talked to two hundred people in a dozen different cities in the South and I never

14

met anyone who said that desegregation was morally wrong. Many said they would like to see desegregation brought about voluntarily, but nobody said that a Negro with his wife or child should be unable to go into a restaurant or a movie house or use motel accommodations for the night. I was therefore optimistic about the chances for peaceful compliance with the Civil Rights Law. This optimism has been borne out.

Lastly, I always pointed out that desegregation is part of our life and times. It is definitely here to stay, and anyone who does not attempt to adjust to the times is in for trouble. Trouble is the last thing most people want.

1.2 COMMUNITY CRISIS IN NEW YORK CITY
1.21 STATEMENT OF CRISIS
JOHN G. FEILD*

In the summer of 1963, the Bronx Chapter of the Congress of Racial Equality picketed a number of hamburger restaurants owned by the White Castle chain as part of the movement to increase opportunities for minority group employment. The employment policies of the White Castle chain were, in the judgment of the Congress of Racial Equality, in fact discriminatory against minority group persons. The picketing was the occasion for an unexpectedly vigorous anti-Negro reaction on the part of hundreds of white youths who assembled at one of the Castles for the purpose of heckling the pickets. A large police force was needed to keep the peace during the first week of demonstrations. Shortly afterwards, the City Commission on Human Rights was called upon to mediate and conciliate the dispute between the two private organizations: CORE and White Castle. This conciliation was effected by Madison S. Jones, Executive Director of the Commission, Irving Goldaber, Deputy Director, Louis M. Zimmerman, Chief of Conciliation, Harold Goldblatt, Chief of Research, and Warren A. Smith, Human Rights Specialist.

The picketing grew out of the failure of negotiations between CORE and representatives of the White Castle restaurant chain. On *June 23* CORE had requested the hiring of four Negro car hops and four Negroes for inside work for the month of July.

---

* Director, Community Relations Service, United States Conference of Mayors.

Subsequently a request to hire five more for the same period was made, and this was agreed to by the management. Later this figure was raised to 25 to be hired during July in the Bronx and 25 a month for the New York-New Jersey area for the next nine months. White Castle rejected this request and the picketing started.

Early Saturday morning, July 6, picketing began in the Bronx at the White Castle restaurant on Allerton Avenue and Boston Post Road. Several thousand jeering white persons, primarily teenagers, pelted CORE pickets with rocks, eggs, and tomatoes from 10:30 P.M. until midnight. A riot call brought 60 policemen to the scene. One youth was arrested, and CORE criticized the police for letting white youths get out of hand.

On *July 7* picketing resumed at 9 A.M. and lasted around the clock. The diner closed and reopened later that day at 2:20 P.M. and eight pickets began a sit-in. At nightfall a crowd began to gather and by midnight a thousand people were milling around outside the restaurant. Approximately 75 policemen were assigned, including 50 from the Tactical Patrol Force, especially trained for handling civil disturbances. Barricades were set up about a block away from the pickets to keep young spectators dispersed. Rain began to fall at 1:15 A.M. and many white youths went home.

On *Monday, July 8,* the Human Rights Commission sent a staff person to the Bronx to gather first-hand information about the situation. In addition, a telegram was sent to the Chairman of the Bronx CORE in an attempt to arrange a meeting to discuss the matter with him.

Picketing continued until 1 P.M. An estimated 1,000 youths roamed the area around the restaurant, hurling stones and vegetables at passing cars occupied by Negroes. At approximately 11 P.M. the police began to clear the area. People inside the restaurant were ordered to leave and no one was permitted to enter. Due to the efforts of 300 policemen, the police and the pickets were the only people in the streets surrounding the restaurant at midnight.

On *July 9* at 9 A.M. 60 pickets were marching in front of the restaurant and picketing continued until 12:30 A.M. A brief free-for-all began at 10:40 P.M., interrupting more than three hours of uneasy order that had been enforced on a crowd of several hundred hecklers

16

by police. Thirty policemen subdued two youths who then fled, and two men were arrested on charges of simple assault. As a result of this incident police blocked off the streets around the restaurant.

Meanwhile, after talking with a CORE representative, the Human Rights Commission wired the president of White Castle, requesting his attendance at a meeting at the Commission's office to discuss the situation.

On *July 10* the number of pickets reached 75, but Wednesday was the first nonviolent night since the CORE demonstrations began. Young white girls carrying signs reading "Vote Right Wing Conservative" and a man representing the National Association for the Advancement of White People arrived on the scene at about 10:30 P.M. The CORE leader in the Bronx threatened to picket all four White Castle diners in the borough unless his demands were met. The lack of violence may be attributed to large police presence. Many were drawn from the Tactical Patrol Force. However, there were also scores of detectives, mounted men, and motorcycle patrolmen. About 300 policemen were assigned to the area around the restaurant.

On *July 11* the assistant general counsel for White Castle, Inc., in Columbus, Ohio, and the assistant district manager for the New York-New Jersey Division met with representatives of the Commission. Company representatives stated that their previous meetings with CORE were very stormy and that they had no interest at all in sitting across the table from CORE to negotiate the matter. They were willing, however, for Commission representatives to be mediators and to keep the matter under surveillance after an agreement was reached.

The company stated they saw no reason to have an agreement with any private organization. They were observing the Fair Employment Practices Law of the State of New York and no private group had the right to tell them what to do.

On *July 12* the same Commission representatives met with Bronx CORE representatives. Also present was an advisor from National CORE. At this meeting CORE presented their demands, which included:

1. Twenty-five Negro and Spanish-speaking people to be hired within 30 days after agreement was reached (excluding the

17

hiring of porters). Such hiring to be based on regular turn-over, normal summer expansion, business conditions and regu-lar company hiring standards.

2. Twenty-five Negro and Spanish-speaking people to be hired per month in the division over a period of nine months, with the same hiring conditions as set forth in Point 1.

3. Special effort to be made to recruit these people by using CORE through the Commission, want ads in newspapers in-cluding the minority-group press, and a statement that White Castle is an equal opportunity employer.

4. The Commission to review the employment policies and prac-tices of White Castle as part of the implementation of any agreement.

5. Positive steps to be taken by White Castle to upgrade qualified Negro and Spanish-speaking personnel.

6. Pickets to cease their activities when an agreement was reached, and picketing would not resume until clearance was obtained from the Commission.

On the *afternoon of July 12* the Commission representatives met with White Castle to review the CORE demands. CORE representa-tives were in the office, ready to negotiate. With regard to Point 1, White Castle representatives offered to try to achieve a goal of between 15 and 25 Negro and Spanish-speaking people; and with regard to Point 2, between 7 and 10 to be reached as a goal. Further points were tentatively agreed to, with the understanding that any offer or accept-ance of terms would have to be cleared with White Castle home office officials in Columbus, Ohio.

(It is to be noted that White Castle gave tentative agreement to the Commission's proposal to meet with CORE representatives across the table at future meetings.)

The CORE group was then met with separately, but the offer of 15 to 25 and 7 to 10 was flatly rejected. This rejection was placed before White Castle and negotiations were suspended pending White Castle's consultation with their officials over the weekend.

On *July 15* White Castle representatives presented their reply to CORE's demands, which had been cleared with their central office.

In essence, all points of controversy had been complied with, with the exception of naming any figures as goals in Points 1 and 2. Throughout the negotiations the company had taken a firm position that they would never agree to specific figures as goals or quotas, since they felt this was illegal and could be the subject of court censure. The company indicated they would try to employ a *reasonable* number of Negro and Spanish-speaking persons in accordance with Points 1 and 2. The entire matter was communicated to CORE at a special meeting that day. CORE stated they wanted to discuss it with White Castle.

On *July 16* a meeting was held with all parties concerned present at the conference table. At this time White Castle verbally agreed to a goal of hiring 25 Negro and Spanish-speaking people in the Bronx over a 30-day period and in the division over a 90-day period, in accordance with Points 1 and 2. They would not specify this in any written agreement or letter. However, White Castle tentatively agreed to have their New York counsel confer with CORE's counsel to define the legality of such a procedure. Other points in the projected agreement were changed only in wording. CORE indicated they were ready to take the entire matter to their membership and policy-making group for consideration.

On the *evening of July 16* the Executive Director of the Commission received a call from the assistant district manager of White Castle, indicating that he was withdrawing his commitment of 25 Negro and Spanish-speaking people as a goal in Point 1 and substituting the figure of 13. On Point 2, White Castle would agree to 25 for the division over a 90-day period. The proposal was then communicated to CORE, whose representatives indicated this was not acceptable.

On *July 17* representatives of White Castle again met with Commission staff to discuss the breakdown in negotiations. At this time White Castle was joined by local counsel retained by the company. After much discussion they agreed to confer again with representatives of CORE. At this meeting the White Castle representatives stated that the figures in the goal requested by CORE were unrealistic. There was further discussion of the figure of 25 minority group personnel in the Bronx over a 30-day period and 25 per month for nine months in the New York-New Jersey division. White Castle kept insisting that these figures were unrealistic, particularly those for the division. However, they indicated they would transmit this information for consideration to their home office.

19

On *July 18* word was received from White Castle that they would not deal with CORE. They felt they were being blackjacked into an agreement with an organization that had nothing to do with their business and that any consideration of goals and quotas was beyond question. This information was transmitted to CORE. This was, in effect, a breakdown of all efforts to bring the two groups into communication with each other through the Commission.

During the week of *July 18 to 25,* the full Commission met and the staff reported that there was an impasse. There was danger that violence would break out again. The Commission announced that it would terminate staff efforts to negotiate and would subpoena the records of White Castle, as preliminary to a public hearing on the entire question.

On *July 25* the Executive Director of the Commission talked to the assistant district manager and arranged to have a representative of the Commission examine the books of White Castle to ascertain the rate of turnover, job opportunities, and all other information which would be germane to continuing to work with White Castle so that their employment policies would reflect the effectiveness of their July 16th proposal to the Commission.

From *July 18 to August 8* negotiations were deadlocked and CORE picketing continued. Violence subsided as a result of the continuing presence of large numbers of police, as picketing spread to other White Castle restaurants.

On *July 20* James Farmer, National Director of CORE, announced the immediate initiation of picketing in all 28 White Castle restaurants in the New York metropolitan area. He also mentioned the possibility of eventually starting a nationwide boycott of White Castle restaurants.

On *July 24* picketing began at a White Castle restaurant in North Bergen, New Jersey, and several pickets were arrested for blocking the entrance to the restaurant. CORE maintained that the White Castle chain had "reneged" on its agreement to settle the dispute.

On *August 2* announcement was made of the scheduling of a mass demonstration for August 8 at the Bronx restaurant which had been the scene of so much community tension.

On *August 9* five weeks of picketing of White Castle restaurants ended with an agreement between White Castle management and

20

CORE on the hiring of more Negroes and Puerto Ricans by the chain. Pickets were withdrawn. White Castle agreed to revise recruitment techniques in their continuing effort to maintain a more realistic ethnic balance in all levels of employment. Within ten days the management would hire six Negroes and Puerto Ricans in the Bronx, bringing the total to ten. The CORE leadership was assured that those workers would have an opportunity for advancement. After ten days a 30-day "crash program" would get under way, to consist of placing employment ads in Negro and Puerto Rican papers stating that White Castle was an "equal opportunity employer." The management would cooperate with the New York State Employment Service in the placing of minority groups. Preferential treatment would be given Negroes and Puerto Ricans who applied for jobs. Representatives of the City Commission on Human Rights would be stationed at all White Castle hiring places to make sure the agreement was carried out.

1.22 "It is Almost Impossible to Solve the Problems of the Whole Community"
Stanley H. Lowell*

In New York we do not have a problem of public accommodations as in Savannah. In most cities in the North we are dealing with problems which involve economics and dollars. Progress will be made when we are able to do something about jobs and job advancement and equal opportunity for employment. Then Negroes will be in a position to compete in the housing market, and the problems of school integration will be that much easier to solve.

Initially, there were four basic problems. First of all, whether or not anybody was willing to listen to the City Commission on Human Rights dealing with a racially tense situation. We had not been in existence long enough within the community to know whether people would come to us when a crisis arose.

We are only now working up to the point where people come to us assuming that we are there expressly for the purpose of resolving these problems. This is part and parcel of the question as to whether the parties involved would be willing to communicate through the City Commission on Human Rights.

* Chairman of the New York City Commission on Human Rights.

21

CORE had engaged in prior negotiations. The organization had made direct appeals to the White Castle chain, without any real progress. They did result in the stereotype response from White Castle, "We never discriminate," and then there was a breakdown in negotiations.

At the point at which the Commission became involved the parties were not talking to each other. For a long period of time, the parties talked through the Commission at separate meetings. The whole problem seemed to center around White Castle asking, "Who are these people? Who is this CORE? What right do they have to tell us anything about our hiring policies? What is their status in this?"

On July 18, there was a breakdown of all the Commission's efforts to bring the two groups into communication.

The City Commission on Human Rights is an unpaid group composed of fifteen volunteers with a staff headed by an Executive Director. All these negotiations were conducted by the staff people on the basis of a pattern which we had evolved in dealing with hotel chains in New York which did not have problems of desegregation, but rather hiring and personnel problems which the CORE Chapter felt indicated a discriminatory hiring pattern. The Commission brought both parties together around a table and eventually worked out a resolution of that problem. The same technique was employed in the White Castle situation.

Between July 18 and 25 the full Commission met and the staff reported that there was an impasse. There was danger that violence would break out once again. At this point the Commission issued a statement saying that they would terminate the staff efforts to negotiate and would subpoena the records of White Castle, which had steadfastly insisted that there was no problem of discrimination. Then a public hearing would be held on the entire question, with testimony from those who were complaining, that is, potential employees.

We had no power over White Castle. We were going to disclose this situation to the entire population of New York City through a public hearing, using the material from the subpoenaed records. We were not in a position to order them to cease and desist as a result of this hearing, but we could issue a public statement and then formally vote to hold public hearings. As Chairman I could appoint a hearing panel of three Commissioners, which automatically would give them

22

the authority to subpoena the records of White Castle. The Executive Director, keeping in touch with the White Castle people in New York, was able to use this possibility as an effective club or crutch, to persuade White Castle to negotiate.

What occurred between July 18 and 25 was material and important in getting the parties back to the discussions with the Commission.

Our second problem in the White Castle situation was the status of The Congress of Racial Equality. What right did they have to question the Commission's practices?

Another major problem was the role of the Commission itself. In this instance, we were acting as a mediator rather than as an advocate.

The New York City Commission on Human Rights prides itself on being one of the most outstanding advocates of equal opportunity in this field. Frequently conflicts develop between its role as an advocate and as a mediator. Thus when White Castle came in, we had overcome the initial feelings on the part of the employer, or respondent, that we were on the side of CORE.

At first CORE felt that they would not be treated fairly by us. However, we have succeeded in getting the parties to the particular conflict to accept the Commission's role as a mediator.

On the other hand, we do not eliminate subjective feelings in a given situation. The problem of conflicting roles is one that must be faced.

A fourth problem that persists, is that what CORE is asking for is illegal. They are asking us to contradict our own laws against discrimination. We have to deal with this problem continually in the areas of housing, the efforts of our Board of Education to desegregate our schools, the efforts of the Housing Authority to desegregate public housing, and the efforts of this Commission to resolve problems of employment discrimination. For instance, a group will come in and claim that a pattern of employment indicates that an employer is not employing Negroes or Puerto Ricans and they want us to demand that within a certain period of time he hire a specific number of Negroes and Puerto Ricans.

We have laws in New York City which require you to be color blind, employment policies which require you to be color blind. In the State of New York we have taken pride for forty or fifty years in

23

these laws, but they have not achieved the purpose for which they were designed. Over the last four or five years they have almost become stumbling blocks to progress.

The White Castle people resisted our demands, claiming that it would be contrary to the laws of the State of New York to hire only Negroes in a given situation.

Nobody suggests that only Negroes should be hired, and nobody suggests that whites should be fired so that Negroes can be hired. It is not suggested that Negroes should be hired to replace competent whites, or that business standards should be reduced.

CORE does not urge such a procedure, nor does the Urban League, nor the NAACP, or any other public agency in this field.

By 1964, American society presumably had come of age and matured to the point where it was willing to do something about a hundred years of discrimination, and to do it on a basis of fraternalism. We are willing to take the steps necessary to remedy the evils of the past. That does not mean firing whites to replace them with Negroes, and it does not mean reducing standards. But when vacancies occur (in the White Castle situation there was a regular turnover), one must contact the sources within the Negro and Puerto Rican communities and recruit personnel from the areas.

White Castle adopted the policy; they advertised in newspapers which reached the Negro and Puerto Rican communities. They went to the Urban League's employment division and to the New York State Employment Service and were able to find a sufficient number of qualified Negroes, once they made an honest effort to do so.

On July 18 the White Castle people advised that they would no longer negotiate, as CORE was asking for something that contradicted the laws of the State of New York. At this point, the Commission indicated that it would have a public hearing and subpoena the records. Under the threat of subpoena, White Castle consented and agreed to open their records to examination.

White Castle's lawyers offered to prepare a statistical analysis of what had been done in the matter of employment over the last twelve months.

The Commission refused the offer as a compromise solution, and we insisted that it would subpoena all the records. White Castle co-

24

operated in producing the figures which enabled us to show that what CORE was asking of White Castle in the New York area was an impossibility.

CORE wanted White Castle to hire 25 Negroes and Puerto Ricans within a month or two months. Our figures showed that this was an absolutely unreasonable demand, as there was no such turnover. On the other hand, CORE also wanted 25 Negroes and Puerto Ricans hired in the whole regional area, including New Jersey and other areas, and this, our figures showed, could easily be accomplished.

As a result of the subpoena, of an analysis of the facts which we transmitted to the CORE representatives, and of the threat that pressure from the Negro community and from CORE would spread to all the other White Castle restaurants across the country — both groups were brought back together and we were able to confine the dispute to a narrower area in New York. The parties sat down to negotiations which lasted from the middle of July until August 9. Finally, CORE and White Castle entered into a memo of understanding rather than a contractual agreement, as to what goals were being sought. In effect, White Castle said that they would seek to change the pattern of employment within the restaurants in this area in accordance with goals.

There was nothing in the memo of understanding with reference to any numbers. There was no indication that any particular number would be achieved; even CORE's representatives felt that there was deep concern about the legality of a specific agreement that White Castle would hire "Y" number of Negroes and others within a certain period of time.

Only the number six was mentioned, because there were six vacancies which had occurred during the period of stress. White Castle indicated they would be able to fill these very quickly, and would try to fill them with Negroes and Puerto Ricans.

Finally, the Commission feels that this whole area of special effort reflects affirmative action and conscious effort on the part of a private industry to give the American Negro the opportunity to achieve economic equality. These kinds of efforts represent exactly what is being sought by President Johnson's anti-poverty program, which plans a broad attack on poverty in our society.

25

The problems of discrimination will be resolved only by constructive action. They cannot be resolved in a vacuum. They can be resolved only with economic means. We must give people dollars to help themselves within our society. Only then will we make great progress. Only then will this country project the kind of image which it deserves but, in a great many instances, does not yet have.

1.23 "Anger and a Lack of Trust on Both Sides"
Louis Zimmerman*

Initially, there was anger and an absolute lack of trust on both sides. Our first meeting was on July 11, at 4 p.m. in the Commission's office. At that time we met only with the White Castle people.

There had been an earlier session with the representatives from CORE. On July 12 there was a meeting in the Commission's office with the Bronx CORE people. Later in the day we held a separate meeting with the White Castle people.

Even though there was no direct communication, an agreement appeared to be in the making, shaped around specific numbers of people to be employed.

On July 15 there was a meeting in the Commission office, with representatives of White Castle. Finally, on July 16 there was an afternoon meeting in the Commission's office where at long last the Commission staff met jointly with the CORE people and the White Castle people.

Communication continued. Then there was a break, followed by communication in the form of letters from the White Castle management. During the interval we made the inspection of the records following the service of a subpoena, and additional activities went on. Our staff made visual checks of the ethnic composition of the White Castle units.

On August 6 we had a meeting with the CORE representatives. Again on August 6 we heard from White Castle by means of a letter in which they indicated a willingness to reach out into the community

---

* Chief, Conciliation Services, New York City Commission on Human Rights.

to hire minority people, but only if CORE would call off the picketing. Finally on August 8 there was another meeting in the Commission office which resulted in the drafting of a tentative agreement.

The final session took place on August 10. This was an all-day session. It was amicable, and an understanding was finally reached at that time.

In a few weeks we went from an atmosphere of anger and bitterness and complete lack of faith to a point where this was dissipated and both sides began to see each other as individuals. A lot of stereotyped thinking had been overcome, some element of humor crept in from time to time, and faith was established.

We do not take all the credit for this. CORE was most cooperative, understanding, and patient, as was management.

The agreement was drawn up on August 10. On August 28 there was a special meeting of CORE and the White Castle group in the Commission office, at which time White Castle presented an interim report on how the understanding was being implemented.

There was another session on September 5, again to review the implementation of the earlier understanding. The Commission was present, as well as CORE and the White Castle people.

Another similar session was held on September 17. On September 20, according to the terms of our memorandum of understanding, additional visual checks were initiated in an effort to identify further the ethnic composition of the working staff of the White Castle units. CORE kept in touch with us continually. On November 18 they reported favorably in terms of their own check.

At that time the point was made that CORE was concerned about white collar jobs. This feeling was conveyed to management. Management reacted by suggesting the distribution of letters to organizations such as the New York State Employment Service, the Urban League, and the New York office of the Commonwealth of Puerto Rico, pointing out that management was prepared to interview qualified females for white collar jobs, and spelling out the specifications for the different kinds of office jobs.

In March and April of 1964, our staff made around-the-clock visual observations of most of the White Castle units in the area. This meant a three-shift inspection on the basis of which reports were prepared and incorporated into the record.

27

As of August 5, 1963, a few days before the understanding was worked out, the four Bronx units employed five Negroes on the porter level.

As of May, 1964, the Bronx units employed 33 Negroes at all levels. Apparently some upgrading had occurred. These people were employed not only as porters but also as car hops and behind the counter.

In terms of all units that were checked as of August 5, 19 Negroes were employed. As of May, 1964 there was a total of 73 Negroes in the various units. These figures indicate a degree of progress that hopefully will be continued in the future.

CORE pointed out, in terms of the over-all situation, that there still was a relative scarcity of Negro people who could be related to the better-paying jobs. It was imperative that something be done at some level to provide jobs for unskilled people, and they pushed hard in that direction.

The White Castle management did indeed make an intensive effort. They reached out into the community, accomplishing things that they had never done before.

They used the minority press, they used agencies which were especially equipped to help qualified minority people find jobs. They changed their recruitment techniques. On the basis of their change in approach and attitude, and their cooperation, we believe meaningful progress was made.

1.3 COMMUNITY CRISIS IN CHESTER
1.31 STATEMENT OF CRISIS
JOHN FEILD*

Chester, Pennsylvania, a port city near Philadelphia on the Delaware River, has a population of about 64,000. One of the most significant changes between 1950 and 1960 was the rapid growth (more than 12 per cent) in the city's nonwhite population. At the time of the demonstrations of 1963 and 1964 approximately 40 per cent of Chester's population was Negro.

---

* Director, Community Relations Service, United States Conference of Mayors.

Although Chester's Negro citizens have always had open access to hotels, restaurants, and other public accommodations, unemployment and poverty have characterized their living conditions. In 1963 at least 14 per cent of the employable Negroes were jobless, compared to 7 per cent of the employable whites. Nearly one-half of the 27,000 Negroes subsist on an annual family income of less than $4,000; 13 per cent of the Negro families live in abject poverty with incomes of less than $1,000. Most of the Negroes live near industrial plants in cramped neighborhoods.

Educational opportunities have also been limited for Chester Negroes. In 1963 Negro children accounted for over half of the city's school-age population. While Chester's schools have generally been operated on an integrated basis, at the time of the demonstrations three schools had all Negro pupils and four others had more than 80 per cent Negro students. Many of the schools, particularly those in Negro neighborhoods, were old and had poor facilities. Although by 1963 $100,000 had been spent on improving the old buildings and three new schools had been constructed, seven school buildings had been condemned and abandoned.

In *July, 1963,* Mayor Eyre, responding to the growing tensions and pressures, created a 16-member Chester Commission on Human Relations to air Negro grievances and improve equal opportunity.

On *July 25, 26 and 27,* Negroes, under NAACP leadership, conducted a sit-in at the Chester Municipal Building to protest the composition of the Chester Human Relations Commission. The demonstrators demanded an equal number of whites and Negroes on the Commission. No arrests were made, and the demonstrators dispersed to give Mayor Eyre time to reach a decision on their demands.

In *September, 1963,* Stanley Branche, in protest against alleged sluggish NAACP leadership, organized a new, more militant civil rights movement, the Chester Committee for Freedom Now (CFFN). Immediately the CFFN began to act. In October the CFFN demanded changes in conditions at the Franklin Elementary School. Failing to receive a favorable response to these demands from city officials and the school board, the CFFN organized a series of mass demonstrations at the Franklin School and in downtown Chester, protesting the *de facto* school segregation, the poor facilities, and overcrowding.

On *November 12,* students from nearby colleges and Negro and white clergymen joined the picket lines and blocked the entrance to

29

the Franklin School. At that time the school board ordered the school closed. At a demonstration at the Chester Municipal Building 158 demonstrators were arrested. The next day 80 more school pickets were arrested for blocking school entrances. State Police were alerted for assistance to local officers but took no part in law enforcement activities. Finally the demonstrations ended after a promise to stop picketing was exchanged for agreements by Mayor and school board to transfer pupils to less crowded schools and to drop all charges against arrested demonstrators.

From *December, 1963, to February, 1964,* there were no more such demonstrations. Invective was increased between Branche and city officials, including the school board, and the school board refused to meet with CFFN leaders.

In *January, 1964,* a newly-elected Mayor, James H. Gorbey, replaced Mayor Eyre and announced a firm policy of law and order and a refusal to tolerate irresponsible demonstrations. It was in this context that new rallies and demonstrations were called by CFFN leadership in February to demand stepped-up desegregation and school improvement efforts and to provide an impetus for negotiation.

On *Monday, February 10,* after an evening meeting of the Committee for Freedom Now to finalize plans for a school boycott, some 300 demonstrators marched downtown to the police station (evidently to protest police arrests during demonstrations earlier that day). A brief scuffle broke out in front of the station as police tried to take one of the demonstrators, who had been arrested earlier in the day in a lie-in, into the station. On the way to the station the demonstrators had been run through by a car whose driver was not apprehended. At least two suffered leg injuries.

On *February 13,* the school boycott was held, with picket demonstrations at the boycotted schools. Wilbur Johnson, a member of the CFFN executive board, was arrested and held on four counts of traffic violation, but no other trouble occurred during the demonstrations. At about 5 P.M., however, CFFN leaders Stanley Branche and Dr. Felder Rouse were arrested and taken from CFFN headquarters on charges of criminal libel and conspiracy to commit an unlawful act brought against them by the Rev. Donald Ming.

Ming, acting Chairman of the Chester Human Relations Commission, had been called an Uncle Tom by Branche and Rouse and hanged in effigy the night before. An explosive situation developed over these arrests but quieted when Branche and Rouse were released that evening on $500 bail.

On *Easter weekend, March 27-30,* three days of demonstrations were held. On Good Friday no incidents were reported. On Saturday, March 28, in the midst of the last-minute shopping rush, a "sit-down" was held at noon in the busiest intersection of downtown Chester. Police waded in to make arrests, allegedly swinging riot sticks. Several demonstrators were hurt. A newspaper photographer was knocked down by the police and taken to the station, held for a time, and then released.

While police were breaking up this demonstration, two others were started in the downtown area. The 77 arrested that day came from all three areas. At least ten persons, including a police officer, were injured, and one demonstrator was hospitalized. Forty-three adults were fined $350 each, plus costs, for ordinance violations and were further held in prison on bail ranging from $500 to $1000, charged with unlawful assembly and affray. The 34 juveniles were turned over to County juvenile authorities.

On *Easter Sunday, March 30,* a quiet protest march was held with about 50 demonstrators, for the first time protesting alleged brutality by Chester police.

In *April* the Pennsylvania Human Relations Commission tried to work out a solution to the dispute, but the attempt was not successful.

On *April 22* daytime demonstrations resulted in the closing of all the public schools. Nighttime demonstrations resulted in mass arrests, the first direct participation of State Police in dispersing of demonstrators, and further charges of police brutality.

In the evening of April 24, after school officials had made application to the Delaware County Court of Common Pleas for an injunction against further civil rights demonstrations, a rally was attended by some 500 persons to plan an orderly protest. Also at issue was the alleged brutality of police treatment of the several hundred persons arrested in a demonstration two nights before and still being held. After the meeting some 50 people blocked traffic at an intersection in one of the predominantly Negro wards. Police arrived in gradual force, warning the demonstrators to leave or be arrested. Scuffling broke out as police began to make arrests and load demonstrators on

31

buses. About 80 State Police arrived, swinging riot sticks and clearing the area. Twenty-eight demonstrators were arrested, six policemen were injured, and reportedly some demonstrators were injured.

Meanwhile, the FBI had been called in to investigate the alleged brutality of Chester police in the arrest of two reporters of the Philadelphia *Bulletin* who were covering the April 22 demonstration, as well as the beating of one of them.

The following day, *Saturday, April 25,* Governor Scranton met with Mayor James Gorbey and the attorney for the Chester school board and ordered the Pennsylvania Human Relations Commission to meet Monday to set hearings on the issue of alleged discrimination in Chester public schools.*

On *Monday, April 27,* the County Court of Common Pleas issued an injunction against further school demonstrations. Branche nevertheless announced scheduling of a mass protest march for Saturday, May 3, although the NAACP announced a seven-day moratorium on demonstrations. At the last moment Branche called it off, saying that "rowdies" from Philadelphia and New York had come in "hell bent for trouble."†

1.32 "Substandard Educational Achievement in Chester"

James H. Gorbey**

Not long ago, the people of Chester felt that Chester had no problem concerning the Negro and white communities. As a result of what has happened, however, it is apparent that there are many problems we simply did not see.

---

* Extensive hearings were held by the Commission, resulting in detailed findings and an order (reproduced as Appendix B, p. 289 herein) directing the local school to adopt a desegregation plan. A lower Pennsylvania court in February 1966 reversed the order on the ground that the Commission lacked jurisdiction.

† A subsequent investigation of alleged police brutality by a Commission appointed by the Governor is discussed on pp. 40-41.

** Mayor of Chester, Pa.

Chester is small in geographical area, four and a half square miles, with 64,000 people. Two square miles of Chester is taken up by industry. We have poor housing. We have schools that need a great deal of improvement.

We have a population that is 40 per cent Negro. This Negro population has an unemployment rate of about 16 per cent, compared to the white population's 8 per cent.

Average educational achievement in Chester is quite substandard. Over half our people have not completed or even attended high school. Since 1940 we have had a large influx of Negroes and whites from the South who are uneducated, untrained, and unskilled.

We find that there are many jobs available in our area, but the people cannot even qualify for training because they lack the basic education, the reading and writing skills, that would enable them to be trained.

Our crisis put me in the middle because it was a school problem. The school board is an independent, autonomous group in Chester. The members are elected by the people; they set their own budget, and carry out their own programs.

We were not in a position to force the school people to sit down and negotiate. Sixty per cent of our public school population is comprised of Negroes, and it is very difficult to strike a balance with that ratio.

One-third of the school children are Catholics, and they attend Catholic schools.

Under our recommendation a commission was appointed by the Governor to review Chester's problems. When the demonstrations against the school district were not effective, and a court injunction forbade demonstrating against the school district, people decided to demonstrate downtown. They did this for twenty-eight straight days and our policemen were on duty twenty-fours hours a day.

We really were powerless to do anything about negotiations. We attempted to negotiate, but for one reason or another we could not effectively communicate. The school board took the position that the problem resulted from people living in a particular area and refusing to take the bus across town.

33

The Pennsylvania Human Relations Commission just handed down an order that directs the school board to follow a specified plan. The school board is appealing the order.*

This city does not appear to have employment problems in restaurants, hotels, or motels. In fact, the local bank needs two tellers whom they would like to be Negroes.

Our problem is one that could be found anywhere in this country. We felt initially that we were picked as a target area for demonstrations because of our geographical situation and the number of unemployed and needy people.

1.33 "A SENSE OF FUTILITY"

LAWRENCE JACOBSON**

At the time of the crisis I was a member of the Chester Human Relations Commission. Very early in February we had met with civil rights groups, who presented to us a long list of complaints and grievances primarily directed against the school board. The complaints concerned the desegregation of facilities. We noted the complaints and we decided to investigate them, unfortunately without the cooperation of these very same civil rights groups.

These grievances were presented in a very general form. We asked the civil rights groups to sit down with us again and make their complaints more specific.

A meeting was set up which the civil rights leaders said they would attend, but did not appear for. This, of course, made it a little more difficult for us. But in spite of all this we undertook to complete an investigation. Approximately two thousand man hours of free time expended by people from all walks of life went into this investigation, which resulted in a fifteen-page report with any number of specific recommendations and findings. The sum and substance of this report was not complimentary to the school board.

---

* The order of The Pennsylvania Human Relations Commission appears as Appendix B, p. 289 herein. A lower Pennsylvania court reversed the order in February 1966, holding that the Commission lacked jurisdiction.

** Assistant City Solicitor of Chester.

In spite of the fact that we met twice with the school board in an attempt to answer some of these problems and comply with the recommendations, the civil rights groups (I do not mean the NAACP, but our own local leaders) again refused to recognize our Commission for reasons of their own. They said that they would meet only with the school board.

The school board, on the other hand, said, "The civil rights commission is the Chester Human Relations Commission, and we won't meet with a lot of different groups." Then a split developed between the leaders of the civil rights groups and the NAACP. Thus we were involved in the problem of just who were the civil rights leaders in Chester. This was a sort of vicious circle, with the school board refusing to meet with civil rights leaders independently and the civil rights leaders refusing to meet with the Human Relations Commission. At this point communications concerning the Human Relations Commission broke down completely.

The demonstrations continued and there were many meetings. Finally the County Commissioners met with the school board in a desperate attempt to get the board to agree to meet directly with the civil rights leaders, excluding the Chester Human Relations Commission. Most of the members of the Human Relations Commission resigned out of nothing more, I am sure, than a sense of futility. Our Commission has never functioned since.

This is the sum and substance of what went on in the way of official governmental action as our Human Relations Commission sought to help these people. Our group comprised almost all the different facets of society. There were Negroes, there were whites, labor, business, and professional people. It was therefore quite disturbing to me as an individual and to other members of the Commission to have a group come to us, ask for help, and then refuse to recognize us when we tried to aid them.

The Pennsylvania Human Relations Commission subsequently issued a report as a result of their own rather intensive investigation. There is a striking similarity between the two reports—the one that we issued and the one issued by the Pennsylvania Human Relations Commission.

Their recommendations were similar. They said that basically there was a power struggle between the NAACP, the liberal leaders,

35

and a lot of civil rights splinter groups. At one time these groups had all merged, and then the tail started wagging the dog. A power struggle was taking place and the NAACP leaders did not know what was going on.

I conclude that the real breakdown in the negotiations as far as our Human Relations Commission was concerned came from a total irresponsibility on the part of our local civil rights leaders, who did not really try to deal with the problem that they themselves had raised. When a group presents you with a problem and then refuses to discuss it, they are certainly not acting responsibly toward their own people.

1.34 "NO RIGHT TO VIOLATE THE LAW"

PHILIP MCMUNIGAL*

The legal policy of the city of Chester was fundamentally as follows: First, it was the Mayor's primary responsibility to maintain law and order at all times. Second, the demonstrators had a legal right to demonstrate. Third, there would be no mass arrests. The civil rights leaders and their groups would be allowed to demonstrate without interference, unless the situation got out of control.

The next premise was that the demonstrators themselves had no right to violate the law. While civil rights people have equal rights, they do not have rights superior to those of the rest of the community.

We had demonstrations for twenty-eight consecutive days. The Mayor, the Solicitor, and the Assistant City Solicitor were present at the demonstrations at all times, so we had first-hand knowledge about the situation.

The various newspapers ran conflicting stories. We were troubled by this contradictory publicity, especially when we went to court. Arrests were made on three or four days, and the legal steps that we took at the time involved the enforcement of two local ordinances. One dealt with disorderly conduct and the second was a traffic ordinance which concerns failure to obey the command of a police officer.

Sometimes we blocked off a street to let people parade. If the situation became intolerable, they were told to move. If they refused, they were held in violation of the traffic ordinance.

---

* City Solicitor of Chester.

36

The Pennsylvania Penal Code also has a provision for unlawful assembly, riot, and affray that was used on several occasions. In two instances we were compelled to resort to charges of the common law crime of inciting to riot. That is not a statutory offense in Pennsylvania. I believe that two or three individuals were arrested for that offense and their cases are now on appeal. That summarizes the basic legal policy and the legal steps that were taken.

As far as legal enforcement is concerned, for almost a month we had demonstrations with two and three hundred people involved in each, totalling roughly six to nine thousand people, with our arrests held down to a minimum. Approximately 350 were arrested. We feel that the legal policy of Chester was put into effect satisfactorily under all the circumstances.

1.35 POLICE POLICY GUIDELINES
JOSEPH BAIL*

It was my first duty as Chief of Police in the city of Chester to instruct my men that these people had a perfect right to demonstrate peacefully.

My next duty was to make sure that each and every man was equipped properly with mask, visor, and night stick and that he knew the proper use of a night stick. After a meeting with the Mayor I asked him to give me the following policy statement on the position of the police in preserving the public peace:

1. The police are the representatives of the government, a government of laws, not men.

2. The police have a sworn duty to enforce the laws impartially, objectively, and equally. This they have done and this they will continue to do, for without law and order there can be no peace, no freedom, no rights for anyone.

3. The police are aware of the significance of the movement for equal rights. They recognize and respect the right of the people to express their views on matters of public concern.

* Chief of Police of Chester.

4. The police will protect the rights of all to assemble and petition peacefully. They will brook no interference with these rights by anyone. The impartiality of their role is clearly set by law.

5. The police will also protect the rights of the people to pursue their lives and lawful occupations free from illegal interference.

6. The police will take appropriate action under law when the rights of anyone are obstructed.

7. It must be clearly understood that sitdowns or other acts which prohibit the safe and peaceful movements of persons and vehicles in public streets and prevent access to buildings are violations of law, and those who use these unlawful means to gain their ends are subject to arrest.

8. It must be clearly understood that police have not only the duty but the legal obligation to meet illegal action to the degree necessary to restore and maintain law and order.

9. It must be clearly understood that the police will not allow themselves to be placed in the false position of "aggressors." The police are aware of and trained to assume their full responsibilities and they expect others to remember and recognize that they also have responsibilities.

10. The police will preserve the public peace by every legal means. They expect cooperation, compliance and understanding.

1.36 PROBLEMS OF ESTABLISHING COMMUNICATION
H. A. MACNEILLY*

During the Chester school dispute, many meetings were attempted with civil rights organizations in Chester. The Mayor was requested by the leader of the Committee For Freedom Now to arrange for a meeting with the Human Relations Commission, and this was done.

At this meeting, nothing was accomplished. Another meeting was set up. The Human Relations Commission met with the school board, and the CFFN failed to appear.

---

* Administrative Assistant to the Mayor of Chester.

The Human Relations Commission and the school board reviewed the findings of the Committee of the Human Relations Commission on the school situation. The CFFN had requested this, but then failed to cooperate in light of the findings. They insisted on meeting only with the members of the school board.

The Mayor called a meeting of the colored clergy of Chester and the CFFN. The colored clergy attended the meeting, but the CFFN did not appear. They picketed instead.

Another meeting was called by the school board with CFFN, and the CFFN walked out. The County Commissioner then called on Thursday morning for a meeting on Saturday morning. On Thursday at 9 P. M. I was told to organize the meeting.

Fortunately, everyone showed up for this meeting. After two hours of discussion the CFFN and the NAACP agreed to meet in private session with the school board to reach a definite conclusion. Nothing was accomplished.

A meeting was then set up by the Mayor and the County Commissioners with a neutral chairman. The CFFN, the NAACP, the school board, and interested citizens were invited; everyone showed up but the NAACP and the CFFN. They demonstrated outside the Municipal Building.

They were invited to come in but their leaders refused to do so until after the meeting was over. Then they came in and sat in secret session.

Shortly after this the Mayor called the Attorney General, who came into Chester on a Friday night and met with the city officials. We contacted the civil rights leaders. The city officials left and the civil rights leaders sat down and talked to the Attorney General. The Attorney General made his report to the Governor. The Governor then held a session with the Mayor and several other city officials when it was agreed that the State Human Relations Commission should enter the picture.

The hearings set by the State Human Relations Commission finally brought about the cessation of demonstrations and other activities in Chester.

1.37 New Developments

David Stahl*

Two significant developments grew out of the Chester incidents.

As indicated in the chronological description of the Chester situation, a basic cause of the demonstrations was the charge of segregation in the Chester public schools. The Pennsylvania Human Relations Commission conducted extensive hearings on these charges. In December, 1964, the Commission issued a comprehensive opinion, including detailed findings of fact and an order (appearing as Appendix B, pp. 289-320 herein) directing the Chester school district to take certain steps to eliminate allegedly discriminatory practices. This is believed to be one of the few instances in which a state human relations agency has issued an order of this nature. However, in February, 1966 a lower Pennsylvania court reversed the order, holding that the Commission lacked jurisdiction to issue it.

During and following the demonstrations there were serious charges of excessive use of force by state and local police and demands by a number of groups and individuals for an independent investigation. Consequently, in July, 1964, Governor William W. Scranton of Pennsylvania appointed a six-man commission comprised of William W. Bodine, Jr., President of Jefferson Medical College, Philadelphia, Pennsylvania; James E. Gallagher, Jr., a partner in a Philadelphia law firm and a member of the Archdiocesan Commission on Human Relations; Thomas W. Pomeroy, Jr., partner in a Pittsburgh law firm and a past president of the Pennsylvania Bar Association; Dr. Ira De A. Reid, chairman of the Department of Sociology of Haverford College; Ernest Scott, a partner in a Philadelphia law firm and former chancellor of the Philadelphia Bar Association; and David Stahl, the chairman of the PLI Special Forum. The Commission appointed a staff consisting of two attorneys and an executive secretary. The investigation continued to the end of 1964,

---

* City Solicitor, Pittsburgh, Pennsylvania, Professor of Law, University of Pittsburgh School of Law, former Attorney General of Commonwealth of Pennsylvania; Chairman of the PLI special forum.

N. B. Mr. Stahl was City Solicitor of Pittsburgh at the time of this writing and at publication, but not in December 1964, when he presided as Forum Chairman; at that time Mr. David Craig was Pittsburgh City Solicitor (see pp. 196, 198).

and a comprehensive report was submitted to the Governor. Several portions of the Chester Investigating Commission report follow.

Another chapter, entitled "Premises of The Discussion", is included in Part III. It contains a discussion of the legal and policy considerations which the investigators used as a guideline for their conclusions.

1.371 Excerpts from the Report of the Governor's Commission to Investigate Charges of Police Brutality in Chester*

DISCUSSION OF MAJOR EVENTS†

The March 28 demonstrations were the first planned attempts at street sit-ins. The demonstrators no doubt were instructed to offer only passive resistance but, perhaps because of their age, immaturity or lack of training, they were not fully disciplined in this technique. Some of the demonstrators left the intersection voluntarily when confronted by the police, apparently preferring to avoid arrest. Some of the participants in the first demonstration who did not leave the street when ordered to do so swung their arms and feet in an attempt to make the policemen's task of arrest more difficult. At least one demonstrator injured two policemen.

The Commission is critical of the judgment of those persons who planned and who led the demonstration of March 28. A street sit-in, a clearly illegal act because it interferes with the normal flow of traffic, is quite dissimilar to the earlier protests carried on at the schools. In addition, the civil rights leaders and those who led the demonstrations erred, in our opinion, in using minors, some only 12 or 13 years old, to perform an unlawful act designed to provoke

---

* This report was submitted to the Governor of the Commonwealth of Pennsylvania by William W. Bodine, Jr., James E. Gallagher, Jr., Ira De A. Reid, Ernest Scott, David Stahl and Thomas W. Pomeroy, Jr. (Chairman) in November of 1964. Another chapter of the report is included in Part III (at p. 107) under the title "Premises of the Discussion." It contains a summary of the legal and policy considerations which the investigators used as a guideline for their conclusions.

† This section originally appeared as Chapter IX of the Commission's report.

arrest. Such young people lack the maturity and discipline that is necessary in carrying out this hazardous form of protest in a peaceful fashion.

The nature of the demonstrations on March 28 took the police by surprise. Although it had been announced that demonstrations would be held on that day, the police did not expect a sit-in at a busy intersection; several policemen were at lunch when the disturbance began. The police responded to the demonstration with determination and dispatch. The manner in which they removed the demonstrators from the intersection was for the most part within the proper limits of the authority of the police to maintain law and order.

The Commission nevertheless questions the conduct of some of the Chester police on March 28. Although it was within the discretion of the police to resort to that force which they used, this was not a wise exercise of that power. The demonstrators in the streets were violating the law and, though the evidence is conflicting, the Commission is satisfied that several were resisting arrest. The demonstrators, however, were not threatening to escape nor, with the exception of one person, did they threaten the safety of the police. The harsh dispatch with which the police effected the arrest of the demonstrators appears to have provoked additional resistance and also to have generated a reaction from sympathizers in the crowd.

The Commission believes there is a substantial difference between the treatment which is properly accorded a resisting felon and that which should be given to a demonstrator protesting, albeit in an illegal manner, what he considers to be a legitimate grievance. In testimony before the Commission the Chester police did not appear to recognize this distinction. Violations of law, of course, cannot be tolerated. But where the illegal conduct is performed by persons who are not engaged in the commission of serious criminal acts, and who are in the course of expressing their dissatisfaction with existing social conditions, the suppression of the violations should be done with minimal force.

General Conclusions

1. As in many other cities, the civil rights demonstrators in Chester had and still have grievances to protest on behalf on the Negro community. These grievances stem from real or assumed

42

denials of equal opportunities in education, employment, housing and fundamental human liberties which have existed without significant change for many years.

2. The crushing burden of these denials is difficult to comprehend by persons who have not been subjected to them. So, also, is the patience of the sufferers. Yet, the Chester demonstrations aimed at these grievances were originally intended to be peaceful protests. These demonstrations are not to be confused with the riots that other Northern cities have recently experienced.

3. In the overriding interest of all citizens, protests by some regarding their grievances, however real, must be carried out in a manner calculated not to interfere with the maintenance of law and order which the police are sworn to uphold.

4. Mass protests concerning such grievances necessarily evoke emotions and attitudes so deep and so sensitive that effective control of participants within the accepted bounds of law and order is difficult to maintain, even under the most favorable conditions, conditions not present in the City of Chester.

5. The demonstrations were on the whole poorly organized despite the good-faith efforts of well-intentioned leaders. On occasion many young children and irresponsible persons were involved. In addition, few demonstrators were thoroughly disciplined in passive resistance techniques, although most of them claimed to have offered no resistance to arrest. When the Chairman of the CFFN, Stanley Branche, was in jail (during the April 22 police station demonstration and on April 24) the demonstrations were neither well organized nor well controlled. Poor judgment was sometimes used by the second echelon of demonstration leaders.

6. The failure of the local officials to pursue timely negotiations with those protesting the inadequacy of educational facilities was partially responsible for the resentments and reactions which developed in the community. As time passed without producing what the leaders of the demonstrations deemed sufficient results, they turned toward more drastic and sometimes illegal means quite unrelated to their grievances in order to dramatize the seriousness of their wrongs and the believed absence of sufficient movement toward their redress. While this is understandable, the Commission cannot condone the shift to such tactics. This means of courting arrest led to

43

THE COMMUNITY AND RACIAL CRISES

the first reported acts of violence on the part of police and demonstrators.

7. The persistence of the demonstrations seems in part to have been designed to harass the police and to exploit a heightening emotional tension. While the leaders appealed to the demonstrators for restraint, they did not discourage the development of the image of the police as hostile to their efforts to obtain redress for their grievances. As a result, the demonstrators vocally and physically abused the police on some occasions. In the three critical demonstrations, violence against the police occurred. Whether such violence originated with the demonstrators or bystanders is for the purposes of this report immaterial, since it was precipitated by the demonstrations and required responsive police action.

8. The Commission recognizes the important but hazardous role of the police as an agency of State and City in maintaining law and order. In the tense situations of racial disturbance, where police sometimes must make arrests, charges of "police brutality" are not uncommon. In Chester, when the purpose of the participants was to be arrested, and when some demonstrators did not cooperate in being arrested, it should come as no surprise that force was required in effecting some arrests.

9. The heavy burden placed on the Chester police by weeks of almost daily demonstrations had exhausted their patience. In like manner, the rigors of manning the demonstrations, added to the humiliations and frustrations of the long-term grievances, had exhausted the patience of the civil rights protestants. The hundreds of hours of overtime which the Chester police were compelled to serve without compensation resulted in serious fatigue and emotional tension. Like conditions of tension and fatigue existed among the civil rights demonstrators who, after work, school or college hours, spent innumerable hours in rallies, marches and picketing. When the three critical demonstrations occurred, the police and many civil rights participants were so overwrought that they were unable objectively to evaluate the dangers. As a result, a sense of hysteria developed among both police and demonstrators.

10. There is reason to believe that the political "power structure" was unsympathetic with the immediacy of demands of the Negro community and that this attitude was to some extent reflected in

44

the methods adopted by the police to repress the demonstrations. An overworked police force, with no real training in dealing with civil rights demonstrations or crowd control, was instructed to enforce the law strictly in order to show that the acts of civil disobedience were not an acceptable way to gain the desired results.

11. The rough police action on March 28, April 22 and April 24 seems to have been used to inculcate fear and confusion in the demonstrators and their sympathizers. It also added to resentments and helped to turn the image of the police into enemies or punishers of the protestants rather than to emphasize their role as defenders of law and order. The Commission believes that such treatment, even though largely within permissible limits, was unwise.

12. Resentments breed hatred, and something approaching open warfare occurred on two of the three occasions above mentioned. On these occasions the State Police were called in when matters were out of hand or so nearly so that the local authorities believed that riotous conditions either existed or were in immediate prospect. Substantial force was required to restore order. Order was restored, but a number of demonstrators, some innocent people and some police, were injured. Some property damage also occurred.

13. The Commission finds that the Chester police, in good faith, believed that they were using the proper means and no more force than necessary to maintain law and order.

14. The Commission finds that the State Police, in good faith, believed that they were using the proper means necessary to back up the local authorities faced with a critical breakdown of law and order.

15. The Commission finds that for the most part, the Chester Police and State Police exercised force within the permitted limits of discretion allowed to them by law for the purpose of preserving law and order. Nevertheless, the Commission finds that some police tactics and actions were unwise and unwarranted. The Commission further finds that in a few instances some members of both police forces exercised poor judgment in determining the amount of force required to restore order. As a consequence, excessive use of force did occur in at least 7 particular instances treated in detail in the Supplement to this report. In some instances, there was provocation for such conduct and those who imprudently gave rise to it cannot escape some part of the responsibility.

45

16. On the nights of April 22 and April 24, when the State Police were called into action, the force used by the State and local police was applied without much distinction as to whether a particular person had or had not given provocation to warrant its use. This seems to have been especially true of the State Police, who used riot-quelling tactics of a military nature. These are established procedures where riotous or near riotous conditions are believed to exist, as was the case here.

17. The timing of the commitment to action of the State Police at the peak of the crises of April 22 and April 24, heightened the tension. It would seem that an earlier, less dramatic and more gradual introduction of the State Police into the situation would have produced more effective coordination of effort, greater protection of the rights of all concerned and less of a feeling of military invasion among the citizens. The State troopers would not then have been intervening as a military group using riot-quelling tactics, and the use of force noted above might have been avoided.

18. The procedure by which persons arrested were brought before a single committing magistrate disregarded sound principles of judicial administration in an emergency situation of this nature. A magistrate invested with sole authority to act as committing magistrate for police arrests had the responsibility for handling hundreds of charges against the demonstrators. There is credible evidence that persons were held incommunicado for periods of 36 hours or longer and that the magistrate was either unable because of the volume of work, or unwilling, to give information concerning the charges and to admit to bail with reasonable promptness. Chester was not prepared for and did not develop or adopt procedures adequate for handling mass arrests.

19. There was credible evidence that representatives of the press were unwelcome to the police as witnesses of the events of the three critical days referred to. Cameras were destroyed or damaged and newsmen physically abused. It is possible that they were in the way of the police. Grave suspicions are created, however, when authorities appear to fear the eyes of the press.

20. The events under review in Chester received extensive news coverage from the mass communications media. The Commission recognizes the importance of such coverage. Because of the nature of the events, involving as they did the concurrent movements and activi-

ties of many persons and groups, and the confusion attendant upon the three critical demonstrations above referred to, especially those of April 22 and April 24 which occurred after dark, some distortions occurred. The Commission believes that the treatment accorded the events of March 28, April 22 and April 24 in the press and on the air was in some instances inaccurate and in other instances colored and inflammatory. Some examples of this kind of treatment are given in Chapters III and IX of this report. The Commission believes that these distortions aggravated the problems of all concerned in Chester.

The foregoing observations are made without impugning in any way the information given to the Commission by representatives of the press during the course of its hearings, upon whose statements we have placed considerable reliance.

21. Having discussed the specific and unfortunate consequences of the demonstration in terms of the use of force by both demonstrators and police, we mention in closing the ingredients which we believe necessary in any solution of the long-range problems facing Chester. Responsible Negro leadership, in Chester as elsewhere, desperately needs the cooperation and collaboration of responsive white leadership in the effort to effect substantial changes in the economic, educational, civic and social conditions. We believe that a sense of urgency must accompany this response. We accept as applicable to Chester the view expressed editorially by *The New York Times* on August 2, 1964 that —

> . . .what is needed is a sense of emergency by all citizens and all public officials on the imperativeness of community action to begin the long task of eradicating the slums, improving the schools and providing genuine equality of opportunity.

22. The formation of the Greater Chester Movement designed to deal with many of the problems which the demonstrators were protesting is a hopeful sign. The Commission is impressed with the calibre and representative nature of its membership and with the scope of the goals of GCM's officials. Attacks on the basic problems of Chester have also begun through actions of the Mayor and other City officials, the Director of Urban Renewal, the Board of Education, the Pennsylvania Human Relations Commission, the State Departments of Public Welfare and Public Instruction, as well as GCM. Implementation and utilization of the benefits of the Federal Economic

47

Opportunity Act of 1964 should prove helpful. Even as this report is being written, it is noted that a new group has been organized in Chester called the Committee of Economic Opportunity which has expressed discontent with the progress of the Greater Chester Movement and is seeking city, state and federal support for its own plan of urban redevelopment. The chairman of the new committee is also the chairman of the Committee For Freedom Now. Thus, it is evident that unity and agreement have not yet been reached as to the most effective means of bringing about needed improvements in the total community. It is to be hoped that cooperation and coordination in these programs can be speedily realized and that further splintering of efforts and organizations will be avoided.

23. While it is too soon for fruitful results to be evidenced by the recent constructive developments in Chester, the Commission dares to hope that with unity, mutual respect, cooperation and patience, progress will be made in Chester in the foreseeable future toward realizing its potential not only as a revitalized industrial center but also as a viable residential community.

Recommendations*

The Commission respectfully makes the following recommendations on the basis of its investigation and report.

A. *Recommendations to Local Authorities*

1. That there be instituted a program of police training in the handling of civil rights demonstrations, in crowd control and in community relations. This program should include instruction in the causes of social unrest and in the nature of civil rights activities and public demonstrations. The training should also stress the desirability for understanding treatment of those arrested in the process of dramatizing what they believe to be unjust conditions, unless the conduct of those being arrested clearly calls for different and more drastic police action.

2. That continuous communication be established and maintained between police and other local officials and civil rights organizations and their leaders.

---

* This section originally appeared as Chapter XVII of the Commission's report.

3. That proper compensation be paid to police for overtime work.

4. That the "deputizing" as special police of municipal employees not trained in police work for duty in connection with civil rights demonstrations be discontinued.

5. That no member of the local police force should hold any official position or office in a political party.

6. That consideration be given to the re-establishment of a Chester human relations commission fully representative of the community, either under the aegis of the Greater Chester Movement or as an advisory group to the new City Human Renewal Director or as an advisory agency working directly with the Mayor. One of the first concerns of a local human relations commission should be the improvement of relations between the police and other city officials and civil rights organizations.

7. That local public officials continue their cooperation with the Greater Chester Movement, and with state and federal agencies, in order to improve the social and economic conditions of the disadvantaged groups in Chester, both white and Negro, and in order to bring these groups more directly into the life of the community in business, industry, housing and education.

8. That provision be made for adequate assistance to the committing magistrate in emergency situations, such as those resulting from mass arrests, in order to expedite the processing and disposition of cases.

B. *Recommendations to State Authorities*

1. That the traditional role of the State Police in supplementing local police forces only when it is believed that the situation has gone beyond the control of local authorities be reviewed and reassessed to find a workable means, acceptable to local authorities, to make the State Police available for a more constructive role before riotous or other unmanageable conditions develop. The State Police with its high standards of training and discipline, if brought in at an earlier stage of mass demonstrations, would better serve to maintain law and order, to protect the public interest and to protect the demonstrators in the exercise of their constitutional right of protest.

2. That the efforts of the Commissioner of the State Police to provide training for State Police officers in the background and nature of the civil rights movement and in the understanding control of civil rights demonstrations be encouraged and accelerated, and that the State Police continue to conduct training programs for the same purposes for municipal police officers.

3. That the Commissioner of the Bureau of Correction of the Pennsylvania Department of Justice study the problem of adequate detention facilities in situations where there are mass arrests, as in the Chester demonstrations.

4. That legislation be considered to broaden the power of the Pennsylvania Human Relations Commission so as to enable it to deal generally with problems of racial discrimination and racial tensions throughout the Commonwealth. It may be appropriate to include in these enlarged powers the authority, when requested by the Governor, to investigate claims of excessive use of force by police in civil rights protest activities.

C. *Recommendations to Civil Rights Organizations*

1. That young children not be used in civil rights demonstrations where arrests are anticipated.

2. That civil rights leaders stress to participants in demonstrations the rights and duties of the police and their necessary and important role in the maintenance of law and order; also that they emphasize the impropriety and futility of focusing on the police general resentment concerning allegedly unjust conditions.

3. That if non-violent tactics are to be employed, more effective training in the techniques of non-violence be undertaken.

4. That civil rights leaders warn the members of their organizations of the dangers and penalties of civil disobedience tactics, particularly those not related to the grievances being protested, and that such tactics be avoided when they interfere with the security, safety and normal functioning of the community at large.

50

5. That open and continuous communication be maintained with police and municipal authorities with respect to all public meetings and demonstrations.

6. That civil rights leaders participate constructively in community efforts in which problems of concern to the Negroes in Chester are being considered, such participation to include, for example, membership in a local human relations commission, if created, in the Greater Chester Movement, and in similar activities; and that, to this end, any splintering of efforts and organizations be avoided.*

1.372 Statement by the Mayor in Response to the Report of the Governor's Commission

JAMES H. GORBEY**

The report of the Governor's Commission to investigate the problems involved in civil rights demonstrations in Chester was too restrictive in its scope.

The Commission members concluded in numerous instances that the demonstrators participated in illegal acts that merited arrest with sufficient force. Despite these findings, the Commission investigators concentrated their attention on each allegation of "police brutality" with little regard for the offenses against police officers and very little concern for the violated civil rights of persons other than non-whites.

The report in general, in my opinion, is a classic example of "Monday Morning Quarterback" activity. After limited consideration of the violent acts committed against the community's peace and tranquility, the Commission made numerous recommendations. These recommendations are worthy of consideration during periods of normal calm but would be of little value in maintaining law and order in a condition that occurs when a portion of a society decides to disturb the peace of a community in anarchical actions.

---

* Mayor James H. Gorbey, a panelist in the PLI forum, took issue with certain parts of the preceding report. His statement follows.

** Mayor of Chester, Pa.

The Commission obtained information from a large number of demonstrators but restricted its effort to obtain statements from other eyewitnesses. The preponderance of statements from demonstrators and their sympathizers produced an imbalance of information that affected the Commission's inquiry.

The Commission's attempt to function as an investigative agency without the authority to subpoena witnesses and without authority to administer oaths resulted in major handicaps. The best investigative agencies in the nation would be powerless without such vital elements.

The report section concerned with the history of developments before the demonstrations mentioned Chester's increasing non-white population, weakening industrial strength, and declining tax base. These are very general conditions that are evident in many other cities in the nation.

Does the existence of these conditions give a portion of the citizenry the right to abandon law and order and riot in protest? Does the Commission's report imply that these persons should be granted special privileges beyond the authority of the U.S. Constitution to protest alleged grievances?

To give illustrations of the Commission's limited interest in matters other than the protection of the rights of demonstrators, I refer to the incident that occurred November 12th, 1963 in the Chester Municipal Building. The Commission made mere passing notice of the incident.

"There were some disturbances at the Municipal Building and about 150 people were arrested," was the report's master understatement. While the Commission consumed pages of the report in a study of the social and economic background of demonstrators, it satisfied its interest in the November 12th incident with brief mention.

On that date a horde of demonstrators swarmed into the Municipal Building in a wild sit-in and stand-in demonstration. The action immobilized the business of all offices, resulted in considerable property damage and threatened physical harm to municipal officials and employees. Female employees were near hysteria. The incident, because of its shocking nature, could have resulted in death for city personnel with certain medical conditions.

Chester police had no alternative but to make mass arrests. The same would result if similar demonstrations occurred in Harrisburg or Washington, D.C. To permit this conduct would be to grant approval of frenzied mob rule over constituted government.

The report's mention of the demonstration of the night of March 27th, 1964, Good Friday, is gentle handling of fact. It mentions demonstrators marching and singing in the downtown business area in a manner that appears harmless to the unknowing reader. The description sounded less disturbing than a high school pep rally.

Instead of being peaceful, the demonstration, the first of an intensive series designed to force the local government to yield to the will of certain civil rights leaders, disturbed the peace of downtown apartment dwellers and those who live in certain residential areas and blocked the use of highways and sidewalks.

What happened to the civil rights of those persons who wanted to walk on sidewalks and wanted to drive on highways in Chester that night?

A large group of demonstrators remained standing and sitting in the middle of the intersection of 5th and Market Streets for more than 1½ hours. They blocked the passage of vehicles and could have caused a serious problem in the delay of ambulances, fire equipment and other emergency vehicles. The police had no recourse but to make arrests. The report indicated that a demonstration leader "called off" the demonstration "after a brief sitdown". Actually the demonstration ended with the arrival of a State Police riot squad and not before.

A portion of Chester's population indicated that they wanted to abandon law and order in an undemocratic attempt to place civil rights demonstrations above and beyond the law. They were seeking a special, super-important civil rights status with court immunity. They sought this undemocratic status rather than place their grievances before the judicial system in a civilized manner.

It is strange that the Commission considered certain facets of the school problem, the original complaint that triggered the entire dispute, but hurried past other important considerations of the same problem.

The closing of public schools, forced upon city school officials in an effort to protect the lives of students and to protect the buildings from damage through violent demonstrations inside buildings, was

53

mentioned in brief. There was no detailed consideration of the invasion of the buildings by demonstrators. The Commission limited its interest to minimal consideration despite the peril to both students and teachers.

Not one school official, with the exception of Clarence Roberts, a school director, was interviewed by the Commission. Roberts apparently was contacted in relation to damage to his auto during a protest demonstration outside his home. Demonstrators displayed particular anger towards Roberts because he is a Negro.

Although countless cries of police brutality have been sounded for propaganda purposes by civil rights leaders, not one single prosecution has been initiated. Not one claimant has undergone oath and made criminal charges before either minor courts or courts of record.

The key to this mystery is realized when it is recognized that unsuccessful pursuit of criminal charges would make these claimants liable to possible civil action. Individual police officers named as defendants in criminal actions would be entitled to seek redress in the form of countersuits, civil actions to obtain damages. This indicates why the demonstrators restrict themselves to public protests of alleged brutality.

They are seeking to avoid the proper function of jurisprudence while attempting to hide in the shadows of allegations. The demand for a special investigation, the demand that resulted in the Governor appointing this Commission, could be interpreted as an attempt to restrain the action of police in future demonstrations. The threat of subsequent investigations would resemble a form of intimidation.

The reasoning of demonstrators seems to attempt to establish a set of double standards that would require other citizens to obey all existing laws but would relieve the demonstrators of the responsibility of compliance. Civil rights leaders encourage demonstrators to break laws. They reason that they can break the laws at will by a mere self-determination of their action as being "right."

The published claims that demonstrators were arrested without advance warning by police on a number of occasions were positive lies. The warnings were given in each instance, usually with public address equipment amplifying the voice order. These police commands were witnessed by many other persons and were ignored by demonstrators who were arrested.

The Commission did establish that a number of organizations, namely the Greater Philadelphia Branch of the American Civil Liberties Union; the Fair Housing Council of Delaware Valley; the Catholic Intergroup Relations Council; and the Inter-Faith Committee for Reconciliation, made reports that generally concluded that an excessive amount of force was used by police. The Commission establishes that these reports were based "largely" on newspaper accounts and "to a limited degree" on eyewitness observation.

The Commission claimed that a comprehensive report by Professor Paul Bender, of the University of Pennsylvania Law School, prepared for the Greater Philadelphia Branch, American Civil Liberties Union, concluded that the allegations of excessive force by police "were supportable in a number of instances". If this organization has determined that prima facie cases existed, why has it hesitated to assist the aggrieved persons in preparing cases for submission before the courts?

The leaders who conducted civil disobedience demonstrations through the use of passive resistance shortchanged their followers. The people apparently received instructions to "go limp" to delay arrest but were not given sufficient instructions for their protection. As a result, some of these people became innocent victims through their ignorance of the law. They were not given the basic information that any flaying of arms or accompanying disorder may be construed as resistance or even as assault if it occurs after a police officer announces a proper arrest.

A description of the "chanting and singing" of demonstrators provided by the Commission is misleading. The Commission accounts make it appear somewhat pleasant in nature. As an eyewitness to many demonstrations, I can say this is very different from the vulgar oaths and obscene curses that were hurled at police. I wonder how certain religious leaders managed to justify their presence in some of the demonstrations. It was awkward to see clerics walking in a demonstration, with some demonstrators shouting obscenities and others showing the effects of alcohol.

While the report made extensive use of published accounts of alleged police brutality, it displayed total ignorance of published accounts of the assaults on white persons by marauding gangs of Negro hoodlums.

Innocent white persons were attacked and beaten on the streets of Chester during the height of the violence fired by demonstrations. Those that perpetrated the attacks were members of the fringe element who were fired by the actions and statements of the leaders. They sought special violence by pouncing upon victims in wolf pack attacks. One of the victims included a soldier who was wearing the uniform of the U.S. Army at the time he was attacked. Not one of the identified victims was interviewed by the Commission. The information of the victims would have been of general interest value if nothing more.

The report made full mention of a street light that was extinguished outside the police station during the April 22nd demonstration. It was mentioned in such a manner that it implied that police may have turned off the light in order to beat demonstrators in the darkness. Actually the flash of photographers' lighting equipment extinguished the light by affecting the sensitive light control device. A mere contact with officials of the Philadelphia Electric Company would have established this for the record and relieved police of the inferred suspicion that police exercised any control of the fully automatic street light.

The veracity of civil rights leaders and certain clergy who told a story about the fate of a pregnant woman allegedly beaten by police can be given serious questioning. They claimed that the woman suffered a miscarriage because she was beaten in the abdomen by a police officer. The Commission report subjected these damaging rumors to the light of truth when it established that rumors about two women being beaten in similar manner actually involved one person who gave birth to a child in August after a normal pregnancy term. The rumor was one of the most vicious used to incite persons. It was accepted without question because the information was presented by persons who should have been above the practice of repeating unfounded rumors.

The section of the report devoted to "Premises of the Commission" was the best received portion. It cited that "Respect for Law and Order is the cornerstone of every free society. This is particularly true of the United States, where the rule of law was the guiding principle in the establishment of our form of government".

I recommend the entire section as required reading for all civil rights leaders and their followers. If they had taken heed of these premises and recognized the inherent rights of others, the demonstrations in Chester would have been peaceful and the Commission's existence would not have been necessary.

"The right to full citizenship, including reasonable and equal opportunity for gainful employment, adequate housing and sound education, increases understanding and appreciation of the necessity for law and order," the report states. It also stated: "Police agencies exist at every level of government for the purpose of preserving law and order, and every police officer stands in the vanguard of the protection of the public peace and the public safety".

This portion of the report accurately portrays the role of Chester police officers during the civil disobedience demonstrations. The police formed the thin line that separated the respect for law and order from those who advocated the rule of the jungle. "The role of the police is difficult, dangerous and demanding and often misunderstood," was one of the most significant statements in the report.

It is puzzling to me that most newspapers elected to emphasize dramatic portions that supported the position of demonstrators and decided to ignore statements that defended the action of police. Some newspapers slanted stories related to the report. These were the same newspapers that leaned in one direction during the coverage of the demonstrations. Apparently some officials of newspapers, television and radio allowed individual beliefs to influence news coverage.

Television stations and networks expended considerable amounts of money and effort in order to obtain films of demonstration activities. The majority attempted to present Chester as a cruel city where innocent demonstrators were being persecuted by evil police and city officials.

Transmission of this inaccurate image was accomplished. Television news crews did Chester a grave injustice with their hit-and-run tactics. The citizens of the City, and especially police, have been subjected to tremendous amounts of unfair criticism because of the slanted presentation of news material.

One network television crew displayed its zest to obtain certain pictures at any price. The crew commandeered a taxi and induced the driver to drive the wrong way on a one-way street. The crew made a distinguished appearance riding on the top of the taxi.

An almost concentrated effort was apparent by the press to present the police in a poor light at every opportunity. Some individual members of the press overextended themselves in their exuberance to present an image of the police as monsters. The Chester police officers were abused by demonstrators and maligned by the press as they attempted a defense of law and order.

The Commission report identified one of the social problems in urban areas as "the tension created when the police are compelled to use force in controlling manifestations of social protest". This section is a very accurate statement of the condition that existed in Chester.

The report declared that the use of force to terminate or prevent breaches of the peace, affray or riot "is proper only to the extent he (the police officer) reasonably believes it to be necessary to preserve law and order". Greater force than this can be considered "excessive". The force applied by Chester police met these requirements and was not excessive. I have found in a study of the individual reports that force was used as a last resort when people assaulted police or resisted arrest.

It must be realized that many persons—I specifically refer to those sympathizers of civil rights demonstrators who claimed to be impartial witnesses—saw violence in the streets for the first time in their lives. Their credibility as witnesses can be questioned because of their personal motives and their shocked mental state.

The accounts of some witnesses when compared to police reports result in wide variation. These witnesses were unusual in that they were able to "see" police brutality but were unable to recognize a single instance of brutality when police were injured. There were some witnesses who made themselves available at various demonstrations. These persons managed to observe what happened in mob actions, such as mass arrests and dispersals, but were unable to observe one criminal act invoked by demonstrators against police.

The report referred to a state court opinion relative to the treatment of bystanders in riots and the hazards of the innocent in situations involving the suppression of disorder. The court opinion that was cited states: "It is not safe even for persons conscious of innocence to resist him (the police officer)". The opinion states further: "In disturbed conditions of society it is not always possible to perfectly protect innocent rights and the maintenance of public order is paramount and must be attained even if innocent individuals occasionally suffer."

I offer this as an explanation for the arrest of photographers and reporters who claimed to be innocent victims. News personnel must obey police commands during a disturbed condition. When the police command that an area be cleared during the time of turmoil, the area must be cleared without any delay or obstruction. Those photographers and reporters who attempted to remain within an area being cleared were arrested for their interference. Their arrests were justified when they prevented police from executing their assigned duties.

The public disorders received vast notoriety and the streets of Chester could not be considered as normal peaceful areas during the demonstrations. Those who ventured into these areas to satisfy personal curiosity did so at their own personal risk. Persons who entered these areas during those hectic hours without good reason displayed poor judgment. If they were injured or arrested they have only themselves to blame. They suffered because of uncontrolled morbid curiosity.

The Commission report mentions a citizen's constitutional right to peaceful protest and describes "street sit-ins and other types of civil disobedience" as "illegal acts". The report said "orders to cease such conduct are appropriate and arrests must be expected where there is non-compliance".

The report was critical of the judgment of leaders of the demonstrations for using young children "to perform an unlawful act designed to provoke arrest". The report absolved police from certain charges of brutality and stated that the Commission "is satisfied that several were resisting arrest".

The Commission determined that police were "justified" in making mass arrests on April 22nd when a large number of demonstrators "blocked the sidewalk and were trespassing on private property in a residential neighborhood". It said the second demonstration on that

59

date, outside the police station, ended with justified mob dispersal. The report stated: "The amount of force used was warranted in so far as it was directed at the rock throwers and other violent members of the crowd".

The report mentioned that Dr. Felder E. Rouse, Jr., a leader of demonstrators, appeared outside the police station and although he claimed he was interested in ending the demonstration, made no attempt to persuade the crowd to disperse and avert violence.

The report explicitly mentioned that Rouse had sufficient time to attempt dispersal through persuasion but "attempted nothing in this direction". The Commission stated that it believes violence might not have occurred if the demonstration had been prevented.

The Commission said Philip Savage, an NAACP official, viewed the April 24th demonstration from a half-block distance. The report accused Savage of "leaving the demonstration without top leadership" although he was aware of the "atmosphere" and the condition of the "fringe element" and the number of inebriates in the area of the demonstration. The report said the leaders "set in motion a chain of events which were started by an illegal act". It said the leaders must share the responsibility for the violence with demonstrators through errors in judgment.

The report confirmed that police "were the targets of bricks, stones and bottles" and termed the condition "near riotous". I contend that the condition was "riotous" at this point. A condition is riotous in my opinion when such missiles are thrown at police, and not near riotous.

I claim that the Chester Police prevented an outbreak of terror like that which has rocked other northern cities by their display of forthright action against the lawless. The action of police here may have caused injury to a few but prevented mass carnage.

The report concluded that the tactics used by police to disperse mobs "were standard procedure for the quelling of riots" and at the same time criticized police for indiscriminate use of nightsticks. With the violence that existed, does the Commission suggest that police should have dispersed rioters with the use of voice and show of badge alone?

The report mentioned that various elements of the press provided a stage for the performance of leaders and demonstrators. I heartily agree with this notation. Furthermore, I claim that a number of press representatives failed to meet the responsibility of faithful reporting of facts in a fair and accurate manner. It is interesting to note that the Commission cited the insertion of "an undue amount of color which tended to be inflammatory" and the "inaccurate" news reports and "distortions".

The report singled out an account by Richard Taylor, executive director of the Fair Housing Council of Delaware Valley, as "another instance of faulty reporting". Taylor claimed that he witnessed police beating a woman with clubs.

The report absolved Magistrate Philip C. Puzzanchera, target of massive criticism by civil rights leaders, of any misdeed. The report concluded that the bail amounts and fines set by Puzzanchera "appear to be within permissible limits". Persons who claimed higher amounts were found to have been arrested several times in separate violations, according to the report.

In conclusion I want to state that I will not initiate any punitive action against the Chester Police on the basis of the loose allegations received by the Commission. The incidents involved merited the use of force.

I commend the Chester Police for their restraint in view of the insults, abuses and degradations from demonstrators. To those who were assaulted and injured, I praise their devotion to duty. The City will be unable to compensate these officers for the valiant service they performed in the defense of the right of liberty and justice for all.

In response to the Commission's eight recommendations made on the basis of its investigation and report, I would like to make the following comments:

1. That there be instituted a program of police training in the handling of civil rights demonstrations.

At the start of my tenure of office on January 6, there was immediately instituted an educational program for all members of the Police Department covering all phases of police work. Since the cessation of demonstrations at the beginning of May, there have been numerous schools that our police have attended, seminars for officers and conferences for city and police officials. All of these conferences and seminars were designed to improve community relations and to give the policemen a better idea of the civil rights problems and the proper enforcement of existing laws.

2. That continuous communications be established between local officials and civil rights leaders.

Communications in the City of Chester between the present public officials and the civil rights leaders have been excellent. Prior to and during the demonstrations, the most militant of the leaders carried on almost daily conversations with us. This friendly relationship exists today and we have succeeded in bringing several of the more militant leaders into the activity of the Greater Chester Movement.

3. That proper compensation be paid to police for overtime work.

According to the Third Class Cities Code, no overtime compensation may be paid to police officers. This is a matter for the State Legislature to correct.

4. Deputizing as "special police" of municipal employees.

According to the laws of the land, we have the right and duty to deputize any citizen to maintain law and order, and in the absence of a better suggestion from the Commission, what other procedure can be taken?

5. No member of the local police force shall hold any official position or office in a political party.

The Code of Third Class Cities does not limit the political activities of any police officer. They have the privilege and right to maintain their freedom of judgment as citizens of the city in which they live. If these rights and privileges are to be taken away, this, too, must be done by an act of the State Legislature. We feel that to do otherwise would be dictatorial and an infringement of their personal liberties.

6. Consideration be given to the re-establishment of a Chester Human Relations Commission fully representative of the community.

The Human Relations Commission that was functioning at the time of the outbreak of the demonstrations was representative of the community and included the leaders of the two active civil rights groups in the City of Chester. The more militant of the leaders refused to work with the Human Relations Commission or to meet with them or members of the Chester School Board who were trying to reach a satisfactory conclusion with regard to school conditions and *de facto* segregation. City Council has created the Department of Human Renewal and employed as its director a former staff member of the State Human Relations Commission to deal directly with all elements of the civil rights movement in Chester. The Director is familiar with our problems after having worked in the Chester area for six years. The results of his efforts are being demonstrated with the more active cooperation of civil rights leaders. When it is deemed advisable to re-establish a full commission, this will be done under the direction of the Chester City Council. When the commission is re-established, it will be composed of representative groups that will be acceptable to all elements involved.

7. That local public officials continue their cooperation with the Greater Chester Movement and with State and Federal agencies.

The Greater Chester Movement was organized through the efforts of the City Council and the Governor's Office, the Secretary of Welfare, Arlin Adams, and interested leading citizens of the Chester area. The aims of the Greater Chester Movement were the planks in my platform when I was candidate for this office last year. We intend to continue our cooperation with the Greater Chester Movement. I am a member of the Steering Committee of the Greater Chester Movement. We have been successful in involving all of the Departments of the City in various Greater Chester Movement sub-committees. We have succeeded in bringing about the cooperation of all elements within the city and we will continue our fullest cooperation with the Greater Chester Movement and the Federal government in its poverty program.

8. That provision be made for adequate assistance to the Committing Magistrate in emergency situations.

Here again the Code of Third Class Cities limits the assistance that can be given the police magistrate in emergency situations. The Code provides for one committing magistrate and he conducts hearings in the Police Station. The other aldermen must sit in their own bailiwicks. Due to the limited strength of the police force, the taking of those arrested to aldermen other than the police magistrate would be impossible. Here, too, the State Legislature would have to act to change the Code of Third Class Cities to make available magistrates sitting in the Police Station under emergency circumstances.

1.4 QUESTIONS AND ANSWERS

Question: Should not advocacy be more properly left to the executive branch of the administration of the City or State of New York?

MR. LOWELL: I tried to make clear the fact that we were acting in the role of mediator-advocate. We have the role of advocate because local law in the City of New York gives us this responsibility.

It gives us broad jurisdiction to eliminate segregation, discrimination, prejudice and bigotry wherever it may arise. It gives us a very broad jurisdiction over business, labor and schools.

We have jurisdiction, but we have no power, and there is a very important distinction between the two. The broader the jurisdiction, the more limited the power, the more difficult the job.

We have the specific power, for example, to remedy evils in the field of housing. We enforce our local fair housing practices law. We have the power to seek an injunction or a stay in the rental of private accommodations under a prima facie case of discrimination in the sale or rental of that private accommodation.

We have power to recommend the cancellation of contracts on the part of a contractor who does business with the City of New York. We have no power over labor unions. We have no power over private businesses. We have no power, for example, over the school system, but we have become deeply involved in the problem of integration in the City of New York. It does present a problem, but in terms of what we think is our responsibility, if we had to choose we would choose advocacy over mediation. We think that the role of advocate is more effective for an agency like ours to play in resolving the problems of our society which local law gives us the responsibility to resolve.

Question: Is it not true that the racial policy of Chester is intransigent; that even after the demonstrations the school board although ordered by the State Commission on Human Relations to desegregate, has decided to fight the ruling in the Court; that the Greater Chester movement has initiated a Negro removal program under the guise of an urban renewal program; that the person appointed to the Chairmanship of the Chester Human Relations Commission has been one of the prominent members of the Chester Parents' Association, the group most actively resisting any change in the existing treatment of Negroes; that Chester has just recently instituted the use of police dogs on regular patrol duty; that there has been for about a year now an apprehension in the Negro and white communities which the present settlement has not alleviated?

MAYOR GORBEY: This business of a Negro removal program under the guise of an urban renewal program is, of course, a falsehood. Recently the Chairman of the Committee for Freedom Now accepted a role on the Steering Committee of the Greater Chester Movement, which two groups merged forces after negotiations of some several hours. I doubt that he would have joined if he had felt that way about the program. Also we have hired a Deputy Director who is an expert and was second in command in Norfolk, where I think that they have one of the best programs. We decided to leave this to the experts.

As for the statement about a prominent member being appointed from the Chester Parents' Association to the Chester Human Relations Commission, I would like to say that I did not appoint the Commission. It was appointed by a previous Mayor and has not functioned since shortly before I came into office. It was really Stanley Branche who did that. However, we are most fortunate now to have Norman Watts as our city human relations man. He has served in the Chester area for six years and was the leg man here for the State Human Relations Commission.

As for the statement that Chester has just recently instituted police dogs, yes we have. I think they have been very effective, but this action was not directed toward Negroes.

It is true that there is apprehension in the Negro and white communities which the present settlement has not alleviated.

Question: If you had it to do over again, Chief Bail, would you deputize civilian untrained police for use as policemen against demonstrators? How much was the excessive force, to use the phrase in the Governor's report, due to panic on the part of the police or to a new policy which was not apparent prior to April 21?

MR. BAIL: I will answer this by saying that I personally would do it over again. I believe every man here would have done the same thing. I had only 82 men on the police force. When you have between three to six hundred people, you have to get help and you cannot get help from men who are inexperienced.

The men that I put in the automobiles were experienced policemen. They were not sent out on the street by themselves. There had to be at least two officers with them at all times.

As for the second part of that question, we had to use force against force, and we are within our power to do that.

Question: What is the panel's recommendation on the handling of publicity and press releases during the time that negotiations are going on, particularly if they are going on in secret?

MAYOR MacLEAN: I would suggest that you have none for the following reason. We tried it both ways. We tried it with publicity and we tried it without publicity, and without publicity was much better.

These negotiations are very much like labor negotiations. You just cannot reach a settlement when one side makes a statement saying, "We'll never surrender," and the other side yells, "You've got to surrender today or else."

However, if you have a quiet meeting the chances are that one side will agree to do something by October 1 or July 4 and all this can be worked out, but it cannot be done publicly.

All the lawyers here understand this. You start off with an insurance company by asking for $300,000 for a broken leg. The insurance company will say, "We'll never pay," but then you get them off to the side and after a few depositions they find out that the plaintiff really broke his leg. Then you learn that the insurance company will pay $25,000, and probably your client will accept it.

This is exactly the same sort of thing. You will not get the dispute settled in public, and especially you will not get it done in a community where the majority of the population is unhappy about changing their current arrangements. So to answer your question, I think it is self-evident that you cannot reach a settlement in the glare of publicity.

MR. LOWELL: I think that you cannot answer this question completely by saying no publicity whatsoever, because publicity may be helpful in a situation where there is potential violence. In a community like New York the build-up of violence may be obvious to the parties involved, to the public and to the Negro community. In this type of situation the people are apt to sit down and try to resolve the problem, even though they know nothing about the substance of what is being suggested. For that matter awareness of the negotiations would be important to keep any additional violence from developing.

Secondly, as I have said, when your negotiations seem to be breaking down the very real threat of exposure to the public of the weakness of one side or another may result in bringing them back to the bargaining table. In general, therefore, I would agree that this is not the place for newspapers or television, but sometimes it is necessary.

MR. SCHERMER: I agree with Mayor MacLean that in a period of negotiation, if you are attempting to deal with representatives of groups in conflict with some degree of integrity, the nature of those negotiations will have to be kept from the public until there is some understanding. But I protest loudly against the thought that race relations matters or community conflict problems can be resolved in a vacuum or behind the scenes.

The essence of good community relations is that a very large percentage of the population knows and understands what is going on. Tension and fear generate in a vacuum of noninformation. Therefore a major challenge to any agency working in this field is to bring the mass media into participation. This is not easy.

In many communities the mass media are more or less captive of one viewpoint or another and tend to misinterpret the information. But this is a part of the job: bringing the mass media into the role of telling the facts, relating them with integrity, and making sure that the whole community is as fully informed as possible.

Anybody who thinks that you disseminate information to a hundred thousand people through informal channels highly mistakes the process. By the time the third person has handled your message for you, it is grossly distorted.

MR. STAHL: I want to give two examples of the mass media problem. After the Harlem, Rochester and New Jersey situations, there were rumors that Baltimore was next. The technique in Baltimore was to saturate newspapers, television and radio with information about the rumors and how the mayor, the police and other governmental and civic organizations were trying to meet the threat. The result, fortunately, was that nothing happened.

In Pittsburgh the procedure was just the opposite. The newspapers were kept informed by the Human Relations Commission, the Mayor's office, and the police of rumors that strangers were coming into town and other intelligence. The newspapers agreed not to print any of this because it was felt that the mere communication or dissemination of rumors might generate further rumors and eventually cause further trouble. These strategies both achieved excellent results.

Question: Is there not a conflict between the goal of maintaining peace and order, and antidiscrimination laws which exist in a good many states? What is the alternative to enforcing the antidiscrimination statutes which have been on the books for a long time but which for one reason or another have not been enforced? What is the alternative to the kind of demonstrations which have preoccupied this conference? Have there ever been major social movements in this country that were constrained within the existing interpretation of law and order?

MR. LOWELL: I think there is not necessarily a conflict between the laws with respect to law and order and antidiscrimination.

The Police Department of the City of New York did a very effective job in the White Castle dispute. They saw a situation develop where over a thousand young white boys between the ages of 16 and 19 were told to arrive on the scene, and the Police Department carefully kept the situation under control.

There were occasional arrests of a few of these boys. There were also arrests which received considerable publicity of a group of American Nazis who were stimulating some difficulty in the area. There was little sympathy on either side for those people, but basically the Police Department did its job of preserving law and order and permitted peaceful picketing and a peaceful demonstration. The Com-

68

mission on Human Rights has found that the majority of circumstances in New York City have been similar. The police have been able to handle their responsibilities, and we have handled ours.

Question: In the course of implementing the New York Commission's policy of urging employers to make an effort to remedy the evils of the past, when compliance is achieved and the Negroes are hired, how would the Commission handle the complaint of racial discrimination by a rejected, qualified, white applicant for the same job?

MR. LOWELL: This is a traditional question. We encountered it when the Commission first enunciated its policies in October, 1963. Countless reporters and television inquisitors posed this question, which the Commission could not answer.

They gave an example of two equal people arriving on the scene, being interviewed. Their qualifications were exactly the same. The only difference was that one was white and the other was Negro. Which one should be chosen?

This is a fiction. There is no such thing as two equal people. It is a fine theoretical question, but we do not have to go into how many angels there are on the head of a pin and how many can fit, because that is not the problem. We have found over the past year that the problem simply has not arisen.

We have found that private industry after private industry, private business after private business has been able to say in the year 1964 they never really did anything about equalizing the employment structure.

We in the Commission are now going back into the clippings of the press all over the country and summarizing what has been publicly acknowledged in this field. I think this is the most wonderful progress that has been made in America over a period as short as one year. Now group after group is making the kind of effort that we are talking about.

We do not ask them, "Do you or do you not believe in discrimination against whites?" You can turn the question around and say that if they choose the white man, this is perfectly all right, because the inquisitor would base his answer on the fact that this was always the white man's job and the Negro is pushing him out of line.

We really are very serious about this. We have found that the problem has not come up. There is no such thing as two equal people. We are not talking about types of persons. We are talking about the fact that American society just never has gone into the advertising industry, into the brokerage industry, to attempt to find a competent Negro or Negroes for these jobs. They never have done this, but now with the publicity they are broadening the base from which they can seek their employees.

We are not asking any bank or stock brokerage firm to take in an incompetent person. We are only asking that these people be given an opportunity that society has never given them before. Tremendous progress is being made in this area. With this kind of progress we are going to resolve this problem in America in a most effective way.

Question: I believe Mr. Jacobson, and I think the Mayor and Mr. McMunigal as well, all indicated that they thought the school board acted with great intransigence in their failure to recognize some of these problems.

They all indicated that they had no legal power to deal with the situation. My question is whether there was any attempt on the part of the administration to publicly condemn or point out these facts through the press, thus indicating what they were trying to do and perhaps gaining some sympathy for the administration. This might have shown that they were attempting to handle the problem with some degree of good faith. Even more important, did they attempt to bring public pressure, as Mayor MacLean did, by going into the community and finding a Committee of One Hundred or Bishops or Monsignors? If not, in retrospect, might these efforts have helped to prevent the kind of impasse that occurred in Chester?

MAYOR GORBEY: First of all, I did not ask or bring pressure to bear on the school board to use their discretion in one form or another. I do not happen to feel that busing is the answer to the problems of the city of Chester. I do not think that sending children from one end of Chester to the other end to school is the answer, and I do not think that we can afford to bus them, if for no other reason than we need the money for our schools. I do not think you can strike a happy balance with 67 per cent Negro and the rest white. I feel that this is important if we are going to spend any money.

I do not think that Chester has an improper balance in the community itself. We would be spending only for Negroes. I think we should spend money for school facilities, and the training of teachers, not to try to get some percentage of black and whites over here and black and whites down there.

I think this is very foolish. I do not agree with the Commission on Human Relations report. If I were on the school board, I would probably be going to court to have it determined whether I can exercise my discretion as a board member or not. That is how I feel it should be. Does that answer your question?

VOICE IN THE AUDIENCE: No, sir. I am not asking about buses. I am saying that you said, and that you feel that the school board was acting with intransigence insofar as some remedies that could have been made at the time. I am asking whether you made these things public, whether you made any public statement criticizing the school board for their intransigent position? Did you try to get public pressure through the community organizations, the Chamber of Commerce, and so forth? In retrospect, if you did not, do you think it might have been a good idea?

MR. JACOBSON: Attempts were made to deal with the school board, as I spent some time telling you. The Chester Commission on Human Relations was an adjunct or branch of the Mayor's office, so that whatever we did, we did on behalf of the city government in attempting to deal with the school board.

There was a problem here in that the school board itself is a somewhat touchy organization. Sometime in October, before the demonstrations, the civil rights leaders raised different grievances against the school board. When that problem arose, the City Solicitor intervened. That particular problem was settled to a great extent by and through his efforts, and he subsequently incurred the wrath of the school board for doing this.

When this particular report of the City Human Relations Commission came out, I also incurred the wrath of the school board because as a city official I was telling the school board what to do. So you see we ran into this problem in spite of the fact that the civil rights groups in Chester say, "Don't give us that nonsense, you're both the same party, you're both the same thing." It just is not so. We really got into a lot of difficulty.

71

1.5 SUMMARY OF DISCUSSION
HAROLD C. FLEMING, *Moderator**

MR. FLEMING: I just want to say a few words to summarize this discussion. One is that it is not easy to resolve such interracial difficulties as we have been considering. I think we have seen from these case studies that in most instances the phrase "power structure" represents something of a fiction. It is too easy a concept. Instead, there is likely to be a "power stricture" in these communities that has to be resolved before you can get at the problem. In each case where there has been a resolution of difficulties, there has been one center of strong, positive leadership. Usually the community and the civil rights groups look to the Mayor as the man on the spot, whether or not he has official jurisdiction over the area that is being contested. Whether he does the job, gets other people to do it, or finds some instrumentality or base of leadership outside the public officialdom, the Mayor more than anybody else is looked to for leadership. It behooves him to use his ingenuity to get as much help as he can.

As Mayor MacLean pointed out, he must be persistent, patient, and often courageous.

Now, in all these cases, it was brought out that there was some division among the civil rights groups, the Negro leadership. We might as well accustom ourselves to this state of affairs. There is no monolithic Negro structure, just as there is no monolithic white structure in which all members of the group think alike and have the same views about tactics and strategy. There also is no single problem at the root of these community difficulties. Conflict arises because of one grievance or another, but very quickly we discover that we have to deal with a multiplicity of ailments in the human relations of a city in order to resolve even that one difficulty.

I have been impressed by the statements of the various panelists about the ultimate importance of economic self-interest as the glue that can bind the community back together when it is fractured by a social upheaval. This was borne out very clearly in two of our cases and perhaps in the third as well. Of course, it has been borne out again and again in other situations that we all know about.

---

* Acting Deputy Director, Community Relations Service, United States Department of Commerce; Executive Vice-President, Potomac Institute.

Only one thing remains to be said. I am sure the panelists who have done such an excellent job for us would agree that none of them feels their respective communities have made more than a beginning in solving the problems of equal treatment and equal opportunity. The kinds of processes we have been looking at today are going to have to be looked at again. Many more learning experiences are going to have to be shared at meetings like this.

1.6 SUMMARY OF WORKSHOP DISCUSSIONS*
1.61 DISCUSSION GROUP A**

The discussion leader suggested as the initial subject the various techniques available to the community in controlling protest demonstrations with a view to protecting both the rights of the public at large and the rights of free speech, assembly, and petition guaranteed by the First Amendment. Mr. Lankenau asked specifically whether arrests and physical removal of demonstrators were the only solutions to the problems of obstruction of public thoroughfares, the danger of violence, or breach of the peace.

Ed Joseph, the City Attorney of Flint, Michigan, pointed out a fundamental distinction between demonstrations which can or may infringe on the rights of the general public and those which affect primarily the rights of only one party. As an illustration of a demonstration of the latter type, Mr. Joseph referred to protest picketing held outside a bank in Flint and directed against the bank's alleged discriminatory employment practices. He observed that while there were minor obstructions of the public's free passage to and from the bank, no arrests were made, because no officer or customer of the bank would sign a complaint authorizing the issuance of a warrant. Mr. Joseph did not comment as to whether in his view arrests would have been appropriate as a matter of public policy.

---

* These workshop discussions with respect to the statements of crisis in Savannah, New York and Chester took place at the Practising Law Institute forum, "The Community and Racial Crises," in New York City on Dec. 4, 1964.

** Discussion Leader: John C. Lankenau, Attorney; former Assistant U.S. Attorney, Southern District of New York.

Reporter: John H. Doyle III, Attorney, Patterson, Belknap & Webb, New York City (on leave); Assistant Director, Lawyers' Committee for Civil Rights Under Law.

Mr. Anderson of Philadelphia, a member of the Commission on Racial Understanding, spoke with reference to the Chester demonstrations. He observed that the hostility to the police and the general state of tension were attributable to a basic lack of communication among the protesting groups, the Mayor's office and the School Board. He stated that in two meetings attended by the Committee for Freedom Now, the School Board was represented only by its attorneys. Further, the School Board invited representatives of the PAT (Parents' and Taxpayers' Association) to join in the meetings, a factor which greatly decreased the confidence of the protest leaders.

Mr. Robert Campbell of the District of Columbia, a member of the staff of the Corporation Counsel and of the Commissioners' Council on Human Rights, gave several examples of demonstrations successfully controlled in his city. Referring to the March on Washington in 1963, Mr. Campbell stated that the successful execution of this massive demonstration was possible as a result of long months of planning and consultation among police and city officials and the groups planning the protest march. Not a single arrest was made during the course of the entire demonstration. The route of the march was well mapped out. The District of Columbia Police were present in the crowd and exercised a moderating influence. A counterdemonstration by Lincoln Rockwell and his Nazi Party group produced no violence and was contained primarily through the efforts of the police officers who were able to anticipate and avert a direct confrontation.

Mr. Campbell also referred to a series of demonstrations against the Safeway Store chain in Washington, protesting its employment practices. The demonstrations took the form of picketing. Police were present at all times and prevented blockage of the store entrances. The demonstrators were told to keep moving, and no incidents of violence occurred. Nor were any arrests made.

Mr. Campbell also spoke of a demonstration which consisted of a march to Lafayette Square and a protest in front of the White House. In order to avoid any disorder, the police blocked off the streets marking the route of the march and allowed speeches to be made at Lafayette Park. As in the other cases discussed, no arrests were necessary.

In the light of the above examples, Mr. Campbell emphasized the importance of careful prior consultation by protest leaders with the police and city officials. Given proper planning, he stated, the demonstration can give effective voice to specific grievances without causing disorder and the necessity for arrests.

Mr. Allan Knight Chalmers, President of the NAACP Legal Defense and Educational Fund, Inc., observed that the discussants were placing excessive emphasis on the necessity of assuring that demonstrations took place smoothly. He noted that the essential purpose of demonstrations is to make the public aware of the protestants' underlying grievances. He suggested that the discussion focus on techniques of maximizing the publicity given to such grievances, consistent with the basic requirements of public order. He observed that in some instances the absolute right of the public to free passage in streets and other thoroughfares might be suspended if the result would permit an effective demonstration along peaceful lines.

Robert Garrington, a Police Captain in Flint, Michigan, stated that it was the duty of the police to arrest anyone acting in violation of the law and that police behavior cannot and should not be tempered by allegations of police brutality. While disapproving of brutality under any circumstances, he endorsed the use of necessary force to avert potential violence and to protect the general rights of the public.

Professor Eric Polisar of Cornell University noted that the problem of lack of communication to which many of the discussants had referred was in danger of becoming a cliché. He observed that in many communities the municipal officials and the representatives of business groups choose for themselves the leader of the Negro community with whom they will deal. He urged greater deference to the Negro community's own choice of leadership and argued that the success or failure of negotiations often depends upon how carefully the participants are selected.

J. Griffin Crump, Executive Director of the Indianapolis Human Rights Commission, argued that both public policy and the Constitution require that an adequate opportunity be provided to protest leaders to express their views. He approved the suspension or waiver, in some circumstances, of technical laws protecting the public's right to use sidewalks, streets, and other thoroughfares. He stated that in 1963 there had been widespread segregation in schools and public accommodations in Indianapolis. Local NAACP leaders conferred with the Human Rights Commission for the purpose of mapping out a program

75

of demonstrations. The Human Rights Commission was able to persuade police officials to work directly with the NAACP. A protest march was arranged, attended by both the Mayor and the Governor. No violence occurred and no persons were arrested.

Mr. Lankenau then asked by what methods effective communication within a community can be achieved. Max Klezmer, Chairman of the Indianapolis Human Rights Commission, observed that even with full communication many communities will still be unwilling to meet the demands of protest leaders unless pressured through demonstrations. He said that the discussion must therefore necessarily reach the problem of whether and in what cases arrests of demonstrators shall be made.

Mr. Campbell replied that his experience in the District of Columbia showed that arrests are rarely necessary. He related that in the District of Columbia there was a recent fund-raising program of the Student Non-Violent Coordinating Committee. The students making the appeal for funds had obtained no permit to solicit for charitable contributions. Nevertheless, a rally was held at which Dick Gregory appeared, attended by five hundred students who sat down at an intersection. The police were able to clear the intersection without making arrests. There was some physical damage to the street and to automobiles at the intersection, followed by a hearing before the Magistrate's Court. The Court lectured the students as to the necessity for compliance with the law, and full reparation was made for the physical damage caused.

The Law Director of Cleveland Heights, Ohio differed with Mr. Campbell, stating that in some situations arrests will be absolutely necessary to avoid loss of life or personal injury to demonstrators or members of the public. He spoke of a demonstration made at the construction site of a school building in Cleveland Heights, in which one person was killed as a result of clashes between the demonstrators and the police. He urged that protest leaders seek relief to the largest extent possible through whatever legal procedures are available in the courts.

Mr. Jacobson, Assistant City Solicitor of Chester, spoke in some detail of the Chester demonstration. He observed that the Mayor and municipal officials lacked authority to speak on behalf of the school board, which is independently elected. He noted that many meetings which had been planned were boycotted by the civil rights leaders. He felt that the actual results of the demonstrations could have been obtained without demonstrations if a proper forum could have been provided for meetings with full representation of civil rights leaders and the school board.

While the District of Columbia has experienced several successful demonstrations without arrests or disruptions of the public order, the same peaceful evolution cannot be anticipated in each community where the need for demonstrations arises. Inquiry must therefore focus not only upon the means by which communications can be established and operate effectively, but also upon the tactics to be used when communications and negotiations fail and demonstrations become inevitable. The available police techniques short of arrest, such as requiring demonstrators to keep moving and to avoid blockage of thoroughfares and business entrances, were generally agreed to be of great utility.

1.62   DISCUSSION GROUP B*

The discussion began with a consideration of the use of children in protest demonstrations. The appearance of large numbers of children in the Chester situation had raised the question of the value and wisdom of their use. The discussion leader opened the session with a quote from the Reverend Robert F. Drinan, Dean of the Boston College School of Law, who has stated that it is a good and ennobling experience for children to protest actively the violation of the nation's basic principles as long as they are not exposed to violence.

Several officials from different cities commented on this topic. Opinions differed widely on permitting the use of children. Some officials thought it was wrong to use children as tools of protest, for it encouraged disrespect for law and order and exposed them to possible physical danger. Many of those who commented, however, agreed with Father Drinan's statement. These officials did empha-

---

* Discussion Leader: J. Robert Lunney, Attorney, Shearman & Sterling, New York City; Member, Lawyers' Committee for Civil Rights Under Law.

Reporter: Lawrence C. Malick, Staff Member, Community Relations Service, United States Conference of Mayors.

size, though, that civil rights leaders ought not actively to recruit children for demonstrations as a general rule. Moreover, the demonstration leaders must be responsible for encouraging orderly behavior by the children and ensuring that irresponsible and unlawful activities will be prohibited and discouraged. In addition, the commentators confirmed that the demonstration leaders must also be responsible for protecting the children and removing them from potentially dangerous and unlawful situations.

Finally, one official noted his impression that children were frequently used in demonstration situations where adults themselves feared to tread. In his city, for example, where mass demonstrations for desegregated public accommodations took place, children demonstrated because adults feared job losses and other reprisals by their employers.

From this topic the discussion moved to a series of broader issues concerned with demonstrations and civil disorder. An official from a state civil rights commission said that the real question before us is how the responsible community leadership can establish and maintain procedures for building mutual confidence and reaching agreements with local Negro leaders. He said that only by providing open, effective channels of communication between local government and Negro groups could demonstrations, and hence the use of children, be prevented altogether.

Another discussant then asked the group to consider the pros and cons of civilian review boards to investigate complaints against the police. He believed they might be one step toward building community confidence in public authority. Several other participants agreed with this statement, and thought more such boards should be established. Police officers and mayors in the group dissented from this point of view, however. They believed that while civilian review boards might bolster public confidence in impartial law enforcement, they would certainly impair the effectiveness of police operations. Several of these officials did emphasize that yet another alternative to the problem of police-community confidence must be sought. In response to this latter point, some discussants said they had found that active police-community relations programs had created a mutual respect between police and public and had, in fact, quieted demands for review boards.

The discussion now turned to a consideration of the need to coordinate official responses to demonstration and disturbance situations. At the Savannah demonstrations the courts and the Mayor pursued different strategies. The result was confusion and a lengthened period of demonstrations. Some spokesmen believed that had the courts and the Mayor been prepared to act in unison, the situation would have been resolved more swiftly and effectively.

Another official attested that in his city, Philadelphia, a similar situation had evolved during the 1964 summer riots. When the riots erupted, officials in the various departments were very much at a loss to move into action and totally unprepared to act together. Hence the official response was delayed and hesitant. Thereafter, he noted, a crash program was initiated to have representatives of several city departments meet together with Negro leaders in the community to evolve broad-based contingency plans. These meetings are on a continuing basis and should allow government officials and Negro leaders to work swiftly and cooperatively to guide demonstrations onto constructive paths and prevent disorders. Moreover, these city-wide meetings are being supplemented with an expanded police-community relations program.

Next, one discussant, referring to the White Castle demonstrations in New York City, cited the inability of minority individuals to negotiate with large corporate enterprises for improvement of minority employment patterns and status. He noted that minority groups rarely have the leverage needed to force management to negotiate at all, let alone swing the negotiations in their behalf. Until this situation is remedied, he said, it will loom large as a source for demonstrations and militancy, the only remaining methods for minorities to gain the ear of management. In response to this statement another participant thought that government should remedy the plight of minority workers by giving fair employment and human relations commissions the power to initiate complaints on behalf of individuals and groups and to issue binding regulations and orders.

Finally, one member of the group wanted to know what steps cities had taken to guard against racial violence arising from isolated incidents such as the accidental shooting of a Negro by a policeman. Several other members responded that active police-community relations programs which build general police-minority understanding were the best means to prevent unexpected and unwarranted racial disorder. A Colorado official then told how violence had been prevented in Denver when a policeman accidentally shot a Negro youth in the process of arresting him. The Mayor immediately called together leaders of the Negro community to explain to them the situation and the administration's actions. The Negro leaders in turn were able to explain the incident to their community, and adverse reaction was avoided.

1.63 DISCUSSION GROUP C*

Discussion Group C consisted of approximately 30 people, equally divided among police officials, attorneys, and human relations commission personnel. In addition there were a few law professors, assistants to mayors, and a representative from CORE. Approximately seven discussants were from the South, and four or five Negroes were represented in the group.

Robert J. O'Connell opened the discussion by stating that the three critical city situations—Savannah, Chester and New York—would be used to explore three issues involved in crisis resolution.

The issues were the roles of (1) communications, (2) the existing legal framework, and (3) planning prior to the emergence of a crisis situation. He stated that solutions tend to assume a pattern. If emerging patterns can be found through discussion, they may serve as guidelines to other communities.

The discussions brought to light many different patterns and attitudes about "The Community and Racial Crises." This variety probably reflected the diverse backgrounds of the discussants. It also indicated a lack of consensus about the extent to which demonstrations and protests *should* be allowed to disrupt normal community activities.

For the most part the discussions centered on three topics. First, a great deal of attention was given to the term "double standard." A second topic was the legally permissible limits to civil disobedience and protest demonstrations. The third major topic was the method of countering complaints about police brutality.

---

* Discussion Leader: Robert J. O'Connell, Assistant Professor of Law, Marquette University School of Law.

Reporter: Melvin Mister, Staff Member, Community Relations Service, United States Conference of Mayors.

Double Standard. The term double standard was used in four different contexts. In discussions of the Savannah situation a corporation counsel said that there is a tendency to forgive violations of law and order in the name of the "higher law of civil rights." A member of a local human relations commission in California stated that Savannah was plagued by a dual legal system involving a conflict between local and constitutional law. In still another context the question was raised whether or not the strategy of arresting leaders of demonstrations should be used. An assistant district attorney asked, "Why single out the leader? Again there is a chance of imposing a double standard." Finally, the concept of the double standard was applied to different legal treatment of whites and Negroes. A Negro dean of a southern law school stated that failure to enforce all laws consistently leads to lack of respect for the law. He mentioned one case in which a Negro woman was attacked and the white attacker went free while his victim was held by authorities.

Some discussants viewed the "double standard" as a reflection of the wide discretionary power of government officials in enforcing the law. An assistant district attorney and a law professor both felt that whether or not there is sympathy with the objectives of demonstrators will influence the type of legal action taken. One of them said, "The issue is sympathy with the civil rights movement." The other said, "Since the cause is just, there is a natural tendency to excuse the actions of civil rights demonstrators."

One member of the group felt that while frequently the administration of the law is tempered for many other issues, "we often become very strict in interpreting law for civil rights demonstrators." These statements indicate that different members of Group C held contrasting views about how civil rights demonstrators generally are handled by local law enforcement agencies.

The discussion of the double standard and discretion in law enforcement involved the mention of specific legal devices that have been used in different cities to halt demonstrations. One discussant was "upset about the apparent view that demonstrations must be controlled." Other members of the discussion group responded by saying that officials have a responsibility to uphold the peace and order of the community.

Permissible Limits to Civil Disobedience. A law professor pointed out that Henry David Thoreau was a proponent of civil disobedience

81

and that punishment should not be looked on as bad, since it is part and parcel of the demonstration technique. He also felt that "on the legal end mitigating circumstances can be taken into account."

Two situations were described by the discussants which illustrated local government reaction to civil rights protests demonstrations. In St. Louis there were only a few arrests despite approximately 170 demonstrations. One of the demonstrations took place in the downtown area during the rush hour. Instead of making mass arrests, the police rerouted traffic. Their policy was to make *no* arrests unless something serious happened. St. Louis has a police-community relations program organized by precincts. Frequently police officials and leaders of demonstrations consult before demonstrations take place.

Another city tried rerouting traffic, but this response proved ineffective when the demonstration lasted for eight weeks. Another situation in this city concerned demonstrations at several banks. Demonstrators would line up at windows, ask for a hundred pennies in exchange for a dollar, go to the end of the line, and then ask to have the pennies changed into a foreign currency. By repeating this process the bank's business could be brought to a halt. The process was dubbed a "coin-in." New laws were passed permitting civil injunctions and civil arrests in situations where demonstrators obstruct the conduct of business. (In this locality policemen cannot make arrests on privately owned property.) Cameras located in the bank were used along with the new laws to achieve one hundred per cent convictions.

The contrast between official reaction to demonstrations differentiates these two cases. However, the two cities had some things in common. In both some demonstrations were directed at private institutions, such as banks. In these cases public officials had neither power nor authority to grant demonstrators their demands. The bank involved in the coin-in was controlled by the main office located in another part of the state. The demonstrations were directed at people who had little power to grant any concessions. Some discussants pointed out that this aspect of the case made it similar to the White Castle restaurant situation.

The disturbances in New York City in connection with protest demonstrations at White Castle restaurants were discussed as an example of the problems of coping with counterdemonstrations. Some discussants felt that everyone, including counterdemonstrators, has the right to demonstrate. Most discussants felt that the various groups of demonstrators had been treated fairly in the White Castle situation. In general the discussants felt that some official action was required when one group of demonstrators started throwing rocks and fighting with another. One person felt that the "demonstrators who get hit are often arrested. Isn't there a duty for police to act against counter-demonstrators instead of getting rid of demonstrators?" One person's view was that all should be allowed to demonstrate and given the widest possible latitude as long as there is no "clear and present danger to a breach of the peace." A police official stated that the police department protects the rights of all citizens, but "when the rights of the wider community are endangered the area should be cleared."

People from some cities mentioned that they have handled the counterdemonstration problem successfully. A police official said, "Agitators and drunks are arrested while the National Association for the Advancement of White People demonstrates peacefully." He also mentioned that negotiation with several groups of demonstrators made it possible to determine locations of demonstrators and keep them orderly. In another city the Ku Klux Klan and young, mostly Negro, demonstrators were engaged in protests on the same street for four hours. Policy decisions by the Mayor, a well-trained and understanding police force, and a great deal of consultation made this event possible, according to one discussant. This lack of violence was remarkable, the discussant said, since many of the policemen were more sympathetic to the Ku Klux Klan than to the Negro demonstrators.

Police Brutality. Most discussants felt that charges of police brutality reflected a lack of confidence in police officials. Some felt that the issue was whether brutal policemen would be dealt with properly. Others felt that the specter of police brutality was raised in order to voice a general displeasure with police-minority group relations. This division of opinion was reflected in the types of proposals made for dealing with charges of police brutality.

Some discussants felt that a civilian review board or opening up of discipline procedures for public review were possibilities for achieving the confidence needed to eliminate charges of police brutality.

Others described wide-ranging police-community relations programs involving police recruitment and training plus a broad-based committee established by the mayor and representing most community groups. One city uses its human relations commission, which has the power to initiate and investigate complaints, to handle charges of police brutality. One discussant felt that the single most important factor in decreasing charges of police brutality is the expressed attitude of the mayor. He said, "The mayor should take positive action to reflect that he will seriously try to do something about it (charges of brutality)."

Two other subjects emerged sporadically in the Group C discussions. These were the usefulness of and the problems involved in using state police, and the use of court injunctions.

1.64   DISCUSSION GROUP D*

The discussion group consisted of approximately forty persons. Mr. Pratt opened the discussion by suggesting that the focus be placed on immediate issues relating to what a city can do with the particularities of racial crises. Basic underlying problems which produce such crises were not to be emphasized at this time.

Mr. Pratt indicated that the first major area for discussion would concern communication between city officials, civil rights leaders, police, human rights commissions, and other interested parties. In each of the three given examples of community crisis situations developed in the PLI Program, there was an ebb and flow of events which presented opportunities for negotiation. Mr. Pratt asked what kind of information a mayor should have received and how he should have been advised when faced with a large group of Negroes asking for freedom now.

Mr. Lee Allen, Legal Assistant to the Mayor of Nashville, Tennessee, responded by relating a crisis incident in Nashville which had been caused by restaurant segregation. He stated that during the course of the crisis the Mayor's Committee on Human Relations was negotiating continuously. Apparently the city had allowed the demonstrators the full exercise of their constitutional rights, but

---

* Discussion Leader: John M. Pratt, Counsel, Commission on Religion and Race, National Council of Churches.
Reporter: John R. Wing, Attorney, Shearman & Sterling, New York City.

would not let them sit on the streets. The major point stressed by Mr. Allen was the necessity of convincing civil rights leaders that officials would be fair in allowing them full and free exercise of their constitutional rights. Once leaders of the demonstration were convinced that city officials were acting in good faith, they would reciprocate by informing the officials about the details of their planned activity.

Eugene Sparrow, Assistant Director of the Mayor's Friendly Relations Committee of Cincinnati, Ohio, emphasized the advance planning aspect of the communication problem. Apparently, in the Cincinnati rent strike potential problems had been eliminated by virtue of the fact that prior to the strike police officials, civil rights leaders, and leading citizens had been meeting together regularly. These meetings had established a relationship enabling the police to have a good rapport with the civil rights leaders. As a consequence, both police chiefs and civil rights leaders felt free to call each other at any time when tension arose. The practical result of establishing this harmonious relationship in the particular rent strike crisis was that the tenants were able to be peacefully evicted.

Terry C. Chisholm, of the Commission on Human Relations of Philadelphia, Pennsylvania, stated that although spelling out guidelines for demonstrations clearly was helpful, the justness of the civil rights leaders' claims was also most important. Thus, in the process of setting up communications the local administrations should concentrate on continually informing minorities of what was being done about their problems. This exchange of information should be sufficiently detailed to convince the people that things were moving as expeditiously as possible.

Mr. Pratt raised the problem of what to do when demonstrations are taken over by outside civil rights leaders with whom no previous lines of communication have been established.

Philip McMunigal, City Solicitor of Chester, Pennsylvania, then raised the problem which was encountered in the Chester situation when one group of officials were faced with demonstrations against particular grievances which had little relation to their particular offices and which they therefore were unable to remedy through exercise of their normal powers. The question was how city officials could negotiate when they did not have the power to meet the demands being made.

A field secretary from CORE pointed out that a popular protest technique was to attack one vulnerable part of officialdom in order to bring pressure on unrelated departments. If the Board of Education would not deal with the civil rights leaders, CORE felt that demonstrating and protesting against school segregation to the mayor was a practical strategy because it was believed that formal government relationships did not accurately reflect the reality. Even though the mayor had no legal authority to influence decisions on the part of the school board, his over-all stake in the city's image required the exercise of informal pressure and influence which could lead to an adjustment of the protested grievances. The civil rights leaders wanted to talk directly with the people authorized to address their particular problems and the city administration was thought to have a duty to insist that the authorized persons meet with the civil rights leaders.

One significantly effective remedy utilized in the Chester situation was to hold public hearings of the grievances in return for an end to the demonstrations. A hearing board selected in part by the civil rights group and in part by the city, with perhaps one disinterested member on whom both factions agreed, could make findings of fact and conclusions of law and issue an order in regard to the particular problem. This was considered more desirable than going to court, and it was thought that respectable civil rights leaders would adhere to a fair proceeding and agree to be bound by the result.

Mr. Pratt then switched the focus to the problems facing police officials, who were often caught in a crossfire between their responsibility to protect the demonstrators and their obligations to city officials and the courts to maintain peace and order.

Captain Thomas Smith, from Asbury Park, New Jersey, addressed himself to the problem of recruitment, and stated that generally a better class of individuals was coming into the police force. Many of the personnel were college educated, and psychological tests were being used to weed out undesirables.

John B. Layton, Chief of Police of Washington, D.C., referred to a police-community relations committee which had been formed in Washington and was a great aid in improving general relations between the police and the community. Good communications established through such a committee often had been utilized in solving problems. In addition, there was a citizens' crime council which functioned as an advisory group in Washington, D.C.

Mr. Pratt asked how assignments were made to particular areas of the city, and whether it was considered wise to allocate primarily Negro police to Negro communities. Chief Layton responded by saying that the traditional practice of assigning Negro officers to the Negro areas was gradually changing, and that at least in Washington, D.C. Negro officers currently operated in all precincts.

The Chairman of the Yonkers Human Rights Commission described the practices of that city's police force which had been worked out in part at meetings called by the Mayor of all city department heads, other officials, and civil rights leaders. At these meetings the possible causes of demonstrations were discussed, and much attention was given to both immediate and long-term remedies. There was also a great deal of discussion on procedures to be followed by police in dealing with demonstrations. Apparently it was revealed in this group that white police were not considered as able to handle the tension areas, because they lacked an understanding of the feelings and motivations of the demonstrators. As a consequence Negro police were shifted to crisis areas when problems arose. It was thought that by so doing both police and demonstrators would be protected. The Yonkers meeting between the Mayor, city department heads, police chiefs, and civil rights leaders is a good example of a pre-crisis operation.

Eugene Sparrow of Cincinnati also mentioned the value of having civil rights leaders talk with police chiefs so that the former would be well aware of the internal problems that police officials face.

It was also pointed out by a police official from Clifton, New Jersey, that the average policeman wants to negotiate rather than arrest when faced with immediate problems of civil rights demonstrations. That is, the *ad hoc* settlement of an incident is naturally favored. In line with this, it was thought that a dialogue should be established between the civil rights leaders and police chiefs to determine policies which could be carried out when problems arose.

Mr. Pratt asked whether it would be a good idea to have a special civil rights division in the police force specifically designed to handle demonstrations.

Captain Smith from Asbury Park, New Jersey stated that the Elizabeth riots had established a prototype of a method of operation which could and should be followed. In this incident only exceptionally stable police personnel were utilized. Pictures were taken of each arrest and only one officer was used to arrest one particular person. In addition, police observers were present to see exactly how and in what manner things were handled.

The use of movies was highly recommended for reviewing exactly what happened in crisis situations. Such movies were considered beneficial for suggesting desirable changes and establishing the truth or falsity of brutality charges.

It was also mentioned that a police complaint procedure with records available to the public was a desirable and useful system.

PART II

LAWS GOVERNING DEMONSTRATIONS
AND OTHER FORMS OF PROTEST

2.1 LAWS GOVERNING DEMONSTRATIONS
AND OTHER FORMS OF PROTEST

ROBERT B. McKAY*

Protest demonstrations are as old as Socrates, as old as Jesus, as American as the Mayflower, the Boston Tea Party, and the Suffragists. Now the protest demonstrations for integration are coming to the fore with more dramatic impetus than anything we have faced before.

The right of protest has been exercised from time immemorial, even in such relatively puny controversies as students signing a petition in objection to the decision of an Executive Committee as to when registration shall commence for the next semester.

I am prepared to think of this as not being very serious. But if these students come to the point of picketing the building and saying "New York University Law School is unfair to students" without spelling out why, or if they take to the streets in violence, I may feel differently. It is in just that kind of context that the issue is framed.

No one is much disturbed by the kind of brotherly love exhortation that is involved in trying to get us to do something better, or by peaceful picketing and rather innocuous and inconspicuous placards.

---

* Professor of Law, Associate Dean, New York University School of Law.
ED. NOTE: For a more extended treatment by Professor McKay of the points he makes here, see his article, *Racial Protest, Civil Disobedience and the Law*, p. 273 herein.

But the situation changes when it really makes a difference, when there is a likelihood that the protestors will persuade those who might otherwise be inclined to protest against them, or when there is danger of disorder or riot or, as the police may feel, something more serious. Then the bite is really sharp.

Everybody in the American community is favorably disposed to the idea of making protests, of complaining, or picketing, or whatever the appropriate device may be in the particular circumstances. But that idea is an abstraction. When it comes down to cases, I am not so sure that most Americans believe in the First Amendment and the rights that are said to be included in it.

For instance, Chief Justice Warren said a few years ago, "If the Bill of Rights as a whole"—and I think he had particular reference to the First Amendment—"were to be put up for majority vote today, it probably would not pass."

We believe in the abstraction, but I am not at all sure that we believe in the concreteness when we get down to particular cases. The one problem that we have to face is one of self-help, but there are very real difficulties in carrying out this program.

Professor Harry Kalven has pointed out that the problem with a do-it-yourself legal remedy kit such as is involved in the self-help movement is that you get rather quickly to the boundaries of what is permissible before you run into trouble with the Courts themselves; that you can't just say "we will do it ourselves" because you are exasperated; that by and large the Courts have been against self-help, and have hedged it in.

What I want to consider is the extent to which the courts have hedged it in, and for what reasons, whether justifiable or unjustifiable. What are the constitutional limits of the permissible and nonpermissible? The dilemma, it seems to me, is that both sides, the protestors and the protestors against the protestors, tend to use too-easy generalizations. They give too-facile answers to problems that really are very complex indeed.

The demonstrators are inclined to say, "You know, we have had a very hard go for a long time, and injustice is something that should be corrected in this democratic civilization of ours. Therefore, if we are a little civilly disobedient, even a little unlawful, please excuse us because this is the only way we can make up for long decades of ill-treatment." This is obviously not a sufficient answer when considered by itself.

On the other hand, those espousing the great wisdom of the majority claim that the democratic ethos will tend to bring about its own solutions, that everything will right itself because we believe in majority rule.

But we know that democratic majorities are not always right, that they need to have their consciences pricked. So the question has been the same in all those periods: Under what circumstances do we tolerate civil disobedience or even encourage it? What do we do with conduct that in another day might have been described as lawless?

The law is an essentially conservative force in society. I am bound to say, however, that the lawyers, too, have recognized that there is a real problem here and that there may be justification for the protest and for occasional disobedience of the law. The American legal system requires that there be a case or controversy in order to answer legal questions. The belief is that in order to know what a statute means, in order to interpret a constitutional provision, we must have an actual case in which there is disagreement as to who is right and who is wrong.

And so the Canons of Professional Ethics permit, almost encourage, the violation of law when there is a serious question posed as to whether that law, when tested against some appropriate higher law, is, in fact, valid.

Thus, Canon 32 of the Canons of Professional Ethics provides that clients must be advised to comply with written law and with the strictest principles of moral law. But Canon 32 reminds us, as well, that until a statute has been construed and interpreted by competent adjudication, the lawyer is free and entitled to advise as to its validity and as to what he conscientiously believes to be its just meaning and intent.

Thus, in order to determine the validity of law, obviously some kind of protest, some kind of disobedience, some kind of what in stricter terms you might call lawlessness, is not necessarily condemned.

The difficulties arise for the protest movements, either as they move on toward greater success with their demands, or as they encounter more resistance. This statement is not as paradoxical as it may appear: Where at first the protest movement may be satisfied with fairly modest demands, and thus secure modest victories, it becomes imperative with each success that a little more dramatic result be accomplished, and that something a little more specific be demanded, and something a little farther out be sought in order to maintain leadership in the protest movement. Quite obviously, we never achieve all our goals, and so long as some goals that might be desirable have not been attained, and the movement seems to be going well, it is natural for the leaders to demand even more. So with the success of the movement—and the success of the protest movement in the United States is a real fact—we tend to move gradually toward ever larger, more insistent, and perhaps more troublesome demands. The question becomes one of determining at what point a halt should be called.

On the other hand, if the protest movement is for the moment content with the peaceful, normal means of objection, it becomes very easy for a majority, cynical or otherwise, to bypass the protest and remain undisturbed by it. After all, you are not terribly upset by a picket line that continues week after week, month after month. You can ignore placards, you can ignore minor traffic inconveniences. Accordingly, when there seems to be no disturbance of the status quo by the ordinary protest devices, the quite natural temptation is to use ever stronger and more dramatic devices.

In this, too, I think there is a potential danger for the success of the protest movement. In general terms, it seems to me, we have not yet reached the point of serious danger in that respect, as is evidenced by the success of the protest movement in accomplishing major objectives during the last several years.

Most dramatic is the Civil Rights Act of 1964. I do not mean simply the fact of its adoption. I call attention more specifically to the fact that the program as proposed in 1963 by President Kennedy was most often criticized for being too tough. Interestingly enough, after the Freedom March of 1963 and the other developments in late 1963 and early 1964, the Act that finally was adopted was stronger in most respects than what was originally proposed. I consider the civil rights protest movement as the impetus that succeeded in achieving this important objective.

Secondly, not very many years ago most people were quite content to say that the Constitution is color-blind and so no complaint was made if there simply was an absence of discrimination against a person on grounds of race or color.

Now the protest movement has seen the possibility and is beginning to suggest that because of the long period of discrimination, the Constitution may permit preferential treatment for a catch-up period. It is possible that a new constitutional doctrine is being shaped. The protest movement has led the way toward suggesting the desirability and perhaps the constitutionality of such a device.

Third, the timetable for school desegregation, which ten years ago we thought might work very well on an "all deliberate speed" basis, has raised similar questions. The protest movement has taken the position that the original timetable has been proved inadequate. The Supreme Court has said, both in 1963 and in 1964, that the time has come for some change.

Finally, in the North, where there is presumably less hostility to the demands for school integration, the school boards in New York, Chicago, and other cities are working toward plans of school integration that far surpass anything that was possible, perhaps even anything that was thought constitutional, a few years ago.

I hold that changes are in the making, perhaps triggered by the protest movements, which have been enormously effective in these areas.

It seems to me that the First Amendment is the most important constitutional provision in the context of protest. Some of it is obvious. In the first place, it is now clear, I believe, that the guarantees of the First Amendment protect the person who protests so long as he does it in moderate, orderly, and reasonable ways and does not interfere with the sacred shibboleths of our society. He is assured protection against the majority, even though they may object to what he has to say. Certainly in New York City it has been the philosophy of the Police Department that where a permit is issued (and there is reasonable generosity in the issuance of permits in New York City), it is the speaker who is entitled to protection from the crowd, not the crowd from the speaker. Accordingly, the threat of disorder that the speaker poses by virtue of the hostile things he

93

may say means simply that a larger police force must be mustered in order to take care of any potential disorder that may follow.

As to the more troublesome problems of the sit-ins, we have seen a very substantial change in emphasis in the law in the last few years, as a result of the sit-ins and related demonstrations. More is on the horizon.

We did not know until 1961, for example, that a peaceful sit-in was not necessarily a violation of a disorderly conduct or a breach of the peace statute. We now know that to enforce such a breach of the peace statute either would be acting without evidence, as decided in *Garner* v. *Louisiana* [368 U. S. 157 (1961)], or in some cases might be a violation of constitutional guarantees against unequal treatment under law. We now know, too, that there may be difficulties with the enforcement even of trespass statutes. The questions have not all been resolved by any means, but the law is moving in new directions.

Where it will end we cannot confidently say at this time, but I suggest that there has been substantial change in the last few years and there is more change on the horizon.

One specific problem that is almost a cliché is often raised in connection with the situation of Governors Barnett and Wallace, who have resisted court orders. The questions are asked: Are not their rights the same? Should they be punished for contempt while other protestors are excused without contempt citations?

The difference is perfectly obvious to me. Governors Wallace and Barnett were challenging and resisting the enforcement of orders which had already been litigated in the courts on issues which had already been decided,—on which, in effect, they had already had their day in court. The peaceful protest demonstrations by sit-ins have been quite the reverse. The challenge has been that the law itself was invalid. And they were perfectly willing, if they lost on the ultimate constitutional issue, to pay whatever the consequences were. But the striking fact is that in a large proportion of the cases they have won their point and proved that the convictions were, in fact, invalid.

The final point is the school boycott. The parents who keep their children out are technically in violation of the compulsory school attendance laws, and thus they make technical truants of their children.

Yet, particularly in New York where hundreds of thousands have joined in such demonstrations, it was not felt that this was an act of lawlessness which deserved automatic censure.

On the other hand, there are dangers that if a school boycott is successful once, the temptation will be to resort to it again and again and again. At some point this amounts to an unjustified interference with the rights of other children, those who do not want to participate in the boycotts, and it becomes a disruption of the school system. Eventually the question becomes the harder one of where the line should be drawn.

The last matter, and the obvious one, is the practical difficulty of the continuance of the popular support which seems to be going in large measure for the protest movement at the present time. There may come a time when the protest movement does a series of things which make it difficult to secure the continued support which is necessary for success. In judging the protest movement we must remember, as did André Gide, that "The world will be saved only by the unsubmissive."

2.2 UNDERSTANDING JUDICIAL REACTION TO PROTEST BEHAVIOR*

Robert G. Dixon, Jr.*

Judicial reaction to protest behavior is generally based upon a distinction between civil disobedience and lawful protest within the framework of the legal system. Henry David Thoreau, an early exponent of civil disobedience, correctly realized that punishment should not be looked on as harmful, since it is part and parcel of the demonstration technique. On the legal end, mitigating circumstances will sometimes be taken into account. On the other hand, there is a well-protected right to conduct lawful protest within the legal order, and the Courts will generally insist that the demonstrator have maximum protection in such a situation.

Civil disobedience has two major elements. One is a disposition to violate unjust law, justifying the violation by appeal to a moral

---

* Professor of Law, George Washington University School of Law.

95

principle which may be called natural law, but which is not positive law or the law of any governmental organ. The second element is the disposition to be arrested and to accept whatever penalty is imposed. I do not think that all our activity in this country during the last two or three years, or even, perhaps, very much of it, falls into this category.

Lawful protest within the legal order in turn has two broad subforms. One subform is to violate unjust or allegedly unjust law, or a mixture of law and custom, under a claim of legal right under a higher, positive law, that is, a higher manmade law such as the Constitution or federal statutes. In this situation, the violation is committed under a claim of legal right with an intent of seeking redress in the courts. If that is the approach, I do not think we can call it civil disobedience. Examples would include the sit-ins which have taken place under an appeal of right under the Fourteenth Amendment. Another example would be the Freedom Rides of two or three years ago, undertaken in regard to interstate travel or interstate terminals—bus terminals, railroad terminals—and made under a claim of right under the Commerce Clause or the supporting federal statutes.

The second form of lawful protest involves the device of marches and picketing designed to call attention to segregation laws and to noncompliance with Supreme Court desegregation decisions, but not aimed at violating any particular segregation law as such. Demonstrations of this sort—marches and protests, if orderly—are held under a claim of right under the free speech principle of the First Amendment.

I think that a great deal of the protest and demonstration activity, perhaps the great majority of it, has been in one of these two categories —to violate an unjust legal command under claim of right under constitutional law, or to protest through marches under the free speech principle to call attention to grievances.

A different situation may arise if there are sit-ins and demonstrations in regard to public accommodations in areas not covered by the Civil Rights Act, if the Supreme Court should declare that those accommodations which are outside the Civil Rights Act are also outside the Fourteenth Amendment. Then there could be no claim of legal right under either a statutory or constitutional theory.

96

The issue of a constitutional right of access to public accommodations going beyond the present statutory language is still unsettled. The last major sit-in case, the *Bell* case, split the Court and the Court avoided the constitutional issue. [*Bell* v. *Maryland,* 378 U.S. 226 (1964)]. But if the Court should decide that there is no Fourteenth Amendment right to be served in an accommodation not covered by the Civil Rights Act—distinguishing the broad power of Congress to act under the Fourteenth Amendment from the more narrow, self-executing force of the Fourteenth Amendment applied by judiciary without Congressional action—then a sit-in might be classified as true civil disobedience, because it would be an unlawful act in protest against a private person's court-supported constitutional right to select his customers.

So far, however, we have not had much of this sort of action. It has been more in the nature of action seeking redress inside the legal order, and this explains, at least in part, the disposition of the federal courts in many cases, and the Supreme Court especially, to sustain demonstrators in the cases that have been litigated.

More difficult in terms of classification would be areas such as the Triborough Bridge sit-down, school boycotts, or the violation of the school attendance law. In such cases there is perhaps only a technical law violation, and the main thrust may be a communication interest or free speech interest, calling attention to noncompliance with desegregation principles.

A further difficult category would be violations by Negroes in the South of injunctions obtained by Southern officials against demonstrators for various practices. This is a difficult constitutional problem. There is a doctrine that a person wishing to make a speech or hold an assembly need not bother to comply with a *permit statute* if the permit statute is void on its face. He may proceed. If he is arrested and can show that the permit statute is void on its face, he will go free.

But, having established that doctrine for the permit cases, could it be argued that there ought to be a similar power to violate a state court *injunction,* or a lower federal court *injunction,* thought to be void on its face? Or would that be rather extreme? Would the better viewpoint be to stay inside the legal order and appeal the injunction?

It may be difficult to separate the power to ignore a *statute* void on its face, which has been settled in the First Amendment Area (the free speech area), from the power or right to ignore an *injunction* void on its face.

I think the following three cases indicate the rather broad and favorable legal basis which demonstrations now have in United States Supreme Court doctrine:

One of the cases is the *Feiner* case, which goes back to 1951.* The other two cases are *Edwards* v. *South Carolina*** and *Fields* v. *South Carolina*†, both in 1963. The *Feiner* case was not a Negro demonstration case, but it did involve the question of freedom of speech and right of demonstration versus police action in the face of possible unrest or mob violence.

Feiner involved only one speaker on a street corner in a Negro section of Syracuse, New York, who was using a loud-speaker mounted on a car. He was speaking to publicize a meeting of the Young Progressives to be held in a hotel that evening. He was protesting against the city administration's cancellation of a permit to hold the meeting in a public school.

The man used rather violent language, calling the President a bum, the American Legion a Nazi Gestapo, the Mayor of Syracuse a champagne-sipping bum, and telling Negroes to rise up in arms and fight for equal rights.

There was a crowd of 75 or 80. Two policemen were present. Evidence later was presented that one person in the crowd said if the police did not act, he would.

The police did make the arrest and the Supreme Court upheld the conviction, saying that Feiner was not arrested for the content of his speech but for the reaction it engendered in the audience.

---

* Feiner v. New York, 340 U.S. 315.

** 372 U.S. 229.

† 126 S.E.2d 1, 6 (1962) ; judgment vacated and case remanded, 372 U.S. 522 (1963) ; adhered to on remand, 131 S.E.2d 91 (1963) ; reversed, 375 U.S. 44 (1963).

In the *Edwards* and *Fields* cases there were Negro demonstrations in South Carolina. In each case the Supreme Court finally absolved the demonstrators without reversing *Feiner,* although I think the distinction between *Feiner* and these last two cases is difficult to make.

In the key case of *Edwards* v. *South Carolina,* 187 Negroes were convicted of breach of the peace for demonstrating at the State House grounds in South Carolina against state segregation practices. There was a crowd of about two or three hundred.

Several policemen were present. There was some evidence of impeding traffic, but apparently no evidence of major violence.

The Supreme Court reversed the convictions that followed arrests for breach of the peace, stressing that though traffic was impeded it was not completely blocked, and also that there were no threats of violence from the crowd. There was no evidence that any one man had said, "If the police don't act, I will," as the Court pointed out was the case in *Feiner.*

But I rather doubt that it makes a difference whether you had or did not have that one strand of evidence.

The Court also said that conviction under a more specific statute would be a different case, indicating a disposition not to sustain a broad breach of the peace arrest in the field of demonstrations where freedom of speech is involved.

The *Fields* case involved a somewhat similar situation, but larger numbers were involved. The Court reached the same decision as in *Edwards,* not with full opinion, but by simply citing *Edwards.*

In *Fields,* which arose in Orangeburg, South Carolina, a city of 20,000, a series of demonstrations came out of two Negro colleges. One demonstration gave rise to the arrests, and involved about a thousand Negro students who marched in three groups toward City Square. There was testimony that traffic on the sidewalks and in the streets was badly blocked. Some pedestrians took refuge in stores to get off the streets.

Again there were arrests and convictions for breach of the peace, but in the end these were reversed by the United States Supreme Court.

What lessons can be drawn from the *Edwards* and *Fields* cases? Large numbers of people were involved in these cases, and I think the cases indicate that it will take a rather extreme showing of incipient violence, or perhaps actual violence, to make a breach of the peace arrest stand up in the United States Supreme Court.

The opinion contains a hint that some cities may act on. If they do, we will have a further round of cases. That is the hint in *Edwards* that under more precise regulations an arrest might be sustained. This hint, it seems to me, may invite consideration of joint action by community officials to prescribe in more detail the times and places where demonstrations may be held lawfully, simply by taking the Supreme Court's language at face value.

There is an interesting short article on the liability of local governmental units under mob violence statutes in an issue of a publication sheet called *The Local Government Law Service Letter,* published by the American Bar Association's Section on Local Government Law. It is in the October, 1964 issue, and it summarizes the picture succinctly.

The article finds that twenty-two states possess some form of statute subjecting a local government to legal responsibility for acts of mob violence and suggests that this is perhaps the first inroad on the governmental immunity doctrine.

Some of these statutes go back to the last century. It may be that in the next two or three or four years, they will be more relevant than in the last several decades.

In the last volume of the *Race Relations Law Reporter,* Volume 8, there is an indication that there may be some North-South distinction between sustaining or not sustaining breach of the peace arrests.

In some of the Northern cases, of course, the demonstrations were more vigorous in the sense of involving obstruction of passage of trucks, construction vehicles, and so on. But I think that there is also some indication, in the context of the Southern scene, of a feeling that a fair amount of adverse "audience reaction" will be tolerated, without allowing or sustaining police arrests. Given the amount of racial tension in the South, a large amount of adverse audience reaction is unavoidable. To put too much stress on adverse audience reaction in the South would mean no demonstrations at all.

100

2.3 RECENT DEVELOPMENTS
2.31 EDITORS' NOTE

Shortly after the PLI Forum the United States Supreme Court ruled in *Hamm* v. *City of Rock Hill* and *Lupper* v. *Arkansas, 379 U. S.* 306 (1964), that the Civil Rights Act of 1964 precludes the states from enforcing criminal penalties arising from convictions for peaceful "sit-in" demonstrations obtained prior to enactment of the statute. The defendants were Negroes convicted of violations of state trespass laws for refusing to leave lunch counters upon request in a five-and-ten-cent store and department store respectively.

Both establishments are covered by the provisions of the Civil Rights Act of 1964 which prohibit discrimination in places of public accommodation. The Court found the conduct of the defendants to be protected by Section 203 of the Act, which provides that no person "shall punish or attempt to punish any person for exercising or attempting to exercise any right or privilege secured by Section 201 or 202." The Court found that under this section a nonforcible attempt to gain admittance or remain in a place of public accommodation in defiance of a policy of segregation is immune from prosecution by state authorities. The question posed in the cases at hand was the validity of enforcement by the states of convictions obtained but not finalized before passage of the Civil Rights Act.

The Supreme Court rested its conclusion on the following points: In federal courts a defendant whose case is on appeal may not be punished if his conduct has been declared lawful subsequent to his conviction. This rule is based on the presumed intention of Congress, unless it declares otherwise, to avoid inflicting punishment at a time when it can no longer serve any legislative purpose and when it would be unnecessarily vindictive. Since the convictions no longer would be valid under federal law, the Supremacy Clause of the U. S. Constitution requires that they also be overruled in the state courts. To enforce pending convictions in state courts for actions no longer criminal would be inconsistent with the purposes of the Act.

There were pending in the state courts over 3,000 cases involving convictions for sit-in demonstrations, a large portion of which were peaceful and, therefore, invalidated by the Court's decision.

101

Four justices dissented, questioning whether Congress had the power to abate *state* criminal prosecutions and, even if such power did exist, whether Congress had declared any intent to accomplish such a result.

2.32   DISCUSSION

JACK GREENBERG*

I hope that the disposition of these cases will be as simple as possible. I see no political or practical utility in dragging these students—most of them are students, and all of them are well-meaning—over the coals to prove that you can prosecute somebody for sitting-in in 1960.

Now, as to the future so far as a sit-in is concerned, even though it affects a relatively small number of communities here, it affects a good number of people under the Civil Rights Act of 1964. Their action would no longer be a crime. The Act says that no one shall be punished for exercising rights that it has conferred. So if someone sits at a lunch counter and demands service and he is entitled to it, under the Act he cannot be prosecuted for it.

It has been suggested that the Supreme Court is viewing different types of demonstrations in different parts of the country in somewhat different ways, and I think that is true.

I think that the only demonstration case that I know of, which the Supreme Court turned down—and in that one they almost granted the release—was the case out of Louisiana involving a student who conducted a pretty riotous demonstration on the Southern University campus. He ran through the classrooms and so forth. At least it was so alleged. The defense which was presented for him was that he had not been properly prosecuted under the law and that the statute under which he was prosecuted was unconstitutionally vague.

During the oral argument Justice Black asked one question of the counsel who was arguing the case. He asked whether or not it was the contention of counsel that while this particular defendant really

* Director-Counsel, NAACP Legal Defense and Educational Fund.

EDITORS' NOTE: Mr. Greenberg discussed the *Hamm* v. *Rock Hill* and *Lupper* v. *Arkansas* cases, described above, which were pending before the U.S. Supreme Court at the time of the forum, and in which he represented one of the ultimately successful parties. Mr. Greenberg's further comments follow.

had not acted properly, he was being prosecuted improperly. Counsel conceded that the defendant was not acting properly, but he felt that the prosecution was technically deficient.

The Supreme Court then entered an order saying that it had decided improvidently to review the case, had withdrawn its decision to review, and would hand down no judgment of the case. In other words, the Supreme Court would neither approve the form of prosecution nor appear to give approval to what this particular defendant had done.

If we look at the bad side, this illuminates what actually has happened in the cases involving these demonstrations. Out of approximately 13,000 demonstrators convicted, that is the only case I can think of at the moment in which a conviction has been upheld upon ultimate review. In one way or another all the other demonstrators have been released by the courts, having been judged as either acting properly under the law or having been prosecuted improperly under the law. That is a fair measure of the conduct of the demonstrators under very tense circumstances and under very adverse conditions.

2.4 QUESTIONS AND ANSWERS

Question: Would you discuss the significance of the clear and present danger test in the civil rights area?

PROFESSOR McKAY: The clear and present danger test originated perhaps only casually with Mr. Justice Holmes in the *Schenck* case.* He said, in effect, that in determining whether the prosecution could be sustained for the use of words—advocacy, as we now call it —the test would be whether those words were used in such circumstances as to create a clear and present danger of the existence of a substantive evil which Congress would have the right to prevent.

The man who was charged with crime in that case was convicted, and Holmes wrote the majority opinion. However, as soon as Holmes and Brandeis came to a case in which they believed that application of the test would result in reversal of a conviction, they were forced

---

* *Schenck* v. *United States*, 246 U.S. 47 (1919).

into dissent. It was not until 1937 that the clear and present danger doctrine was ever used as a basis for reversing a conviction.

The truth is that if you examine the cases in which the test has been used, and there are only a very few, the result in every case would have been the same without the application of the clear and present danger test.

Obviously, it is a balancing test, one that says that you must weigh the free speech rights against the rights of the community. I suggest that the test of clear and present danger looks more to the restriction on speech than to the preservation of the right of demonstration. I believe that is particularly true in the protest area, because those who wish to make ineffective the protest movement can always find some kind of disorder that is likely to result from any effective protest or any effective demonstration.

And so I am personally very much inclined to believe that the clear and present danger test is less than useful, indeed that it is scarcely more than useless, in protecting First Amendment rights.

Question: What suggestions would you have for dealing with the following situation? A Negro in a southern community seeks service in a tavern. We will assume that it is a tavern in a hotel clearly covered by the Civil Rights Act of 1964. The Negro is advised by the bartender that under the law prohibiting service to persons who have had too much to drink, he will not be served in that place. The patron alleges that he has had nothing to drink and demands service.

MR. GREENBERG: What you really have posed is the type of issue that we begin to get into once we establish certain rules of law.

A rule of law requiring nondiscrimination quickly begins to run into problems of whether or not there has been discrimination on the grounds of race. The isolated case is clearly going to be a tough one, there is no question about it.

THE CHAIRMAN: A problem that arises from one basic feature of our American legal system is that normally a legal question or a statute's constitutionality cannot be decided, or the statute interpreted, until there is an actual dispute.

Question: Is it possible to develop test cases to interpret local statutes or local ordinances that may be controversial, cases which could not subject the person testing the statute to the harshness of arrest, to remaining in custody, and so on?

PROFESSOR DIXON: Yes. Let me first back up to the clear and present danger doctrine for just a second. I think it is very often as important to look at the actual result of a case as to look at the language the court used. And given the actual facts of the *Edwards* case and the result reached, it would seem to support the idea that the Supreme Court is inclined to require a rather strong showing of a clear or present danger of mob violence before it will sustain a breach of the peace arrest in a demonstration.

The opinion does not discuss doctrinal matters, but on the facts I would say it is a fairly strong case.

I am doubtful on the degree of flexibility left in the clear and present danger doctrine by the recent cases in this field.

On the hypothetical case being raised by the question, it is important to stress that there is in law no such thing as a test case. There must be a full, complete, conventional cause of action in terms of injury already occurred, or about to occur, before the person will have standing to sue.

We often use the term "test case" to refer to the first actual case that raises a legal question or a constitutional issue, but it is a real case. Somebody has his neck out, and if he is wrong on a constitutional plea, he will pay whatever price is involved in terms of criminal penalty, if he has violated the law, or civil damages and so on.

Therefore, it is no easier to think of a painless test case in the area of desegregation than in any other area.

The device of an injunction may be considered. One reason for the equity device which we call injunction is to allow a person to litigate an issue where he can show that harm is about to occur, without first sticking his neck out and violating a law.

The possibility will vary a great deal from statute to statute whether there can be a fact situation that will justify an injunction suit. I would certainly consider that as the first step. There could be a class action, perhaps, or an individual action by a Negro or a couple of Negroes, or others seeking to enjoin the enforcement of an ordinance or statute which is felt to contravene the Constitution or some other higher law, i.e., a federal statute or regulation.

Beyond that, I would just suggest this. Insofar as the *Edwards* doctrine filters down fairly quickly—and, of course, it may not filter down fairly quickly—demonstrations—even though massive and therefore calling attention to a problem, and even with large numbers involved—cannot lead to valid breach of the peace convictions if the demonstrators are peaceful and no specific law violation occurs. A fairly harmless but large demonstration may be a good way of calling attention to a problem. However, in order for a test case to get an official ruling you have to either violate the law or seek an injunction.

PART III

RACIAL TENSIONS AND THE POLICE

As clearly emerges from Parts I and II, the police have a pivotal role as governmental and community agents and representatives, both in the handling of racial crisis manifestations and in all-important day-to-day relations with Negro citizens. Crucial issues have arisen as to the proper guidance, training and control of the police in these tasks, which limited time did not permit to be sufficiently developed at the forum. We have accordingly assembled here pertinent materials which give the necessary background and sometimes differing viewpoints on these issues.

We start, as "Premises of the Discussion", with an excerpt from the report of the Commission appointed by the Governor of Pennsylvania to investigate charges of police brutality growing out of the events in Chester described and discussed in Part I. We have included the statement made at the forum by Glen Murphy of the International Association of Chiefs of Police, the pertinent forum discussion, materials supplied by Mr. George Schermer, a panelist, and by the United States Conference of Mayors, among others, and conclude with "The Case for Civilian Review", a paper especially prepared for this publication by Dr. John Morsell, Assistant Executive Director of the N.A.A.C.P.

3.1   PREMISES OF THE DISCUSSION*

Respect for law and order is the cornerstone of every free society. This is particularly true of the United States, where the rule of law was the guiding principle in the establishment of our form of government.

---

* This chapter originally appeared in The Report of The Governor's Commission to Investigate Charges of Police Brutality in Chester, Pennsylvania as Chapter VIII, "Premises of The Commission", pp. 64-69.

The rule of law is predicated upon the consent of the governed. The people do not consent unless the laws are administered fairly and firmly and thereby command respect and confidence. Respect and confidence for the law are necessary to its effective operation and to insure observance of the law by the overwhelming majority of our citizenry. Unjust or discriminatory administration of law by excessive force or otherwise tends to create hate, distrust and the threat of anarchy.

The right to full citizenship, including reasonable and equal opportunity for gainful employment, adequate housing and sound education, increases understanding and appreciation of the necessity for law and order. The lack of such full rights inevitably leads to discontent and motivates acts for the redress of real or imagined grievances.

Police agencies exist at every level of government for the purpose of preserving law and order, and every police officer stands in the vanguard of the protection of the public peace and the public safety.

The role of the police is difficult, dangerous and demanding and often misunderstood. Urbanization intensifies police problems, thus requiring strong community support and understanding if police forces are to be maintained at sufficient size, with adequate training and equipment, and with high morale. In lower income areas of urban centers, the position of the police officer is especially difficult because he is the symbol of what are conceived to be the oppressive forces of the community, forces over which the police in fact have little if any control. The police officer is thus placed in a buffer position between the disadvantaged groups with their resentments and the community "establishment". One of the social problems arising in this situation is the tension created when the police are compelled to use force in controlling manifestations of social protest.

Without undertaking to make a full statement of the law relative to the amount of force that may be used by a peace officer in terminating or preventing breaches of the peace or preventing or suppressing affray and riot, we note that the use of force by a police officer is proper only to the extent he reasonably believes it to be necessary to preserve law and order. When force greater than this is applied to accomplish this purpose, such force is excessive. Excessive force is improper and unlawful.

108

Almost a century ago a Pennsylvania court stated the governing principle of law which still pertains today:

> As a general rule, it may be safely affirmed, that an officer of the law whose authority to arrest or imprison is resisted, will be justified in opposing force to force, no matter what may be the consequence; but in any case, he ought to act with extreme caution, and should not resort to excessive violence (i.e. force) until it is impossible to avoid it.

The necessity for the use of force often requires an immediate decision by a police officer in the face of physical danger to himself or to others. The privilege of hindsight and leisurely contemplation is not afforded a policeman faced with a split-second decision. For this reason, the law gives him an area of discretion within which his judgment may be exercised. In exercising this discretion, a police officer may in good faith err in evaluating the threatened danger, but if under the circumstances there was reasonable justification for his apprehension of harm he does not abuse his prerogative.

On the other hand, while a police officer has considerable latitude, his decision as to the amount of force required in a particular situation is not conclusive of the propriety of his conduct. Thus, it is not enough that the officer believe the force he is using be necessary; his belief must be reasonable. Reasonable belief is generally considered to be that which an ordinarily prudent and intelligent person would have had under the circumstances. The determination of reasonableness is subject to review by higher authority. Where the conduct of a police officer is unreasonable or improper, he is subject to censure, and where appropriate, to disciplinary or other action as provided by law.

It should be emphasized that police officers have no authority to punish persons for crimes or offenses for which they have not been convicted in court. Their function is rather to maintain peace and order in the community, and to this end to apprehend those who violate or are reasonably believed to violate the law.

With respect to the treatment of bystanders, a Pennsylvania court has spoken of the hazards of the innocent in situations involving the suppression of disorder:

> It is not safe even for persons conscious of innocence to resist him (the peace officer).

109

In disturbed conditions of society it is not always possible to perfectly protect innocent rights and the maintenance of public order is paramount and must be attained even if innocent individuals occasionally suffer.

The right of peaceful protest is constitutionally guaranteed. Law enforcement officers must protect citizens in the lawful exercise of the right of protest. When protests take the form of illegal acts, as in the case of street sit-ins and other types of civil disobedience, orders to cease such conduct are appropriate and arrests must be expected where there is non-compliance. Even here, however, the carrying out of an order for the dispersal of demonstrators or the making of arrests should be accomplished with the minimum amount of force possible and in strict observance of individual rights.

Arrest, fines and incarceration are the penalties for violations of the law. Civil rights demonstrators, in many instances, are willing to undergo these consequences in order to dramatize conditions which they sincerely believe to be unjust to them or their cause. We should never forget that this nation was founded in protest, often strongly expressed, against injustice and oppression.

3.2 THE POLICE EXECUTIVE
Glen R. Murphy*

Community law enforcement officials are sworn and are duty-bound to uphold the Constitution of the United States as well as their state constitutions and local laws. Yet, avowed civil disobedience presents them with the dilemma of which laws they are to enforce. Are they to enforce the moral law, are they to enforce the First Amendment with regard to persons who are protesting, or are they to protect the individuals who want to protest against the counter-demonstrators?

This is the dilemma that confronts the law enforcement officials in the United States today. This dilemma was dominant in the Savannah situation where the courts held to one set of laws, and the city administration held a different point of view as to the proper tactics or procedures that should be used in civil disobedience cases.

---

* Research Consultant, International Association of Chiefs of Police.

The Savannah Chief of Police went as far as he could with the city administration without violating a court order.

It is without question the responsibility of the law enforcement agencies to protect the demonstrators and the human dignity of everyone involved. Yet, much discussion focuses on the police tactics that are used in dealing with civil disobedience. The claims directed against the police are generally symptomatic and not the actual causes of the problem that we are trying to resolve in the United States today. Yet the tactics themselves continually become the point in question. Obviously, police tactics will result in arrest if the demonstrators want to be arrested, and many of them avow just that when they start a demonstration. Perhaps police tactics should not be discussed as much as the initial causes of the problem.

The police, who must protect everyone involved, are frequently charged with brutality. Police brutality is a violation of the Constitution; it is a federal charge that can be investigated by federal authority. Nearly 2,700 cases of alleged police brutality were investigated by the Justice Department in 1963. Only 25 cases, or less than one per cent, were substantiated by investigation.

Some of the brutality charges may be just a smoke-screen. The charge can be an illegitimate tactic to foster civilian review boards to check police practices.

As a group, the police in the United States are very conscious of the problem of civil disobedience and civil rights. The police are attempting to upgrade selection methods and develop better command officers by appointing competent men to responsible positions, men who understand the need to protect the rights of all citizens. These attempts will help law enforcement agencies to assist impartially in civil rights programs. I hope that impartial law enforcement and the development of better community relations throughout the country will allow police to be of greater assistance in the future in our civil rights problems.

3.21 QUESTIONS AND ANSWERS

Question: Many police officials argue that a civilian review board would impair police morale and has not been effective in those cities in which it has been tried. These officials, who do a fine job themselves, are understandably hurt by and do not understand the lack of public confidence in the police. But whether or not this feeling is justified, it is a reality in many cities. What suggestion do these officials have for gaining public confidence in the manner in which complaints of police brutality are evaluated?

MR. MURPHY: Actually several questions are posed here. First, police chiefs generally have a pretty good idea of whether the public does or does not have confidence in their departments. Some police officials can do more to develop confidence, and in cities like Washington, D. C., St. Louis, Syracuse, and Chicago many have already done so.

Some of these cities have developed a police-community relations organization which covers the entire area of law enforcement and is not restricted to civil rights. These police-community relations units have probably been as successful in developing a better climate or image of police as anything that has yet been tried. Beyond that, the police and the IACP are experimenting constantly with ways to develop better relationships within the communities.

As for the function of the civilian review board, the responsibility for discipline within the Police Department rests with the Chief of Police. He cannot delegate this responsibility even if he wants to. The civilian review boards abrogate some of this responsibility.* They have been established to review one aspect of police activity, civil rights, but that does not get to the real problem of law enforcement. The problem is bigger than civil rights and is the chief's responsibility.

Question: Does the Association have an official position either in favor of or against civilian review boards?

MR. MURPHY: Yes, we have definitely stated our position as being opposed to civilian review boards.

VOICE: I would like to make just a brief observation on what I believe to be the role of a police department in policing and regulating demonstrations and various other forms of activities. I come from Toledo, Ohio. It is my understanding that in the principal demo-

---

* For an extensive analysis of the theoretical and practical problems of the administration of civilian complaints against the police, see 77 Harv. L. Rev. 499 (1964).

cratic societies in which we live the fundamental obligation of law enforcement lies with the individual citizen. Otherwise we would develop a police state which we, as police officers, do not want.

In other words, it is the responsibility of the citizen to know the law and to obey it. That is how we can ultimately prevent a police state from arising. With that idea in mind, I think the role of any police organization in dealing with demonstrations has to be one of strict neutrality. I do not think that we should be either the protagonist or antagonist on any particular issue.

Our job is to maintain peace and protect lives and property. I do not believe that any well-intentioned police department thinks that the only way to handle a demonstration, whether it is a religious or labor demonstration, is to arrest the leaders.

The duty of a police department is to arrest those who are actually violating the law, not to rationalize that it is better to arrest a leader or a particular individual. But when a situation gets out of hand or is about to and certain individuals are working toward that end, possibly even being carried away by the emotions of the situation and actually advocating acts which are in definite violation of the law, then they must be removed from the scene.

This is necessary to protect lives, maybe the lives of the very individuals whom you have to take into custody. Again, I do not think it is the object to arrest the leaders, but you cannot avoid arresting a leader if he happens to be violating the law. On the other hand, no enlightened police department intends to pick out the leaders and arrest them merely because they are leaders.

3.3 UTILIZING COMMUNITY RESOURCES: A REPORT FROM ATLANTA*

Herbert T. Jenkins**

In Atlanta, the racial and emotional problems of today can be compared in many respects to those of a hundred years ago—with this difference: today the city government and state government have combined all their resources to join with the federal government in an effort to find an honest, decent and legal solution.

---

* Reprinted, by permission, from *The Police Chief*, September, 1964.
** Chief of Police, Atlanta, Georgia.

113

The Federal Civil Rights Law can be compared with the law against robbery, or the federal law against counterfeiting, in that a great majority of the citizens of the United States do not need such a law. However, there is a small minority who must have the support, the authority and the prestige of the federal government to force them to do the honest, fair and legal thing. Once a law is adopted, it must be applied to and obeyed by all citizens. The Civil Rights Law of 1964 is now the law of the land. Those of us in the field of law enforcement at the federal, state and local levels have no choice but to enforce all of the laws, for the law is our strength and our justification — and the highest value of the law is the keeping of the peace.

The Civil Rights Law has caused only minor changes in the lives of most of Atlanta's citizens. This is the result of the city government, the Chamber of Commerce, various civic groups, the press, and business men trying to do over a period of years what the Civil Rights Law now requires. The Hon. Ivan Allen, Jr. was the first Mayor of a major city to appear before the national Congress and urge adoption of the Civil Rights Law. We believe the adoption of the law will mark the beginning of the end of second class citizenship and discrimination in this nation because of race, creed or color.

The civil rights movement, as we have known it in recent years, first came to my attention in 1933 when a committee of Negro leaders requested the late Mayor James L. Key to employ Negro policemen. The Mayor advised them the request was not unreasonable, but an educational program for both white and Negro citizens would be necessary; and he urged them to start such a program, promising his help to make it succeed. In 1947 a resolution was adopted by the Aldermanic Board to employ eight Negro policemen. The Chamber of Commerce and other civic organizations adopted resolutions approving this action. The eight Negro policemen were employed with many restrictions imposed on their activities. Since that time Negro policemen have expanded in number and rank. In fact, Atlanta was one of the first cities in the South to make wide use of Negro policemen. In 1962, with the full support of Mayor Ivan Allen, Jr., all restrictions imposed on Negro policemen were removed. Today, we have 72 Negroes in the department, including eight detectives, one lieutenant and one sergeant. This emphasizes how the thinking and the attitude toward the Negro in Atlanta and the South has changed in a few short years.

114

I am happy to report that our experience with Negro policemen has been most successful. The cardinal rule to follow is the same as it is in any other police detail: proper screening and selection, adequate training, and proper and constant supervision.

Although the Gallup Poll indicates the Civil Rights Law and the race issue is the biggest problem facing the nation today, the City of Atlanta has considered this a major problem for a good many years.

Atlanta made its first big decision on how to deal with this problem when we received a federal court order to desegregate the golf courses on December 22, 1955. There was wild debate on the subject and Governor Marvin Griffin suggested that all of the golf courses be ploughed up and planted in peas. Atlanta rejected such suggestions and desegregated its golf courses without demonstration or disturbance. This set our procedural policy which has been followed successfully in dealing with demonstrations, civil disobedience and segregation. The City of Atlanta has never abandoned any public facility because of the necessity to desegregate.

The following public facilities were desegregated—with some arrests, but without serious incidents; some with a court order and some without: buses, airport facilities, libraries, city courts, baseball and football stadia, theatres, parks, bus terminals, lunch counters, schools, swimming pools, and many private business establishments, such as hotels and restaurants. This was accomplished long before the adoption of the Civil Rights Act of 1964.

The gradual desegregation of public facilities in Atlanta did not just happen, but was designed and guided by community leadership. I believe I personally developed early a sympathetic understanding of the purposes of the civil rights movement, and I have made every effort to direct the training in the Atlanta Police Department so that every member of the force could develop a similar understanding.

Perhaps the single greatest problem was in desegregating the schools, but when Mr. John Sibley, a distinguished attorney and executive of the Coca-Cola Company accepted the chairmanship of a committee organized to find the answer to this complex problem, he clarified it by removing propaganda and half-truths from the discussions to define the issue. The definition was as simple as this: (1) accept the U.S. Supreme Court's decision and desegregate

115

the public schools, or (2) abandon and destroy public education. All of our PTA's and civic clubs gave freely of their time and money to establish the organizations known as Organizations Assisting Schools in September (OASIS) and Help Our Public Education (HOPE). The Atlanta newspapers gave full support in both news coverage and editorials.

When the mission was accomplished Mr. Sibley publicly stated it was a community project, but if the police had ever hesitated or shown the least sign of weakness, the mission could have failed.

Those of us in the Atlanta Police Department recognize that our primary responsibility does not include the solving of all racial and psychological problems in the community, nor does it relieve us from our duty to participate with others in finding a solution. A common mistake made in dealing with civil rights demonstrations by white police officers is that we do not always thoroughly understand and appreciate these people, their motives or desires. We, as police officers, are trained to deal with criminals and to meet them with whatever force is necessary in order to take them into custody. Civil rights demonstrators are generally good citizens, with a non-violent attitude, who sincerely believe they have the law and right and justice on their side. To cope successfully with this kind of problem, we must change our tactics. We must approach it with moderation, tolerance and restraint.

The real conflict develops when in the midst of a demonstration the police are confronted with an individual or a group of individuals who refuse to follow the instructions of non-violence given by their leaders and bring in to the demonstration violence, resistance and force. Under these circumstances the police have no alternative but to apply all the force at their command to keep the situation from getting out of control.

We experienced such a demonstration last January at Leb's Restaurant, located in the center of downtown. The question is still being debated whether or not the police were slow or hasty in applying force and making wholesale arrests. We think our timing was good and the press and the public appeared to agree. James Forman had become the local leader of the Student Non-Violent Coordinating Committee (SNCC). He was a tough, violent leader, determined to integrate Leb's Restaurant, and led a group of demonstrators to

116

Leb's every day at noontime. Charlie Leb, the owner, was just as determined to keep his restaurant segregated. Large crowds of spectators gathered on the streets just to see who was winning. On January 25th about 30 of the demonstrators were successful in entering the restaurant for a sit-in demonstration. The restaurant was immediately closed by the owner. The group of spectators outside became an angry mob of both white and Negro citizens. This was a real threat to the peace and security of the community. Police reinforcements, including about 40 Negro policemen, were called and a riot was prevented. The next day the demonstrators were informed by the police that only a limited number of legal and orderly pickets would be allowed. They refused to cooperate and 85 of them were arrested, but they were allowed to sign their own bond and released when they promised that all future demonstrations would be orderly and adhere to the rules and regulations. The next day a mass demonstration was attempted, with both white and Negro, male and female, participating. They went limp when the police attempted to move them and 114 were arrested and jailed. The Negro leadership cooperated by refusing to post bond or pay their fines and many of them served time in the city stockade. Charlie Leb charged that the police failed to protect him and his property; the demonstrators charged police brutality and declared some female prisoners were improperly handled. Admittedly, we have been unable to design a graceful method to remove a fat lady who goes limp. The demonstrations, however, ceased and Leb's Restaurant remained segregated until the day after adoption of the Civil Rights Law by Congress, and then every one was served regardless of race, creed or color.

The Chief of Police can only establish and execute successfully such policies and procedures as the Mayor and the Board of Aldermen or City Council and the public will support.

But it is the responsibility of the Chief of Police to keep the city fathers and the business leaders informed of the potential dangers and the great need for their advice and assistance.

A business leader, a civic leader, or an officer in the Chamber of Commerce is the most logical person to go to a restaurant operator and explain the necessity of making his services and facilities available to all citizens. He can better explain that the alternative

117

in many cases has been demonstrations, violence and even riots. It is not difficult for a businessman to understand, especially if it is pointed out to him by another businessman of broad experience, that a breakdown in law enforcement is very bad for business.

Atlanta's business leadership was by no means thoroughly familiar with all the grievances of the Negro community, and many would prefer "business as usual" to the difficult task of solving the race problem. But it at least recognized that it had the problem and was determined not to wait for violence before attempting solutions.

Following the lunch counter sit-ins of 1961, which had resulted in the closing of several retail store lunch counters, Negro Attorney A. T. Walden, Robert Troutman, Sr. (a partner in one of the city's leading law firms), and Ivan Allen, then president of the Chamber of Commerce, formed a biracial committee comprised of Negro preachers, civil rights workers, students and retail store executives. This committee promptly negotiated the immediate reopening of store eating facilities, the re-employment of several hundred restaurant employees, and the elimination of boycotts and picket lines. Court cases which had resulted from the demonstrations were dropped by restaurant operators.

As a result of careful planning and agreements among all of the town's leading merchants, all retail department and variety store lunch counters, rest rooms, drinking fountains, beauty parlors and other customer facilities were desegregated in the fall of 1961. Proceeding out of an abundance of caution, final action was delayed until after the first desegregated schools had opened and the fall elections had been held.

The Chamber of Commerce, the city government, the Retail Merchants Association, and other groups applauded the action and urged hotels, motels and restaurant operators other than those located in retail stores to follow suit. Many did but others held back, and some who had opened their doors to all citizens re-segregated, perhaps because they did not then have the benefit of careful planning, through negotiation and conference, or the strength of organization which characterized the desegregation of the retail store facilities. The confusion which resulted from this lack of agreement or concerted action was undoubtedly one of the prime factors underlying the sit-in demonstrations which ultimately took place last January.

118

Meanwhile, several civil rights organizations, some of whom proposed the conference method, while others preferred direct action, had banded together to form the Atlanta Negro Summit Leadership Conference. This group published a statement outlining an eight-point program of objectives.

Mayor Allen, under authority granted by the Board of Aldermen, appointed a coordinating committee of white citizens, representing religious, business, civic, health and government groups, to facilitate communication and negotiation in the specific areas outlined in the Summit Statement.

The lines of communication were therefore open and ready for action before the passage of the Civil Rights Act of 1964. To prepare the climate of opinion for prompt and voluntary compliance with the Act, and to avoid the possibility of a leadership vacuum during the period immediately following enactment, two members of the coordinating committee—an architect and a corporation lawyer —assumed specific responsibility in the fields of employment and public accommodations. They called an advance meeting to see what could be done by government, the news media, business, religious, professional, labor and human relations groups to promote prompt observance of the law once it became effective. Attending this meeting were city officials, the clergy, newspaper and television and radio representatives, professional and business men, and various civil rights groups, including the Southern Regional Council, the American Jewish Committee, the National Conference of Christians and Jews, and the Potomac Institute. A portion of the meeting was video-taped and later included in a television program entitled, "New Law in Town." At the meeting specific plans were made to mobilize as many community resources as time would allow, to meet and publish statements promoting law and order, and urging voluntary compliance "in the Atlanta way."

The subcommittee, which has no budget or paid staff, set up an office in City Hall, staffed by a volunteer and the executive director of the National Conference of Christians and Jews for the follow-up work.

Meetings were held in quick succession by the Bar Association, the Medical Association, the Hotel and Restaurant Association, the Convention Bureau, the Chamber of Commerce, the Council of Churches, the tri-faith group, and other organizations. All released

119

statements—and a flood of publicity followed. The Governor, both Senators, the Mayor and the Grand Jury all spoke out for peaceful observance. Negro Summit Leadership and Atlanta's Negro State Senator urged restraint. The Summit leaders, including a representative of SNCC, agreed upon an orderly and carefully planned approach for service at four establishments whose proprietors had been known as leaders of the resistance.

Did it work?—at all except one, and I wish to assure you he does not represent the Atlanta spirit and attitude.

3.4 "UNJUSTIFIED CHARGES OF BRUTALITY..."*

Quinn Tamm**

I know of no period in recent history when the police have been the subject of so many unjustified charges of brutality, harassment and ineptness. It almost seems that the better we do our job of enforcing the law the more we are attacked. The more professional we become, the more effective we become and the more effective we are, the more we impinge upon the misbehavior of society.

But for this we should offer no apology. A police force is established, among other things, for the purpose of enforcing existing laws. In this respect, we are duty-bound.

Those who damn our actions in this regard must be made to understand that the police do not make the laws, that laws are the direct product of public desires and if the public does not like those laws or believe them to be fair, then the public should change the laws rather than criticize the police.

It is in this context that I offer the fervent hope that we will not be known as the "Silent Generation."

The time has passed when we can sit silently by or protest feebly to those who unfairly criticize us when what we do is legally and morally right. We can no longer afford to answer unjust criticism with thinly veiled innuendos and pusillanimous generalities. If we are right, let's say so.

---

* Reprinted, by permission, from "Police Professionalism and Civil Rights," *The Police Chief,* September, 1964.
** Executive Director, International Association of Chiefs of Police.

This was the philosophy behind one of our recent editorials in *The Police Chief,* entitled "Police Brutality—Or Smokescreen?" In it we referred to baseless charges of police brutality which have been made to cover excesses and illegal conduct on the part of some demonstrators involved in the current racial tension.

The editorial† is, I believe, forthright and simple enough in expression. It is merely an assertion of fact, and it needed to be said. Of course, it would have been politic to say nothing, and some of our leading law enforcement executives have chosen this tactic. At the same time, other practicing police executives have had the courage, if indeed that is what it takes, to speak unemotionally and factually of our responsibility of upholding the law. To do so is not to align oneself with one side or the other of a sociological argument. It is merely to state the police position with regard to breaking the law, whether the violation be robbery or illegal conduct while engaging in a public demonstration.

Columnist David Lawrence wrote an understanding analysis recently when he commented, "Perhaps the most difficult phase of the whole problem is the situation which confronts the local police. If they do not arrest the demonstrator, lots of innocent persons are injured, but, on the other hand, if the police try to use force to deal with those who are threatening violence, these same law officers are accused of 'brutality.' "

Never before in the history of the police service have we been singled out so mercilessly and so wrongfully as the whipping boys by demonstrators for so-called sociological evolution and by out-and-out hoodlums who have abandoned the banner of civil rights to engage in senseless insurrection.

The police of the nation have no quarrel with peaceful demonstrations by responsible groups. An excellent example of planning and purposefulness was the "March on Washington, D. C." last August, at which time demonstration leaders and the authorities charged with maintaining law and order insured peace through cooperation and planning. That human dignity prevailed is a tribute both to law enforcement and to the leaders of the March.

---

† *The Police Chief,* December, 1963.

A moment ago I used the term insurrection. I can think of no other word which would describe the recent outrages against life, property and authority which we have seen perpetrated by hoodlums in Harlem and other sections of New York City and in Rochester, New York. It has been clearly established, I believe, that these mob actions involving destruction of property, looting and assaults on peaceful citizens and the police have transcended the hopes and purposes of responsible civil rights leaders. Cloaking themselves falsely in the mantle of civil rights, the rabble of society in these two communities have used so-called resentment against police to engage in savagery seldom witnessed in this country's history.

One lachrymose female reporter for a Washington, D. C., newspaper, who became an "expert" on the cause of Harlem's riots in something like a 48-hour visit to that area, has opined that, "In the beginning, both the good and the bad in Harlem had a common bond and it was not so much their color as it was their seething rage at the New York City police force." She also quoted a Harlem youth worker who declared that the riots were a rebellion against the New York City police and that they were the result of "act upon act of police brutality." She added that "True or false, Harlem believes that it is a fact of life that cops are on the take and cops will 'brutalize' you—bash your heads in for no provocation."

She, like so many other journalistic observers, cites the slaying of a 15-year-old Negro youth by a white police officer as the spark which ignited the dry tinder of so-called frustration in Harlem.

And, like so many other erudite, journalistic observers, she dips deeply into her store of sensational adjectives and adverbs to describe the police action. The state of our so-called objective press is sad to behold as one peruses the mostly biased and tongue-clucking accounts written by journalists whose writing prowess appears to be titillated only by violence and sensationalism. Subtly, too many so-called objective news writers attempt to excuse the actions of minorities even when their unlawful rioting causes death, injury and carnage which no other society would condone for a moment. For instance, the female reporter wrote, "And they (Harlem's inhabitants) again renewed demands for a civilian review board to guard against any cover-up. Instead, the city answered their requests by sending wave after wave of white-helmeted, white-faced police officers into Harlem."

122

She continued, "And a Negro youth said: 'When I see a helmet I think of war and so I act like it is war.' Thus, bottles, bricks, stones, garbage, even lethal Molotov cocktails were thrown on police from the rooftops and the cellars." Abruptly, this reporter changes her mood and goes on, "Police retaliated by scorching the air with round after round of ammunition, fired over the heads of the rioters." She then deplores this police tactic apparently to back up her earlier contention that "billy clubs and bullets are not the way to halt New York City's hemmed-in youth."

At the same time, however, she offers no alternative which might have had the immediate effect of containing and restraining the rioters.

This pompous tone of reporting and the avid search by movie and still photographers for pictures of police battling "frustrated" rioters are an appalling and dishonest journalistic treatment of the police and the mission which they are duty-bound to carry out.

Try as I might, I cannot accept the so-called news media's contention that the police are responsible for society's failures to provide better opportunities for minority groups, and it is hypocritical and morally wrong for the police to be singled out by virtually all factions as the symbol of all society's failures.

Louis Lomax, a Negro journalist and author who writes for the North American Newspaper Alliance, Inc., has injected some reason into the Harlem picture. He said in a recent article, "The killing of a 15-year-old Negro boy by an off-duty white policeman was not the cause of the riots; rather, this incident was only an excuse for the rioting to occur. For Harlem, USA, is little more than a bloody race riot looking for somewhere—and a reason—to take place."

He goes on to say, however: "Then there are, to be sure, the police. Most of them are white, many of them are rookies, and so many of them seem to have what New Yorker Barbara Benison called 'an irrational fear of black men.' Harlemites disrespect the police with vigor and hate them with passion. They disrespect the police because they know—after all, they see it with their own eyes every day and night—the police are in league with the vice and crime that flaw their community; they hate the police because most of them

123

have either experienced or witnessed some act of flagrant police brutality."

Such a sweeping indictment of police is a smear of the first magnitude. Such general comments beg specifics to be brought to light and presented to the proper authorities.

It is not surprising that these charges come from a group which Mr. Lomax describes as follows: "The Harlem masses, more than any people I have encountered anywhere, simply don't believe in anything or anybody. They applaud but do not follow Malcolm X and the Black Nationalists; Harlemites rejoice when there is a victory by their brothers in the Deep South, but they refuse to support the organizations involved in the civil rights struggle; Harlem's newspaper has a smaller circulation than either of the white dailies in the community; the area brims with churches and bars, but the ministers have no more community-wide influence than the bartenders. . . . The ultimate irony is that Harlem rioted at the very time when its citizens have more opportunities available to them than they have ever had before."

Rather than sensationalizing myths and rumors which sell papers and stir further violence in such tense situations, the news media could perform a more valuable service by focusing the spotlight on proven police brutality supported by the workable process of justice which is represented by American courts.

As I mentioned a moment ago, the female reporter in Washington cited as one of their reasons for rioting the failure of the Harlem group to have their demand granted that a civilian review board be established to inquire into alleged acts of brutality by police.

Strangely enough, however, the riots in Harlem were shortly echoed in Rochester with even more ferocity and viciousness against the police. I say strangely enough because *Rochester has now and has had for some time a civilian review board of the type advocated by the Harlem element!*

The charge of "act upon act of police brutality" is aired in the newspaper, on the radio and on television when this country has the most efficient machinery of any in the world for the discovery of deprivation of civil rights under the color of law. It is a violation of Federal statute to maltreat anyone under the color of law. If such rampant police brutality exists, the U. S. Department of Justice should have been notified of each and every incident. The FBI, the investigative arm of the Department of Justice, is in Harlem, and it has the responsibility of inquiring into such charges. It will be interesting indeed to see how many authentic cases of police brutality emerge as a result of FBI investigation.

Where such brutality exists, the administrators of the New York City Police Department and indeed the police of the entire Nation would want to see the perpetrators punished because there is no place in professional law enforcement for brutality. But, at the same time, unless the charges are substantiated by convictions in our impartial courts of law then it would seem that the false criers of police brutality are doing a disservice to their fellow man, to their Nation's police and to their country. But perhaps this is their aim.

In 1963, there were 2,692 allegations of civil rights violations of all kinds handled by the U. S. Department of Justice. Following appropriate investigation of these matters, less than 25 resulted in indictments of police officers. This is less than 1% of the total civil rights matters investigated.

Rumor which is viciously detrimental to the police establishment has no place in our society, and opportunism which singles out the police officer as the villain in society's failures is reprehensible. The dedicated and honorable police executives of the country have traditionally condemned and taken severe action against officers guilty of brutality. They are willing and desirous of being governed by the law; it is high time that other segments of our society also seek to accomplish their goals through the courts rather than through insurrection and baseless character assassination.

Where police brutality actually exists, may it be deterred and stamped out by stern retribution in the courts; where public brutality against the police exists, may it also be deterred and stamped out by equally stern retribution in the courts.

To endure, this Republic must be governed by law; no proponents of any cause can achieve their goals through the commission of serious crimes against their fellow men.

The police are obviously the symbol of the law, and a breakdown in public respect for the law is apparent in the senseless assaults upon our policemen. When public respect for the law is regained, then human dignity will be restored in New York City, in Rochester and in other areas of our country which are being blighted by hoodlums who cover their excesses by falsely flying the banner of civil rights.

3.41 DEVELOPING GUIDELINES FOR POLICE PRACTICES*
NELSON A. WATSON**

End Police Brutality has become a battle cry ringing out from one end of the land to the other. It is repeated parrot-like by hundreds of thousands who have never had any personal experience which could even remotely serve as a basis for the charge. It has become a commonplace and almost automatic accusation attached to any physical action taken by an officer to control disorders. It has been plastered in garish posters in public places for all to see. It has been chanted tauntingly in the faces of officers assigned to prevent violence at scenes of demonstrations. It has been used by supposedly responsible Negro leaders to whip up support among their followers. Police have been charged with verbal abuse of minority group citizens, with beatings, and even with murder.

It was reported in a major eastern newspaper that Harlem takes it for granted that "cops are on the take" and "cops will brutalize you"— bash your head in for no reason. This paper reported that James Farmer, Executive Director of CORE, said he saw a white policeman shoot a Negro woman who had asked his help in getting a taxi to escape the riot area. The woman is supposed to have screamed, "You shot me" and the policeman is reported to have replied, "Well, lay down and die then."

I charge that this story represents irresponsibility at its worst. The writer is guilty of at least cheap sensationalism for putting into print a charge that on its face is preposterous. I charge that James Farmer is guilty of the most serious dereliction of duty as a citizen for not having instituted action against the offending officer if his accusation is true and, if not, then he is guilty of the most damnable irresponsibility. As a matter of fact, investigation by proper and com-

---

* Reprinted, by permission, from *The Police Chief,* September, 1964.

** Project Supervisor, Research and Development Section, International Association of Chiefs of Police.

petent authority has disclosed that the incident as described did not occur. Trifling with the truth and playing upon the emotions of the masses cannot help but create confusion and disorder. The blame should not be put upon the police, but rather on the heads of those who play fast and loose with the facts. And let us be mindful that these people—who are so ready to exaggerate and distort—are the same people who want to be given the power to review complaints against the police.

But, wait! Let us take a sober look at this question. We ourselves must avoid sensationalism and emotionalism, and I hope you will forgive me if I let my resentment show through.

The control of violence often calls for extreme countermeasures. No officer is expected to stand by passively and allow himself to be injured. We do not send men into the streets to be cursed, spat upon, assaulted or killed. Vilification and oaths will not hurt them, but bottles and bricks will. They should not be targets for either. They are there to prevent or to quell disorders, to protect life, limb, and property. Whether or not the action they take is brutal, whether or not the force they use is excessive depends upon the viewpoint. I dare say the owners of the looted businesses do not regard the action taken by the police to be unwarranted. And in the heat of the conflict, only the officer can judge the necessary force behind the stick. It is he who must decide when he is in danger of injury or death. If the people of the community expect him to do this rough and dangerous job to protect them and their property, then they owe him their support. Unfortunately, there are all too many unthinking persons who are willing to believe charges against the police without looking into the facts. There are more people who are apathetic and who accept no responsibility in what is, after all, a problem for the whole community.

Our topic is Developing Guidelines for Police Practice, and I can think of no better place to start than the Law Enforcement Code of Ethics. This is no time for playing ostrich and hiding our heads in the sand. We have to face our problems objectively and dispassionately. We must acknowledge our mistakes frankly and honestly. There have been policemen who turned burglar. There have been policemen who extorted money and merchandise in return for winking at violations of the law. Badges have been tarnished by inexcusable abuse of power. The unpardonable and outmoded third degree reaches out from history and continues to plague professional police everywhere. Officers here and there have undoubtedly used abusive and injudicious language. After all, policemen are subject to many of the human frailties that have beset mankind from the beginning of time. It is remarkable, considering the nature of the police job, that transgressions are as infrequent as they are. To the everlasting credit of the police service, it must be acknowledged that there are literally hundreds of thousands of honorable men who have spent a lifetime serving their communities without deviation from the basic tenets of our Code of Ethics.

When we talk about developing guidelines for police practice, we seem to imply that such standards do not now exist. Such a conclusion is, of course, erroneous. Police literature abounds in statements of philosophy and policy. Nevertheless, it is a profitable investment of time for us to turn our thinking in this direction for a few moments with a view to reviewing, reorganizing, and strengthening our position.

Our approach to police problems must be based upon a well-conceived set of beliefs and convictions. The intellectual embodiment of these concepts and principles constitutes a basic police philosophy. Let us recite a few of the philosophical concepts pertaining to the subject matter of this meeting:

1. In human society, the unrestrained expression of selfish impulses cannot be permitted and everyone must learn to accept restrictions for the good of all.

2. In all civilized societies, man has found it necessary to explicitly define certain of these restrictions in a formal code known as the law and to establish machinery for its implementation.

3. In our democratic society it is acknowledged that everyone is entitled to equal opportunity and to equal protection under the law.

4. National policy decrees that neither race, color, national origin, nor religion shall in any way modify or limit one's right to the enjoyment of these blessings.

5. No person and no group may be permitted to disregard the law for to do so threatens the foundation of the freedoms of all.

6. The law specifies not only certain things that people may and may not do, but also specifies many requirements and restrictions relative to its enforcement—requirements and restrictions which apply to the police.

7. The job of the police requires that action be taken within the limits imposed by the law when violations occur.

8. Under some circumstances, police power may be employed in the interest of preserving public order and safety and to prevent unwarranted interference with the liberties of others even though to do so results in curtailing the activities of some. For example, in a demonstration the number of pickets may have to be limited and the area within which they may picket may be specified. It would not be proper, however, for the police to ban posters or signs no matter how distasteful unless they are obscene.

9. We hold, as a matter of policy in relation to offenders, that the police are not in the punishing business any more than they are in the rehabilitating business. The police job is to prevent crime and to detect and apprehend offenders. Treatment of the offenders is some-one else's job. Similarly, it is not the police function either to promote integration or to maintain segregation. These are broad social problems, the resolution of which involves the populace in general.

To sum up, the words of Police Commissioner Michael J. Murphy of New York are appropriate and significant: "The police do not serve one segment of society as against another. Police protection extends to all people. Police protection means fair and equal treatment; no special privileges. The mandate of our duty as police officers is clear. We must observe a position of neutrality and impartiality. Our primary concern is the preservation of the public peace."

In developing our guidelines for police practice, we must recognize certain realities of life. We must keep in mind that we are dealing with a highly explosive issue on which nearly everyone has some kind of a strong opinion. We must understand that the actions of the police as viewed in the light of these strong opinions will be criticized from many sides. We must recognize that there are certain basic psychological principles at work which directly influence police planning.

First, there is the matter of suggestibility and contagion relative to uprisings and disorders. In all parts of the country, there is the potential for demonstrations and for reactions to demonstrations. The demonstrations and the reactions which they generate present a potential for possible violence and riots. Many chiefs of police feel that the local situation is well under control and that such possibilities in their jurisdictions are remote. Don't count on it. An unexpected incident can trigger violence before you know it. What happens in one community may easily spread to another. The leadership may or may not come from local citizens. People do move from one place to another and national organizations sometimes send individuals or "task forces" to various sections of the country. Moreover, people see what is going on elsewhere and these things have a way of catching on. Police are well aware of contagion as a psychological phenomenon. We know that certain kinds of crime have a tendency to breed more of the same. So it is not safe to assume that "it can't happen here."

Police experience has shown that the participants in demonstrations and violent disorders are largely youths and even juveniles of a very tender age. They are often reckless and appear to be "out for kicks." It is a common observation in police work that juveniles will do things in groups which they would not do when alone. A boy who is otherwise well-behaved may, when showing off in his gang, toss a rock through a window. When you ask him why he did it, he says he doesn't know. The same is true in public demonstrations. Some of these young people will hurl insults at officers—or maybe even stones—things they would never do if they were alone. In other words, the excitement, the large numbers involved, the cloak of protection the crowd offers, all serve to generate behavior that would not normally occur. The important thing for police is to expect and plan for such behavior. When a demonstration is peaceful and orderly, the police problem is to see that it remains that way, but, at the same time, we must be alert to all influences that could turn it into violence.

A routine arrest of a drunk can serve as the springboard for hotheads to trigger a violent disorder. When the situation develops into looting and pillaging, violent assault on police officers and others, and the destruction of property, we have what amounts to complete breakdown of law and order. These acts are just plain crime and must be dealt with accordingly. They cannot be excused on grounds of racial unrest or anything else. The redress of grievances arising out of social inequality does not justify burglary, thievery, arson, vandalism, assault, and other crimes.

A very important psychological principle is that people react not to objective reality but to their perception, their interpretation of the world. As we all know, people see things differently. What seems fair and reasonable to one person may be regarded as gross injustice by another. The interposition of the police power, seen by the police as a necessary measure for the preservation of the peace and protection of the rights of persons not involved in a demonstration may be seen by the demonstrators as unfair interference with their right to demonstrate or even as extreme provocation on the part of the police. Deliberate violations of certain laws during acts of civil disobedience are perceived by the perpetrators as a highly moral duty, and by onlookers, as incomprehensible attacks on established social order. Arrest and jail under certain circumstances are valued as a badge of honor and are deliberately sought. Those who engage in these acts often regard themselves as martyrs to a cause, whereas other people may look upon them as criminals, communists, anarchists, subversives, and so on. These divergent attitudes illustrate the depth of the cleavage. Thus it is that police see as an inescapable duty the removal of a nonviolent but limp and uncooperative person from a public street— an action which may be viewed by those engaging in civil disobedience as an unfair application of police power or even as brutality.

The function of the police in society is a role that is unfortunately not always correctly defined. The ambiguity arises in part because of differences in jurisdiction that exist. For example, some police have very limited powers. Railroad police and building guards would be examples. Some state organizations are limited to policing the highways and concern themselves only with traffic. Municipal police, as a rule, have wider powers. However, even here the actions they can take vary considerably because of differences in the statutes and ordinances under which they work. Still another factor producing variation in police practice results from different methods employed in applying police power. Some administrators are more aggressive than others. Training of officers differs. Emergencies present situations for which there is no precedent and decisions must be made without adequate guidelines. And, of course, personalities differ greatly. All these factors have a tendency to becloud the police role. Yet, to the average man, a policeman is a policeman and differences in powers and practices create confusion in his mind. Many people will assume, for example, that it is any policeman's job to enforce the provisions of the recent Civil Rights Bill.

It is generally conceded that among the common elements in the police role are such things as the following:

1. Police are sworn to enforce and uphold the law.

2. The law must be applied impartially to one and all.

131

3. Police must take appropriate action to prevent crime.

4. Police may not generally interfere with a citizen's pursuit of his goals unless the citizen's actions violate the law.

5. When a violator must be apprehended, police are required to effect an arrest and such physical force as is necessary to consummate the action must be employed.

6. Police, as enforcers of the law, must not themselves break the law.

7. Police must act within the restrictions placed on them by the law as interpreted by the courts.

8. Police have no choice as to which laws shall be enforced nor when except that discretion residing in the intelligent and trained judgment of the individual officer as he interprets the situation.

We could go on listing other elements descriptive of the police role but these will serve sufficiently to illustrate the point.

While we are on the subject of role, we should note that we must concern ourselves with more than the police role. Other people have roles to play also. Now, it is a psychological fact of life that when an individual is convinced that he is or should be a certain kind of person, he will act accordingly. In other words, he will live up to his concept of his role. If a juvenile is convinced that he is no good and will never amount to anything, he certainly will not try very hard in school. If a Negro is convinced that he is a hopeless victim of a caste system, that all whites are enemies, that the police exist to keep him down, and that he will never get anywhere except by slyness and cunning, the role he assumes will be very different from that he would play if he believed he had a chance to make something of himself. The behavior of any person is determined to a large extent by the role he is then playing.

In developing guidelines for police practice, it is important for us to realize that today's widespread social revolution is creating a new concept of role for a large number of people. These changes affect people who are partisan to both sides of the question. They produce tremendous pressures for accelerating change and heavy resistance to change. Pressures from both directions focus on the police and the problems of preserving peace and order are, consequently, made more difficult.

132

We need to train our men and to plan carefully for any eventuality. Neglect of either of these angles is a serious dereliction of duty. As you already know, training is being given and planning is being done by persons and groups who intend and expect to create disorder. One manual used by persons engaged in demonstrating and in civil disobedience describes what they call the Alabama System and the Mississippi System. The pertinent portion reads as follows:

> " 'Tough' policing of civil rights generally falls into two types: the 'Alabama System' and the 'Mississippi System.' The former involves the *lack* of police protection for legitimate demonstrations—it permits the formation of mobs, as in the case of the Freedom Riders in 1961. The latter system forbids the formation of mobs, and uses police authority to crush civil rights demonstrations. This has the advantage of being not only more efficient, but also proceeding under the protection of 'law and order.' While Northern police do not use the 'Alabama System,' it should not be thought that they never use the 'Mississippi System.' There are at least two variations upon this system—the straight-forward, 'hard' line: disperse, or else. Period. The other variation appears soft on the surface and attempts to disarm, psychologically, the leadership and rank-and-file by being polite first, and only later pulling off the soft gloves. For example, the police command may appear to side with the demonstrators, asking them to sing a few songs or lead the group in prayer (this happened on the part of the Maryland State Guard in Cambridge in May, 1964), before asking them politely to disperse. This can be coupled with veiled threats to have leading demonstrators committed for observation to mental institutions, which also happened in Cambridge—this threat seems to be more severe than simple prison. But the objective is the same: to disperse demonstrators at all costs."

The manual also discusses police tactics. Among the items mentioned the following few are of interest:

> "Intelligent officers have learned that to break up a crowd an officer does well to pick random citizens off the edge and arrest them, rather than attempting to move into the center to arrest, say, a street speaker."

133

"Accepted American police practices include having a plan, and acting with all the force necessary to carry out the plan. Intelligent officers do not bluff. They make their intention clear to the crowd or the demonstration, allow time to clear out, and leave avenues of escape (unlike a recent Peruvian sports stadium tragedy in which gas panicked a crowd against barred doors)."

"A crowd is usually attacked opposite the direction in which police want to drive it. A skirmish line, wedge, or diagonal line is formed across the street, and State, National Guard and Federal troops usually fix bayonets. The effort will be to drive the crowd or demonstration away from the sensitive areas, street crossings, objectives of demonstrations such as stores, and to break the crowd up into its individual units by the use of gas, horses, dogs, fire-hoses, etc. Individuals can more easily be controlled and sent home than larger groups. Civil rights workers, under such circumstances, may want to consider the use of 'sleeper' elements to divert an attacking police unit by demonstrating in its rear, thereby keeping the demonstration going a while longer and taking the pressure off the group under immediate attack."

Regarding tear gas, the instructions read in part,

"Grasp hands of demonstrators near you, and avoid running into the street (and risking getting run over since your visibility is impaired). Retreat in an orderly fashion from the scene. An assembly area should be picked beforehand and demonstrators should reassemble for further orders out of range of the gas."

At another place the following appears,

"Do not assume that because an officer is a Negro he is also a sympathizer. Some Negro police officers 'lean over backwards' to be tough."

Through informants police officers have learned that demonstrators have been trained to go limp and to engage in other tactics designed to make the police task more difficult and embarrassing. One informant advised a police chief that demonstrators had been

134

taught to make grimaces and to throw up their hands as if warding off a blow when news photographers were taking pictures.

Since this kind of preparation is being made, the urgency of police training and planning is all the more acute.

Let us now take a few specifics relative to the police role in enforcing the law and preserving order. . . .

1. With regard to the behavior of individual officers under our command, I hold the following would be essential. Every officer must put aside his personal feelings and prejudices when he puts on his uniform. He is a policeman for all of the people. He is a public servant who represents the impersonal majesty of the law. He must apply his police powers without regard to race, creed, religion, or situation in life. He must strive to be both impartial and impersonal. We cannot permit officers to render judgments and to discharge their duties on the basis of personal likes or dislikes.

2. As public officials acting within the law, we must resist with all the logic and strength at our command pressures from partisans of any conviction. The law may not be perverted any more than it may be ignored. We must not be sandbagged or coerced by any pressure group.

3. We must refrain from all acts that are, in fact, brutal. I am sure everyone here will "buy" this statement: Any officer who would hit a man just because he is a Negro or who would use more force than necessary to effect an arrest just because the subject is colored is a disgrace to the uniform and should be dismissed.

4. Verbal abuse is no less reprehensible than physical abuse. The impartial and equal application of the law knows no color or race. Profanity directed against anyone by an officer on duty deserves disciplinary action. The derogatory term "nigger" has no place in the *police* vocabulary.

5. Every officer must be trained to keep his head. All must understand that an impulsive act, a thoughtless act can serve as the trigger for a riot in a tense situation.

6. In our advanced planning, we must establish and keep open channels of communication with the responsible leaders of all kinds of groups. It is only by knowing what is going on that we can

135

intelligently plan. Planning without communicating with the interested elements in the community is like flying blind. We are liable to run smack into an unexpected crisis.

Now, you say that many of these leaders are not responsible individuals. Well, that may be, but we must still make the effort to communicate. We cannot expect them to know or to care about police problems unless we try to inform them. Nor can we accurately assess their potential and anticipate their actions if we remain aloof.

7. We must give increased attention to the police image. By word and deed we must convince the people that we are enforcing the law impartially for the benefit of all. At the same time, we must let it be known that officers will defend themselves when it is necessary. We must remain calm and controlled in the face of verbal abuse, but physical attack must be met with effective measures for the protection of the men.

8. In our training courses, officers should be educated in the essentials of the social movements of our time so they will have a better understanding of the whys and wherefores of the current situation. Training in police tactics alone is not enough. We need men who can act intelligently and judiciously under a variety of circumstances.

9. As administrators, we must give other community officials the benefit of our professional appraisal of the situation from the police point of view. Their decisions should be made with full appreciation of the problems faced by the police—the very men they are depending upon to do the job.

10. Even though enforcement of the Civil Rights Bill is not within the jurisdiction of local police, our officers must be acquainted with its provisions. They must understand its relationship to local law enforcement. They must be in a position to handle and refer correctly complaints arising under it. They must be kept abreast of developments as they arise, court decisions, threatened and actual disorders resulting from both compliance and defiance of the law.

As a final point, I want to return to the concept with which we began this discussion, police brutality. In my opinion, it is not enough just to tell a group of officers in a training school that they must not be guilty of acts of brutality. We need to be more specific. We need to lay down some guidelines, to provide them with some ground rules. I shall, therefore try to construct a framework around which guidance can be given.

To begin with, we will all agree that it is a forlorn hope to expect that we can get such divergent groups as those we have to deal with to agree on a definition of brutality. But, if we face the issue squarely and calmly, I think we can arrive at a concept that has utility.

What does it mean to be brutal? One who is brutal is savage, cruel, coarse, insensitive, vulgar, inhuman, ferocious, barbarous—obviously, all qualities undesirable in the police service. Whether or not these adjectives can be correctly applied to a given act is a matter of interpretation. As I said in the beginning, whether or not an act is regarded as brutal depends upon the viewpoint.

I would propose as guidelines the following:

I. No action taken by an officer in defending himself, up to and including the death of his assailant, is brutal provided

   a. He is acting officially as a policeman within the boundaries of his legal powers.

   b. He has sufficient cause, as would appear real and reasonable to a prudent man, to fear for his personal safety.

   c. The means and the force employed by him are not such as a prudent man would consider excessive, unreasonable, or unnecessary.

   d. There is no acceptable alternative available to him considering his obligation not to retreat from his official mission and his inherent right to protect himself.

II. When it comes to bringing a specific police mission to a successful conclusion—getting the job done—and there is no immediate or apparent danger calling for self-defense by the officer, his actions should be tempered by good judgment, common sense, restraint, and understanding. His actions would not fall within the definition of brutality provided

   a. He is acting officially as a policeman within the restrictions imposed on him by law.

   b. He conducts himself impartially and dispassionately.

137

c. He is firm without being angrily unreasonable.

d. He provides reasonable opportunity for compliance with the law.

e. He uses force only after other means have failed.

f. The force employed is not more than is required to produce compliance.

g. The force is not of an uncivilized or cruel nature.

This proposed framework leaves no room for "bashing in heads without provocation" as has been charged by some. It rules out any application of force after a person has submitted to arrest or complied with legal police orders.

You may or may not find it possible to agree with the details of these guidelines for practice and, of course, you are at liberty to make such alterations, additions, or deletions, as your conscience dictates. The point is that for the sake of younger, less experienced men, *do something*. Give them something on which to base their conduct. They need guides based on your superior judgment.

In conclusion, permit me to say that the police problems generated by social unrest are chronic. Like an infection, there will be acute flare-ups from time to time, but the chances of imminent relief are remote. We must, therefore, intensify our efforts to meet the situation in a truly professional manner with justice for all.

3.5 POLICE, LAW AND ORDER, RACIAL TENSIONS*

The problems of maintaining order and the conflicts and tensions that often characterize relationships between police and citizens, particularly Negro citizens, are symptoms of underlying causes. Unless the problems of employment, education, training, housing, etc., can be resolved and reduced, the problems of law and order and police-community relations will persist.

* Reprinted, by permission, from *GUIDELINES: A Manual for Bi-Racial Committees* by George Schermer, published by the Anti-Defamation League of B'nai B'rith, New York City.

However, the hostility between Negro citizens and police is so deep-seated in some communities that, unless special measures are taken to promote understanding and cooperation, the attitudes will persist whether or not the underlying causes are removed. Also, even if the other cause factors cannot be affected in a short time, overt hostilities can be substantially reduced through appropriate measures.

There are several separate and distinct elements of tension-conflict, any of which may occur separately; or there may be combinations of two, three or more. The principal elements are:

1. White hostility and overt attacks upon Negroes. These usually occur when Negroes violate the status quo or normal pattern, e.g., when Negroes move into a formerly white neighborhood, when Negroes seek service in formerly "white only" facilities, when Negroes seek to vote or attend formerly "white" schools in communities where such forms of behavior are contrary to the established norm. White behavior is often overt, as a mob; or it may be covert as in hit and run vandalism, shooting, bombing or lynching.

2. Negro hostility and overt attacks upon whites. The Negro community has rarely acted as a mob in attacks upon whites. Attacks upon one or a few whites by roving gangs of Negro boys or young men are a common symptom of rising racial tensions which may reach riot proportions if some triggering incident occurs.

3. Police hostility, abuse and brutality toward Negroes countered by hostility, sullen unresponsiveness or open resistance toward police. If this pattern is prevalent, rioting against the police can be readily triggered by an incident. (Cause and effect become confused. It is rarely a simple case of initial misbehavior by either police or citizens producing an understandable or justifiable response. The usual pattern is a mounting series of incidents with rising feelings of injury, and a desire to get even.)

There has been a tendency among official human relations agencies and civic groups to launch specialized programs to treat one phase or another of the general problem; a police advisory or review board to investigate complaints of police brutality; a police human relations training program; a community tensions control program. Each of

139

these has some value, but the results are likely to be disappointing if there is not a comprehensive approach to deal with the total problem.

The first requirement for wholesome race relations is good local government. Where there is honest, capable, democratic, responsive government, there is likely to be an efficient, well-trained, fair police force, justice in the local courts, and general respect for the law and the forces of law and order. If the local government is weak or corrupt, the police will be weak and inefficient at best and may, themselves, be corrupt. In some cities the city administration and the police are well administered, but the lower judiciary is insensitive, inefficient or corrupt. This invariably leads to demoralization of the police.

In the absence of efficient and honest government and police administration, it will be extremely difficult to command the respect of those elements of the community that fall prey most readily to fear or demagoguery. A local human relations agency will be at severe disadvantage under such circumstances. This is not to say that any effort will fail. The agency must always do the best it can. This guide-book must necessarily assume that reasonably responsive and honest government prevails.

The municipal human relations agency should seek at all times to supply the forum through which fear, tension, misunderstanding, complaints and hostilities can be voiced, ventilated and resolved. It should also advise and assist the city administration and the police force with the objective of maintaining order, assuring due process of law, establishing justice, and promoting public confidence in and respect for the law.

The program must be comprehensive and continuous. It is never done. There is never a time when the danger of new misunderstandings and conflict is past. The program must reach all elements of the population; it must be dramatic enough to command attention and have depth enough to have meaning.

A community relations program to reduce tensions and to promote order and respect for the law will have many elements. Some of the most important might be:

1. *A Police-Community Relations Program.*

To a large extent the police department must develop and conduct the program for itself. However, the human relations

140

agency can supply the initiative and guidance. The police command should publicly announce its principal policies and orders, and interpret them to the community. The police commissioner and chief deputies should seek every opportunity to appear at meetings and before civic and religious gatherings, making sure to reach those groups that are farthest from the center of power and prestige.

Ministers, civic leaders, and any citizen or group of citizens with a concern or a complaint should be encouraged to come to the police headquarters or district station, be treated with courtesy, and have their complaints heard attentively.

A small group of police officers should be trained to appear in uniform at schools, recreation and civic centers, to speak to and show motion pictures to children concerning law and order, and to answer questions.

Groups of ministers and others can be encouraged to be present at police stations, and at magistrates' and police court hearings, particularly on weekends when many arrests for disorderly conduct occur.

2. *Police Recruitment and Training.*

The police should set up standards of recruitment and a system of examination and psychological screening to assure recruitment of well qualified and emotionally stable officers. Police training should be comprehensive, embracing all aspects of police work. Such training should *include* training in human relations, but it should be much broader than that. Teaching an otherwise poorly trained officer how to deal with human relations problems is not likely to do much good.

Since most young officers are much more influenced by senior police officers than by initial training, it is usually necessary to start the training program with the top command, and to include the entire force in an in-service training program.

3. *A Community Forum on Tensions.*

The human relations committee should establish a continuing forum for the airing of complaints, concerns and tensions. A special committee on community tensions, representative of the

141

law-enforcement agencies, business, civic, religious, labor and minority group leadership should be appointed to conduct formal hearings, consider the information and make recommendations.

The committee should establish a few basic and firm rules to assure orderly meetings and hearings. With that assurance it should conduct many hearings in public although it should reserve the right, also, to meet in executive session. If it establishes a reputation for orderly deliberations and scrupulous fairness, it can command respect and exercise tremendous influence for the correction of misunderstandings and practices which do not readily fall into the arena of the formal procedures of the courts.

4. *The Mass Media.*

It has been stated repeatedly . . . that communication is the essence of wholesome community relations . . . . Judicious candor with the press and other media will usually cultivate trust and respect. If candor is lacking the media and the public will sense that something is being hidden and suspicion will result. The mass media must be an ally, not an enemy.

5. *Incident Control.*

. . . Tensions and conflict generate in a vacuum; that is, in the absence of authority and official activity. In large and crowded cities, in particular, the potential for incidents of tension and conflict is extremely high. It is predictable that there will be many incidents in any one day, especially at the end of each school day and on Friday and Saturday nights. The police can and should be trained and instructed to handle such incidents with fairness and firmness. They are the first line of prevention and cure.

However, the very fact that the police represent authority and force prevents them from bringing the underlying feelings and hostilities into the open, so they can be ventilated and resolved. It is extremely important that the human relations agency provide for prompt, on the spot attention and communication. This can be done best with a small, well-trained field staff. A team of volunteers can provide the same service, but it is difficult to sustain such a service on a voluntary basis for any length of time.

142

3.6 POLICE-COMMUNITY RELATIONS POLICIES AND PRACTICES*†

Brief Summary of Findings

I.   Less than a third of the police departments studied have continuing, formalized community relations programs.

II.   Two-thirds of the departments studied now have, are adapting or are developing plans to cope with racial demonstrations and disturbances.

III.   In cities with more than 5% non-white population, 70% of the studied departments reported that they are experiencing difficulties in recruiting non-white officers.

IV.   While more than 60% of the reporting departments indicated that they offer some training in police-minority group relations, there is wide diversity in the type and quality of training involved.

V.   In only two regions did the responding departments report that they restrict the power of arrest of non-white officers — 10% of those in the South Atlantic and 14% of those in the West South Central. Assignment of officers either on a non-racial basis or to racially mixed teams is becoming increasingly general.

VI.   More than half of the departments studied are being charged by racial groups with police brutality and/or differential treatment. Nearly two out of ten reporting departments indicate such complaints are increasing; about the same number report them to be decreasing.

Implications of Findings For Mayors and Police Executives

The racial demonstrations and riots of recent years, exemplified both by the peaceful March on Washington in August, 1963 and by the violence in several Northeastern cities this past summer, have

---

* The International Association of Chiefs of Police and the United States Conference of Mayors have collaborated in this study which was designed to gather information on police policies, practices and problems with respect to community relations and racial demonstrations in U.S. cities of over 30,000 population. In addition, an attempt has been made to assess the needs of law enforcement agencies in this sensitive area and to determine what service could be rendered that would be most helpful both to Mayors and Chiefs of Police. It is anticipated that supplemental reports and studies will be issued at a later date based upon materials gathered in connection with this national survey.

† EDITORS' NOTE: With the exception of introductory material on study design and Tables 1 and 2, this report is reproduced in full.

143

dramatically portrayed the scope, depth, and volatility of the current racial crisis in the United States. At the same time, the handling of these demonstrations and riots has brought the actions of local police departments into the forefront of public interest and has raised fundamental questions as to the proper police role in quelling racial disturbances, in handling racial demonstrations, and in mitigating community racial tensions in general. In light of such understandable public concern, the results of this study should be both timely and useful in resolving some of the new policy questions now confronting many Mayors and police executives throughout the country.

Present Context

In analyzing the results of this survey, however, it is important to consider police-community relations activities within the broad context of present day circumstances. Public outcries to the contrary, it is unreasonable to expect that police policies are the sole or even the major source of most minority group grievances. Nor can it be assumed that improved police-community relations programs alone will solve all local racial problems.

In appraising the police role in handling racial problems, whether they be legitimate demonstrations or street violence, certain key principles stand out:

1. Every city administration needs to have a clearly defined strategy for the handling of racial demonstrations and a clear public policy on civil rights problems.

2. Police at all levels, from top to bottom, need to know in advance what the city's policy is and what is expected of them.

3. Cities need to redouble their efforts to assist their police departments in attracting competent personnel to man their metropolitan police forces.

4. All police officers must be well trained, especially at the command level.

5. Both city officials and police executives must take the initiative in establishing programs that will result in good communications between citizens of all backgrounds at the precinct as well as at the city-wide level.

144

Failure to discharge these important responsibilities exposes the police, acting as the visible agents of community authority, to the type of public criticism that has characterized many recent incidents.

Beyond this, it is the responsibility of the civic, political and economic leadership of the community, not the police, to provide answers to the other basic conditions which affect community relationships — equal employment opportunities, good education, decent housing and adequate health, welfare and social conditions for all persons to enjoy the rights, privileges and responsibilities of citizenship.

Within this context, then, the major implications which arise from this survey include the following:

I. *Programs to Build Communications*

Perhaps the most important finding of this survey bearing on the state of police-community relations is the fact that less than one-third of the responding departments have established formalized community relations programs. While this number is disappointingly small, it is encouraging to note that those cities that do have such programs have established them on a basis that is well organized and comprehensive, providing for police-citizen communication at both the precinct and city-wide levels. Clearly, the long-run impact of these programs has been beneficial and their development poses a major question as to why more of the departments have not felt it necessary to establish similar programs of their own. Detailed reports on some of these programs will be published by the United States Conference of Mayors.

In contrast to this small number of formal programs designed to strengthen communications and build mutual confidence, the survey revealed that some two-thirds of the departments have developed or are developing crowd control plans especially designed for racial demonstrations and disturbances. In many instances official Human Relations Commissions are now assisting in the planning process. In addition, it appears that these departments are beginning to communicate with non-government civic groups, such as the NAACP, CORE, National Conference of Christians and Jews and Chambers of Commerce. This degree of police-citizen communication is, of course, important to the effective handling of racial demonstrations and disturbances, but the question remains whether police-citizen exchange of information in just this limited area of the racial problem is sufficient.

II. Recruiting Good Police Officers

A second survey finding with important implications for police-community relations was that 70% of the reporting departments are having difficulty recruiting qualified officers, both white and non-white. This finding raises questions as to whether present recruiting techniques, including press announcements, speakers, employment services, and the like, are sufficient to draw out prospective qualified applicants. It also raises the question of whether the public image of the police is one that appeals to prospective recruits, especially minority group candidates, effectively enough to meet the competition from other professions in terms of salaries and opportunities for equal employment and advancement. In addition, because the majority of the departments attributed their recruiting difficulties to applicant failures, what can be said of the employment standards and testing methods themselves? Does the current basis of rejection necessarily mean that these men do not have the *potential* to be good officers, or does it suggest, perhaps, that the basis of some selection procedures may be in need of review? Could present procedures for acceptance to training conceivably be altered or adjusted without undermining the quality of the recruit, the training he needs, the effectiveness of law enforcement, or the maintenance of department *esprit de corps?* This is an area for review that would seem to be deserving of high priority in the case of most departments experiencing such difficulties.

III. What Kind of Training?

A third important finding bearing on the police role in race relations was that 62% of the reporting departments offer some sort of human relations training. This figure, while impressive, tells us little of the quality of the human relations training being given or of its bearing on actual law enforcement activities. What must be asked is whether this training, in general, is designed and implemented with sufficient expertise to aid the police officer in understanding the problems of community relations and his role in them or whether it is training largely of a superficial nature contributing only marginally, if at all, to impartial and effective law enforcement. The detailed findings are worthy of careful study by the Mayor or police executive who would like to improve their training efforts. Because of its importance, it is contemplated that a special separate report on this subject will be issued in the very near future.

IV. Contrasting Views on Complaints

A fourth finding revealing the large number and the kinds of complaints being voiced by both racial groups and police officers indicates and dramatizes the extent of the communications gap between the police and the public in many communities. Viewpoints as to the status of police-community relations are widely divergent and several responding departments indicated that the differences appear to be growing. These findings point up the urgent need for comprehensive police-community relations programs.

Only two of the responding departments process citizen complaints through citizen review boards. This indicates that an overwhelming majority of departments do not view such extra-departmental review procedures as a satisfactory means of providing an impartial handling of complaints. Clearly, however, this aspect of police-community relations remains a continuing question — and the means of securing public confidence in complaint review procedures remains to be found. The fact that a great many departments emphasized that "court review" or other "appeal procedures" were available indicates that departments are sensitive to the issues involved.

V. Assignment Practices

A fifth finding, indicative of current trends in administration, was that an extremely small percentage of departments in only two regions of the country reported that they restrict the power of arrest by non-white officers to non-white citizens. This would seem to imply that police departments have overwhelmingly decided that to restrict the power of arrest by non-white officers will undermine impartial and effective law enforcement, hinder recruitment, and, in general, weaken the foundations of good police-community relations.

In addition, an increasing number of departments appear to be following assignment practices designed to make maximum use of minority group officers. Assignment without regard to race, to all divisions, to all geographical areas of the city and to regular and special details are indicative of the current trend.

147

National Survey Findings
A. Planning

The results of the survey indicate that slightly more than half, 59%, of the departments in the primary study group have fundamental crowd control or riot plans. An additional 26% are in the process of developing plans or of adapting their basic crowd control plans to racial problems. Only four departments reported that they have a special planning division which, among other functions, makes plans for handling racial demonstrations. Three of these departments are in cities above 1 million population, one is in a city of between 500,000 and 1 million.

City departments other than police are involved in the planning process in 52% of the reporting departments. Communication with non-government civic groups in the planning process has been established by 38% of the primary study group departments. This 38% appears to have adapted basic crowd control tactics to account for the racial situation. When those which are now "in process" complete their planning programs, an additional 41 departments, or 26%, will have similar special plans, bringing the total which have special plans to 64%.

Table 3 presents information on the extent to which the police departments in the 165 primary study cities are planning in advance for handling and controlling racial disturbances and demonstrations.

Three types of plans have been distinguished.

1. *Basic Crowd Control Plan.* This designation refers to those department plans which are basic police crowd and riot control schemes, based on fundamental crowd control tactics; they generally are not race disturbance plans *per se.* They involve little communication and coordination with other city departments and leaders of minority groups and are adapted on an individual basis from disturbance to disturbance.

However, some departments whose plans fall within this designation have begun to recognize the fundamental differences between racial demonstrations and disturbances and others and have begun to adjust their crowd control schemes to account for these differences. That is, they follow the practice of consulting with other city departments and with non-government civic groups and of planning ahead for the handling of racial disturbances. Their standard plans have

148

been adapted to the special conditions that accompany racial disturbances in contrast to labor conflicts or unruly sports crowds.

2. *In Process.* This designation refers to those departments which have no race disturbance plans as yet but are establishing them.

3. *Special Planning Division.* This designation refers to those departments which have created a special unit with the function, among other things, of planning for the handling and controlling of racial demonstrations and the prevention of disturbances; the function of the division, through constant contact and coordination with minority groups and other city departments, is to keep the department informed in advance of all demonstrations and to be ready with alternative and specially designed methods for handling them. These specially designed methods are calculated to de-emphasize the racial implications of the disturbances and to account for the special difficulties inherent in racial demonstrations. These units are called Tactical Force, Riot Squad, Special Intelligence Unit, etc. and are often limited in their function to the physical tactics to be employed on the street in handling a violent disturbance. Some units, designated as Human Relations Units, have a broader planning function emphasizing primarily the prevention angle.

The very few departments in which a formal planning bureau or division exists have highly organized standard plans which are adapted to each new situation by the planning unit. This is but one function among many performed by such planning units. Only the departments having formal planning divisions are designated as such in the chart.

Table 3

No. Cities Reporting 165
Cities Having:
   Basic Crowd Control Plan............................ 97
   In Process 41
   Special Planning Division 4
Plans Involving Other City Depts.[1]...................... 86
Plans Involving Non-Govt. Groups[2]...................... 60

---

[1] The other city departments most often involved in the planning process were fire, public works, local Human Relations Commissions and the Mayor's office.

[2] The non-government groups most often involved were NAACP, CORE, church groups, NCCJ, and business groups. These departments appear to be modifying their standard riot plans to include provisions for handling racial problems.

B. Human Relations Training

Virtually every police executive responding to this survey agreed that there must be good training, including comprehensive curricula and competent instruction, if the police are to be prepared to cope with difficulties arising from racial tension. Such preparation cannot be undertaken after trouble starts; it must be made well in advance. Many of the responding departments attested to the fact that good training had made it easier for their men to handle the problems that arose.

Yet, while 143, or 86%, of the responding departments in the primary study group offer some training in human relations for their officers, a review of the kind of training being offered reveals a wide diversity in both scope and quality. In examining sample course outlines it appears that some of the courses are rather sketchy, leaving much to the individual imagination of each officer. Others seem very well conceived and some are highly specialized. (In at least one department specialization in training extends to giving foreign language training to those officers assigned to a section of the city in which much of the population speaks a foreign tongue.) Some departments consider training in riot control formations and tactics the major and sufficient component of a training program, while in other cases emphasis is also on human relations courses—psychology, minority group relations, civil rights and constitutional law. The topic which dominates police-human relations training is "public relations"—63% offer instruction in this area. The lack of consensus as to what constitutes adequate and proper training poses a real problem. Because of its importance, a special report dealing with training programs will be issued jointly by the International Association of Chiefs of Police and the United States Conference of Mayors.

Of the 143 departments offering human relations training, 78% employ outside instructors for their programs. Some departments utilize a cross-section of sources such as professors of psychology and sociology, state police and FBI instructors, businessmen, church officials and others. Some departments send their command officers to college-sponsored police-human relations programs, such as those at Michigan State University and others. A few departments have sent key men to other cities where riots have occurred in order to observe and learn so they could pass on their observations and contribute to their departments' planning.

150

Table 4 presents information on police department human relations training programs in the primary study group.

Table 4

No. Cities Reporting 165

No. Cities With Human Relations Training................. 143

Average Recruit Hours Per Department 11

Average In-Service Hours Per Department................. 9

Average Command Hours Per Department................. 15

No. Cities Using Outside Instructors [1].................... 111

---

[1] Of the 111 departments, most drew their instructors from the ranks of local government officials, including city attorneys, judges, and members of Human Relations Commissions, and from the FBI. Many, however, utilized a cross-section of sources, including sociology and psychology professors, college training courses and businessmen.

C. Recruiting

The results of the survey revealed that of the 165 departments in the primary study group, as many as 87% have a civil service or merit system of employment.

Yet despite these impartial selection systems, designed to guarantee equal employment opportunities, 71% of these departments are finding it difficult to attract non-whites into police work. Departments in some regions appear to be having more recruiting difficulties than departments in other regions, but in no region do less than 42% of the reporting departments experience recruiting problems. More than two-thirds of the departments attribute their difficulties to the inability of candidates to pass the written and oral exams and the background investigations, while more than one-third attribute the difficulties to a scarcity of applicants or to a combination of both.

The steps which have been taken to surmount these recruiting difficulties include press announcements, speakers at high schools and civic gatherings, the use of employment services, and radio-TV advertisements. At least 72% of the primary study group departments undertake one or more of these recruiting activities.

Table 5 contains information on department recruiting problems in the primary study group.

Table 5: *Police Recruiting*

No. Cities Reporting.................................... 165

No. Departments With Civil Service or Merit System........ 144

Departments With Recruiting Difficulties................... 117

Reasons for Recruiting Difficulties:

Too Few Applicants................................... 48

Applicants Fail Exam and Standards..................... 83

Departments Using Special Recruiting Methods:

Speakers 66

Press 117

Employment Service 58

Radio-TV-Posters 41

D. *Assignment Policies*

The responses of the departments in the primary study group indicated only slight variations in their assignment policies with regard to non-white officers. Of the 165 departments, only 4%, all in the South Atlantic and West South Central regions, reported that they restrict the power of arrest by non-white officers to non-white citizens. In addition, 22% reported that they assign non-white officers only to predominantly non-white sections of the cities. Only four of the departments reported that they never pair white and non-white officers, while nearly one-half reported that they make no distinction as a general rule. The remaining departments have mixed crew assignments only occasionally or under special circumstances.

In general these patterns appear to be indicative of current administrative policies, and only eighteen of the 165 departments are receiving complaints about them. Most of these complaints are from non-white citizens who request that more white officers be assigned to their districts.

152

Table 6 reports the number of departments in the primary study group which restrict the power of arrest by non-white officers, the number which assign non-white officers only to predominantly non-white sections of the cities, and the extent to which departments have mixed crew assignments.

Table 6: *Police Assignment Policies*

No. Cities Reporting...................................... 165
Departments Restricting Power of Arrest of Non-White Officers 6
Departments Which Assign Non-White Officers to Predominantly Non-White Sections of City...................... 34
Departments Which Pair White and Non-White Officers:
Special Details 40
Occasionally 54
Generally 74
Never 4
Cities Experiencing Difficulties With Their Assignment Policies[1] 18

---

[1] Mostly complaints by non-white citizens requesting white officers in their sections of the cities.

E. Police-Community Relations Programs

The survey revealed that 46, or less than one-third, of the responding primary study group departments have developed extensive police-community relations programs. Of these 46 departments, 37 have specialized community-relations divisions to administer the formal programs. While some departments assign as many as ten men to staff these units, the average number of men per each of the 37 units is three.

Active police-citizen committees exist in less than half of the 46 formal programs. Nineteen have such committees on the city-wide level, and eight on the precinct level.

One-third of the primary study group departments reported they have representation on the official community relations agencies in their local communities. Some of these departments consider this representation as a substitute for police-community relations programs of their own; others use such representation as a supplement to their own formal programs.

Table 7 presents information on police-community relations programs for the 165 primary study cities.

Table 7

No. Cities Reporting	165
No. Departments With Formal CR Programs	46
No. Departments With Specialized CR Units	37
Average No. Men Per Special Unit	3
Units Under Command of:	
Chief	30
Asst. Chief	5
Other	6
Depts. Having Police-Citizen Committees On Level of:	
Precinct	8
City-Wide	19
No. Departments Represented on Official Inter-Racial Councils	55

F. Complaints

This section of the study presents information on the state of police-community relations in the primary study cities as it is reflected in the extent of both citizen complaints against the police and of police against the public. There are marked contrasts in the two points of view. In many places, demonstrators and civil rights workers have been critical of police actions, while, on the other hand, the police have often been critical of the tactics employed by demonstrators. Frequently the actions which police consider necessary and proper for preserving public peace and order are the actions against which bitter complaints are raised. While a more complete analysis of this subject will be included in a subsequent separate report, a brief listing of the complaint findings follows:

Complaints Against the Police

The charges most frequently levied at the responding departments in the primary study group were brutality in the handling of demonstrators and/or differential treatment of non-white citizens. Slightly

154

more than half of the departments report they are being charged with either differential treatment or brutality or both. Police experience shows that these charges range from vague opinions to fully justified cases involving excessive and unjustified use of force.

Other charges against some primary study group departments include the "over policing" of minority group districts, the discriminatory assignment and use of non-white officers, and the improper policing and suppression of legitimate demonstrations. Charges of this kind, however, were more infrequent than those of brutality and differential treatment. Only four departments, for example, report they have been charged with the suppression of legitimate demonstrations.

Complaints by Police Officers

More than one-third of the departments in the primary study group reported that their officers are voicing complaints. The most frequently mentioned complaints were (1) the leniency of the courts in decisions concerning racial matters, (2) the general lack of community support for police authority, (3) the lack of respect for police officers in minority group districts, (4) inaccurate and unfair treatment of police actions by the press, and (5) the attachment by the public of racial connotations to every police action involving non-white citizens.

Complaint Review Procedures

In two of the 165 primary study group departments complaints are initiated and settled in extra-departmental citizen review boards. All other departments process complaints through internal departmental machinery, usually supported by appeal procedures to the courts. Less than one-third of the 165 departments use special procedures to handle racial complaints.

Table 8 contains information on complaints against police action arising from racial demonstrations and on the police department procedures for handling and processing those complaints. Information is also given on the number of departments in which police officers are voicing complaints about racial problems and about public reactions to police authority.

155

Table 8

No. Cities Reporting...................................... 165

Departments Being Charged With:
Brutality 48
Differential Treatment................................. 46
Suppression of Legitimate Demonstrations................. 4
Other[1] 7

Departments With Special Procedures for Handling Racial
Complaints 15

No. Depts. With the Following Complaint Procedures:
Department Referral................................... 163
Citizen Review Board[2]................................ 2

Cities Where Racial Complaints Are:
Increasing 27
Decreasing 22
Same 115

Cities Where Police Officers Are Voicing Complaints[3]......... 68

---

[1] The "other" charges consisted primarily of complaints against police tactics at demonstrations such as the use of dogs and cameras.

[2] The citizen review boards consisted of a cross-section of the community including ministers, minority group leaders, businessmen, city officials, etc.

[3] The complaints were generally:
A. Leniency of the courts in racial issues.
B. Lack of community support for police actions.
C. Lack of respect from minority groups.
D. Biased press reporting.
E. Attachment of racial connotations to every action involving non-whites.

G. *The Supplemental Study Group Cities*

The 145 responding cities with total populations less than 100,000 and non-white populations less than 5% were separated from the main body of statistical data because of a unique and common lack of racial tensions and problems. Most of the police departments in these cities have not yet found it necessary to plan for racial demonstrations and/or disturbances nor to establish community relations programs. More specifically, however, the responses of these departments indicated the following:

1.   Of the 145 reporting departments in the supplemental study group, 10% are establishing, or have established, riot control plans which include special provisions for handling racial problems.

2.   Slightly more than one-tenth of the supplemental study departments offer training in police-minority group relations. As in the primary study group departments, the topic which dominates these human relations training programs is "public relations."

3.   Nearly one-tenth of the supplemental study departments are experiencing difficulties in recruiting non-white officers. Most of these departments attributed their difficulties to a scarcity of applicants.

4.   None of the departments reported that they restrict the power of arrest by non-white officers.

5.   Only 6 of the reporting supplemental study departments have continuing, formalized community relations programs.

6.   Of the 145 reporting supplemental study departments, five are being charged by racial groups with police brutality and/or differential treatment. One department indicates that such complaints are increasing, and one department indicates they are decreasing.

7.   In one-tenth of the reporting supplemental study departments, officers themselves are voicing complaints of their treatment by racial and civil rights groups.

Table 9

Number of Cities Reporting	145
Departments Having Special Race Plan or In Process	15
Departments Offering Human Relations Training in:	
Police-Minority Group Relations	16
Public Relations	27
Departments With Recruiting Difficulties	20
Departments Restricting Power of Arrest of Non-White Officers	0
Departments With Formal Community Relations Programs	6

Departments Being Charged With:
Brutality 2
Differential Treatment 4
Departments Where Complaints Are:
Increasing 2
Decreasing 1
Departments Where Officers Are Voicing Complaints........ 12

3.61 Current Approaches—Police Training and Community Relations*

CURRENT APPROACHES

BACKGROUND

In our recent national survey Police Chiefs were invited to:

1. Describe any programs they have developed which have prevented or aided in the reduction of racial tension.

2. Describe any tactics or procedures they have found to be effective for handling racial disturbances.

3. Give examples of ways in which the officer's job has been made easier in their departments.

A large number of individual comments and suggestions were offered on these three points, and, in addition, many departments sent in manuals, training program outlines, lesson and lecture plans, and other documents pertaining to police activities in the area of community relations. Information from these sources has been summarized in this report.

There is one important factor which Mayors and Police Chiefs should keep in mind when considering the techniques and suggestions which follow: No careful scientific determination has been made of their actual effectiveness. In most cases the techniques and practices seem to have worked well, but the evaluation is largely a matter of opinion and intuition rather than objective measurement. Often the programs have been devised to fit individual situations and techniques have been employed on an *ad hoc* basis with limited resource

---

* Survey Supplement Jointly Conducted by: International Association of Police Chiefs and United States Conference of Mayors.

and manpower. Moreover, it should be noted that as there is a wide diversity of viewpoints and approaches by law enforcement officials, no easy answers to police problems can be presented and no attempt is made to deal with the various techniques and suggestions in a quantitative manner. They are reported here so that Mayors and police executives might know what others have tried.

I. Communication

The most frequently mentioned practice considered helpful by police in maintaining peace and order was the establishment of active communication with community leaders including local minority groups. Such communication has been established in a variety of ways:

1. *By the creation of official local Community Relations Commissions, Bi-Racial Committees, or Community Relations Bureaus, usually operating at a city-wide level.* In many communities the police departments are formally represented on these commissions. Yet, even in communities where the police do not have such formal representation, several chiefs noted that the very existence of these commissions has simplified the police role in racial conflict. For these commissions, speaking for the city government as a whole, in addition to providing a forum for discussion, deal with such broad community problems and sources of racial frustration as unfair employment practices, discrimination in housing and public accommodations, school desegregation, and the like. These commissions have varied titles: Bi-Racial Committee, Commission on Community Relations, Brotherhood Council, or Citizen's Advisory Committee. (See U.S. Conference of Mayors report: *Official Local Community Relations Commissions—A National Survey, 1964.*)

2. *By the creation of a formal police department community relations program, operating on either district or city-wide levels or both, with or without the active participation of other city-government departments.* Our survey revealed that 37 of the responding police agencies are now operating formal police-community relations programs of various types. Many of the programs, for example, do not seek to deal solely or even primarily with racial groups and racial problems. These programs are aimed at promoting better, closer, and more workable relations between the police and the entire community, including business, racial, religious, and ethnic groups, in the interest

159

of the welfare of the whole community. Naturally, smoothing of racial tensions is an important and welcome by-product of such programs. (See U.S. Conference of Mayors report: *Police-Community Relations in St. Louis,* Experience Report 103, Service Series.)

On the other hand, some of the programs are designed specifically to deal with race relations. Among their functions are the maintenance of contact with local racial leaders for the airing of mutual grievances and misunderstandings and the handling of peaceful, orderly demonstrations. Police executives who operate both types of programs say they have been instrumental in easing police-community tensions in general and racial conflict in particular.

3. *By participation in annual Police-Community Relations Institutes.* These institutes are frequently sponsored regionally by the National Conference of Christians and Jews, the Southern Police Institute, and various University Schools of Police Administration. The Institute at Michigan State University, for example, attracts police officers from the entire country. Such meetings provide a forum for the exchange of viewpoints and of police experience. The participants at these meetings often include, in addition to police officials, leaders of Negro groups, educators, city officials, church leaders, and other influential citizens.

4. *By establishing personal contact between the chief and/or other ranking officers and racial group leaders.* Such contact ordinarily is accomplished without an institutional framework such as a formal police-community relations program. Thus, in many police departments one officer may act as Community Liaison Officer to represent the department in meetings with other community leaders. These meetings, usually on an *ad hoc* basis as the situations require, have often been instrumental in preventing racial crises. In at least one instance, police initiative led to the voluntary desegregation of various facilities prior to the passage of the 1964 Civil Rights Act, thus warding off trouble. Other meetings have aired grievances and allowed for the planning of demonstrations in such a way as to minimize the police problems.

5. *By police participation in various community programs involving youth.* One large department sponsors Precinct Youth Councils, composed of local citizens organized on a neighborhood basis, working toward the betterment of the city's youth. In another case, a department sponsored a summer vacation job program on a non-segregated

160

basis. This provided a constructive outlet for the energies of the young people and promoted better relationships with police officers.

II. *Police Attitudes: Fair and Equal Treatment*

Most responding police chiefs stated that one of the most essential practices in handling racial demonstrations and disturbances was adhering strictly to a policy of equal treatment under the law for all people. The chiefs often noted that their training programs are designed to instill the spirit of impartiality in every officer. The respondents also listed several courses of action or approaches which they found helpful in implementing a policy of impartial and objective law enforcement at demonstrations . . . Those most often cited were the following:

1. *Most chiefs noted that peaceful demonstrations are a normal part of our democratic system and that demonstrators must be protected from violence by onlookers. At the same time it should be clear to demonstrators as well as onlookers that all illegal acts will be met with prompt and decisive police action.* Such a policy, it was noted, has rallied responsible local citizens in many communities to the support of the police in the interest of responsible and orderly conduct. This policy also tends to discourage demonstrators or onlookers who might otherwise be inclined to become disorderly.

2. *Another policy found helpful by several departments was to commit to a large demonstration only the minimum number of officers that adequate control would permit.* This was done in order to avoid the appearance of police harassment and of impending violence. In most cases these departments maintained larger concentrations of officers and riot squads several blocks from the scene of the demonstration, where they could be immediately mobilized if necessary.

In addition, in the face of riot situations themselves, it was noted by many chiefs that manpower limitations required them to draw a clearly defined *priority* for police actions. For example, in connection with one serious disorder, officers did not arrest looters under certain conditions. Taken at face value by much of the public, this appeared unconscionable. The fact of the matter was, however, the time and manpower needed to arrest and book these people would have left other more important and urgent aspects of the riot untended by the police. In other words, they had more serious problems demanding their immediate attention.

161

3. *If it should be necessary to make arrests during protest demonstrations, it was the general feeling that prompt, cool, decisive action is the most effective procedure.* The fact that demonstrators must sometimes be arrested is no source of satisfaction to police, according to the comments of the respondents. It is the prevailing opinion that the best policy for the police vis-a-vis demonstration arrests is to take action only when the cause is clear-cut and perhaps even aggravated.

4. *The respondents also noted that restraint should be an officer's first rule* in the face of name calling, spitting and other forms of ridicule and taunting. Several chiefs reported they had issued orders that their men were not to retaliate, even verbally, in absence of outright physical attack; they were to maintain their dignity and composure. Such restraint, it was believed, indicated to the public the absolute impersonal and impartial intention of doing the job strictly according to the law. Such dignified behavior generates public respect and support.

5. *Another policy followed by several chiefs, designed to demonstrate police impartiality and objectivity in law enforcement, was to have at demonstration scenes as observers representatives of various local minority and other interest groups.* One chief asks members of the Human Relations Commission to aid in controlling demonstrations. Another chief invites representatives of the press, the prosecutor's office, and the court to see for themselves the reality of police behavior. Also, in this instance, the prosecutor is available for on-the-spot legal advice. Some chiefs have found it helpful to invite leaders of minority action groups to address the departments' top command and participate in give-and-take discussions.

6. *Many respondents recommended the assignment of both white and Negro officers to police the demonstrations.* This gives the public another outward sign of the attempt to be impartial and objective.

7. *Other chiefs stated that it was helpful to their departments to follow up carefully and objectively all complaints and to take prompt disciplinary action when justified.* Some departments have established special Internal Affairs divisions to process such complaints.

III. Supervision and Command

Unity of command and proper supervision were frequently cited by the responding departments as required administrative factors in police handling of disturbances.

1. The responses indicated that *the desired procedure is to vest the ultimate decision-making power in one supervisory officer at the scene of the disturbance.* This supervisor is responsible for such actions as calling in the standby reserve squad or special tactical unit being held in readiness "around the corner." It is he who issues the orders to the crowd to disperse. He must also decide when, where, and to what extent police pressure against the crowd or mob is required. In one department "arrests are made only with the approval of a supervisor, preferably a lieutenant or higher. This . . . minimizes the possibility of false accusations of brutality and is a tempering influence for the line officers."

2. *Below the commander must be a precise and responsive chain of command.* In some of the more elaborate department plans, the hierarchy of command responsibility is spelled out in great detail and differs according to the magnitude of the disturbance. At any rate, most responses indicated that the duties and responsibilities of first- and second-line supervisors must be clearly defined and adequately rehearsed. To improve the functioning of the command structure, several chiefs noted the advisability of reducing the span of command for supervisors when engaged in highly charged emergency actions. Whereas a platoon of ten to twelve policemen may be adequately supervised under normal circumstances by a sergeant, he may be able to direct only four to six under riotous conditions.

3. *The departments also indicated that a smooth, sensitive communications system was necessary to support the chain of command.* Commanders must know what is developing from moment to moment and keep their forces advised. Many departments have found that Negro officers are very useful and often essential to an effective information gathering system. These officers can easily pick up rumors and rumblings of impending trouble among Negro demonstrators. Similarly, white officers in civilian clothes can perform well among white agitators. Several chiefs recommended using officers in civilian clothes as much as possible, especially during the early stages of a developing incident. Also many respondents cited the value of radio communications at observation points and police headquarters.

4. *Another element of supervision cited as indispensable at disturbances was support and backing of the community for the officers on the scene.* It is important to the operation of the chain of command and to the officers' morale that they be supported when acting

163

in accordance with established policies. *Relief of officers at disturbances is also an aspect of good supervision.* As one chief said, "Since duty at a tense demonstration is generally quite arduous and fatiguing, we attempt to provide frequent relief for all officers. By doing this a more objective and professional attitude can be maintained by the men while they are on the line." Especially when a line of officers is facing an excited crowd that is shoving and name calling, supervisors must keep careful watch over their men in order to replace them when they show signs of strain and stress. An intemperate act by a fatigued or highly aggravated officer can be the trigger that sets off actual violence.

5. *Finally, many responding departments noted the importance of assigning a number of officers commensurate with the size of the disturbance or demonstration.* The number of officers assigned will also be influenced by the nature of the crowd, the past history of police handling of such incidents in a given community, and the preparation and capability of the officers. Many chiefs have found it necessary to get assistance from nearby large departments and/or state police for handling emergencies. Cooperation among neighboring departments in training is a common practice. Cooperation in planning for mutual assistance is apparently growing.

IV. Press Relations and Publicity

Police are often distressed and angered by press coverage of their activities at riots and demonstrations. Authorities believe they are often unfairly criticized when they were doing the best job they could under trying conditions. Police often cite examples of distortions in text and misleading captions or photographs. Many feel that pictures showing police using night sticks, dogs, or tear gas are often placed out of context to make emotionally exciting stories which portray the police in an unfair manner. It is seldom possible to put into a picture the circumstances which made the use of the night stick necessary, and the only thing the public sees is the policeman "beating" someone. Police are disturbed because they usually have little choice but to use forceful tactics when facing civil disorder.

Police also have expressed concern for what they think is a tendency on the part of the press to exaggerate or overplay the importance of demonstrations. Reporting of statements made by militant leaders can convert a relatively harmless protest into a serious disorder. Also, the practice of the news media indicating that additional acts of violence are expected in the near future can incite certain individuals to show up looking for trouble.

In dealing with such problems in press relations, several chiefs noted they have worked directly with local press officials to reach some mutual understanding. Other chiefs indicated they have published press releases refuting false charges and describing police responsibility and intentions. An excellent example of one such release is contained in the Appendix. Often attempts to deal with the press may be fruitless, but usually through direct cooperation much greater objectivity in reporting can be achieved.

V. Special Considerations and Tactics

Police plans for controlling the public behavior of people must take into account the circumstances under which the behavior is produced, the nature of the behavior (i.e. whether it violates the law or for some other reason warrants police intervention), and police capacity for handling it. The plans must be flexible and include preparations for handling minor picketing up through major riots and civil commotion. It is beyond the scope of this report to attempt exhaustive analysis of such plans. The best we can do in this final section is to recount some of the observations and suggestions made relative to police performance in connection with the problems under consideration.

1. *Police officers regard the availability of manpower to be one of the critical problems.* It is obvious that in a serious riot situation officers may easily be outnumbered one hundred or more to one. In all cases, special training of men as well as adequate equipment for this kind of police duty is necessary.

Many departments have organized special riot squads. In one report the chief said, "We have available a squad of selected young men who have been trained in crowd control and are reasonably equipped with helmets, riot sticks, and tear gas and are supplemented with canines and fire-fighting equipment." Emphasis is placed on rapid mobilization and transportation of these special units. Men are chosen for their physical prowess and their psychological stability.

As was indicated previously, some departments try to get one or two competent officers to the scene fast so they can take immediate steps to prevent the situation from developing into a full-blown riot. This is the procedure followed in connection with racial demonstrations where violence might erupt. In one reply, the following appeared: "Our plan at present is to assign to any racial demonstration one or two three-wheel motorcycle units to do nothing except observe and keep headquarters informed of the situation. The participants on both sides are admonished against a breach of the peace and advised that arrests will be made for such action committed in the presence of officers."

The policy in another department is stated this way: "If the demonstration is in progress, the Watch Commander shall direct the District Sergeant to make an immediate and thorough reconnaissance of the scene and to report back as soon as pertinent facts are obtained. The report should contain the location and disposition of the demonstration, the sponsors, number of onlookers and such other facts as are readily available." In this particular department each district commander has an intelligence unit, a communications unit, a surveillance unit, and a uniformed tactical unit. The tactical units are mobile four-man squads under a sergeant or other officer. Some plans provide for special radio signals for emergency mobilization of variously-sized task forces. The code signal, ordered by the personnel on the scene, is sent out via police radio, and those involved proceed as rapidly as possible to their assigned mobilization points. Quite a few of the plans specifically noted the need for plainclothes personnel to circulate among the crowd, gathering intelligence.

* * *

2. *Special equipment is often required under extreme conditions.* We have already alluded to some of this. The items used by the responding departments range all the way from helicopters to hand cuffs. A number of reports made specific mention of public address systems, bull horns, walkie-talkies, helmets, long batons, gas masks, bullet-proof vests, wooden barriers, special busses and trucks, movie and still cameras, and so on. There are sources in the police literature where detailed discussion of equipment may be found.

3. *Much is heard about putting on a "show of force." A show of force can be effective, but in several reports the chiefs cautioned about overdoing it.* Large numbers of police cars converging on an area

with sirens and flashing lights in operation will attract the curious, and what was a relatively minor incident can easily wind up with a crowd of a thousand people milling about. A show of force does not necessarily mean large numbers of police. Nor does it mean only physical prowess or impressive equipment. A well-trained officer can put on a show of force all by himself through his calm but determined and sensible application of police power. An officer who "takes command" of the situation and "cools off" a potentially dangerous incident has put on the best kind of a show of force. At any rate, the effective deployment of available manpower is a matter requiring careful thought and should be appropriate to the situation.

CONCLUSIONS

When police action is aimed at the protection of the rights, life, limb, and property of all citizens and when police officers do their job impartially and competently, they should and usually do receive the full support of city officials and all citizens. Police officers are not expendable, and when they are assigned to tasks exposing them to injury or death they must be given the training, equipment and support that will enable them to handle the situation successfully. Citizens must understand and support this in the interest of an effective police service. All must realize that the general nature of the police job involves restraint and at times produces conflict. The people are paying officers to enforce the law. As they do their job, there will be complaints about what they do and how they do it. When they act properly and within the law, they must be supported. O. W. Wilson, Chicago's Superintendent of Police, has put it this way: "I will always support the police officer who, in the performance of his assigned tasks, exercises what he believes to be his legal authority in a reasonable manner. Such an officer need not fear complaints filed against him. He need not fear the threat of a lawsuit. *The department and the city will defend the officer against any legal action brought against him and, by statute, will assume liability for any damages which might be assessed.* The only difficulty which an officer can incur is if he intentionally exercises his authority improperly or resorts to procedures which he knows to be in violation of departmental regulations. Anyone can make an occasional error. This is human. But a well-intentioned and well-trained officer has nothing to fear."

3.7 THE CASE FOR CIVILIAN REVIEW
John A. Morsell, Ph.D.*

It may have been inevitable that the issue of a Civilian Review Board should get bogged down in a morass of emotion, but there is all the more reason on that account to press the case for it soberly and reasonably. The emotion has come largely from the instant reaction of policemen everywhere to what they regard as a dire threat, but some proponents have also unwittingly helped by envisioning millenia in police-community relations which no civilian review board can possibly produce.

That the issue has been most broadly discussed in a period of heightened racial unrest, evidenced by such events as the summer riots of 1964 and 1965, further complicates the matter. One consequence is that the question of whether to have a civilian review board has been made into a battleground, in which the final decision is to be interpreted as bitter defeat for one side and exultant victory for the other. In this kind of atmosphere, a decision either way could carry with it the seeds of failure.

Historically, the idea of civilian review did not emerge in a racial context. It arose, simply and inevitably, from the need for some agency whose evaluations of alleged improper conduct by police officers could be proclaimed and accepted as beyond the influence of group loyalty or self-interest. This need exists irrespective of the race or color of the alleged victims, although the preponderance of cases would be among the poor. (Most crime in which the individual policeman is pitted against the offender has always occurred in the crowded areas inhabited by the poor; the swindler, the stock fraud, the bank embezzler and the anti-trust law violator not only enjoy a special immunity from the epithet "criminal" but are usually arrested—if they do not make an appearance in counsel's custody—quietly and without disturbance.)

This is another way of saying that those elements of the population with whom the police are most frequently involved are also those least able to defend themselves against improper treatment through

---

* Assistant Executive Director, National Association for The Advancement of Colored People.

the established law-enforcement channels. The civilian review concept was developed in this context, and it has acquired its contemporary racial and ethnic connotations from the pressure of events.

Concerning the basic facts there can hardly be any dispute. Police brutality does occur, and the only question is how much of it there is, and where. Conversely, the police are often subject to harassment and are frequently assaulted or otherwise impeded in carrying out their assignments. Unnecessary force is sometimes used in making arrests, although the determination of what is and is not "unnecessary force" is often extremely difficult.

Neither can it be denied that, at present, large numbers (majorities in some instances) of Negroes have come to regard policemen as oppressors rather than as protectors. While this feeling is greatly intensified by the fact that most policemen are white, Negro policemen are by no means excepted. It must be taken for granted, furthermore, that, if only to the extent that they constitute a cross-section of the white community, some white policemen are racially prejudiced and will find themselves unable to surmount these feelings, especially under stress.

It is also a safe assumption that at least some of the accusations brought against policemen are groundless, and that the accused officers in some cases are blameless.

Finally, it is clear that no police force, operating under conditions short of a police state, can hope to function effectively for very long in a situation of crisis deriving from resentment or resistance on the part of massive proportions of the community in which it works.

Given these factors, no further case needs to be made for determined, speedy and intelligent measures to clear the air and to create or restore a climate in which the normal functions of the police can be properly performed. A civilian review panel is one such measure.

The assertion that criminal prosecution makes a civilian review board unnecessary is not realistic. In the first place, such prosecution is inevitably restricted to only the most serious offenses. In the second place, the prosecutor's office is, in the public mind and in actuality, part of the same law enforcement entity; it does not possess the image of objectivity which a review board would have.

169

Policemen are accustomed to argue that a civilian review board would weaken or supersede the authority of the departmental heads, who are responsible for the training and discipline of the police force. But the proposals currently under consideration would confine the review board to investigation and determination of the facts and to recommendations based thereon. Assessment and application of penalties would remain the function of the department itself.

Policemen also contend that knowledge of the existence of a review board would inhibit the individual officer in doing his job; that he would be reluctant to use his best judgment or would fail to take necessary action lest it be misinterpreted by the review board. This contention does not hold water. The policeman is already, we are assured, deterred from wrongdoing by the fear of interdepartmental punishment. If he distrusts the review board, therefore, it must be because he anticipates that it will judge him by a different (i.e., unfair) standard. But there is no reason why this has to be so, and, in the meantime, the more policemen use this argument the more firmly their critics are convinced that what is feared is an end to the department's "taking care of its own."

Just as we take for granted that an employer (or a union) is likely to do a better job of observing fair employment rules if there is an outside agency to weigh the evidence when discrimination is charged; just as no one suggests that adulteration of food is best prevented by giving the food processor the responsibility for checking on his product and penalizing himself if something is wrong; so, a finding on a charge of police brutality will inevitably carry greater weight if it does not issue from the police fraternity itself.

It is of the utmost importance to expand the focus of attention beyond the review board's function of finding policemen guilty of misconduct. It would have an equally vital function in *exonerating* policemen when the evidence established that a complaint was not justified. Indeed, one of the anomalies of the whole debate is the failure of the police to recognize that a civilian review board would hold substantial benefits for the police themselves. A properly functioning civilian review board would be a source of security to the officer doing his job conscientiously and effectively. The knowledge that baseless charges against him would be exposed as such, upon review by a panel whose good faith was accepted by the public, would be a positive aid to police morale.

170

It is equally obvious, it seems to me, that the establishment of a civilian review system and the installation of a review panel would not, *ipso facto,* bring about all these desirable results. Time would be needed for the panel to establish its competence and its fairness, and to develop the tools and procedures best calculated to promote both. It is unfortunate that we have had to concentrate almost entirely on the question of "Whether or not," and have thus far been able to devote little or no attention to the "How best," in the case for civilian review. Let us hope that the first question will soon get an affirmative answer, so that the next step will no longer be delayed.

PART IV

LAWS AGAINST DISCRIMINATION, FEDERAL, STATE, AND LOCAL; ENFORCEMENT PROBLEMS

4.1 THE CIVIL RIGHTS ACT OF 1964

HAROLD H. GREENE*

The Civil Rights Act of 1964 represents our third opportunity to make some progress in solving the racial problem that has been with this nation since it was first founded.

The first of these opportunities came, of course, when we became a nation, but that opportunity was not grasped.

The Declaration of Independence was silent on the subject of slavery. On the other hand, the Constitution accorded it recognition. It is true that there was a movement for abolition even before the United States was formed, but it achieved no great momentum until considerably later in the history of the United States.

These built-in conflicts between a legal system which recognized slavery and the aspirations of many of the people led to the Civil War.

After the Civil War there was a second opportunity to do something about the racial problem. Again there was a great initial effort to solve the problem. The Thirteenth Amendment abolished slavery, the Fourteenth Amendment gave rights of citizenship to the former slaves, and the Fifteenth Amendment provided the right to vote.

---

* Chief, Appeals and Research Section, Civil Rights Division, U.S. Dept. of Justice.

172

A great body of enforcement legislation was enacted, but the difficulty was that after a fairly short time the consensus was against giving to the freed slaves what these constitutional amendments and this legislation promised.

The result was that the laws were either not enforced, repealed, or were declared unconstitutional by the courts. Twenty-five to thirty years following the end of the Civil War, only two statutes remained on the books. These were criminal statutes.

One punished conspirators who deprived citizens of their rights (the so-called Ku Klux Klan Act), and the second (Section 242 of Title 18, which has been most used prior to the present legislation) punished deprivation of rights of citizens by official action.

These two statutes were largely ineffective, essentially because there was no great will to enforce them. The courts read very stringent requirements into these statutes. The kind of proof that was required of the government was almost overwhelming. Under these post-Civil War statutes the intent had to be proved more convincingly than any comparable type of intent under any other criminal statutes.

It is almost impossible to prove, for example, that a sheriff intends to deprive a prisoner of his specific constitutional rights when he beats the man up. Thus by their interpretation of these laws the courts themselves rendered them ineffective.

Finally, the great difficulty which has deluged all criminal laws in this area is that they require a jury trial for enforcement.

It is certainly no secret that when you operate in the civil rights area in a state or a county which is unsympathetic to the cause of civil rights, and the achievement of equal opportunity for Negroes, it is very difficult to get a jury to convict someone who is guilty of depriving a Negro or some other minority group member of those rights.

In fact, it is difficult even to get an indictment. Before you can get a conviction or a trial, you must have an indictment from a grand jury. Of course, the members of a grand jury have to be drawn strictly from the district in which the crime was committed.

This is true for both state and federal offenses. As a practical matter, the criminal statutes have not been terribly effective even in recent years. In the five-year period from 1958 to 1963, when there was considerably more will and effort to enforce these laws, there were 116 prosecutions and only 16 convictions. This is a much lower ratio than you would find in any other kind of criminal law enforcement.

Therefore, the task was to find an alternative to enforcement and to the protection of the civil rights of citizens through the criminal laws. The prerequisite was a change in climate.

Congress does not suddenly develop a feeling for civil rights. It has been and will continue to be difficult to enact legislation in both this and other fields. You need a change in climate, and I suggest that that change in climate was brought about largely by the courts, particularly starting in 1917 with the Supreme Court decision outlawing restrictive residence ordinances. This was followed by the restrictive covenant cases, the white primary cases oulawing discrimination in voting, the cases involving segregation in institutions of higher learning, and finally in 1954 the *Brown* case [*Brown* v. *Board of Education,* 347 U.S. 483 (1954), 349 U.S. 294 (1955)] outlawing segregation in public education.

All these cases, in addition to laying down rules of law, had a great educational value. So did the action that was taken by the executive branch — the wartime FEPC, the establishment for the first time under President Roosevelt of a civil rights section in the Department of Justice, charged with the specific duty of looking after, enforcing, and helping to achieve civil rights for citizens, and various executive orders in regard to federal employment in government contracts.

These steps finally led in 1957 to the first new civil rights statute. In addition to creating a Civil Rights Division in the Justice Department and a Civil Rights Commission, the statute had one main substantive aim, to protect the right to vote by the means of civil instead of criminal remedies and by means of injunctions issued by the federal courts.

Injunctions have two basic advantages, depending, of course, on the point of view of the enforcing or the receiving end. At least from the point of view of enforcement, the advantage of an injunction is that the burden of proof on the government is much less than in the criminal case. Secondly, if an injunction is disobeyed, a criminal trial with a jury is not required. Instead there is a contempt proceeding which is conducted solely by the court.

An injunction is tailor-made for this type of situation. The 1957 Civil Rights Act does offer the remedy of injunctions in cases of intimidation or deprivation of the right to vote by either public officials or private persons.

This remedy was further perfected by the Civil Rights Act of 1960, which permitted the appointment of voting referees when there was a pattern or practice of discrimination in registration or voting.

These laws work quite well. Some 65 to 67 cases have been brought in as many counties in a number of southern states. A number are still pending, but those that were concluded by and large have been successful.

Injunctions were issued and a substantial number of Negroes in some areas were added to the voting rolls. Macon County in Alabama is one prize example. In 1960 there was hardly a Negro registered to vote. Now about 50 per cent of those eligible are registered, and several Negroes actually were elected to local office in this last election.

So, with the right kind of determination and will, something can be done under these statutes. But then we are dealing with a limited field (voting) and the 1957 and 1960 laws also contain some defects and weaknesses. The 1964 statute is designed, first of all, to perfect, implement, and make more workable the earlier laws.* It also deals, of course, with a vast array of other civil rights which previously had received no real protection from the federal government.

On the subject of voting, Title I of the new act deals with specific abuses and difficulties we have encountered in enforcing the older statutes, particularly the use of the double standard.

In most of the southern states the literacy test was devised and used to disenfranchise Negro citizens. A Negro college graduate would be rejected on the ground of illiteracy, although white persons who had barely completed the fourth grade and could not sign their names were registered by the hundreds of thousands.

The Act of 1964 specifically outlaws the use of double standards of that kind. It also prohibits the use of immaterial errors for rejecting an applicant. For example, there are some parishes in Louisiana where the administration of the literacy test is part of the application form, as well as a question asking for the race of the applicant. In

---

* A summary of the Civil Rights Act of 1964 appears as Appendix D herein.

some parishes if a Negro writes "brown," he is rejected because "Negro" is the proper answer, while in other parishes the answer "Negro" is rejected because "black" is the proper answer. This is a flagrant example of the type of thing that is and has been going on in many places. Under the 1964 legislation immaterial errors of this kind may not be used to deprive someone of his right to vote.

There are other voting provisions, such as the sixth grade standard. Anyone who has completed the sixth grade is presumed to be literate, but the state has an opportunity to prove, if it can, that such a person is illiterate. Initially, however, anyone who has completed the sixth grade in any accredited school is presumed to be sufficiently literate to be allowed to vote.

The second and perhaps the most controversial of all the titles of the 1964 legislation deals with public accommodations.

Title II arose largely out of the demonstrations and demands in the summer of 1963 for humane treatment in places which were otherwise open to Negro trade but would not sell Negroes a cup of coffee. The protest demonstrations were concerned largely with department stores, dime stores, and similar establishments.

Title II declares it to be a federal right for anyone to remain free from discrimination in certain specified places of public accommodations, hotels and places of entertainment.

This statute, like the voting law, is enforced basically by injunction. It can be enforced either by the victim himself or by the Attorney General acting on behalf of the United States.

If the victim of discrimination wishes to bring a lawsuit in federal court, generally he must first exhaust any state remedy that may be available.

Where there is a state or local law against discrimination, usually the victim may not sue immediately in federal court. Where there is no state or local law, the court has the option, if such suit is brought, to refer the matter to the Community Relations Service which was established by the 1964 Act.

When the Attorney General sues, he is not required to go into the state procedure first. Nor is he required to communicate and to deal with the Community Relations Service before bringing the lawsuit. As a matter of policy, however, the Department of Justice has taken the position that where there is any kind of effective state body that will deal with this kind of discrimination, the Department will not bring any lawsuit of its own, even though the law does not require such disclaimer. The Department has no interest in bringing lawsuits for the sake of compiling litigation statistics. Where there is a state law and some effort to enforce it, the Department will not bring any lawsuit on its own.

Two cases are pending before the Supreme Court, one from Atlanta and the other from Birmingham, concerning the constitutional basis of the public accommodations title.*

We who worked on the bill, drafting it and writing some of the background briefs to defend it, never had any doubt about the constitutionality of this legislation.

It is squarely based on many laws that the Congress has passed in the exercise of its commerce powers, such as the labor laws, Agricultural Adjustment Act, and the Pure Food and Drug Act. This is on essentially the same kind of constitutional basis, that is, where there is some artificial impediment, some artificial restriction on the free flow of goods in interstate commerce, the Congress can pass legislation to remove those restrictions. In regard to the Civil Rights Act of 1964, there was ample testimony before the Congress from Franklin D. Roosevelt, Jr., the Under Secretary of Commerce, and others to show that discrimination was a real impediment to the free flow of goods, not only from the point of view of the Negro traveler who cannot travel as easily and probably will not travel as much because he cannot find motel or restaurant accommodations on his trip, but also from the point of view of industries not locating in areas where there is discrimination, conventions not being held in New Orleans or in Mississippi because large companies feel that they should not subject their Negro employees to this kind of discrimination.

All of this was taken into account and is the basic, fundamental support for this title. This is what we argued in the Supreme Court.

Titles III and IV give the Attorney General power to bring injunctive suits to realize the Supreme Court decisions regarding public schools and public facilities.

---

* Title II of the Civil Rights Act of 1964 was upheld in *Heart of Atlanta Motel* v. *U.S.*, 379 U.S. 241 (1964), and *Katzenbach* v. *McClung*, 379 U.S. 294 (1964). These cases are discussed on pp. 180-181.

177

Public schools, of course, may not segregate their students. Public facilities, court rooms, libraries, and so on may not segregate. This, unfortunately, is more true in theory than in practice. Over 90 per cent of the Negro children in eleven southern states are still going to segregated schools, and it was felt that the private lawsuit approach was too slow, too burdensome, and too expensive to make a real dent in this situation.

Therefore, the Department of Justice was given the authority, subject to some limitation, to bring lawsuits in these areas on its own. The educational title does prohibit use of this particular statute to overcome racial imbalance or to require school busing. The Department of Justice cannot sue to overcome racial imbalance under this title, nor can the Commissioner of Education grant financial assistance to overcome racial imbalance. This does not outlaw state or local efforts to overcome racial imbalance, by any means.

This matter simply is not dealt with at all.

Whether this may ultimately be done or not is a matter which has not been finally decided, certainly not by the Supreme Court. The point is that the Civil Rights Act does not preclude a city or state from taking measures to overcome racial imbalance in the public schools.*

The employment title, Title VII, is a very important addition to the law. It does not take effect until July of 1965. It will be administered basically by a commission without enforcement powers except for the power to conciliate.

The commission does have the power to subpoena witnesses and records, however, and the Attorney General again has been given the authority to bring lawsuits in the case of private persons.

Potentially, the great significance of the employment title is that it is one of the few federal laws in this field that have been aimed at a practice which exists in both the South and the North.

The economic consequences of the employment title provisions are great. It has been estimated that the use of full employment of Negro manpower without discrimination would add thirteen billion dollars to the gross national product annually and about 50 per cent to the average income of Negro families.

---

* See, e.g., *Balaban* v. *Rubin,* 14 N.Y. 2d 193, 199 N.E. 2d 375, cert. den., 379 U.S. 881 (1965).

178

Title VI deals with the fact that federal financial assistance no longer may be used for discriminatory programs. Title X sets up a Community Relations Service which is most important and which, insofar as federal assistance is concerned, is the first line of any possible federal action.

It is the definite policy of the federal government to permit conciliation, persuasion, and voluntary efforts to work their way first before litigation and compulsion are used by the court.

On the other hand, if conciliation and persuasion do not work, we are fully prepared to bring the kind of lawsuit and to effect the kind of enforcement that is necessary. The Act of 1964 really is a charter that Congress has given us to make another start toward solving the problem that has plagued this nation all this time, that is, to integrate properly into the economic, social, and political life of this nation the 10 per cent group of Negroes who have been excluded from all of these areas solely because of discrimination.

How successful this third effort will be in relation to the others no one can foretell. We have been surprised and delighted with the ready acceptance that the public accommodations title has found throughout the country.

Voting and educational difficulties seem to be greater.* No one knows yet what the acceptance will be in regard to employment, but I think with the change in climate, with the consensus that exists today as distinguished from the consensus that existed in this country in the eighteenth century and again after the close of the Civil War, it is realistic to expect that this time our efforts will succeed.

I believe that the Civil Rights Act of 1964 will have an enormous impact, though not entirely because of the specific enforcement provisions that it contains. Everyone knows that you cannot change widespread practices simply on the basis of one lawsuit after another, just as you cannot collect income taxes if you have to sue every taxpayer.

Success depends to some degree on public acceptance and the fact that the Congress by an overwhelming majority did pass legislation which truly reflects public opinion. All three branches of the

---

* The Voting Rights Act of 1965 almost eliminates state and local discrimination against Negroes in the field of voting rights. Of course, the question of how the Negro will benefit from his ballot power remains to be seen. See Summary of the Act, pp. 352-358 herein. The key portions of the Act have been held constitutional by the Supreme Court. *State of South Carolina* v. *Katzenbach,* 86 S. Ct. 803 (1966).

federal government, as well as the press and educators, are behind it. These factors tend to encourage much needed public acceptance and support.

[EDITORS' NOTE]

Shortly after the PLI Forum the United States Supreme Court upheld the constitutionality of Title II of the Civil Rights Act of 1964 in two landmark decisions.

In *Heart of Atlanta Motel, Inc.* v. *United States* [379 U.S. 241] the Supreme Court upheld the public accommodations title of the Civil Rights Act as applied to inns, hotels, and motels. In order to be covered, an establishment must either affect commerce or discriminate because local law requires it to do so. The Heart of Atlanta Motel serves transient guests, is easily accessible to interstate highways, and advertises on national media. About 75 per cent of its registered guests come from out of the state.

The Court found the Act a valid exercise of the power to regulate commerce. The unavailability of hotel accommodations restricts a Negro's freedom to travel, often forcing him to go great distances for lodging. Transportation and the travel of persons among the states are traditional concerns of interstate commerce. Local businesses, each acting independently, though in the same way, may together obstruct commerce. The power of Congress to remove obstructions to interstate commerce includes the power to eradicate moral and social evils incident to commerce. The Court cited other instances of the exercise of this power, such as regulation of interstate gambling, deceptive practices in the sale of products, wages and hours, and fraudulent security transactions.

The Court also upheld the constitutionality of the public accommodations section as applied to restaurants in *Katzenbach* v. *McClung*, [379 U.S. 294]. Ollie's Barbecue in Birmingham, Alabama, is eleven blocks from an interstate highway and was not shown to serve or offer to serve interstate travelers. The restaurant argued that its operation therefore affected interstate commerce very slightly. The Court found, however, that Congress was justified in taking into account the total impact on interstate commerce of all restaurants like Ollie's Barbecue. Negroes spend less in areas where discrimination is widely practiced, thus reducing the flow of merchandise, causing unrest, and depressing business conditions. Lack of adequate restaurant facilities also discourages interstate travel by Negro citizens. Racial segregation's total dislocation of commerce thus provides a basis for the regulation.

Forty-six per cent of the food served at Ollie's Barbecue is meat from out of state. The restaurant argued that this fact does not affect commerce. But such presumptions have justified regulation designed to eliminate many other evils, such as the payment of substandard wages to employees producing goods for commerce. The Act applies only to establishments serving interstate travelers or serving food which has moved in commerce. The Court held this a reasonable basis for regulation.

4.11   FEDERAL PROGRAMS AND CIVIL RIGHTS
WILLIAM L. TAYLOR*

The most disturbing problem in the area of federal government policies and civil rights centers around the involvement of the federal government in grant-in-aid programs. Throughout the years, it has operated these programs, as a silent partner in discrimination.

This subject was touched upon by the Civil Rights Act of 1964. There has resulted an official policy which prohibits such federal subsidization of discrimination.

We are aware of the increasing importance of grants-in-aid from the federal government, that is, aid from the federal government to states and localities as a way of meeting public needs.

In statistical terms, in the fiscal year 1963 the government appropriated some eleven billion dollars for these purposes, and for the fiscal year 1965 the sum that is estimated will be about fifteen billion dollars.

These funds are very important sources of state revenues. In 1964, for example, federal grants-in-aid constituted about 15 per cent of all state and local revenues. In some states, particularly, but not only, in the South, one dollar out of every four or five that a state received for revenue purposes came from the federal government.

---

* General Counsel, United States Commission on Civil Rights.

In general, grants-in-aid may be viewed as a rather positive example of cooperation between the federal government and state and local governments. The federal government provides the means for meeting the very important needs of these other governments and, of course, they are protected by the rules and regulations which act as a safeguard against undue federal control. But this policy of non-interference by the federal government in connection with the administration of grants-in-aid has been misused for years to permit so-called neutrality with respect to the racial practices of states, communities, and institutions which receive such assistance.

The result of this policy of so-called neutrality on the part of the federal government has been to perpetuate inequality in education, to build all-white suburban neighborhoods, to provide employment opportunities for whites only, and in general to subsidize the discriminatory practices of state and local governments and institutions.

This has been a subject of particular interest to our Commission under its mandate to appraise the laws and policies of the federal government with respect to equal protection. For example, libraries which receive federal aid in some parts of the country have not allowed Negroes to use their facilities and have subjected them to segregation once they are allowed to use the facilities.

Elementary and secondary schools which are built with federal funds in impacted areas are discriminating and not giving equal treatment to their students. Hospitals which have been constructed with federal funds either have refused to admit patients because of their race or have discriminated against them in placement once they have been admitted. They have also refused to allow Negro physicians to practice in such hospitals.

Vocational training which has been established with federal funds has not been available to all students. Employment offices which are financed entirely by the federal government have refused to refer all job applicants to available openings on a nondiscriminatory basis.

In the field of agriculture, the Agricultural Extension Service operates offices with federal funds. They have been established on a segregated basis and often they provide unequal services to Negroes.

Again, employers who received business loans from the federal government which are designed specifically to increase employment opportunities have discriminated in their hiring practices.

In recent years the executive branch of the federal government has begun to abandon this false neutrality and to adopt a new policy under which President Johnson said recently that "all members of the public should be equally eligible for federal benefits which are financed by the public." As a California judge once put it, when someone dips his hands into the federal treasury, "a little democracy should cling to whatever is withdrawn."

Now, in some areas this policy has been well established for a number of years, for example, in federal contract employment, an area where executive orders have been issued starting with the wartime FEPC and after that by President Truman, President Eisenhower, and President Kennedy.

Starting about 1960 or 1961, there was increasing activity in this area. President Kennedy did a good deal more than most, and the most dramatic action taken was his housing executive order that said that federal assistance should go only to those members of the housing industry whose homes were made available to all persons without regard to race. There have been various other policies dealing with such matters as state construction employment for the building of highways and hospitals where such employment was assisted by the federal government and which have operated since 1930 under the so-called merit standards. These standards have now been amended to require no discrimination on grounds of race. Previously they required only that there be no discrimination on grounds of religious or political opinion.

In issuing such orders and regulations President Kennedy acted in part on his authority to establish reasonable conditions in government contracts, in part upon the implied and sometimes expressed intent of Congress that facilities provided for with federal funds would be available to all persons, and in part upon his constitutional duty to see that the laws are faithfully executed.

The President was supported in these actions by a growing body of judicial law which recognizes the increasing involvement of the federal government in the activities and operations of major private institutions and public agencies.

As these relationships have developed and become more complex, the judiciary has had to subject them to constant reexamination in trying to interpret and make meaningful the "state action" concept of the Fourteenth Amendment.

This has been necessary to assure that acts of discrimination, which the government is prohibited from engaging in directly, shall not be accomplished indirectly through private institutions. So the test now is whether to some significant extent the state has become involved in private conduct which abridges an individual's rights.

There have been a number of judicial decisions on this point. Perhaps the most recent is the decision by the Court of Appeals in the Fourth Circuit which prohibits discrimination by private hospitals which receive federal assistance under the Hill-Burton Law [*Simkins* v. *Moses Cone Hospital,* 323 F. 2d 959 (1963)].

With the passage of the Civil Rights Act of 1964, all branches of the federal government will have participated in formulating that national policy. Congress has declared that no person shall be denied the benefit of any program of federally-aided financial assistance because of his race, and it has established an orderly procedure for assuring compliance with these provisions.

The regulations covering seven agencies were recently approved by the President. These agencies are the Departments of the Interior, Agriculture, Labor, and Health, Education and Welfare, the General Services Administration, the Housing, Home and Finance Agency, and the National Science Foundation.

The regulations for other agencies are now being drafted and probably will be issued within a short time. When these are all completed, they will apply to a list of about 190 federal programs, and they will cover, without going into too much detail, major programs of education (the building of college facilities, college dormitories, research grants and equipment) and various kinds of aids to communities in the form of accelerated public works projects and urban renewal projects.

They will cover various kinds of aid to health, such as Hill-Burton hospital grants and vocational rehabilitation grants. They will cover aid to employees under employment security programs, training and recruitment programs, such as the Manpower Development Training Act, and various kinds of aid to agriculture.

In short, citizens in every walk of life will benefit from these programs and in one way or another will receive service as a result.

What do these regulations provide? They say that no person shall be denied or be excluded from participation in the benefits of or be subjected to discrimination on the grounds of race, color, religion, or national origin under any program or activity receiving federally-aided financial assistance.

The regulations spell out the types of discrimination problems. For example, a recipient of federally-aided financial assistance violates Title VI if because of race, color, religion, or national origin he denies an individual any service, financial aid, or other financial benefit under a federal program or activity.

The new law and regulations prohibit a federally-aided state employment service from refusing to place a qualified job applicant or a National Guard unit from rejecting a volunteer on the ground of race.

The law will be violated if an agency receiving federally-aided financial assistance offers aid or other benefits which differ or are provided differently from aid provided to others in the program. In other words, if an agricultural extension agent encourages and teaches the white farmer but not the Negro farmer to grow a variety of crops which will increase his potential income, this will be a violation of the law.

It will also be a violation if a recipient subjects an individual to segregation or separate treatment in any manner related to his receipt of such service or financial or other benefits. Again, if a federally-aided state employment service or an Agricultural Extension Office maintains racially separate facilities, or if it assigns employees of a particular race or color to serve only those of the same race or color, this will violate the law.

It will be a violation if a recipient restricts an individual in any way from the enjoyment of services or facilities or any other advantage or benefit provided by the recipient to others under the program. For example, if a college were to admit students of all races but then go on to discourage their participation in particular events such as sports events, this would be violation of the law.

It will be a violation of the law for a recipient to treat an individual differently in determining whether he satisfies any admission, eligibility, membership, or other requirement which is a prerequisite to the service that is involved. This means that if a federally-assisted

185

hospital refuses to permit a doctor to practice in that hospital because he is not a member of the local medical association which does discriminate, this again will involve a violation of the law.

The act or regulations will prohibit a recipient from using the kinds or methods of administration that would defeat the objectives of the act by subjecting an individual to discrimination. For example, a vocational education program which seemingly is not discriminatory but which counsels Negro students out of the program because there are not employment opportunities for them will violate the act.

It will be a violation of these regulations for a recipient to discriminate against an individual in any program or activity which is conducted in a facility constructed in whole or in part with federal funds. For example, it will be a violation if federal funds are used in the construction or improvement of a hospital and the hospital segregates patients because of race.

And finally it will be a violation of the law for a recipient to subject an individual to discriminatory employment practices under any program or activity which has as its primary objective the providing of employment. For example, if an employer receives small business loans or an area redevelopment loan, he must hire on a nondiscriminatory basis.

These examples do not represent the full scope of the law by any means, but I think it is fair to say that whatever the federal aid program involves and whatever form the discrimination may take, the purpose of Title VI is to assure to every individual equal opportunity and equal access to federal funds.

This law will apply prospectively; it will not apply to commitments or contracts that were signed before the effective date of the regulations. However, in the case of a continuing contract where payments are still being made, such as an annual contributions contract for public housing, the recipient may well be required to adjust his racially discriminatory practices.

During the course of the debate on this provision of the law, there was a great deal of discussion and controversy over what was meant. I think there were some misrepresentations stemming from a dispute over the applicability of this statute. It is directed only toward recipients of federal aid who are conducting programs or activities for the benefit of other people. The term "recipient" will not include

186

an ultimate beneficiary of the federal program, such as the person who receives unemployment insurance or social security. He, himself, is not prohibited from doing anything. Secondly, it does not cover direct federal programs formulated by the federal government. These already come under the federal nondiscrimination law.

The law does not cover the employment practices of a recipient unless the primary objective of the program is to create employment. It is well to understand that a great deal of the federal policy already has been directed toward employment, so where these federal aid assistance programs involve employment, existing executive orders that have been issued will remain in effect and may well apply.

The law also does not cover and, in fact, specifically exempts federally-insured bank loans or contracts, for example, an ordinary FHA contract on private housing. But with certain exceptions, such as transactions by individual home owners, federally-assisted private housing already is covered by the executive order issued by President Kennedy. This order, too, will remain in effect, as it covers federally-assisted private housing.

Procedures for compliance under this law contain very careful safeguards to protect all the parties concerned. The first step is the issuance of regulations which are now partially completed. Second, the complete regulations will require that all contracts under the law contain a specific assurance that the recipient will afford equal opportunity in his program. In many cases, even before that, there will be discussions and negotiations between the federal government and the recipients on the means by which compliance will be effected.

The federal government will attempt to assist the recipient in making these changes. There will also be the usual procedures for monitoring compliance. An effort is being made and will have to be made to see that employers and other recipients are not required to file voluminous reports to numerous federal agencies.

If any person believes that there is a violation, he will be able to file a complaint with the agency which has this responsibility. Ordinarily the complaint will have to be filed within 90 days of the date of discrimination.

When a complaint appears to be well grounded or when a full review or a compliance report indicates a possible violation, there will be an investigation.

187

If a violation is found, an effort will be made to adjust or eliminate it through negotiation and persuasion. If all these efforts fail, then the normal enforcement proceedings will go into effect. These take the form of an order by the agency involved to terminate the program to the discriminatory recipient or to refuse to grant funds in the future.

This action will be taken after a fair hearing has been afforded to the parties concerned and after the appropriate congressional committee has been notified that such action will be taken. The action also is subject to judicial review.

In lieu of taking the kind of action which would result in a termination of the funds, the Justice Department could take other actions authorized by law. For example, it might sue on behalf of the agency which has made the contract to enforce the terms of the nondiscrimination assurance.

In quick summary, this is what these laws and regulations provide. We are really just at the beginning. The policy issue has been settled, but the question of implementation has just begun. The responsibility for implementation, of course, rests primarily with the federal government. But the goals of the policy establishing equal opportunity for all citizens—while maintaining and improving the programs which are designed to meet public needs—can only be achieved through full cooperation between all of the federal, state, and local agencies which are involved, plus the private institutions and the public interest groups which are striving for a full realization of constitutional rights.

How this is going to work out at this point is difficult to say. The usual argument is that you may well wind up interfering with important public needs by establishing this condition of nondiscrimination.

I would think that our experience over the years with this kind of policy as well as the general lack of any massive resistance to the Civil Rights Act of 1964, would indicate the contrary. We are dealing here with a set of ground rules, and I think that discrimination in federal programs is really a symptom of the exclusion of minority groups, particularly of Negroes, from the life of the various communities. This new policy is an effort to reverse that situation. It is really an instrument to try to bring them within the mainstream of community life.

I think that as a result of our experience thus far, we can say with some confidence that Title VI will not result in any disruption of federally-aided programs but will accomplish its objective—enlarged opportunity for all Americans.*

4.2 STATE LAWS AGAINST DISCRIMINATION
Gerald B. White**

In the State of Michigan we have a Constitutional Commission which, in keeping with the Chairman's admonition, is attempting to arrive at new techniques for dealing with the problems of discrimination in every field. Thus, in 1963 the Constitutional Commission wrote into the Constitution a rather liberal clause stating that the Civil Rights Commission would have jurisdiction over civil rights that have been created by law and those civil rights that were included in the Constitution.

The State Attorney General held that the Commission had jurisdiction over both civil rights created by State law and civil rights created under Federal law. He began to enumerate those rights as being civil rights in the areas of housing, education, employment, and public accommodations.

I think the measure is unique in providing a Constitutional Commission, and I think that it is significant to look at the various kinds of state commissions that have been created through state legislation and to rethink some of the problems that they have experienced.

Historically, discrimination was regarded in our country as contrary to the public policy of most states in the Union.*** Traditionally, two types of remedies were permitted. First there were criminal penalties that were handled by prosecutors and subject to jury trials. Experience indicates that in many instances the prosecutors gave birth

---

* See Appendix E for an analysis of Title VI of the Civil Rights Act of 1964 entitled *Civil Rights Under Federal Programs*, prepared by the U.S. Commission on Civil Rights. This explains the kinds of discrimination prohibited, the federal programs covered, and compliance procedures.

** General Counsel, Michigan Civil Rights Commission.

*** For a comprehensive treatment of the legal dimensions of discrimination see *Discrimination and the Law*, edited by Vern Countryman, University of Chicago Press, Copyright 1965 by The Anti-Defamation League of B'nai B'rith.

to the process of conciliation that is written into most of our laws. If we were to poll the 83 counties in Michigan, it would be interesting to note that in almost every county, including the largest and not excluding Wayne County, most prosecutors dealing with civil rights violations have adopted a policy of conciliation with the wrongdoers in preference to fighting the cases, because of the ineffectiveness of the jury trial.

In addition, civil remedies are available under most statutes, but these remedies were found to be expensive. Theoretically, damages would be inadequate in those cases where redress was being sought, as for instance, in the case of the right to a job or housing. Also, we find juries reluctant to make awards sufficient to redress the enormity of the problem of discrimination. In 1945, we found that the New York State Commission Against Discrimination was established as the forerunner of the various types of commissions now active in most if not all northern communities and many southern communities.

Most of these commissions have various defined powers. In most instances the implementation of their power and authority is initiated by the complaints of an aggrieved party.

The concept of an aggrieved party is narrowly defined and generally does not include community groups. Thus, I should say that very few commissions have the power to initiate complaints. Almost all of them are empowered to conciliate. A few of the commissions with enforcement powers have the power to hold public hearings after a finding of probable cause. Through experience we have found that probable cause also has been narrowly defined and in some instances has meant almost absolute proof of guilt or an admission of guilt.

This shows that as a regulatory body, we probably have not made a great deal of progress. We ought to give a lot of consideration to whether our general concept of what is probable cause functions even more strictly in administrative agencies than in the courts.

In addition, most state laws provide for exemption of religious and nonprofit organizations. They also provide exemptions for domestic and family employees. In one instance there is an exemption for agricultural workers.

These exemptions arose in most instances because of the political climate prevalent in the states where passage of these laws was attempted. In order to make the specific features attractive, these exemptions had to be written in as a part of the political realities of those various states.

In the matter of processing complaints, the complainant usually is represented by some state-appointed lawyer, generally an Assistant Attorney General, and a paid nonlegal staff member. The complainant makes certain general allegations about the experience that he has suffered.

I think a better process is developing in most of these states, or at least the trend is developing, to have the commission state a more formal, sharper type of complaint, such as setting forth the specific kind of discrimination suffered.

In most states the investigations are carried out by staff members under rather adverse circumstances. In some states it is not clear as to the scope of the power to subpoena either persons or records. This means that an investigator may become the strongest man in the process and in his attempt to gain information about various nebulous allegations.

When this kind of procedure is tied in with a concept of probable cause, it means that there must be a preponderance of evidence in order to issue a complaint or to hold a public hearing on the complaint.

Many people feel that these various legislative agencies are ineffectual. However, we must recognize that many respondents rightfully escape unfair public ridicule in those situations where the mere fact of being named as a respondent would indicate to the public that the respondents were discriminating, when ultimately the proof will be that they were not.

In most instances the various legislative agencies created to deal with discrimination have the power to draft conciliation agreements. These agreements generally are treated as confidential, and they are difficult to enforce or even to review because of staff and budget limitations. We should probably review the efficacy of these agreements, unless they are entered into as a stipulation, as part of an order in the case, which would give them a great deal more enforceability than some kind of private contract entered into without the status of a formal order.

One problem has been that the professional groups in the field have not generally agreed upon or developed clear concepts regarding the kind of evidence necessary to prove a case of discrimination. There is a great feeling throughout the United States that discrimination consists primarily of circumstantial evidence. Very little thinking has been given to the concept that discrimination by its very nature is made up of a number of independent acts that taken together would cause a person to conclude that discrimination was a factor in the conduct of a party involved in a transaction.

Therefore many people have been led to assail the process as too vague and to state their feeling that the standards of discrimination should be more clearly developed by those professional organizations. We need to crystallize our thinking in this regard and to project a clear concept of the fact that discrimination is fundamentally circumstantial. There is seldom either an admission or a clear-cut case that is not made up of a continuous chain of related events that are indicative of an intent to discriminate.

Most commissions that we deal with have rather strong enforcement powers when they have the power to issue an order, because these orders can be taken into court and enforced by the processes of various courts.

As we look at the various problems of legislative agencies in the field of discrimination, I think that we have to develop some concept about what constitutes discrimination. From an evidential standpoint we must rethink the concept of probable cause.

More consideration should be given to the question of jurisdiction, especially in those situations where companies or parties are discriminating. Some of these have only a limited role in the particular jurisdiction or city or state, and their primary location is outside the state. They may engage in only a minor transaction within the jurisdiction of the commission, and most of their assets are outside of the State. This creates a serious problem in terms of enforcement.

In addition, we will have to rethink the concept of the statute of limitations. In most instances, the Commissions hold that there is such a thing as a continuing violation which persists until the time when the discrimination has ceased.

We have educational problems that need rethinking in terms of clearer rules concerning election of remedies, whether a complainant

192

can elect a criminal remedy, for instance, as against an administrative or civil remedy. We must develop ideas as to when he should be permitted to pursue each remedy.

It is pretty clear that a man may file with the Civil Service Commission and then file with a public human relations agency. We have continuously held almost unanimously that civil service hearings were just a part of the employment process and did not constitute an election of remedies. However, we must rethink whether or not there has been an election of remedies with regard to the relationship of local agencies to state forums. There is the problem of whether or not arbitration agreements constitute an election of remedies. One of the most serious problems that I have seen is whether or not in a particular employment case the union should be named as a party-respondent in order for a person to gain certain legal equities in a job.

I am thinking of those situations when a man files a complaint with a commission dealing with employment in one year. The determination occurs a year later. The commission orders the employment of that individual and the union takes the position that they cannot give him security because they were not part of this proceeding and his seniority must date from the most recent date, rather than a year ago.

This is a vital consideration in most employment cases. In addition, the long period of time which transpires between the time a case is filed and the time that it is finally adjudicated and disposed of means in many instances that we must rethink the concept of how to stay the equities of a party in the interim. This would be true in employment and more particularly in those areas where housing jurisdiction is exercised.

Another rather unsettled problem in the field is what weight should another administrative agency give to the findings of discrimination by a formally constituted body dealing with discrimination. Should the Real Estate Commission immediately revoke a license because a certain realtor has been found to discriminate, or should it hold an independent hearing? The general tendency among federal agencies and some state agencies has been to give credence to the findings of state agencies in the field of discrimination and to honor them as such.

193

Yet they make investigations and submit certain findings, and we must determine whether or not the financing or the underwriting of the financing should be withdrawn from the realtor who discriminates, or should be withheld until such time as he has proven that he is not discriminating.

This would mean that local agencies without enforcement powers could at least assist on an ancillary basis some of the federal agencies dealing with discrimination.

We need to rethink, in the light of current federal programs, what kind of formal finding must occur in order to invoke the jurisdiction of federal agencies, such as the FHA, in a situation where the human relations commission has no power to adjudicate.

With regard to the relationship between state and local human relations commissions, it is my feeling that perhaps the most desirable situation is one where local commissions are permitted to operate on a concurrent jurisdictional basis with parent state agencies.

In Michigan, unfortunately, we have been the subject of quite a bit of deliberation, because under both the Fair Employment Practices Commission and the current Civil Rights Commission the various attorneys have ruled that the local agencies have no power or authority to investigate, process, and make findings in these particular areas of employment where discrimination is now classically defined.

What has happened in Michigan is that the local agencies have not been a party to the forming of the parent authority or other source of power. The local agencies in Michigan attempted to have a recognition of their existence inserted into the constitution or the Fair Employment Practices Act, and I think that it should have been at once apparent that there was concurrent jurisdiction and they could function simultaneously.

With regard to the role of concurrent jurisdiction of the state agencies, in Michigan we have had a problem similar to that of California in terms of the Rumford Amendment to the state's constitution.

The Rumford Amendment reads that neither the state nor any subdivision or agency thereof shall deny, limit, or abridge, directly or indirectly, the rights of any person who is willing or desirous to sell, lease, or rent any part or all of his real property or to decline to sell, lease, or rent such property to such person or persons as he in his absolute discretion chooses.

In other words, in the constitution you find a basic right to discriminate if you choose in the sale of real property. It is my feeling that the Rumford Amendment and the ordinance recently passed in the City of Detroit will fail in the light of the previous decision of the United States Supreme Court in *Barrows* v. *Jackson* [346 U.S. 249 (1953)], whereby no state can give any enforcibility to an action that denies equal protection of laws to any person.

In addition, I think one case that will be of value is *United States* v. *Morris* [125 Fed. 322 (E. D. Ark. 1903)], wherein the court held that the Thirteenth Amendment is applicable to the private acts of individuals where they attempt to deprive a party of his right to sell, lease, rent, and otherwise deal with property.

This case gives credence to the concept that we live in a community where we have dual citizenship, both federal and state, and that there are certain rights, or inalienable rights as the case cites, which cannot be taken away even by individual citizens in a community when the deprivation is based on race.

Even at such a late date this seems to be a novel theory, despite all the conflict which caused its evolution. We find that in most jurisdictions which have housing legislation, there will be a strong reaction or an attempt to amend the constitution, if necessary, or to pass ordinances where indicated, in order to take away the authority of the commissions to deal with racial discrimination. I am satisfied, however, that in an ultimate test both the Rumford Amendment and the local ordinance in the City of Detroit will be found wanting in the face of both current and older opinions of the United States Supreme Court.

In conclusion, it is my impression that one of the reasons for our present failure is that we have permitted a climate to persist in which we have been uncertain what our standards of conduct should be. We have permitted laws to put us into a position of narrowly defining rights. The general impression has been that the only civil rights that an individual enjoys in his particular state are those which are enforceable.

I think agencies will have to be more imaginative in the pursuit of remedies in the federal courts. We must encourage state attorneys general to file more expansive litigation to redress these rights, and sometimes we may have to give up the prerogative to make adjudications in our local commissions.

We must become part of a total attack on discrimination which will be resolved in the federal courts, outside of the jurisdiction where it has had very little, if any, effect other than to suggest to the various parties that they ought to engage in this kind of litigation. Most important of all, we must attempt to regain our concepts of the Constitution and the Declaration of Independence so that people will begin to recognize that they have a civil right to housing and employment and that there is no such thing as the right to discriminate. Unless we attack this concept with renewed vigor, I think it is fairly clear that we will begin to lose some of the things we have gained in the last two decades under state and local agency rule.

4.3 LOCAL LAWS AGAINST DISCRIMINATION: SALIENT LEGAL ISSUES

David W. Craig*

The first problem that arises in local anti-discrimination legislation concerns the enabling legislation. Exactly what is the statutory authority for non-home rule cities in this area? In all cases, express authorization is highly desirable. Otherwise, the state-wide or region-wide nature of the public interest in equal rights is often used as an argument against local power. In some cases, where no enabling laws specifically allow equal rights ordinances, general statutory powers to regulate for the health, safety and welfare of the general public have been used as a basis of power. Finally, where state laws directly implement equal rights, local action may be excluded.

Once these initial problems are overcome, the administration and enforcement of civil rights legislation at the local level presents substantial problems. A widely representative voice-of-the-community commission is always helpful. Positive processes, with an emphasis on education of business groups (e. g. multilists, etc.) have been found helpful in utilizing a community conscience as a basis for compliance. When conflict arises as to the constitutionality of legislation, it is of primary importance that strong fact cases be used as a basis for judicial tests of constitutionality. Where strong sanctions become neces-

---

* City Solicitor, City of Pittsburgh.

sary as a last resort, especially in housing purchase cases where bargaining is incomplete, it is often wise to seek an injunction requiring "bargaining in good faith."

In the area of public accommodations, the club device has kept alive disputes as to what accommodations are public. However, actual instances of unrest provide part of the reason why the right to equal treatment over-balances any pretext of private business choice under the broad police power of the local government.

In the area of equal employment opportunity, the Federal government is even now engaged in controversy over the status of discrimination on account of age or sex, the logical outcome of early rulings concerning discrimination on the basis of race, color, religion, or national origin. Training programs and apprenticeships remain the most pressing problem with respect to racial discrimination.

In all cases, there is substantial dispute whether there is a presumption favoring the minority applicant where subjective considerations for selection are involved (personality, etc.). There is often ground for evasion under the doctrine of rational relevancy, when religion or national origin are claimed to be relevant to selection. The courts have been moving towards a policy of prohibiting circumvention through the use of limited resources. If this policy is extended, there is a possibility that all specialized placement services will be outlawed. In the area of labor organizations, where union membership is a practical necessity, what weight should be allowed union constitution provisions, such as those which provide a membership vote as a condition of membership? And finally, is forfeiture of a contract a feasible penalty when a public contractor discriminates illegally?

In the area of open occupancy legislation, there is some question as to the inclusion or exclusion of one-family dwellings under a "public accommodations" analogy. In fact, under a business licensing theory, it is possible that realtors can be regulated more extensively than transactions conducted by private parties. However, if in some situations where the landlord continues to reside on the premises he is exempted because of personal residence, there is a problem concerning the exemption of one-family dwellings. When the "economic confession" is found in the claim that discrimination is practiced only because of the threat of a loss of clientele (tenants, etc.), tests of discrimination become especially difficult. Can a benign quota be validly

197

authorized in any situations, such as pilot integration projects? Since most of these are questions of degree rather than of kind, they are likely to remain uncertain for a long time to come. For this reason, it is increasingly necessary for city attorneys to be willing to take risks in these areas, rather than adopt traditional wait-and-see attitudes.

4.31 "WE MUST TAKE SOME LEGAL RISKS"

DAVID W. CRAIG*

The doctor and his wife noticed new houses going up in the area, and they decided that their family needs called for them to consider moving there.

The doctor made an appointment through the developer's office to meet a salesman there one weekday evening. The salesman missed that appointment, so the doctor made another. Finally negotiations for a lot commenced. They went on and on. All these discussions came to naught, simply because the doctor was Negro.

He got nowhere in trying to purchase the house. Fortunately, for the last decade, Pittsburgh has had a Fair Housing Ordinance under which you may file a complaint.

The doctor filed a complaint. After earnest and extensive efforts at private conciliation failed, our Commission on Human Relations held a comprehensive public hearing and concluded that the developer was in violation of the ordinance for discriminating against the doctor because of his race. We then initiated an enforcement and penalty proceeding which caused the developer to attack the constitutionality and statutory authority of our Fair Housing Ordinance.

After further hearings in our Common Pleas Court, Judge Weir handed down an extensive opinion upholding the Fair Housing Ordinance on all counts and requiring the developer, by injunction, to proceed in the negotiations and sale.

The decision was not appealed. Shortly after the appeal time ran out, the doctor and his family acquired a suitable lot and home in the development and they now live there without incident.

The chief point that I think needs to be made, is that in the civil rights area my fellow city attorneys must be willing to take some legal risks. By contrast, when it comes to local taxes, I am

---

* City Solicitor, City of Pittsburgh.

very concerned about the legal risks which the City Council of Pittsburgh takes, because if I make a mistake in allowing a classification or an exemption, the entire tax may fall and Pittsburgh will lose that revenue. However, I do not think that I should be as conservative in the matter of local civil rights regulations.

I do not think that local municipalities need to wait until they get an express authorization from their state legislatures. Even though I grant that all municipalities in most states are creatures of the state and have only such powers as the legislature gives them, or such powers as can be necessarily implied from those grants, we need not wait for express authorization. Very few cities wait for express authorization to adopt ordinance regulations pertaining to other sorts of conduct, such as loitering and so on, so why should they wait for explicit authorization to get into this field, which has been proved by our common experience to be of heartfelt concern to American cities?

Our Pittsburgh ordinances are not based on any explicit grant of power from the state but upon the general health, welfare, and safety ordinance-adoption power in our City Charter. The substance of the words of the charter reads something like this—to make all such ordinances, in addition to the special powers in this section granted, for the proper maintenance, care of the city finances, and the maintenance of peace, good government, and the welfare of the city and its trade, commerce, and manufacturing.

Can anyone in this day and age, realizing the importance of a fair and equal shake in public accommodations, employment, and housing to the peace and good government and welfare of the city, and realizing further the figures demonstrating the importance of equal treatment in terms of the economic welfare of a city—can anyone overlook in that language the clear power to have local regulations on equal employment and equal housing with teeth in them?

We are also somewhat aided by the fact that the Pennsylvania Human Relations Law explicitly states that the operation of that law shall not repeal or supersede any local ordinances or regulations affording equal rights. The state law language was adopted long after our city ordinance had been in effect, but we pointed out, when our ordinance on housing was attacked, that the state legislature had thus recognized that we did have power all along to get into the equal rights field with respect to housing.

The existence of a state agency (although I feel that it is essential and important for local agencies to have local regulations with teeth in them) is a great blessing to us.

When our housing ordinance was attacked, in the case of the doctor that I described, one of the more ludicrous arguments against our local power was that equal civil rights are not matters for city concern but are only of regional concern. They argued that, if we were to enforce equal housing laws against developers within the City of Pittsburgh, the existence of such local regulations in the City of Pittsburgh would necessarily mean that all white house buyers would flee to the suburbs. This argument, ridiculous as it was, clearly was refuted by the fact of statewide regulations. There soon will be no place for the prejudiced to flee to. Therefore the existence of state regulations is of great importance to civil rights issues concerning the central city surrounded by lily-white suburbs.

If city attorneys must interpret state laws as to when they operate to preempt local power, it seems to me that they should give the benefit of doubt to the local regulations with respect to equal rights and then let the matter be settled in the courts.

In the choice of test cases, I do ask that our co-workers in the civil rights movement appreciate the importance of choosing the *best* test cases when the statutory authority or the constitutionality of local regulations is attacked, for usually they are attacked by some of the best-equipped law firms.

It is only good strategy to choose the strong test cases, such as that of the doctor I described. I considered that to be a strong test case partly because it involved an empty lot; there could be no quarrel about whether or not we were dealing with an owner or landlord who objected to children, the sort of thing that comes up as an excuse in rental cases.

The test case was also aided by the fact that this was not a penniless person but a doctor with means and income, who was well able to afford a dwelling in the $35,000 class. That fact permitted the final decision, which upheld our ordinance, to make clear that discrimination against anybody—rich or poor—is wrong. A whole series of acts, not just one, is our real target. Just as in zoning, we are not content merely to eliminate nuisances, we want to achieve a communitywide effect. We are not in the equal rights regulations field merely to help downtrodden individuals, but to eliminate the tacit conspiracy in the white community.

Such legislation is well supported by the general police powers granted by statute. This kind of legislation is essential, not only to the "peace and good government" of the cities of this country, but also to their very existence.

4.4 CRISIS
JOSEPH P. WITHERSPOON*

One thesis of this discussion is that disobedience of the law is a major and dominant fact in a community crisis. I think the following observations must be made.

Firstly, protest actions employed in crisis situations in communities have, often, been quite legal in nature. The situation is not so much a question of what to do about disobedience of the law; it is rather how do you resolve the underlying problems that caused the crisis.

Secondly, crises tend to pass, while the problems that underlie them remain. The adjustments achieved as a result of crises are generally only temporary and short range. They tend to be poorly formulated, no matter how salutary.

Finally, it seems to me that crisis is only one dimension of a community problem; the great social upheaval which should come about generally does so only after a great deal of time, effort, and discontent.

The picture in Texas is quite different from one of crisis. It is apathy, and to me the most pressing problems in this area lie not in dealing with crises but rather with apathy toward the human relations problem.

The Southwest and the South have the greatest problems. What confrontation I have had with human relations in the North and West convinces me that in these areas, too, apathy is the problem.

How do you get the minority group started toward doing something about an obviously present, difficult human relations problem? Whether you have apathy or whether you have crisis, and usually

---

* Professor of Law, University of Texas.

you have both in any one community regardless of its location, how do you solve the problem? There is a great lesson in our federal system, for in the past two decades, while the South was doing very little about the problem, 22 or 23 of our state governments were addressing laws to the solution of this enormous public question of human relations.

The years from 1940 through about 1945 saw the genesis of the idea of using an official agency of the law to solve human relations problems, including that of discrimination against minority groups.

I feel that the more we know about the law the more we realize that the concepts that have been built into it are by and large not only outdated but also overrated.

The federal law that was enacted in 1964, however necessary it was, will make little change in the South and Southwest. Substantively it is good law, but from the standpoint of the legal institution that has been developed to enforce it, I think it is greatly lacking.

It is built in large part upon the model state legislation in this field, and at the present time the law is largely a failure in terms of changing the picture of the Negro with respect to discrimination in the last twenty years.

In North, South, East and West, the Negro holds substantially the same position with relation to white persons in employment and in housing, for example, as he did twenty years ago.

Therefore, it seems to me that the great challenge to an institution like this is, how do you reinstitutionalize? What kind of institutions do we need today to make this law substantively good and realistic in the long run in order to achieve its proper objectives?

4.5 "THE CRISIS IS THE LACK OF DEMONSTRATIONS"

Eric M. Mann*

There has been inordinate emphasis on the concept of law and order as an intrinsic good in the community. I certainly feel that law and order have a valid place in the community and should be enforced. But the concept of law and order is a very amorphous thing,

* Field Secretary, Congress of Racial Equality.

for instance, to the police officials. We have been in many situations with police officials in which a very strict definition of law and order has been imposed upon demonstrators and upon civil rights groups who are attempting to achieve what they consider valid goals. As a result, I feel we have lacked the presentation of an adequate picture of the motivations and the reasons for the conflict.

It is not simply that each of us judges a problem from his own particular point of view. This, of course, is inevitable. Nevertheless, I think that a police officer who is coming in conflict with a civil rights group needs more insight into why the demonstrators are there. I find many times that the police have taken a very myopic attitude toward civil rights demonstrations and have seen them as an invasion upon the over-all equilibrium of the community rather than as a positive attempt to achieve certain important goals.

Secondly, although we may have a commitment to preserve law and order, we must realize that law is a very amorphous and constantly changing concept. This does not mean that where a law must be enforced, the police officer should decide that since there may be a change in two years, he cannot enforce it. It does mean that in terms of certain laws which we consider unjust but which nonetheless have to be enforced, we feel that many times these laws have been enforced with a fervor and enthusiasm which is not commensurate with the over-all value of these laws for the community.

Therefore, we feel that the police department should evaluate the laws that they are enforcing and, without trying to stretch the law, at least give us the benefit of the doubt before they are compelled to enforce them.

Thirdly, we must deal with the concept of crisis. There is too much concern over crisis in terms of the manifestations of public demonstrations and strikes, picket lines, sit-ins and lie-ins. These are unhealthy forces in the government. The crisis in the community is not the crisis that confronts human relations people, peace officers and other city officials. We have been considering crisis in terms of disturbance of the community equilibrium, when the crisis, as I see it, *is* the community equilibrium.

The crisis lies in the fact that the white community as a whole has not accepted the responsibility for total integration in all its dealings. One often encounters stories of a man attempting to rent an apartment to a Negro or of people on the job or in non-civil rights occupations attempting to integrate a company. How many people in white communities—whether scientists, teachers, or anyone else—have made civil rights an integral part of their way of life? The Negro community is guilty, too, but for different reasons. What we consider the crisis from our point of view is not the demonstrations. *The crisis is the lack of demonstrations.*

The crisis is the fact that CORE and the NAACP and other civil rights groups of comparatively small membership have not been able to involve the large-scale community in the problems of discrimination. Therefore, I contend that the civil rights demonstrations present Negro communities with a positive way of releasing an active creative force. Unless we can encourage this rather than inhibit it, the total effect will be narrowed.

There must be a civil rights struggle, but many people are resentful that the CORE groups were not willing to cooperate fully. Perhaps the reason why we were unwilling is that we have different goals. The business community acts within a specific area with regard to a human relations committee or a human rights committee, and seeks to get the most that it can in terms of its own goals. I do not see why a double standard should be imposed upon a civil rights group.

Supposedly the human relations committees seek the same goals that we do. When we disagree, it is not because we are irresponsibly intent on keeping tensions at a high pitch but because we have responsibilities to our own members whose goals may differ from yours. We would like to work with you, but there are many times when we must oppose you. Although in theory we may endorse the same goals, in practice, however, there will be times when we come into direct conflict with you and are not willing to reduce tensions in the community until our demands are met.

4.6 QUESTIONS AND ANSWERS

Question: Does the Civil Rights Act of 1964 open the doors for Negroes as qualified apprentices or journeymen in lily-white building trades unions? How long do you estimate it will take a Negro applicant to get through these doors?

MR. GREENE: As to the first part, it is clear that the 1964 Act does give the right to anyone who is qualified to become a member of any union, including the building trades unions. The Act states explicitly that it is an unfair employment practice to bar a qualified person from membership in any labor organization. That would include any building trades union, as defined here.

As to how long it will take and how a person would proceed, this is more difficult to answer. The employment portion of the Act does not become effective until July, 1965. Unlike the remainder of the Act, which became effective immediately, the employment portion has a one-year lag. Once the Act does become effective, there are essentially two ways in which an individual can proceed. First, he can file a charge with the Equal Employment Opportunity Commission or he can file a complaint with the Department of Justice, either directly or through the local United States Attorney.

There is a provision for going through with local or state procedures first. Certainly if the Equal Employment Opportunity Commission received the complaint, there would have to be a waiting period, sixty days, I believe, until the local or state procedures can be tried. If that procedure was unsuccessful, of course the Equal Employment Opportunity Commission would proceed with the charge. The Department of Justice is not so restricted, but if there is an effective commission, it would also wait for local state efforts. How long it would take after that no one could tell, because the Act has not been tried.

I would suspect, however, that if there is a local or building trades union that has a long history of white-only membership, it should not be too difficult to prove discrimination, no matter what kind of test or what kind of evidence, circumstantial or otherwise, you would require. Therefore, as to getting a court order or short of a court order some administrative adjustment, I do not think it would take too long, but the exact time is impossible to estimate.

MR. WITHERSPOON: I think we can add to that reply that Section 706 puts a time limit on the processing of a complaint once it has been brought back from the state agency having jurisdiction over it, or once it has been referred to that agency by a commissioner who has filed a complaint. I think that is very clearly defined in the Act of 1964, but state agencies usually borrow from the federal terminology.

Question: Would you comment on the potential scope of application under Title VI of the Civil Rights Act of 1964?

MR. WITHERSPOON: I think that the device of sanction which has been worked out in Title VI, while not entirely new in civil rights law, is new in its potential scope of application. From the standpoint of administrative law I think that this device promises to take its greatest effect with the enactment of the Civil Rights Law of 1964.

I think the device of sanction suggests action at both state and local levels. That is, when you have local or state funds, those funds certainly ought not to be utilized to promote a system of discrimination and segregation. Therefore this is a suggestive step for those at the state and local level.

Question: What is the most serious problem presently facing us?

MR. WITHERSPOON: I would say it is apathy. There are several ways of solving that problem. One is by direct action, a method which has been discussed.

I know that on my own local front in Austin, Texas, the Police Department has been extraordinarily cooperative each time direct action was used by a particular civil rights group. By and large the plans have been cleared with the Police Department and at the beginning, about two years ago when it was a much more difficult problem than today, the Police Chief carefully selected from among his officers those who were at least neutral or sympathetic, to monitor the situation as it presented itself. So far as I know, we have yet to make an arrest on the local front.

Question: Can you project how far the newly pronounced policy will go toward withdrawal of aid for discriminatory practices by groups which are not directly aided by the government, but which are suffered to exist as bodies related to those receiving the aid? What about college fraternities?

MR. TAYLOR: This is not a question that you can answer categorically. It will depend to a great extent on whether the related bodies the questioner is talking about are themselves involved in the conduct of a program which benefits a segment of the public. For example, where we are talking about federal assistance to employment in various ways, it would, of course, defeat the policy if union practices of discrimination were allowed to impair the employer's intent to hire on a nondiscriminatory basis. So in a case where the union has a share in both policymaking and assistance, obviously the policy will have to guarantee that there would be equal opportunity on the job which is federally assisted.

Now, as to colleges and fraternities, this is becoming a complicated question, too. Perhaps I should not comment on this because one of the provisions of the 1964 law prohibited our Commission from investigating college fraternities.

It was the product of very intensive lobbying on the part of the fraternities. But as far as fraternities are concerned, here again I think the question turns on whether they are involved in some function which relates to the provision of services to students or other members of the college community. In other words, if at a particular college or university a fraternity has some function in providing housing dormitory space for students, which sometimes it does, it seems to me that this may well be covered by the new policy. On the other hand, purely social functions, which are unrelated to this policy, are not likely to be covered.

One final point: Apart from the coverage of the federal policy, it is quite conceivable that the state government can take action to secure nondiscriminatory treatment by fraternities of individuals in state-supported universities. In some cases that has been done.

Question: What is the status of federal aid to California since the Rumford Act was voted out?

MR. TAYLOR: This has been a subject of some intensive consideration by the Housing and Home Finance Agency, which recently issued a determination with which I am not completely familiar. In essence, I gather that the urban renewal assistance program in California has been curtailed but not completely cut off. The program will probably remain in this status until the California Supreme Court has had an opportunity to resolve the issues which are involved in litigation out there.

I do think that there is little question that where we are dealing with urban renewal or public housing, it will either be determined that Proposition 14 does not apply to publicly assisted housing of this kind or else it will be determined that it is unconstitutional to place these limitations upon developers and the people who live in the housing.

Question: What is the value of conciliating cases after a finding of probable cause when such respondents frequently are multiple offenders and simply conciliate each case by agreeing to terms which do not in fact deter subsequent acts of discrimination?

MR. WHITE: None. There is no value in that. I think that we have seen that such a conciliation pattern would probably lead to a community crisis. I think that in most instances where you have conciliation agreements, there should be a provision to reopen the case in the event that the party does not live up to the standards which you have set.

Where you have small staffs it is slightly impractical to go back and review your conciliation agreements, but certainly the review factor should be included in your agreements.

In addition, generally speaking, if you find a person who is making conciliation agreements just to avoid a public hearing, and this does happen, you probably will find that he is not entitled to his second conciliation effort. If you do not review the case, I think it will lead to a crisis.

Question: In the matter of the election of remedies, does the filing of a complaint with a local commission such as the City Commission constitute an election of remedies which would preclude a party from filing a complaint with a State Commission that has enforcement power?

MR. WHITE: This is a very complex question. Simply stated, I would say that in my opinion the United States law favors concurrent jurisdiction. The only thing that would lead to a concept of preemption is the kind of situation where you find that the State Commission has a more complete enforcement authority than a local commission, and the state feels that public policy or some other reason will demand that the City Commission impose a five-year jail sentence, whereas a cease-and-desist order would result at the state level. This would be too dramatic a difference to allow the City Commission's order to stand.

Frankly speaking, I would say that any City Commission confronted with a problem like this probably should have a judicial determination. I feel that a city attorney would not be afraid of such a test.

By the same token, I do recognize that in our own State of Michigan we have many precedents involving minimum wage laws where the cities attempted to pass a minimum wage law and the State Supreme Court said that even though the state had no such minimum wage law, this was an area that was exclusively in the state's authority. In current thinking, based upon the attitude of the federal government towards the states, I think that you will find that concurrent jurisdiction is a pretty good risk to attempt.

Question: Assuming you have a strong state enforcement law, why have local enforcement agencies? Why not instead have just a local commission created to assist in voluntary educational activities in the spirit of the state law?

MR. CRAIG: Particularly in states with a large geographical area, the state investigative commission seldom has a big enough staff to cover the entire state with the sort of detailed, investigative activities that are necessary in many enforcement cases. Moreover, one of the important roles of a local commission is to develop programs and policies with labor unions and employers. These people just will not come in and sit down with our local commission unless we have an armed fist behind the kid gloves and unless we have enforcement teeth in our local laws. I think that a local official can participate in this head-knocking a lot more effectively than an official situated more remotely at the State Capitol.

We do not regard our Commission as being out in left field away from the administration of the city. These negotiations are participated in by people from the Mayor's office and from my office, as

209

parts of the administration. When an employer or union leader comes in to negotiate with us, he is negotiating face to face with the same local officials with whom he has to deal in other matters.

Contrary to what might be the view of the political scientists, I am very much for concurrent jurisdiction at the state and local levels.

Question: How can the state or city involved in a test case of constitutionality choose a strong case when the action is brought by the person or firm attacking the measure? In other words, are not test cases chosen by the plaintiff?

MR. CRAIG: The answer is that test cases usually are not chosen by the attacker. In our experience he has usually not been the plaintiff. At least in the north, it is not fashionable to nominate yourself as the person to attack a civil rights measure.

In our test case the developer did not receive the financial support he expected from his fellow members of the real estate community. He was hard put to get a real estate man to come in and testify as an expert. He could get no expert witness other than a part-time dabbler.

Hence, in our city and in our atmosphere it is unfashionable to attack the legality of the civil rights measure. Usually the attacker is a defendant, a person against whom we are taking enforcement action.

Question: Would you please define "blockbusting"? How does this differ from "panic-peddling?"

MR. CRAIG: In our part of the country, panic-peddling and blockbusting are the same thing, although I know that in other parts of the country blockbusting is synonymous with integration and has no bad connotation.

In a new draft, not yet adopted, we define blockbusting to mean panic-peddling, to refer to any real estate broker who, for economic purposes, induces directly or indirectly, or attempts to induce, the sale, or listing for sale, of a housing accommodation by representing that a change has occurred or will or may occur with respect to the racial, religious, or ethnic composition of a street or block, neighborhood, or area in which the housing accommodation is located.

210

Question: When can so-called "benign" quotas be validly authorized?

MR. CRAIG: This is related to the preservation of integrated housing projects for demonstration or pilot purposes. We have had quite a debate on this subject, particularly in the north, between those well-intentioned people who believe that it is essential to preserve an integrated project in public housing areas and the equally well-intentioned people on the other side who point out that a benign quota is still a quota. I join with those who take the latter view. I think it is very difficult to deny housing to a young Negro husband, whose wife and children are living in a ratty slum, on the ground that the quota in this housing project has been filled. To refuse him because this is a nice integrated project which demonstrates how the races can live together is unjust. It is too easy to talk about demonstration projects when you yourself are not asked to sacrifice the health and welfare of your wife and children.

Question: Could the Attorney General's office seek an injunction on the basis of a prima facie case filed directly in that office, or under the present circumstances would an injunction be obtained more speedily if the State Commission had power to seek an injunction directly?

MRS. SHIRLEY SIEGEL*: Where very clear evidence of discriminatory conduct is brought directly to us, and we have had at least 10 such instances involving employment agencies in the last couple of years, we go directly to our Supreme Court (the court of original jurisdiction in New York) for a permanent injunction against any further violation of this kind. We have also obtained costs in such proceedings in amounts ranging up to $2,000, our statutory limit.

In each of these cases, we had a better than prima facie case. As a practical matter, under those circumstances, it was not difficult to obtain immediate consent to a permanent injunction. Of course, if the employment agency continues to violate the civil rights law and practice discrimination, it would be in contempt of court.

---

* Assistant Attorney-General, State of New York, in Charge, Civil Rights Bureau.

211

It may be that the question referred to our recent activity to obtain an entirely different kind of injunction, namely, one requested by the State Commission in order to preserve the subject matter of a housing complaint proceeding then pending at the Commission.

In other words, if the Commission finds probable cause, or if somebody comes in with a pretty good complaint, and it seems imminent that the apartment or home may be transferred to someone else, we go into court at the request of the State Commission and obtain a temporary restraining order and then an injunction which will hold that housing accommodation off the market until the State Commission has had an opportunity to make its final determination and obtain whatever order is appropriate.

We do this under a New York statute which provides that at the request of the Commission we may go to court and take whatever proceedings are necessary for the effective enforcement of the law.

The legal action that I described as used against the employment agencies came up under quite a different statute and was enacted at a different time and under different circumstances. It is, perhaps, a codification of a common law principle that the State Attorney General may go to court to enjoin persistent illegal conduct.

As to whether an injunction would be obtained more speedily if the State Commission had power to seek it directly, that is hard to say. We get a result within 24 hours. We think that we have made a good record of getting fast injunctions and serving them quickly on respondents whenever we have received the request to act.

Question: What about instances where accreditation will be denied or withdrawn from Negro schools for the purpose of denying people who graduated from those schools the benefit of the sixth grade presumption for voting purposes?

MR. GREENE: The fact is that many Negro schools, even public schools, are not accredited by their own states. Even if the assumption in this question were true, they would not be denied the benefits of this law.

You do not have to attend an accredited school to get the benefit of the presumption. The statute provides that anyone who attends

212

any public school or any accredited private school gets the benefit of the presumption, so even with respect to a public school which is not accredited, the sixth graders are entitled to the presumption of literacy.

Mr. Taylor is really responsible for putting this provision in the statute. When the bill originally was drafted, it only mentioned accredited schools. He called one day and said that this situation was likely to arise. As a result of that call we had an opportunity to redraft the bill and present the language in the statute to permit use of the presumption for anyone attending any public school, whether or not it is accredited.

DEAN TYLER:* I would like to comment on Mr. Mann's statement. I agree very much with the spirit of his presentation, and I think he made some very important points, but as a Professor of Law I take umbrage with his first point. I have certain theories about law that go very much against what Mr. Mann says, namely, that the police should evaluate the laws that they are enforcing. This gives rise to considerable difficulty. I think judges have trouble enough trying to evaluate laws. In fact, I am very skeptical of their doing it. Certainly, I would be very suspicious if policemen were to evaluate laws.

In the first place, they are not competent to evaluate in an effective manner. In the second place, implicit in this evaluation is a principle analogous to interposition, that is, policemen interposing themselves between the citizens and the law and doing what they think is best for society.

This position has been rejected in constitutional law. The only instance or case where an official of the state was justified in evaluating the law, is the instance which occurred right after the Civil War when President Johnson challenged Congress with invading the prerogatives of the President. The result of such invasion could be that everybody would have to violate the law in order to make it a judicial question for consideration by the courts.

The law cannot be so used. The only way it can be challenged is if we disobey the law. The only way an official could challenge the law would be for someone to disobey it. It is not the position

* Professor Tyler is Dean of the Texas Southern University Law School.

213

of an official to evaluate the law. In my opinion that would be unconstitutional.

In the third place I think if a police officer should be permitted to evaluate the law and he was biased and hostile to the civil rights movement, his evaluation would be more against the interest of the demonstrators than for it.

Therefore I would like the police to be neutral, even more so than other officials. I would say that these policemen should use common sense and decency in treating individuals with a certain amount of respect.

Question: What is the administrative value to a federal agency of an affirmative opinion by an attorney general?

MR. TAYLOR: As for the federal administrative policy that I was talking about, I think that the determination of a state law official would certainly be valuable evidence in any proceeding, whether or not it would be dispositive of the case.

The other point that I would make is that the complaint procedures established under these regulations could be filed by any party. They do not necessarily have to be directed to the victim of the discrimination. I think what is happening is that in a legal sense, perhaps, there is a new relationship between state, local, and federal agencies. In a less legal sense this involves the concept of cooperation between federal, state, and local agencies in trying to solve some of these same questions.

MR. STAHL: If I may try to answer that question, I think an opinion of any state attorney general generally would be binding on the executive and administrative officials. It would not in any way, of course, be binding on the courts. In many cases the courts have overturned opinions of state attorneys general.

With respect to state administrative agencies, that sometimes raises a difficult question. If you have a quasi-judicial agency, such as a public utility commission, or perhaps a state human relations commission which has its own quasi-judicial function, while normally they would accept the opinion of the attorney general, there might be an adjudication in which they choose to ignore his opinion. Many

214

state laws permit one state agency to appeal to the courts from the decision of another state agency which exercises quasi-judicial powers. In some cases a state attorney general may have his people on both sides of the question. In summary, while state agencies and state officials will generally be bound by the attorney general's opinion, it is not binding or dispositive of cases that eventually get to the courts.

Question*: There has not been a single case in which we have had public hearings within the last eight years in Pennsylvania where the respondent has not at one time or another— whether he took an appeal eventually or not—raised the question of constitutionality of the law on the old grounds that our Commission not only investigates the facts but actually tries the case and then makes the adjudication. In your comment on the fact that we have to rethink our basic procedures, have you ever given thought to the fact that in practically all these cases, in all the states, our Commission really does investigate the facts on behalf of a complainant (and the law itself says that general counsel has to present it, just as he does in an ordinary case representing the plaintiff) and then, knowing all these facts right from the beginning, makes the adjudication?

MR. WITHERSPOON: I think that the Supreme Court of the United States has indicated, at least since 1950 (and we have had indications since that time), that there is a problem of wisdom involved here. Perhaps in an extraordinarily acute case there may even be a constitutional issue. Invasion of the decisional process was undertaken by a subordinate administrative agency within the Department of Justice or even by the Attorney General himself. I think that kind of case may well involve a constitutional issue outside the context, of what you might call an action similar to pardoning on the part of the Chief Executive. A typical adjudication of that situation would be the Supreme Court's statement in the *McGrath* case [*Joint Anti-Fascist Refugee Committee* v. *McGrath*, 341 U.S. 123 (1951)] that this is not a constitutional problem. Therefore, the problem is one of wisdom, and I would suggest that it can be solved by what we call a principle of internal separation of functions. It seems to me that it might be

---

* By Nathan Agran, General Counsel, Pennsylvania Human Relations Commission.

wise to separate a portion of the Commission members from other Commission members so that some would be assigned to negotiations and would not participate in the decision-making process.

Here you can utilize the principle of internal separation of functions. Precisely how that would work out, I am not sure. However, I feel certain that you could separate your own office along the lines of the division within the National Labor Relations Board.

PART V

FEDERAL, STATE AND LOCAL RESOURCES IN RESOLVING RACIAL CRISES

We are concerned with the primarily nonlegal resources available in dealing with racial problems. This has to do with the federal, state, and local official programs to help overcome some of the root causes of unemployment, bad housing, and inadequate education that often lead to the more direct symptoms of racial problems. We have also included a discussion of nongovernmental agencies that may be available to help local communities.

5.1   FEDERAL PROGRAMS: "THIS CRISIS WILL NOT BE SOLVED ON THE BASIS OF MORALITY ALONE."

BERL I. BERNHARD*

Quite often the symptoms or outcroppings of racial unrest and discord take the form of accusations against the police. With or without a civilian review board, it appears that the real issue or crisis is caused by alleged police brutality, when actually these allegations often mask underlying problems.

Some of these underlying problems are economic, training, and educational problems. For a long time there has been a failure on the part of the national leadership to assert the whole issue of race relations as a moral one. Now it is accepted as a moral crisis, but it is far more than that.

We know that this crisis will not be solved on the basis of morality alone. When I was in the government service during the discord down in New Orleans, I went there to see someone in the Chamber

---

* Executive Director, Lawyers' Committee for Civil Rights Under Law.

of Commerce. They were having a very difficult time because of the loss of business. This particular man said that he believed that segregation was morally right, but that this whole situation had deteriorated so badly that it was costing him a great deal of money, and he was prepared to help because, as he told me, "sometimes you have to rise above your moral convictions."

An essential reference for anyone concerned with this problem is *Catalog of Federal Aids to State and Local Governments.* It was prepared by the Subcommittee on Inter-Governmental Relations of the Congress and it is published by the Legislative Reference Services, Library of Congress. This is a catalog listing every conceivable type of federal aid, cooperation, and technical assistance that exists.

Another publication is *The Handbook of Federal Aid to Communities,* published by the Area Redevelopment Administration of the U.S. Department of Commerce. It deals with every conceivable type of community problem from long-range planning to low-cost public housing to library assistance.

A new function has recently been given to the U.S. Commission on Civil Rights. It is a clearinghouse function. Under the 1964 Civil Rights Act, the U.S. Commission on Civil Rights was assigned the task of acting as a clearinghouse to provide aid and assistance to communities who wish to learn more about what other communities have done when confronted with particular types of protests, demonstrations, or basic difficulties.

While there are federal programs that deal with labor, education, and various other community problems, they are rarely used in certain instances because of the lack of knowledge about them and the failure of a local community to initiate interest.

These programs do not simply descend upon a particular community. They come about because that community has done prior planning and determined to go to Washington or write to Washington and say, "We have inadequate libraries and our people do not have sufficient facilities to be well educated; can you help us?"

There happen to be some very good federal programs dealing with libraries, particularly in the new Office of Economic Opportunity. But help does not come about simply because programs exist. It does not just attach itself to any community. The community must initiate action and specify its own needs.

5.11 THE COMMUNITY RELATIONS SERVICE: "WE TRY TO BUILD UNDERSTANDING."

DR. JOHN GRIFFIN*

The Community Relations Service was set up under Title X of the Civil Rights Act. It was set up to provide assistance for persons or communities in disputes arising from discrimination which affect or may affect commerce. This is a very broad mandate. We have the responsibility for going into communities when we are asked to mediate, concilate or bring about some settlement of the differences. This is direct field work.

But a second major part of our enterprise is the affirmative program which attempts to build a larger understanding of the Civil Rights Act—what it means to local communities, how it is interpreted and how it is endorsed.

We have assigned several of our 26 paid staff members to develop this facet of our work. Another division of our enterprise fits somewhere between the field conciliation work and the affirmative program. This is our Liaison Department, our Program and Community Planning Department, which is headed by Roger Wilkins.

Mr. Wilkins' special responsibility is to bring together a group of persons who are competently informed about the various programs of the federal government, wherever these programs develop. Thus we will be in a position to support field conciliation activities by relating communities to the various agencies of the federal government, whether they are in the Office of Economic Opportunity, the President's Committee on Equal Employment, the President's Committee on Housing, or the Urban Affairs Administration. We feel that one of the special competencies that we must develop in our agency is a liaison with these various government departments and an ability to relate quickly the kinds of complaints or questions that may come to us.

As part of our work in trying to build understanding of the Civil Rights Act, we have conducted meetings about the law in a number of southern states and in one border state. The first of these meetings

---

* Director of Conciliation Services for the Community Relations Service of the United States Department of Commerce. *Ed. Note:* In April 1966 the Community Relations Service (directed by Roger Wilkins) was transferred to the Department of Justice.

was held in Atlanta in August, when some 500 persons turned out at the invitation of the Civil Rights Commission.

These people were deputy sheriffs, police officers, attorneys, employers and various persons running public accommodations who wanted to know something about the law. The meeting was so successful that it has now been repeated in several other cities and states: Newark, Delaware; Nashville, Tennessee; Columbia, South Carolina. The U.S. Civil Rights Commission assists in setting up such enterprises.

As the law provides, our complaints may come from an individual, a local citizens or civil rights group, a mayor, or a police official. These are the sources of the work that has come across our docket so far.

But the law also provides that court cases may be referred to us by federal courts. When a civil rights suit appears before a federal judge, he may set the matter aside for 60 days and call upon the Community Relations Service and its conciliation activities in an effort to achieve either a settlement or compliance in the matter.

We have been very careful in the few instances of this kind that have arisen not to let our agency serve as an instrument of delay nor a device by which a settlement could be achieved that would fall anywhere short of compliance.

We have been functioning since October, 1964, when Congress appropriated us money. As of December 4, 1964, some 73 complaints had come from North, South, East and West. I believe the count broke down to a little more than half from the South and a little less than half from the North and West. Thus we have more work south of the Smith and Wesson line, as we sometimes call it, than north of it, but we have had calls from all over the country.

How do we proceed? First we ascertain the nature of the complaint, to decide whether or not it is bona fide, whether there is a proper role, whether it is a case that should be undertaken. And then we proceed along several different lines of action.

We may refer the case to another federal agency or to a state agency. Only 19 states do not have a public accommodations law of some kind on the books, so we may refer a case to a state or local agency or even to a volunteer agency in a state that does not have a public accommodations law.

Sometimes we are even able to handle the matters by telephone. Sometimes we are able to call upon a very distinguished group of about 400 people that President Johnson appointed to our National Citizens Advisory Committee. They have been most valuable to us not only in the conciliation effort but also in terms of the effort to achieve a spirit of compliance within the nation.

There are other ways to handle complaints. We may send a field conciliator—although our table of organization calls for only seven field conciliators from our central office—or we may call upon an *ad hoc* conciliator.

We started out with names of 2,000 persons drawn from all over the country who have had experience in these kinds of matters and can be called upon to go into the communities as conciliators. We have whittled this list down gradually and given some specific on-the-job training or in-the-office training to about 25 of these people. They form our blue ribbon cadre of conciliators. We have referred a number of cases to these persons, asking them to go into the field to follow the matter through, make a report to us, and sometimes continue the follow-up until the case can be closed.

Our first business came from some fairly simple situations. We were able to handle them relatively easily, sometimes by telephone. But then, as more complaints were received, some came from the deep southern and hard-core states, and these were more challenging.

We have not yet been of much help in the big cities. We are attempting to build up a capable staff, and we may well be able to assist as our staff grows in competence and in experience.

The strength we bring to the conciliation process is the fact that we are housed in the Department of Commerce. Commerce is a nonthreatening federal agency. Commerce is associated with good business. Our being housed in the Department of Commerce is an asset because it allows us to go into communities in a nonthreatening, supporting way.

Another consideration which is a real help to us is the fact that the law requires in no uncertain terms that we conduct our work in confidence. It even provides that if we should reveal information obtained in a confidential interview and conciliation, we may spend a year in a federal prison.

221

Once you put this point across in a conciliation effort, you can persuade some of the most difficult persons to talk freely and to communicate with you about the real nature of the problem.

Therefore, it is my feeling that the Community Relations Service goes into difficult situations as a supportive federal arm which offers experts who are competent to help persons seeking to help themselves.

To date we have had six complaints concerned with employment and labor practices. We have had nine concerned with housing and real estate, four with law enforcement, 21 with public accommodations, four with public facilities, 13 with school desegregation and 18 with community tension and miscellaneous matters. There is some overlapping in these categories, so that the number does not add up to exactly 73.

We have closed nine cases after assessment and determination that there was no appropriate role for our agency. We referred eight cases to either state or other federal agencies. And 45 cases are under active conciliation activity. Nine have been closed out.

Some cases have been closed out successfully, some unsuccessfully. One of our early cases called us into a Southern city where a good deal of tension and picketing was being caused by *de facto* segregation in a local drive-in theater.

The theater management had built a fence down the middle of an outdoor theater. The admission on one side was $1.00 and the admission on one side was 50 cents. So the Negro community was picketing the theater, claiming that this was a segregation practice, and they wanted something done about it.

We sent in two field conciliators and on the very day that they arrived in this town, Hurricane Cleo, which had been lingering out in the Atlantic, turned inland. By the time Cleo had passed that afternoon, not a board of that fence was left standing. We thought this was a magnificent example of interoffice cooperation.

We are firmly convinced that there is a need for our agency. We have found that we can accomplish some things that perhaps no other federal agency can. I hope that we will develop a reputation as the repository at the federal level of expertise and skill that may be called upon to tip the balance. We have found that we can go into a community and move it toward compliance and some kind of community reorganization that will solve some of its human relations problems.

222

We have also learned how terribly important it is in civil rights matters that there be active and informed members of the local bar. We have faced situations in some states where the bar associations or the members of the bar have been reluctant to take cases involving civil rights—at least, the white members of the bar. We have been in some places where the members of the bar have actually been unwilling to stand up and be counted, even for law and order. Obviously this is a terrific handicap, an inexcusable one.

We have been in some places where the sheriffs were good and some where they were rednecks. We find that if our work is to be effective, it is imperative that there be mayors, police chiefs and sheriffs who at the very minimum will insist on law and order in their communities, whatever their sympathies happen to be in terms of civil rights.

We find, on the other hand, a great deal of strength across the country, even in some of the hard-core states. We find members of the bar who stand up to be counted, men who take cases from which there can come little fee money, if any. Certainly they risk the disapproval of their colleagues, their communities and perhaps even the courts before which they practice.

We find attorneys who give of their time and energy to move into some of the hard-core areas and represent clients who would not otherwise have their day in court.

The story of compliance is already gratifying. In some big cities, even in the South, we find 75 per cent compliance. In some small towns we find 100 per cent compliance in the matter of public accommodations. But there is still much to be done.*

5.12 THE OFFICE OF ECONOMIC OPPORTUNITY

JAMES A. MADISON†

Participation of enrollees in community activities is a desired objective of our community relations plan. We promote such activities, for we recognize the need to have Job Corpsmen practice their newfound social skills. In small communities we will be looking

---

* See the Annual Report of the Community Relations Service—Fiscal Year 1965 (March 1966; Supt. of Documents, U.S. Gov't Printing Office, Washington, D.C.).
† Of the United States Office of Economic Opportunity.

to them as a primary resource in our effort to establish Community Advisory Councils. We anticipate that these commissions will be invaluable, since they are abreast of the local community climate and temper.

In reference to the Office of Economic Opportunity programs, I stress that: (1) the program depends upon community initiative and (2) there are a number of autonomous agencies with which we must work to accomplish the aims of the Economic Opportunity Act. Following is a brief outline of the Act:

THE ECONOMIC OPPORTUNITY ACT

Joint Federal-State-Local Programs:

The Office of Economic Opportunity (OEO), an executive agency headed by a director reporting directly to the President, will have over-all administrative responsibility for programs under the Economic Opportunity Act.

However, participation at the local level in planning and operating the projects will be encouraged in all programs, required in most.

Each governor will have 30 days in which to give consent to proposed Youth Programs and Community Action Programs in his state.

A governor, by not acting within 30 days, may permit a project to begin.

A governor may expedite a project by giving his consent before the 30-day period is over.

Youth Programs:

The Job Corps:

Will enroll, in 1965 and 1966, up to 140,000 young men and women, ages 16 to 22, for up to two years' service in conservation and training centers.

The centers will emphasize basic education, skill training, and work experience.

Job Corpsmen will be recruited through U.S. Employment Service offices, schools, churches, settlement houses, public and private welfare agencies, boys' clubs, selective service boards.

Corpsmen will receive room, board, and travel allowances while in the Corps.

Upon completion of their terms, they will be allowed $50 for each month of satisfactory service.

Or, Corpsmen may contribute to their dependents $25 per month (to which the government will add another $25) and receive $25 for each month of satisfactory service when separated from the Job Corps.

The Neighborhood Youth Corps:

A work training program for unemployed young men and women, ages 16 to 22, in public service projects such as at parks, playgrounds, hospitals, and libraries.

Examples of work training include nurses', librarians', and teachers' aides; nursery school and playground attendants; hospital orderlies; assistant dietitians; mechanics' helpers; landscape assistants.

Projects will be developed by state and local governments, and by private, non-profit service and welfare organizations.

The agency developing the work training project will be responsible for recruiting the young people to work in it.

Up to 200,000 young people will be enrolled in the Neighborhood Youth Corps each year.

Enrollees will work and live in their own communities.

They will be paid wages based on local rates for beginners in similar work.

They will be encouraged to continue or resume their schooling.

Work Study Programs:

Will operate through, and be administered by, colleges and universities.

Will provide on-campus and off-campus part-time work for deserving students selected by participating schools.

Local Community Action Programs:

Locally planned, locally administered direct attacks on any poverty-promoting community problem.

Will require comprehensive community action plans, developed by local community action organizations which may be formed by government agencies, private non-profit agencies such as volunteer or civic groups, or a combination of public and private agencies.

Will emphasize programs designed to produce "a permanent increase in the ability of persons to deal with their problems without further aid."

Examples of such programs include job training, counseling, vocational rehabilitation, remedial education, home management, health improvement, family planning.

Federal government will bear up to 90 per cent of the cost during the first two years, 50 per cent thereafter.

Communities' contributions may be in cash, facilities, and services.

Participants in the Job Corps, Neighborhood Youth Corps, and Work Study programs will be available for work on community action projects.

Other Economic Opportunity Act Programs:

Grants and Loans to Combat Rural Poverty:

Will aid low-income rural families and migrant workers.

Will loan up to $2,500 to such families, payable within 15 years, for certain home and farm improvements, if they cannot obtain funds elsewhere.

Will provide similar loans for local marketing and purchasing cooperatives.

Through the Job Corps program we are including and giving advice to the very smallest of communities. This requires a considerable amount of educational work with the basic institutions in the community.

The Act provides specifically that a governor be given 30 days in which to consent to the location of a center in a particular place in his state. For that reason, when the proposals come in from the various departments, agencies, and contractors, the first thing we want to know is what kind of an educational program has been done in the community concerned to gain acceptance of the Job Corps project. To date, of the 42 sites announced, we have had two where the local opposition was generated by real estate interests who had speculated on the land in the vicinity.

The implication in the stated opposition was that Negroes would be included in the Job Corps. This is true. The Job Corps will be representative of a cross section of the United States. And as so often happens, the presence of Negroes is taken to mean that the prices of houses and lots for sale within anywhere from five to 15 miles are going to be affected.

So, we are doing educational work in these communities. We will be leaning heavily on the various civil rights commissions, committees, and private groups interested in our common objectives to assist in the education of the community so that they will provide not toleration, but support for these programs.

5.2   STATE HUMAN RIGHTS COMMISSIONS

5.21   THE WORK OF THE NEW YORK STATE COMMISSION

GEORGE H. FOWLER*

On March 12, 1945, the New York State Legislature enacted under bi-partisan sponsorship the first law against discrimination in the nation designed to assure equal opportunity in employment to all persons, regardless of race, color, or national origin.

The Commission now called the New York State Commission for Human Rights was established as this law's enforcement agency. In 1952, some seven years later, the law was amended to include under Commission jurisdiction the right of all persons to equal access to and utilization of places of public accommodation, resort, or amusement without regard to race, color, creed, or national origin.

In 1955 the first antidiscrimination housing law was enacted, assuring to all persons equal rights in the rental of specified publicly assisted housing accommodations. A year later, in 1956, this jurisdic-

---

* Chairman, New York State Commission for Human Rights.

tion was expanded to include housing accommodations receiving publicly insured financing, and in 1961 the housing section of the law was amended to include the sale or rental of all accommodations, except the sale of homes with fewer than ten contiguous units and the rental of apartments in owner-occupied three-family homes.

This amendment brought under the coverage of the law the activities of real estate brokers and financial institutions in housing and extended the Commission's jurisdiction to include commercial space.

In that same year, 1961, the age-in-employment factor was brought in to cover workers in the 40-to-65-year age bracket. In 1963 it was made an unlawful discriminatory practice to retaliate or discriminate against a person because he opposed practices forbidden under the law, or filed a complaint, or testified, or assisted in a Commission proceeding.

Another 1963 statutory amendment expanded the housing section of the law to cover all sales and rentals, excepting only rentals of apartments in owner-occupied two-family homes and the rental of rooms in an occupied house or apartment.

Finally, in that year a further amendment to the employment section of the law made it unlawful to select persons for state-registered apprentice training programs on any basis but objective criteria.

We started with employment and then went on to the places of public accommodation, resort and amusement, to housing, to age, and to apprentice training. What does all of this mean?

In my judgment it means from a philosophical point of view that the Legislature of the State of New York recognized that equality is indivisible, that you cannot assure to a person certain rights and deny him other rights and thereby, in effect, separate him from the mainstream of our democratic society. It means that it would be fruitless to permit a person to obtain employment commensurate with his skills and abilities and then deny him the right to housing accommodations which he can afford or the right to spend his leisure hours in the pursuit of relaxation enjoyed by others.

These rights are interrelated and intertwined and the denial of any one of them amounts to a denial of all, for freedom is indivisible.

You cannot call a person free if he is given the right to use both hands and one foot while the other foot is shackled to a wall of prejudice. A man is altogether free or he is not free.

228

The procedures provide for an aggrieved person to seek redress, as set forth in Sections 297 and 298 of the Executive Law of New York State. At the present time any person who believes that his right to equal opportunity has been denied in any of these areas may file a verified complaint with the Commission. The complaint may be investigated by one of seven commissioners with the assistance of the staff, who determine whether or not there is probable cause to credit the allegations of the complaint.

Should probable cause be found, the commissioner attempts to eliminate the discriminatory practice complained of through conference, conciliation, and persuasion. If these efforts fail, he must order the case for a public hearing.

A public hearing under our set-up is a quasi-judicial proceeding conducted by three members of the Commission, excluding the investigating commissioner. These three commissioners are appointed by the Chairman, who designates one as the Chief Hearing Officer. If the Commission finds at the public hearing, or if the three commissioners find that there is guilt, an order is issued to cease and desist and to take affirmative action to eliminate the cause of the complaint.

A complainant or respondent or any person aggrieved by such an order of the Commission may obtain judicial review of such order in the Supreme Court of New York State. Should the respondent ignore or violate the Commission's order, the Commission may seek a court order to enforce it. Any violation of such order may lead to contempt proceedings with the accompanying fine or jail sentence.

In all these proceedings the complainant need never incur one cent of the cost. The Commission's legal division represents him at all times.

A noteworthy example of this was a case in which the complainant alleged that he was denied equal opportunity to rent an apartment because of his color. The investigating commissioner found probable cause. A public hearing determined that an unlawful discriminatory act had occurred and the State Supreme Court sustained the order of the Commission. Some of the other tenants in the building acted as intervenors and challenged the constitutionality of the law. The ramifications of that case carried all the way up to the Supreme Court of the United States, but the Commission ultimately was victorious.

229

On all matters involved in the issue, the legal cost, which ran into the thousands, was borne throughout by the Commission. Even if the final result had been adverse, no court costs could have been assessed against the complainant.

Because of its preeminence in the field of human rights, the New York State law, which was the first of its kind to be enacted in the nation, has been serving continuously as the model for state laws today. Twenty-four other states now have equal opportunity laws with enforcible provisions modeled after the New York law.

The passage of the 1964 Civil Rights Act is a historic achievement in enforcing the equal protection clause of the Fourteenth Amendment. It is unlikely, however, that the federal law will be utilized to any great extent in New York State for various reasons. The first is that the New York State law is more comprehensive and in most areas, particularly in employment, our jurisdiction covers employers with as few as six workers.

The federal law, effective July 1965, covers employers with one hundred or more workers. This will be lowered in July, 1968, to cover employers of 25 workers.

The second reason for the limited use in New York State of the Federal Equal Opportunity Law is the fact that the legal cost to secure the rights of a complainant is borne by the State Commission for Human Rights, while under the federal law a complainant is left to his own resources in court, except for the discretion of the Attorney General to provide counsel. In the event of an adverse decision, the complainant, unfortunately, may be liable for his adversary's legal fees.

Throughout the two decades of Commission administration of state law, a vast body of interpretive law has been built up which runs to several volumes. This collection may have value as a quasi-precedent to a commission that will be set up to enforce the federal law.

These volumes make reference to Commission use of injunctions obtained through the cooperation of our local state attorneys general and local courts in forestalling the sale or rental of a housing accommodation until the Commission's final disposition of the complaint.

A case in point was a complaint by a man who had been denied the opportunity to purchase a home in Westchester County simply because he was a Negro. At the request of the investigating commis-

230

sioner the Attorney General's Civil Rights Bureau obtained an injunction against the owner, forbidding him to sell to anyone else until the complaint was thoroughly processed by the Commission. The case never went to a final determination because the owner agreed to sell.

This developing body of interpretive law is highlighted by the Commission's handling of a complaint by the Attorney General. This complaint charged that a union of sheet metal workers systematically excluded Negroes from membership, after being given an opportunity to qualify them for membership through the apprentice training program administered jointly by the union and the employer. In a public hearing the Commission found that such exclusion had been practiced throughout the union's 76-year history. One of the main obstacles for Negroes was the union's practice of nepotism in admission to the apprenticeship training program. After taking voluminous testimony in this landmark cease and desist order, the Commission asserted the right of all applicants for apprenticeship to be evaluated equally on the basis of objective criteria and ordered that the father-and-son pattern of admission to apprenticeship be abandoned. The respondent challenged the Commission's order in the court and the Commission moved to enforce the order. Under the terms of a consent order later entered into, the union has formed a new class of apprentices, and every applicant for that class has an equal opportunity to qualify regardless of race, creed, color, or national origin.

Decisions such as this serve to underscore the continuing progress in the area of human rights, but the Commission cannot and does not stand alone in furthering the cause of equal opportunity. It has the active support of vast numbers of people of all races and religions, people who are committed to the proposition that equal opportunity is inherent in the rights of all men throughout the state.

Advisory Councils to the Commission, composed of prominent citizens of the community, bring to the attention of the Commission local attitudes and activities in the field of human rights. They also serve the community by spreading information about the law, and the justice and morality that it guarantees.

It is through such Councils as well as the Commission's own educational program that communities are made aware that human rights laws help them to grow and prosper. All citizens are involved in the activities of furthering community progress.

231

In June, 1963, Governor Rockefeller sent a letter to the heads of all municipal governments urging the formation of local human rights commissions and assuring them that the State Commission for Human Rights would provide these agencies with advice and assistance. Almost fifty such commissions are now in existence and more are being formed.

The Commission also conducts police training courses. We have wonderful cooperation with the police officials here in New York City and in some other areas of the state. These training courses in every major community in the State of New York seek to provide information on both the letter and spirit of the law against discrimination, so that police officials at every level of responsibility can give correct and complete information about human rights when required to do so in the line of duty. Yet, much more needs to be done.

I have repeatedly urged that the practicing lawyer familiarize himself thoroughly with human rights laws. Lawyers have a responsibility to their clients to be able to interpret the law in relation to their individual rights or business practices. As officers of the court, lawyers are responsible for assisting in the enforcement of the law.

It may well be, that a body of law has been developed requiring the specialized practice of attorneys in this field. I am sure that with the passage of the first labor laws, few persons foresaw that someday a specialist in labor law would take his seat on the United States Supreme Court.

I believe the day has come, at least in New York State, when the emphasis of governmental agencies responsible for administering human rights law has passed from the educational phase to strict enforcement where conciliation has not been accomplished. Enforcement serves as a warning to violators that they cannot drive across the mainstream of American thinking.

No motorist can plead with a traffic policeman that he did not understand the meaning of the red light, and no violator of human rights can plead that he has been unaware that he has trespassed on the legal rights of others.

The State Commission for Human Rights will continue to use education in the community to foster acceptance of the law. It will continue to use education as a preventative against violations, but where the sociological approach fails to meet with compliance, the Commission will insist on a strict and creative interpretation of the law.

5.22 THE WORK OF THE KENTUCKY HUMAN RIGHTS COMMISSSION
GALEN MARTIN*

The Kentucky Commission on Human Rights has the responsibility of trying to eliminate all forms of discrimination, but has no enforcement powers and only three professional staff people to do this job. We are endeavoring to work within this framework, especially with the city commissions that are in existence.

We have 18 official city human rights commissions and four volunteer membership groups in other cities. Two of our cities have their own professional staff and we cooperate closely with them, but our primary interest is naturally in assisting those commissions without staff.

Compliance with the public accommodations law has been extensive. Kentucky cities are empowered to enact their own laws prohibiting discrimination in places of public accommodation, but so far only Louisville has enacted such an ordinance.

We have had a wide variety of experience with local commissions. Several of the 18 commissions are simply ineffective, and thus we would be better off without them. The key determinant of effectiveness of these groups is whether or not there is strong Negro leadership; they are not as likely to be effective where there is no local Negro leadership to encourage the commissions to act and to provide affirmative leadership.

We have worked particularly with the local commissions to try to get them to encourage compliance with the public accommodations section of the Civil Rights Act of 1964. Many commissions have invited local proprietors and others to involve themselves or have encouraged Negro groups to become involved in testing programs to see whether or not the establishments really are complying.

---

* Executive Director of the Kentucky Commission on Human Rights.

Our most extensive role with regard to municipalities has been in the communities without human rights commissions. We have found most of our problems in this area. Where there is an effective working group, few instances of discrimination occur, and if they do occur, they are taken care of through the efforts of a local group.

The complaints that come in to us are largely from areas without effective local groups. For instance, we have had one complaint from a town having only two restaurants to begin with. In this situation it would be pretty difficult to show a pattern of resistance to the federal law. One of the restaurants was already serving on a non-discriminatory basis. By the time our Commission had made three visits to the noncomplying restaurant and the F.B.I. had made three, we were able to secure a promise of compliance.

One respondent had refused to serve without discrimination before the Civil Rights Act, despite the efforts of both the local NAACP group and our Commission. This was one of the first places against which we received a complaint. The proprietor started off by telling me that the Federal Civil Rights Act did not apply in Kentucky because Governor Breathitt had not passed it.

We sent all 7,000 places of public accommodation in Kentucky a copy of the full text of the public accommodations section of the Civil Rights Act. We worked it into a "Memo to Managers." In addition to sending out the full text of the Act, we tried to answer some of the questions that had been raised by proprietors in our previous experience. We stated what was required of them, explaining that they must serve mixed groups and that they could not serve Negroes and turn away whites in the same group. We tried to explain the law to them with regard to serving disorderly persons and the other rules of their business.

I recently received a letter which may have been written in response to this memo. It suggested to me that maybe the towns that are changing are not encountering too much difficulty. The letter reads:

During the absence from my place of business of a regular employee, a temporary employee mistakenly declined to serve food to two Negroes on Tuesday, November 24. I had specifically instructed all regular employees that they should not decline to serve anyone who presented themselves in an orderly fashion.

234

This incident may be reported to you and immediately I want to assure you and your commission that I have taken all precautions and every measure now to see that there is no like occurrence in my place of business. If further explanation is required, please let me know.

We take this as a sign of encouragement in Kentucky. We had no contact with anyone in this small county seat of about 3,000. We know of no particular reason why this person decided to write us this kind of letter, but we are certainly encouraged that he did.

We in Kentucky have a continuing strong interest in obtaining a state law on public accommodations and employment. We made efforts in this direction in the last regular session of the General Assembly in 1964. We tried for a special session on public accommodations and we will try again during the regular session in 1966. We are painfully aware of the inadequacies of the new federal law. We are pleased that we have it, however, for we think that the federal law is our best hope. But we will continue to work for a state law, because we feel that every level of government carries the responsibility to eliminate discrimination and that the existing federal law continues to keep the primary burden on the shoulders of the aggrieved, who are less able to carry it and who should not have that responsibility in a democratic society. We are also concerned with the inadequate coverage of the federal law.

5.3 THE ROLE OF VOLUNTARY AGENCIES
SOL RABKIN*

The term "voluntary agency" covers a very broad gamut. It starts at one end with the Black Muslims and the tenants' councils in Harlem, and runs all the way to the National Association of Manufacturers. The latter Association has recently devoted a session at its annual Congress of American Industry to the need for employers to recognize the impact of the FEPC laws on their operations. They are smart to do this.

---

* Director, Legal Department, Anti-Defamation League of B'nai B'rith, New York.

Although the range of all such organizations is very broad, it is difficult to ascertain which is the best resource, because the NAM may be the best resource in one community, and the tenants' councils may be the best resource in another.

Most of the so-called "minority" agencies began as defense agencies. The NAACP began as an agency to defend Negro rights, as did the Urban League. Most of the Jewish agencies—the Anti-Defamation League, the American Jewish Congress, the American Jewish Committee—started as defense agencies created because the groups sponsoring them recognized that the government agencies which were supposed to be blind to distinctions of race or creed might not actually follow such a pattern, since they were a reflection of general community attitudes. Hence, there was a need to get those attitudes to jibe more closely with what our system of government called for.

The religious agencies are another group of major voluntary agencies. Jewish defense agencies, while stemming from Judaism, are not religious but rather are general community service agencies. In the case of the Christian agencies, the churches undertook to deal with civil rights problems because they were concerned with the need to implement the basic preachments of their faith, which taught the dignity of the individual, the value of each person, and the need to guarantee equality of treatment to preserve this dignity and value.

There were civic agencies that came into being because they recognized a gap between our democratic preachments and our practices. All these in a sense came together in the *Guidelines* pamphlet. Most of them joined to work together in large organizations, like the Leadership Conference on Civil Rights, which was one of the major contributing forces in bringing about the broadest federal civil rights law that had ever been adopted.

The size of the network of voluntary agencies is coextensive with the American population. The ADL has 26 regional offices, one in every major city in the country and some minor ones. The NAACP has offices all over the country. The Urban League has offices all over the country.

All these voluntary agencies have offices that serve large and middle-sized communities and they also have contacts that reach down into the rural areas. Even before any people were sent into Mississippi I suspect that there were voluntary agencies which had resources

236

in that state. But sometimes resources have to be employed very carefully, lest they be destroyed.

The voluntary agencies have these resources available to work with the public agencies in many other ways. What is their function? What can they do to help public agencies?

When our government set up a system for maintaining law and order and safeguarding individual freedoms as guaranteed in the Constitution, it sought to insure that the government would remain neutral between racial and religious groups, an arbiter insuring fairness. One function of the voluntary agencies is to act as a kind of starter to get the government moving to close the gaps between what the Constitution and our laws maintain are the rights of every individual, and what people really regard as the rights of others.

In this respect, for example, they have often served as starters of drives for needed civil rights legislation. The New York State FEPC law, adopted in 1945, came about because voluntary agencies recognized the need for some kind of legal protection of the right to equality in employment opportunity, and they began to agitate. Then a temporary commission was set up by the state legislature to hold hearings. The voluntary agencies, both local and national, appeared before this commission and submitted evidence to demonstrate the need for an FEPC law.

In addition to the Leadership Conference on Civil Rights on the federal front, the voluntary agencies serve various other functions. They can warn the public agencies of the development of situations that may lead to violence. They can also serve as a communications medium between the public agencies which enforce the laws and those groups whose rights are to be protected by that enforcement, but who may often feel that the protection is not sufficient. Thus they can help public agencies to anticipate trouble and head it off by applying the appropriate preventative. The voluntary agencies can also act as middlemen.

Every law enforcement agency operates within the community. Most local police departments recognize that an essential aspect of their activity is to keep in touch with the community they police. Many of the major police departments in the country have set up community relations divisions within the last eleven or twelve years because they have recognized the need to maintain relations with all

237

sections of the community. They need to create channels of communication that do not involve the man on the beat talking to people with whom he has contact but rather require thinking and planning communications on higher and broader levels.

These voluntary agencies can serve as the media for the community relations groups to work with the police departments and other human relations agencies. They can also maintain contact with the people and thus help overcome the inevitable distrust between the law enforcer and law enforcee, which includes everybody, not just criminals. An element of distrust develops between the person charged with the enforcement of the law and the person who may be complying with the law, but who even in a small way may not be sure that he wants to. In some ways the voluntary agencies can help minimize that kind of distrust.

One example of a middleman operation occurred in New Orleans. The Negro community was very unhappy about the fact that there was employment discrimination in most of the large stores in an area of New Orleans that served mostly Negro customers. One voluntary agency arranged for quiet discussions between the owner of one of the stores involved and representatives of the Negro community. The result was an agreement to abandon this pattern of employment discrimination. This action headed off plans that were being developed for mass picketing of these businesses and thus helped to resolve what might have become a crisis situation.

The voluntary agencies may also prove helpful in working with government leaders to head off the possibility of increased distrust of the police. For example, in Fort Worth the B'nai B'rith arranged for a civil rights training course for the police department which was attended by every sergeant and officer of higher level to discuss the role of the police and general law enforcement, as well as those laws involving the equality of protection. This came about because a Negro had been shot and killed by a policeman, which caused a great deal of resentment against the police in the Negro community.

The police training course that resulted was organized at the request of the Mayor of Fort Worth with the aid and financial support of B'nai B'rith. It resulted in eliminating this source of intercommunity friction by demonstrating to the entire community that the police in Fort Worth wanted to do a fair and honest job, and were doing everything they could toward this end, and were sensitive to

238

their responsibilities to treat every citizen decently, whether or not he was a member of a minority group.

There are all kinds of voluntary agencies on the job. Not all voluntary agencies have the money to pay for such a course. Because they have been in operation for many years, some agencies have experienced staff who have been working in this field for a long time.

Sometimes they also find time to sit down and develop a philosophy of operation. For example, one of the great difficulties in maintaining the successful operation of our democracy is to ensure that people have mutual respect for each other. It is such mutual respect and confidence that makes our system work.

The people who endanger our pattern are those who try to polarize our society—the radical left, the communists, and the radical right—who try to spread the notion that you cannot trust the police, that there is a conspiracy, that the people are the victims of an alleged conspiracy that is undermining the government. This kind of polarization may well make more difficult the job of the police in maintaining law and order.

The voluntary agency, by thinking ahead and recognizing these activities when they are still in the initial stages, can begin to educate the people to these dangers. The book, *Danger on the Right,* published by ADL, says, in effect, that there are people on the right who are good and well-intentioned, but there are also people who are doing the same thing on the right that the communists are doing on the left.

This book tries to point up the danger so that the people of our country and the law enforcement agencies will be aware of it. This is evidence of our thinking through a philosophy of operation and presenting it by educational means to the people.

5.4 PROBLEMS WITH BASIC COMMUNITY INSTITUTIONS

George Schermer*

Ultimately, racial harmony depends on the work done at the local level. We need the power, the law, the force and the support of the state and national governments. We need the understanding and

---

* Human Relations Consultant, former Executive Director of the Philadelphia Human Relations Commission and former Executive Director of the Mayor's Interracial Committee in Detroit.

support of industrial corporations and the national communications media, but the job itself must be done in the municipality and county. Community relations cannot be compartmentalized, and a single human relations committee or mayor's committee cannot affect a problem that requires all of the community's resources.

The basic institutions of the community, which include the local government itself, the police department, health and welfare agencies (both public and private), the courts, public, parochial and private schools, the local media of communications, business and industry, trade associations, the Chamber of Commerce, labor organizations and churches—are the primary local resources through which the problems of race relations, discrimination, and racial conflict must be managed, controlled, and resolved.

If these basic institutions are properly supported, responsibly led, capably managed, and committed to serving the needs of the entire community, including persons of all races and religious and ethnic groups, they can probably resolve most racial problems.

The problem is that in so many communities these basic institutions are *not* well supported, *not* alert to the racial problems and are poorly managed. In many cases the resolution of community racial problems depends on improving and reforming recurrent defects in these basic institutions.

For example, managers of particular institutions, whether they are the local police command or local school management, often respond to complaints about race relations by throwing up their hands and saying, "We're doing the best we can; we don't have jurisdiction." City Hall may refuse to meet a school problem because of this "lack of jurisdiction."

Though the schools may not be technically under the jurisdiction of City Hall, the people look to their elected mayor for responsible leadership, and will not understand or appreciate his denial of jurisdictional power. The community wants its elected officials to provide leadership as well as government.

Other problems arise in connection with municipal civil rights commissions. Some of these are empowered to administer and enforce statutes which prohibit discrimination in employment, housing, public accommodations, education and the like. Some have narrower juris-

240

diction relating solely to employment. Others are only advisory to the mayor, or paper organizations without any power. A mayor may respect and consult his committee, or he may ignore it and hope that it will not bother him. However, regardless of organizational structure, someone must have the ultimate responsibility.

The mayor may handle racial problems out of his own office and do it very capably. He may not feel that he needs an advisory committee. He can become the focus of the community relations program. A responsible and capable mayor usually can stay on top of the situation, and some of the best community relations programs have operated in this way. However, such a method does not institutionalize the operation. If a good mayor is replaced by a disinterested one, the entire program is upset. I think it is wise to institutionalize the operation by creating some sort of a permanent body.

Further problems may arise out of the competitiveness between state and municipal activities for improving community relations. An astute public administrator or executive of a human relations committee will see strength rather than weakness in an abundance of concerned groups.* An important requirement for wholesome community relations is the involvement and participation of the largest possible number of citizens and citizen organizations, both for the discussion and the implementation of the program.

Meaningful citizen involvement on a mass basis through a single organization, or even a few of them, is almost impossible. Most people will work with an organization with which they can identify in a personal way. They will join an organization because they think that it is unique and membership imparts to them a distinguishing individuality.

Not everyone will belong to the same civil rights organization; there must be a variety to serve the whims of the people. People lose interest if they feel there is nothing unique about an organization. At the same time, people want to feel that their particular organizations are effective and powerful and lend a sense of power by virtue of membership.

---

* There is an abundance of specialized agencies and services that deal with specific problems of race relations. For a listing of national private civic organizations, see GUIDELINES FOR THE FORMATION OF BI-RACIAL COMMITTEES by George Schermer, Anti-Defamation League of B'nai B'rith, New York, 1964, p. 58.

It is inevitable and essential, therefore, to have a great many organizations, but only those organizations that are effective will survive.

A degree of conflict among organizations need not be disquieting. This also is inevitable.

Effective programming for promoting equal opportunity, reducing tensions, and developing positive community relations requires an extremely broad range of services and skills. It is desirable, therefore, to have a number of organizations working on problems in order to reach the greatest possible number of people.

Many of these organizations have special skills, such as the legal defense capabilities of the NAACP, the ACLU, and kindred groups. Many times a government agency cannot initiate a defense case where a private group such as the NAACP can. The research and communication skills of such groups as the American Jewish Committee, the American Jewish Congress, the Anti-Defamation League, the National Conference of Christians and Jews, provide skilled resources that the astute public administrator will want to use.

All these are resources of which a locality ought to take advantage. However, these resources are limited. I have heard mayors say, "Well, we're working with the Urban League," or "The ADL has come in to give us a hand," and they think that is the answer. It is neither wise nor possible to turn a problem over to such a group, because it does not represent a cross section of the community. These are resources to be tapped, not to assume the tasks of responsible elected officials.

Questions arise as to when state commissions assume authority and what are their respective areas of jurisdiction. With the exception of a few big cities, a state commission that is adequately empowered under the law is better equipped to conduct regulatory functions. The only exceptions would be those instances in which the state is not doing the job well or where the city itself is in many respects a larger power than the state.

The control of conflict and the maintenance of the peace are local police functions. This is the traditional view and it has firm legal foundations. I suspect, however, that we will need to reexamine this over a period of time.

242

The local police should have the responsibility for preventing conflict, that is, for handling specific breaches of the peace which, if permitted to continue, could generate into larger public disturbances.

However, the experience of the summer of 1964 and previous occasions indicates that few local police forces are adequately manned or trained to control major outbreaks of violence. For that reason, we need specially trained, high mobile units of state police ready to deal with major disturbances. Local government and police officials should be conditioned to call for assistance in good time, rather than to feel that a request for assistance is an indication of local failure.

The community that can prevent an outbreak of general violence is very fortunate. For some years to come there will be the possibility of major outbreaks of conflict, and all our metropolitan communities will need adequate police forces for such emergencies.

5.5 QUESTIONS AND ANSWERS

Question: I think that in some areas of organizations giving technical assistance or with specialized skills—educational, legal, and so forth—this is obviously to be encouraged. On the other hand, however, we have organizations whose purpose is to be the focal point of power in terms of communicating to the public as well as representing the Negro community before government and interracial agencies.

I do not think that anything said is going to seriously affect the way these groups behave. But just in terms of general principles, do you think that we can apply the idea of the survival of the fittest, that somehow or other the most powerful, resistant, and effective ones will survive? And is it most helpful for the organizations themselves to seek a common ground and to become, at least before the public and insofar as the government is concerned, as much of a coalition group as possible?

MR. SCHERMER: There are no clean-cut answers to that question. It seems to me that one of the great challenges, one of the great problems we have to deal with in the 1960's, is the extent to which we actually can be a democracy in the sense of providing

243

opportunity for tremendous numbers of people to participate in decision-making, in the implementation of community decisions, and the like. We certainly are in an era right now where the question is not whether we want a multiplicity of organizations or not. We have them. A community organization has neither merit nor integrity unless it truly speaks for a group of people.

We have a tendency to treat each problem as it arises. At that point an organization tends to crystalize and leave a lot of people out. Somehow the other people will find a voice.

Invariably I see that the existing organization speaks for only a fraction of the people. There are tremendous numbers of other people who also want to speak but who cannot speak through that existing structure.

As an administrator, as a public official, I always saw the necessity of communicating with whatever organization sought to have a voice in the community. I think a public official ought to be realistic about that. Let us assume that in a given community the NAACP says that it has 20,000 dues-paying members, but the CORE chapter refuses to say how many dues-paying members it has. Perhaps we can assume that there are a few hundred.

I do not think that either organization has the right to say that it speaks for the whole of the Negro community. The NAACP chapter president speaks for 30,000 or 20,000 dues-paying members, period. CORE speaks for a few hundred.

I think each ought to have the right to speak and each ought to be heard. Each deserves courtesy and recognition, but the public administrator must always try to learn how many other voices there are in the community.

When groups like these present programs to the community as a whole, they, as well as the public officials, need to make an effort to discover a consensus. It is not important who speaks for how many. The administrator must weigh their statements against a fairly broad range of opinion in that particular racial or ethnic group and in the community as a whole.

The public administrator, the mayor, the police commissioner, the human relations executive—each needs to know that if he is really to reach and work with a large number of people in the community, he will have to work with a large number of organizations. There is no way out of it.

Question: Where you have many organizations with the same membership, and that happens in many cities, they have different identification labels for the same purpose.

Would you care to comment on the advisability of a total effort in this connection, or whether it should be discouraged?

MR. RABKIN: Actually, this is an extension of the same question. What we are really talking about is the function of the voluntary organizations as against the responsibility of public officials to deal with them.

Under our system, practically every popular movement really starts as a voluntary organization. The political parties are voluntary organizations. Even voting is voluntary. In some European countries you are fined for not voting, but in this country it is a voluntary act.

It seems to me that to talk about a multiplicity of organizations or the question of who speaks for whom is to ignore one basic distinction. First, a public official has the job of enforcing the law as he sees it, of carrying out his responsibility as a public official.

He should try to learn the impact of his job, so that he can do it as effectively as possible. He should consult with any voluntary organization that approaches him. He should be well aware of the fact that a larger organization like the 20,000-member NAACP may reflect the point of view of a larger portion of the community than a smaller organization, but he should also recognize the fact that even the size of the membership is not the proper standard to use. Some voluntary organizations consist of people who are interested enough to join an organization because they feel strongly about it, but there are a tremendous number of people who in terms of voluntary organizations or initiative do nothing. But they have feelings and they react. How do we know they react? Because we see the effects, like the white backlash which begins to operate when the people are about ready to vote, even though they do not belong to voluntary organizations.

245

When we begin to talk in terms of planning the operations of voluntary organizations, in terms of multiplicity of organizations, we begin to act as if we have not a democratic society but rather a society in which certain people at the top can begin to formulate plans. If there is a multiplicity of voluntary organizations, it is because the need for them is felt by some individuals.

I do not think that anyone can successfully take over control and eliminate the multiplicity. I think that people in the voluntary organizations, if they themselves recognize that they may be wasting energy in their multiple memberships, will do it themselves.

I do not think that we can talk about voluntary organizations in social planning terms. Voluntary organizations by their essence *are* voluntary, and when we begin to talk about controlling and combining them, I think we are talking in contradictions.

Frankly, it would be nice if we could plan and control everything rationally. A democracy is an inefficient way of operating in terms of the amount of output that you get from the input, but it is a technique that allows the maximum amount of freedom, despite the waste of energy. I think we should continue to operate democratically, particularly by means of voluntary organizations. This is why I think the kind of question which asks whether we organize and control democracy really is not meaningful. Even if we succeeded in eliminating a multiplicity of voluntary organizations in one area, two months later that multiplicity would be back because the people feel that these various organizations must exist to reflect their points of view.

Question: In our State of Minnesota we have two very distinguished and able types of public agencies, regulatory agencies enforcing antidiscrimination laws, and the public agencies that are primarily educational and social but non-regulatory. We feel that at the state and municipal level these two agencies are separate and distinct.

In your experience with this type of public agency around the country, is this the best or preferred kind of arrangement, over and above combining these two functions of education and regulation in the state agency, either at the local or state level?

MR. SCHERMER: This is not the first time that question has come up. I have been doing some research in the area to see if I could discover an answer. The evidence is not in yet. As a matter of logic, it would seem unlikely that a strong regulatory agency can also be a community relations agency. This was the reason why under the Civil Rights Act the Community Relations Service was put into the Department of Commerce and why the Equal Opportunity Commission is to be a separate and independent agency, administering the fair employment phases of that law.

The fact is, though, that some of the most effective agencies in the country, state or local, have combined powers. I speak with a little bias because I have always thought that our Philadelphia Commission is a very effective agency. It has administrative powers; it administered a fair employment law; it now administers a fair housing law. It is also a very effective community relations agency.

I did find in that situation that we tended to swing like a pendulum. One year the emphasis would be on compliance and enforcement and we would underplay community relations. In another year we would feel that community relations were more important and that area received greater emphasis. This resulted to a considerable extent because of inadequate resources.

An agency with adequate resources and competent divisional heads in community relations and compliance activities certainly can do a better job than two separate agencies with inadequate resources.

It is my impression that if a state agency has adequate resources, it will do a better regulatory job than a municipal regulatory agency. By the same token, a state agency suffers limitations in community relations work at the local level.

There are so many ways in which you can divide up this function. I think that we are far from having established a body of experience which says precisely this or precisely that is the better method.

Question: What efforts are being made by any intergroup relations official or agency to get available information about organizations that are either advocating or aiding and abetting segregation and discrimination, like the John Birchers?

MR. RABKIN: This is one of the reasons that I mentioned the book *Danger on the Right*, which has a chapter on the John Birch Society and accumulated information on the radical right organiza-

247

tions. This information is not given in terms of segregation as such. For example, the book does not have a chapter on the white citizens councils, because that information is contained in another book that was published last year, but certainly such material is available. One problem, of course, is that the information is not filed officially, so it must be obtained in various indirect ways. Therefore, you cannot get a complete rundown. You cannot get an official financial report, for example.

All the book gives you is an estimate based on what information can be accumulated by the private agency. Research Associates is another agency which is compiling information on this kind of problem, and this is available.

I would like to state that we have had cases which directly involved the white citizens councils, but we had to be convinced that the cases disclosed some kind of discrimination in employment or in one of the areas in which we operated.

I know of three or four cases, for example, similar to this where applications for membership in a white citizens council have been distributed among employees of a firm. We will take jurisdiction to handle this type of case, because we feel this is a form of aiding and abetting that is contrary to the laws regulating employment.

We have had similar cases dealing with advertisements. In one interesting case near Pittsburgh a person published a magazine in which an advertisement would not actually say, "Do not list your house for sale with anyone except the people on this sheet." But in every other way he made it clear that unless his subscribers listed their houses for sale with those particular people, they would be subject to the provisions of our law. It was on that basis that our Attorney General permitted us to put an end to that kind of advertisement. The Civil Liberties Union might have objected, but it is right in our law that any kind of advertisement that either directly or indirectly causes persons to act in a particular way is illegal. That is the rationale that a public agency can take in dealing with the white citizens councils and other groups provided there is a direct relationship between those councils and the kind of work we are supposed to do.

MR. SCHERMER: I would think from the point of view of public agencies, particularly at the municipal level where community relations gets greater emphasis, that if a commission is reasonably well staffed and financed, it ought to have what I call an intelligence operation to keep itself fully informed about the groups in the community, both the legitimate groups and the suspect groups.

You need to know what is going on. You should be familiar with every organization that operates in your community whether openly or secretly. You should know its leadership, its activities, its connections, and so forth.

It is easy to develop a cloak-and-dagger complex in this business. A lot of people like to function in terms of a conspiracy theory of history. They are persuaded that prejudice and discrimination are brewed by these secret groups. Actually most happenings in this country are the result of stupidity or clinging to ancient, conventional, and respected norms.

I would say that 75 per cent of our problem is caused by the respectable people in the community. So this cloak-and-dagger idea of spying around for secret groups will serve no purpose.

MR. FEILD: Mr. Bernhard, do you want to comment on this, inasmuch as the U.S. Commission's function has been enlarged to the clearinghouse area now?

MR. BERNHARD: It really has not been tried. I have the feeling that it would not be an unlawful act on the part of the U.S. Commission on Civil Rights to question organizations which show themselves to be operating in an unlawful manner where they are disrupting a community. I think it might be a good effort on the part of some state governors or their local component parts to have even some of the private groups write and ask for this information. You might get some interesting results if you asked for this information.

Question: I would like to suggest, and I hope that this idea is growing, that the police departments themselves become increasingly aware of dissent- and tension-producing organizations. Both Detroit and Minneapolis have full-time department heads on duty so that when a call comes in for community protection, they already have people out looking at the various forces and organizations in the community capable of stirring up racial unrest or racial divisiveness. Whether or not there is an implicit or immediate violation of the law at hand, they are there.

This method is being discussed by chiefs of police. They are sharing their experiences, and this sharing becomes very helpful to the public and useful to all agencies, private groups, and public groups. It also serves as a very helpful adjunct to the kind of question that was just asked.

MR. RABKIN: That last comment makes me wonder whether we might not be playing with a double-edged sword. I like to think the police departments should know every possible incipient, subversive operation, but the trouble with that is that it is sometimes difficult to determine what is an incipient, subversive operation as contrasted with one dealing in honest controversy. Suppose this is a new group that is just pushing an unpopular concept.

Once you have the police undercover operator involved, how can you be sure that he will not destroy the right of the organization to operate, the right of association, and the civil liberties of the persons involved?

So, as I listen to this, it sounds good, but on the other hand I begin to worry about it. I think we should keep in mind that before we take any action, we must decide that this is a necessary and desirable police function.

Question: I think that one thing Mr. Schermer fails to realize is the very simple fact that the Negro is just coming out from under a hundred years of oppression. As a result, I think he is not only beginning to realize that the American community owes him something but he is also beginning to develop an ability to sympathize with other Negroes throughout the country in all the different situations in every community in America. There is bound to be a difference of opinion as to which direction to take. A great deal has been contributed by the resources available to the leadership in each community. The Negro is totally segregated in employment, he is segregated in housing, he is segregated in schools, and in my opinion it is an awful presumption on Mr. Schermer's part to think that all this is not going to result in a multiplicity of organizations and leaderships.

Attempts will be made by the NAACP and attempts will be made by CORE to represent the Negro community because first, there is an awareness of the problem, especially in the Negro community which represents the lowest sociological scale of the ladder, and second, the predominant feeling among Negroes is to emphasize sympathy with a community.

I think that the NAACP, CORE and the Urban League realize that they do not speak for the entire Negro community. I think they do speak for the majority of the Negro community, because their problems are common. If you act on the assumption that because of multiplicity of organizations and because of the difference of direction by these organizations, there is not a tone of cohesiveness, you are terribly mistaken. If you assume that because of multiplicity no progress is going to be made, you are mistaken again.

MR. SCHERMER: I thought I was emphasizing the inevitability and the importance of working with a multiplicity of organizations. This is a matter of reality in this day and age, so I see no difference of opinion between us.

Question: I think there is a need for clarification of terminology, especially in the protest area where a neutral is not clearly defined for the police, delinquency is not defined, where children participate in a demonstration, and other terms simply are not clear. I think you need more clarification of the roles of organizations, whether they are advocates or mediators. What research projects currently are being conducted at universities and by various commissions which undertake to study either the protest movement or the broad range of human rights commissions?

MR. BERNHARD: There are a proliferation of groups that have programs to research this question. As I understand it, the U.S. Commission on Civil Rights is attempting to do something in the area of both biracial groups in various communities and some of the protest groups, although it may be limited to the former.

251

There are continuing projects going on in terms of research as to delinquency. The present Committee on Juvenile Delinquency is about ready, I think, to issue another report on the various standards of delinquency. They should be contacted.

A new effort is being made by the U.S. Commission on Civil Rights to collect this type of information as soon as it comes out from independent research groups, from universities and colleges, from all the federal governmental agencies. If you were to direct a question involving clarification on existing research to the Commission, I think you would be most apt to get a broad response.

MR. FEILD: I think utilizing the U.S. Commission on Civil Rights for information in this area is an excellent suggestion. They have improved their staffing a good deal and they can help you more directly than was formerly the case.

MR. ERIC POLISAR :* I would like to make two brief comments, one in view of the fact that there are a great many law enforcement officers here. I call your attention to a fascinating dichotomy that has emerged in this discussion. When the discussion focused on problems of demonstrations, it veered only between whether the demonstrator should be arrested or other forms of control were desirable and possible, but not whether or not the law should be enforced.

I think there was consensus on this. When the discussion turned off, however, to the work of human relations commissions, we suddenly veered into a tack called education, conciliation, and persuasion. This, I submit to you, is a fascinating dichotomy which requires a little more thought than we have thus far given to it.

In one area we are quite clear-cut in our determination to enforce the law. In another area, although the law is equally comprehensive and equally strict, at least in terms of the way in which it is written, our approach is that this is a problem in the hearts and minds of men. Somehow it becomes a problem of persuasion rather than of law enforcement.

---

* Associate Professor and Extension Specialist, New York State School of Industrial and Labor Relations, Cornell University.

In addition I would like to call attention to this dichotomy again —particularly that of the law enforcement officers—to endorse most enthusiastically the determination made by Chairman Fowler of the New York State Commission that they are going to deemphasize somewhat the sociological approach, as he described it, and become an enforcement agency, as the law under which they operate empowers them to. I would also submit that this would have a salutary effect on the educational and conciliatory process as well.

In other words, if you enforce the law in one case, you will be able to conciliate elsewhere much more quickly and expeditiously.

Let me suggest that if, as of today, every state instead of only 24 had mandatory antidiscrimination statutes, and if as of the day after tomorrow, discrimination were completely obliterated and there were no need for statutes whatsoever, you would still have a major problem concentrated among Negroes, Puerto Ricans, and members of other minority groups simply in terms of their background, economic opportunity and training. The legal approach or the approach through legal institutions is itself inadequate to deal with as fundamental a problem as the one we are attempting to deal with today.

Question: I am a private practitioner here in New York City. I was very much disturbed by the genesis of some of the comments here. For instance, from what I heard, I thought we were heading back to the '30's with strike-breaking and so forth, but today we have to demonstrate in terms of the many facilities that deny service to people purely for reasons of their own and we have to break that up. I heard a discussion of whether or not it was better to arrest the leader or not and the tactical advantages in either case.

I heard a discussion over whether it is better to get a civil injunction or a criminal injunction. Then someone wondered if it is better for the Bank of America to get its own injunction or make a citizen's arrest or whether the police should make the arrest on the outside.

I found this really very shocking.

I am also disturbed by the attitudes of the human relations commissions. I feel that they are missing one very important point.

253

I feel it is also their function to find what they have bliss-
fully called the responsible leadership in the Negro community.
I do not believe that it is their function to take refuge behind
the excuse that this particular group coming to us is not
responsible, or that particular group coming to us is not responsible, and therefore they must actively look for consensus. I do think it is a function of the human rights commissions to go into the community and to organize and to help
to organize action groups. I am not discussing action groups
who will lie down in front of stores, because this is being very
well taken care of, but in terms of the people who cannot take
part in this kind of demonstration but very much want to
participate in their communities and just do not know how.

I think this is a facet of the work of rights commissions,
of local community organizations, of state and city operation
which has not been touched on. I think it is a major failing
on the part of these commissions, who generally are fat cats
sitting back and waiting to see what they can do if somebody
puts enough pressure on them. What do you feel about these
kinds of activities that should be undertaken by state or city
agencies or not at all?

MR. RABKIN: As a voluntary agency I say that I think we
would be unhappy if public agencies which were supposed to enforce
laws suddenly also undertook the job of creating action agencies
outside of the law. I certainly think that the job of the public agency
is to enforce the law. One of the points that I have tried to make with
the New York Commission is that it should stop being a judicial
agency and start being a police agency.

What has been happening is this: When they started in '45 they
feared that if they enforced the law vigorously, they might well be
faced with some kind of revolt. They decided to sell the law by
education instead of enforcement. They sought to convince employers
that the law would not interfere unduly with their hiring practices.
They avoided public hearings, stressing conciliation.

They did a good job of selling the law in this fashion. Once they
had it sold, they failed to realize that they no longer had to continue
to keep selling it.

254

I happen on occasion to wear a hat as a member of the Civil Rights Committee of the New York County Lawyers' Association. Two years ago a subcommittee of that committee met with the Chairman of the State Commission to discuss what was wrong with the way in which the Commission was operating. We came up with a report suggesting that the first step was for the Commission not to view itself as an educational or judicial agency, but to operate as a law enforcement agency. Second, in order to meet this need, we said, "Separate the function of investigation from your function of adjudication."

Just a few months ago this report was approved by the Board of Directors of the New York County Lawyers' Association, which is not a radical group. Chairman Fowler got in touch with the Chairman of our committee, Whitney North Seymour, Jr., and said, "You know, I like your report. We like it, we studied it." On December 9 the subcommittee which originally was responsible for the report discussed with Chairman Fowler, how he could implement these recommendations administratively rather than legislatively.

There is an awareness of this problem. There is an awareness on the part of the New York State Commission, which for a long time has been the bellwether of the educational or judicial approach as contrasted to the enforcement approach, and something is beginning to happen. Of course, I think it is long overdue.

I listened to Chairman Fowler discuss that Sheet Metal Worker Union case. I thought that it was a wonderful success, except that it was ten years too late. Connecticut did the same thing with respect to an electrical workers union about eight years ago.

New York should have done it a long, long time ago. I am glad that it has been done at last. But this, too, was part of the pattern of temporizing on the tough cases because it might make some people mad and taking the easy cases and operating on a basis of selling itself to those it was supposed to police.

I think it would be disastrous if state agencies which are charged with enforcing the law against discrimination began to set up action groups to needle them to do the job which they have been doing without needling. This would destroy the essence of our whole legal system, which is that even the policeman on the beat has to enforce the law. Certainly, but he must be neutral in enforcing the law and

255

not allow himself to be affected one way or the other. If a law enforcement agency undertook to create action groups to needle it to do its job, it would lose its neutrality.

That is the job of citizens, of volunteers, of people who have enough get-up-and-go, and too few people have that. The trouble must be solved by the people with drive, not by asking state agencies to do the job for them. I think that is the road to disaster. In our democracy this work must be voluntary, not by state agencies.

MR. MARTIN: I certainly can say for Kentucky, where we are not an enforcement agency, that we do see it clearly as our responsibility to help locate, motivate, and strengthen local leadership, especially in those areas of the state where isolation of the Negro is staggering and overwhelming.

The complaints that we have received did not come from strangers, they came because of the contacts that we had established with people who were in a position or had been in a position or who might get into a position to file a complaint with us.

It is not so much that we are trying to encourage people to drive us to do what we are supposed to do. We are trying to work with them, to help them to file complaints with us or with other agencies in the areas where experience shows that we cannot function effectively. We try to help people, especially those in isolated situations, to file complaints so that we can then move in to do the job that we are supposed to do.

COMMENT: One concept has disturbed me. As a Director of the Commission Against Discrimination in Minnesota, if I were to sit and listen to many of those city officials and municipal officials who spoke, I wonder whether I would be a part of the "we" or a part of the "they."

I think that somewhere along the line we had better realize that it is in our enlightened self-interest to work with people who are upset about their second-class citizenship. This will aid the general good health of the community. With reference to methods of dealing with people, how to pull a strike, etc. which was mentioned earlier, I am not nearly so much concerned with how to break a strike or demonstration as I am with how to eliminate discrimination and give people freedom so that there will be no need for demonstrating.

5.6 USES OF THE MASS MEDIA*

Many government officials and civic leaders underestimate the task of communicating with the population. The most common error is to believe that "quiet, behind-the-scenes action" is better than open public debate and that it is safer to have word passed along through "responsible channels" such as cooperating organizations.

Actually, the informal channels of communication are extremely unreliable. The only reliable way to reach an appreciable number of people is through the press, radio and television. If factual information is regularly carried to the public through the media, the committee members and cooperating organizations are aided in their role as interpreters. Without the mass media, only a few of them will command attention.

Communicating as much as the local press and broadcasting media will carry with integrity is the wisest possible course, and the most efficient method of reaching the public. Those who fear that telling the public the facts of the situation and what is going on will stir up tension and possible conflict should know that misunderstanding, suspicion, and unlawful conspiracies fester in a vacuum. If a community is unaccustomed to public discussion of racial issues it is possible, of course, that there will be a stormy verbal response when the process is first introduced. This will normally be constructive since it will serve as a safety valve for those tensions that have been seething beneath the surface. Once the community becomes accustomed to having the facts publicized and the issues debated in the open, the process will become commonplace and the danger of physical violence is reduced.

It is important, however, that the local mass media should themselves be responsibly managed and that the agency, public officials, and civic leadership learn how to work with and through the media toward constructive ends.

The Philadelphia Commission on Human Relations sponsored a seminar on The Mass Media and Intergroup Relations in 1961. The managing editors and station managers of all the principal news-

---

* This and the two following sections (pp. 257-260) are reprinted from *GUIDE-LINES: A Manual for Bi-Racial Committees* by permission of the Anti-Defamation League of B'nai B'rith, 315 Lexington Ave., New York, New York.

papers and radio and television stations met with representatives of civil rights and human relations organizations, and engaged in completely candid conversations over a period of several weeks. The two groups then jointly issued this set of useful "guidelines."

5.61 SUGGESTED GUIDELINES FOR NEWSPAPERS, RADIO AND TELEVISION STATIONS

1. The city's newspapers and radio and television stations can be powerful instruments for helping to create a climate of opinion where understanding and harmony can flourish. They have a key role in informing the public of the problems, the issues and developments of intergroup relations. In time of intergroup tension, conflict or violence, they have a responsibility to inform the public and to do everything in their power to help contain violence.

2. In "hot" racial or intergroup incidents, "flash" or "bulletin" reporting may stimulate crowd formations and wider tensions. When there is a danger of increasing tensions, such as in the case of a Negro family moving into a hitherto white neighborhood, it may be advisable to wait until the move has been effected and the family settled before carrying the story. Announcing the move in advance may invite the presence of hoodlums and trouble makers. Similarly, the obvious presence of numbers of reporters or cameramen can excite exhibitionist crowd behavior or create greater disturbance. On the other hand dangerous rumors and tensions can fester and spread in an informational vacuum. Objective, factual reporting is the best antidote to false and dangerous rumors.

3. An understanding of the issues and developments of intergroup relations is crucial to the welfare of the nation and community. "Depth" or "background" reporting of intergroup news should be used to present both sides of the issues and get at the factors behind news events. Such reporting may help to prepare the public for positive social changes and minimize tension and conflict.

4. Care should be used in identifying persons by race, religion or national origin. Such labelling is sometimes necessary, however, to give sense to the story. The value of labelling criminals at large by race to aid in their apprehension is always questionable. Labels

should never be used except when other identifying characteristics are also reported. There is no justification for labelling in news stories after a suspect has been apprehended.

5. Negroes or other racial, religious or nationality groups should be treated as integral parts of the American scene. Their social functions, church sermons, and achievements warrant publication whenever "news judgment" would dictate coverage if the people involved were not of minority groups.

6. In reporting cases of altercation between citizens and law enforcement authorities both sides of the story should be carried.

7. Professional bigots and hate-mongers depend on publicity for an audience. They obtain followers and income from notoriety. Such rabble-rousers may profit if given a free forum through the news media for their propaganda. Incidents involving such bigots may merit concise and objective news coverage but "advance" coverage usually contributes to the stature of such persons and their ideas. (Care should be taken in applying the term "bigot" or "hate-monger." The term "bigot" might properly be applied to a person or group which seeks to advance itself by generating hostility or hate toward particular religious, ethnic, social class or political groups. There is likely to be little attention to issues or to documented fact and extreme resort to falsehood, innuendo and half truth.)

8. "Depth" reporting in the form of exposés of extremist movements may serve a valuable function in informing the public of the significance of such groups.

5.7 SUGGESTED GUIDELINES FOR INTERGROUP RELATIONS AGENCIES

1. Intergroup relations agencies should communicate with and confide in the mass media by anticipating events, briefing the media with facts and background material and suggesting how the events could be handled. Constructive criticism is also welcomed by the media.

2. Agencies should avoid giving the impression of having special axes to grind. They cannot expect all intergroup relations activities to be reported.

259

3. Intergroup relations agencies should familiarize themselves with what is regarded by the media as news and should present their materials in clear, simple language, avoiding technical terms and jargon.

4. Agencies should be prepared to furnish to the media pertinent quotations on the issues they want reported. Utilization of well-known persons in the community will help draw the desired attention. Agencies can alert the mass media to good material (speeches by prominent personalities, picture subjects, etc.).

5. Since some of the media warn that they cannot be committed to treat off-the-record material as such, agencies must use their judgment in releasing For Your Information items. In many cases agencies may find they can send out general material without spotting a particular incident.

6. Agencies can interpret to the community and to their constituencies the limitations and opportunities of the media in publicizing intergroup relations programs, activities, personalities and events.

Part VI

SUMMARY

David Stahl*

6.1 ENFORCEMENT OF CIVIL RIGHTS LEGISLATION

When the first antidiscrimination ordinances and statutes were adopted back in the late '40's or the early '50's, they probably could not have been enacted unless the emphasis had been, as it was, on education, conciliation, and negotiation rather than on strict enforcement of the law. We realize now that when you enforce a law against unlawful affray or against riot or any of the other laws that have been utilized in connection with demonstrations, you must also enforce a law that prohibits discrimination in employment and in public accommodations.

We have to remember the history of how the antidiscrimination legislation was passed. For example, I recall the situation in Pittsburgh in 1953 when we enacted one of the first fair employment practices ordinances in the nation. If the emphasis then had been on fines and jail sentences rather than on education and conciliation, I doubt that the ordinance would have been adopted.

Certainly the emphasis is different now. I think we are approaching the time when enforcement will be accepted just as automatically as if we were to enforce a law prohibiting discrimination against people engaged in union activity.

---

* PLI Forum Chairman.

261

6.2 DEMONSTRATIONS

When we discuss the problem of demonstrations, we are neither discussing nor trying to find methods of suppression. We are trying to find ways in which those participating in demonstrations can be given the full scope of their constitutional right to express their protest while at the same time we can provide protection not only to the public at large but also to the very persons who are demonstrating. Thus their safety will be assured. We have had a number of examples in various cities where additional training on the part of the police, additional recognition on how to handle demonstrations on the part of municipal officials, would have been helpful both to the public at large and to the demonstrators who were trying to express their views.

The following strategies have been suggested in dealing with demonstrations—that is, dealing with them in the sense of trying to help both the demonstrators and the public to preserve law and order—

6.21 COMMUNITY TENSION ALERT

Mr. Schermer's *Guidelines* talks about maintaining a constant alert. It is a good technique to have a municipality maintain an alert for possible trouble which could cause incidents, with the police, human relations commission personnel, and others in the governmental and community framework trying to find sources of trouble.

A good example of this, if I may refer again to my own community in Pittsburgh, occurred after the New York, Rochester, and New Jersey problems during the summer of 1964. The Pittsburgh Human Relations Commission, in cooperation with the police, maintained a tension alert system, on-the-street detective work, to see where trouble spots were developing. I understand there were incipient incidents that might have led to further trouble, but they were nipped in the bud by this kind of constant alert system.

6.22 POLICY GUIDELINES ON DEMONSTRATIONS

It is important to have a fixed policy for dealing with demonstrations or other forms of protest and to have clear instructions from the head of the municipality, the mayor, or other head, to the police and to the human relations agency. The policy might be divided into several parts:

(1) The legal policy, handed down by the city attorney, should clearly delineate both the legal rights of those who want to protest, and the limits of the right to engage in direct action.

(2) There should be a policy for dealing with the particular manifestations of direct action, where discretion may be exercised. For example, in some municipalities, if there is a sit-in or an attempt to block traffic as a means of expressing protest, the policy may be to arrest immediately those who are engaging in this action. In other cities a number of police officials take the position that they can better avoid trouble by rerouting traffic.

The discretion we are talking about is in the legal steps taken to control demonstrations. The importance of a clearly delineated policy is that you have instructions from the top as to how this discretion should be exercised. Where there is such an area of discretion, it may be possible to preserve the public peace and at the same time allow full play to the expression of protest.

For example, you may have demonstrators entering and conducting sit-ins in public buildings. Certainly such action has an element of illegality, but many municipal and state officials have avoided the problem by actually providing facilities for those who are sitting in to be more comfortable, and permitting them to remain there for a reasonable period without utilizing the extreme power of the law to compel immediate departure on the pain of instant arrest.

When you decide that arrests have to be made, and this may be an unpleasant prospect, the decision should be made firmly and clearly so there will be no uncertainty or misunderstanding on the part of either the police or those engaged in the protest as to where the police will draw the line. This kind of communication is helpful to all parties. If the demonstrators believe the police are exceeding their legal powers, they have a basis for seeking judicial relief. In addition, violence can be minimized or avoided when the police indicate clearly when and how they will act.

6.23 POLICE TRAINING

It is also important to discuss the need for training police to recognize and respect the techniques of passive resistance and nonviolence.

In other words, it should be made clear to the police that when a demonstrator goes limp and has to be dragged off the street, this may be his way of expressing the theory of passive resistance. He should not be suppressed by the excessive use of force.

Unfortunately, in some demonstrations it has not seemed entirely clear to the police whether it actually was passive resistance when a demonstrator went limp or refused to cooperate in being removed. If the police understand, through their training and through communication with the civil rights groups, what is being done, physical violence may be avoided.

Equally important is the selection of stable police officers and human relations commission personnel to be on the street to deal with these problems. Trained, stable, unprejudiced personnel can deal with these problems much more capably. It is a good idea to have human relations commission personnel right on the street with the police when problems arise.

6.24   DETENTION FACILITIES

Another important point in the general discussion of demonstrations is planning ahead for proper detention facilities. I can attest to this need from my experience in the investigation of the Chester demonstrations. If arrests ultimately have to be made and there are no proper detention facilities, that lack creates an entirely needless problem and generates additional ill feeling which only makes it more difficult to correct the underlying causes.

So, if large-scale arrests are even remotely anticipated, it is well to know how proper detention facilities will be provided. In Chester, unfortunately, an empty garage had to be put in use to take the overflow of those who were arrested. I am not discussing the propriety of the arrests. I am discussing a realistic situation where you fail to provide proper detention facilities to take humane and proper care of those persons who are arrested pending release on bail.

6.25   LINES OF COMMUNICATION

Effective communication is essential not only before a demonstration but also during the conduct of protest activities. When trouble develops, the police and human relations commission staff should be in constant touch with the demonstration leaders to try to keep the protest within legal and peaceful bounds.

The essence of good community relations is that a very large percentage of the population knows and understands what is going on. Tension and fear generate in a vacuum of noninformation. There is a major challenge to anyone working in this field to bring the mass media into participation. That is not easy. In many communities, the mass media are more or less captive of one viewpoint or another and tend to misinterpret the information. But this is a part of the job: bringing the mass media into a role of telling the facts, relating them with integrity, and making sure that the whole community is as fully informed as possible.

6.26 CHARGES OF EXCESSIVE USE OF FORCE

The most desirable approach in police operations would be to bend over backward and to exercise the discretionary legal limits to avoid the use of force.

What is the excessive use of force? When a group of us were investigating the charges of excessive force in Chester, Pennsylvania, the first thing we did was try to determine what the law is. The law is deceptively simple.

A policeman may use as much force as necessary to carry out his duties. What does that mean? We concluded there is a considerable area of discretion. We also concluded that when you are dealing not with criminals, not with escaping felons, not with persons who are violating conventional criminal laws, but rather with people who are willing to risk arrest and hardship, fines and jail sentences, then you should use a different standard to determine when force may be used. You should use force only as a last resort, if at all.

In order to act promptly on claims of police brutality, it is a good technique to try to track down such charges as they happen or as they are reported, even while the protest activity is taking place. Whether or not the charge appears to be unfounded, it is well to investigate immediately and impartially. It is most difficult to resort to hindsight and to investigate a charge of police brutality weeks and months after the incident happened.

The subject of use of force again suggests the subject of proper police training. Certainly the growing emphasis of the International Association of Chiefs of Police, state police, and local police organizations throughout the country on human relations training reflects a recognition of the problem. Perhaps soon we will no longer have to caution against using untrained police because, hopefully, all police officers will receive training in this important area.

We found in Chester that other municipal employees were pressed into service when the police could not muster sufficient forces due to personnel shortages or long hours on demonstration duty. This is a questionable device, to use refuse collectors or other municipal employees for police purposes, western style, by deputizing them in an emergency.

6.27 REPORTING AND INVESTIGATION

Finally, with respect to demonstrations, it is essential that a complete, detailed report be made by every official, by the police, and by the human relations personnel present or otherwise involved in the protest incident.

What happens after a demonstration ends? How do you try to ameliorate the harsh feeling that has developed? Maintaining and reestablishing communications has been one of the most important parts of the discussion here.

One device was used in connection with the Chester demonstrations. I am not necessarily recommending it, but simply reporting what happened. When the complaints of alleged police brutality began to flow in, not only from those who had participated in the demonstrations but also from various other groups, religious bodies, the American Civil Liberties Union and a number of other civil rights organizations, the Governor of Pennsylvania appointed an *ad hoc* civilian review board, composed mainly of lawyers and educators, to review the whole Chester situation.

Apart from the findings of the investigating committee, the mere appointment of such a body had a salutary effect in calming the situation in Chester and at least partially reestablishing communications between the civil rights groups and others and the power structure. I am not suggesting that it solved any of the problems permanently, or even temporarily, but it was a start on the road to an eventual solution.

6.3 LOCAL RESPONSIBILITY AND LEADERSHIP

Perhaps too little attention has been paid in this volume to getting at the underlying causes of our racial problems. By and large, it is the responsibility of government at all levels—federal, state and local —to eliminate these root causes, by taking action to prevent and end discrimination in employment, education, and housing, the most important areas at the present time.

We have tried briefly to provide local officials with some idea of the resources available at the federal and state levels, both governmental and nongovernmental resources, to help the mayor, the police departments, and the local human relations commissions to deal with racial problems. The need for dynamic community leadership in these troubled times cannot be overemphasized.

For instance, mayors do not have jurisdiction over problems of *de facto* school segregation. They may not have direct jurisdiction with respect to public accommodations. In spite of the scattering of legal power, it has been urged that the mayor is the elected official on whom the focus of community action is centered. Whether or not he has the legal power to deal with racial problems, he has or should have sufficient influence and sufficient desire to improve his community, to use the power of his office to bring together all the elements of the community, and to try to deal with all aspects of discrimination.

The day of the mayor who sees himself responsible only for maintaining law and order in a community, and not for worrying about the issues that generate unrest and crisis, may well be over.

6.4 LEGAL APPROACH

Any dichotomy in law enforcement is of particular concern to lawyers, who are the first to insist that we maintain law and order but are perhaps not as quick to say that we must comply with the Civil Rights Act of 1964 and with other antidiscrimination legislation. I mention this point by way of emphasizing the role of the city attorney, who is legal advisor to the mayor and the human relations commission and likewise legal advisor to state agencies.

I know from my own experience that sometimes it is the inclination of the municipal attorney to wait and see what happens and then give

267

legal advice. This is a pleasant way of avoiding a problem—at least for a while. We are beyond such an approach, however, because police officials, human relations personnel, and others properly feel that they must have advance legal guidance as to what they can and should do. If the local solicitor is not willing, or perhaps not able, to give advice in advance, he should be at the side of the mayor in dealing with these problems.

In municipal law circles there is some disagreement, of course, on the approach to take. One approach, that described by David Craig of Pittsburgh, is to interpret the powers of the municipality broadly. The conventional legal maxim is that a municipality, in the absence of home rule powers, has only those powers that are expressly granted by state enabling laws. In the civil rights field, on the other hand, many communities have been sufficiently progressive to innovate, to take legal risks, if you will, just as we have already in urban renewal and in other new frontiers of the law. This approach is not to wait for express state enabling legislation that may never come but to proceed to interpret and apply existing powers broadly.

6.5 LOCAL RECOGNITION OF PROBLEMS

Perhaps the main point is that municipal officials should recognize that they have a problem. We have heard several persons here say, "We don't have a racial problem in our community," but many of them come from communities where there have been demonstrations and charges of discrimination.

We should be sophisticated enough by now to realize that the fact that minority groups appear to be happy and satisfied with their lot, does not mean that there is no problem. The experience of many southern and northern communities should have dispelled this delusion long ago.

Perhaps in northern communities where there have not been manifestations of unrest the municipal officials should seek out the problems that may exist in their communities. The statistics on inequality in educational opportunities and in the economic well-being of the Negro in northern cities seem to indicate few, if any, communities with no potential unrest.

There is a pressing need to reevaluate the structure and authority of state and local human relations commissions in terms of their powers, in terms of the relationship between state and local commissions, and in terms of the need for stronger laws to make these commissions operate more effectively.

6.6 SANCTIONS

Finally, what sanctions and weapons do we have for enforcing antidiscrimination legislation? I want to discuss briefly three types of sanctions.

First is the direct legal sanction you have in your state and local antidiscrimination laws. There are also direct legal sanctions, whose potentiality we may not fully realize as yet, in the new regulations adopted by the federal government to implement the 1964 Civil Rights Act.

These regulations, which make it possible to withdraw federal financial assistance for programs where there is discrimination, can work a tremendous change in the educational and economic opportunities now denied to minority groups.

In the next category are legal but indirect sanctions. By these I mean utilization of the powers of state and local agencies that do not have direct responsibility for enforcement of civil rights legislation but nevertheless do have some impact in that area.

One example is in the field of real estate. Normally we have tried to deal with real estate brokers through fair housing legislation at the state and local level. A local or state real estate examining board which licenses brokers, agents, and salesmen, may be extremely helpful. If these agencies could be brought into the picture, and could condition the issuance of real estate licenses on compliance with antidiscrimination legislation in the field of housing, a big step could be taken toward securing compliance with fair housing laws.

Other indirect weapons have to do with municipal, state, and federal contracts, that is, the refusal to enter into contracts with or withdrawing contracts from those contractors who fail to abide by nondiscriminatory hiring policies.

The final sanction, a nonlegal one, is economic pressure. We should be willing to use the segments of our society that can exert economic pressure to open up opportunities for minority groups.

6.7 ROLE OF STATE POLICE

One point worthy of consideration is the relationship between state and local police forces. Normally, the feeling is that you should not call in any state militia or state police until the local police force no longer can handle the situation. This is the historic concept of the use of state forces in many states. In Pennsylvania, for example, the traditional feeling about the state police no longer is justified. We had the famous, or infamous, coal and iron police in our earlier days and unfortunately there still lingers in the minds of some the memory of a state police force acting in the same way.

Actually, one recommendation of the investigating commission in Chester has been to determine whether the state police forces, which often are better disciplined and better trained in human relations, should come in at an earlier stage in a demonstration. They could act as a supplementary force to help in controlling the demonstrations so as to permit them to go on as peacefully as possible.

6.8 POLICE-COMMUNITY RELATIONS

A final point to consider is the matter of police-community relations. The function of the police should be not only to suppress violations of the law, but also to help in securing the full rights of all citizens under the law.

It is essential that all groups in the community, particularly minority groups striving for full citizenship, be made aware that the police recognize this obligation. The symbol of the police as the oppressor in a particular community, a symbol generally unwarranted, should be eradicated as quickly as possible.

To do this, a number of cities have initiated community relations programs in their police departments. The purpose of these programs is, by word and deed, to remake the image of the police in the eyes of the entire community, wherever such change is indicated.

6.9 CONTINUING PROBLEMS*

Despite impressive progress in some areas, urban communities are experiencing ever-increasing racial tensions. Hard-core poverty and unemployment, particularly in the juvenile and young adult Negro

---

* David Stahl, Frederick B. Sussmann and Neil J. Bloomfield.

group, have responded slowly, if at all, to the many Federal, state, and local remedial programs. The hard fact is that interracial violence could break out in almost any U.S. city. Relatively minor incidents have touched off trouble in Rochester and Jersey City in 1964, and in Chicago in 1965 and Los Angeles in 1965 and 1966. These outbreaks are often of a different nature than civil rights demonstrations, but cause a closely related range of problems for the public and private groups attempting to achieve interracial cooperation in improving the lot of minority groups in urban America.

Since actual benefits from civil rights programs have often appeared more slowly than expected, frustration at the grass roots level will probably grow and grow. There is some likelihood of an increasingly wide breach between the ghetto community and its leaders. A comprehensive report analyzing the causes of the August 1965 Los Angeles riot in the Watts district, issued by a blue-ribbon Commission appointed by California Governor Edmund G. Brown, confirms the continuing difficulty in bringing the deprived Negro community into the mainstream of American life.*

It is therefore of increasing importance to reach the unrepresented members of minority groups, i.e., those who are not affiliated with or even mistrust the recognized civil rights organizations. As some members of minority groups are able to break away from the ghetto as a result of new opportunities, the feelings of others who have been left behind—after having their expectations raised—may become even more embittered. Unless sincere and fruitful efforts are made to reach these persons as well, their frustration may erupt into uncontrollable violence.

While the immediate dangers posed by violence in race relations have been dramatically impressed upon the public mind, the continuing necessity of racial demonstrations and civil disobedience in many parts of the country to press for equality signifies a wide range of problems that are no less disquieting. There is an attitude still prevalent in many Northern cities that race problems are a purely Southern phenomenon. This attitude obscures the immediacy of the problems and hampers Northern communities in their attempts to solve pressing problems such as *de facto* school and housing segregation and the high incidence of unemployment amongst minority groups.

---

* A summing-up of the Watts report appears as Appendix G, p. 359.

271

Never before in our history have we come so close to reaching the ideal of equal opportunity. The aim of THE COMMUNITY AND RACIAL CRISES is to aid in developing local leadership and responsibility in this new era of race relations by (1) identifying the problems communities must face, and (2) examining practical methods of dealing with these problems.

How rapidly will this ideal be achieved? Will we achieve it peacefully, or must we continue to suffer the delay and resistance experienced in the past? The answers to these questions depend in a large part on the methods and goals of community leaders. Will many communities continue to be simply neutral bystanders or will these same communities learn to play an affirmative role in solving the problems of the minority groups?

It is sincerely hoped that this book will in some measure help bring about a change from community apathy to dynamic and fruitful efforts to integrate the Negro into the mainstream of American life.

APPENDICES

Appendix A

RACIAL PROTEST, CIVIL DISOBEDIENCE, AND THE RULE OF LAW*

Robert B. McKay**

It now seems remarkable that the institution of slavery was tolerated in the United States for more than three quarters of a century; and the fact that the badges of servitude are still evident one hundred years after the formal ending of slavery would seem incredible if it were not all too plainly true. As plans were laid in 1963 for the centennial celebration of the Emancipation Proclamation, that anniversary was also celebrated by a mounting storm of protests, both peaceful and violent, against seemingly ineradicable forms of racial discrimination.

Nine years before the emancipation centennial the United States Supreme Court announced unequivocally that state-required segregation in public schools affronts the equal protection of the laws clause of the Fourteenth Amendment to the United States Constitution. Soon the Court made it clear that segregation in interstate transportation also violated the Constitution and various provisions of federal statutory law. But in 1963 desegregation of the public schools was still at the level of tokenism in the eleven states of the Old South; and freedom of movement without racial oppression was still being tested in the courts in cases arising out of the freedom rides of some years earlier.

---

* Reprinted, by permission, from *Arts and Sciences,* Winter, 1964.
** Professor of Law, Associate Dean, New York University School of Law.

273

It is small wonder, then, that the Negro freedom movement, which had principally relied on judicial vindication of its lawful demands, became impatient with the courts. In increasing numbers Negroes took to the streets, the schools, and the lunch counters in protest. The Southern Regional Council has reported that in 1963 alone an estimated 930 individual public protest demonstrations took place in at least 115 cities in the eleven Southern states. More than 20,000 of these demonstrators, Negro and white, were arrested and charged with offenses ranging from disturbing the peace or trespass to insurrection; and a substantial number of arrests were made outside the South as well. Ten persons died during 1963 under circumstances directly related to racial protests, and 35 known bombings took place. "The long hot summer" of 1964, with the massive attempts then made to lighten the burden of discrimination in Mississippi, was no different in kind. The time of the protest is upon us.

The reasons for protests and demonstrations against racial discrimination are known to all who are willing to comprehend with their minds what they know in their hearts is true. Despite the nearly one hundred years since this nation solemnly declared in the Thirteenth, Fourteenth, and Fifteenth Amendments that Negroes should be not only technically freed from bondage but as well from the symbols of serfdom, that brave promise has failed of fulfillment. The simple truth remains that Negroes as a class, twenty million strong, are denied equal dignity, equal participation in the public life of the community, and equal access to public accommodations. After years of litigation to reverse the pattern, Negroes have understandably tired of "all deliberate speed" as a formula that seems all promise and no performance. Dr. Martin Luther King, in his 1964 book, *Why We Can't Wait,* has stated forcefully that "the time has come for our nation to take that firm stride into freedom—not simply toward freedom—which will pay a long overdue debt to its citizens of color." Self-help more drastic than he and other moderate leaders of the freedom movement recommend will be the inescapable result unless these voices of protest are promptly heeded.

There are, however, great problems in the way of any policy of self-help. As Professor Harry Kalven has reminded us, "the problem with a do-it-yourself legal remedy kit, such as is involved in the self-help movement, is that you get rather quickly to the boundaries of what is permissible before you run into trouble with the courts yourself. . . . You can't just say we'll do it ourselves because we're exasperated by having to wait for the courts. . . . By and large the courts have been against self-help; they have hedged it in."

The front line of race relations is now drawn where the ranks of the demonstrators confront the tangible resistance of the police and the intangible, but significant, force of public criticism, even from those sympathetic in the abstract to the freedom movement. Demonstrators and critics alike all too often rely on facile articulation built upon shaky premises. Thus, demonstrators are apt to justify their acts of civil disobedience, sometimes bordering on outright lawlessness, by reminding us of the fact of racial discrimination, present and sorely remembered, without proper allocation of blame or realistic appraisal of the avenues of remedy. Unfriendly, or even unthinking, critics are prone to seek refuge in the sanctity of the law, branding as impermissible all acts of civil disobedience. If criticism is made of protests without first inquiring whether the law protested against is invalid or lacks moral justification, without asking whether the protest against enforcement is peaceful or violent, and whether the rights of others are interfered with or not, the critical reaction lacks reasoned basis. Nor is it sufficient to say that all unjust laws are subject to correction in a representative democracy. We know that is not automatically so, at least not until the unjustness has been called dramatically to the attention of the power-wielding majority.

To put these issues in proper perspective it is appropriate to examine the various aspects of protest, from the most innocuous to the most destructive; to study the justifications advanced in support of civil disobedience; and, finally, to place these answers into the framework of the rule of law to which the United States aspires.

The right of protest is all things to all people. It includes the harmless self-indulgence of a letter to the editor complaining about a change in parking regulations; strikes, parades, and picketing; nonviolent civil disobedience; and the ultimate defiance of law, conspiracy for the violent overthrow of government. Obviously, those who wish to protest existing law and those who object to that defiance must alike be discriminating about the form of protest supported or criticized.

The act of protest is as old as Socrates and as new as the abortive stall-in at the New York World's Fair of 1964. Between those times the forms that protest has assumed have been varied and the counter-measures have often been drastic. Until recent years the most important protests have been those in which an attempt was made to upset existing government, whether the effort was by a minority claiming oppression or by a majority seeking to upset the authoritarian rule of the few. In the name of religious differences the world has been stirred by such events as the crucifixion of Jesus, the martyrdom of the early Christians, and the excesses of Inquisition and Reformation alike. The economically oppressed have sometimes sought to take matters into their own hands, often unsuccessfully, as in the revolt of the Roman slaves, the peasant revolts not uncommon in medieval Europe, the bonus march on Washington in 1930, the Montgomery bus boycott of 1955, and the New York rent strikes of 1964.

It is tempting to relax in the warm glow of belief that in the truly democratic state all wrongs will be somehow righted—at least ultimately, if not quite in the immediate present. It is only too easy to forget the possible tyranny of the majority. It is scarcely enough to say that the majority is itself made up of a congeries of minorities. If a complacent majority prefers not to be reminded of minority complaints about the way in which the society is ordered, the dissenters can be rendered impotent or even punished for their opposition to the majority, all in the name of national security. Unless the conscience of a religious majority is unusually pricked by its religious leaders, it is all too likely to relegate the non-believers to positions of social exclusion, economic disadvantage, or worse.

The socially useful role of protest cannot be denied and should not be minimized. Realistically, there is no other way to awaken the conscience of the complacent majority to the demands for simple justice of an easily ignored minority. It makes no difference whether the matter is one of race, religion, politics, or national origin. Whenever men have strong convictions about these or other issues, it is perfectly natural for the dominant group to find disquieting any public articulation of opposed sentiments. Mr. Justice Holmes said it well:

> Persecution for the expression of opinions seems to me perfectly logical. If you have no doubt of your premises or your power and want a certain result with all your heart you naturally express your wishes in law and sweep away all opposition. . . . But when men have realized that time has upset

many fighting faiths, they may come to believe even more than they believe the very foundations of their own conduct that the ultimate good desired is better reached by free trade in ideas—that the best test of truth is the power of the thought to get itself accepted in the competition of the market, and that truth is the only ground upon which their wishes safely can be carried out. That at any rate is the theory of our Constitution. It is an experiment, as all life is an experiment. (*Abrams* v. *United States,* 250 U.S. 616, 630 [1919] [dissenting opinion]).

Human nature, if unrestrained by force, law, or moral command, quite readily turns to suppression of attempts to overthrow the established order. And of course it is proper to ensure the stability and ongoing character of established government. The difficulty, however, is that the tendency to suppress dissent all too often—and again quite understandably—goes far beyond the needs of national security. If Mr. Justice Holmes was correct in his belief that truth will emerge from a fair exchange in the marketplace of ideas, the fundamental democratic principle offers its adherents no choice but to allow free expression of ideas that they do not share—or at least believe they do not share, for the possibility of persuasion to discard old principles for replacement with new ideas should not be discounted.

The difficulty lies outside the notion just expressed. Nearly all Americans profess agreement with the right of free expression. Exception is taken rather to the manner of its exercise. Little fault is found with publications in obscure journals, gentle exhortation from the pulpits in behalf of brotherly love, or even orderly meetings and speeches, at least so long as they do not attract too much public support, and even more particularly, so long as they do not evoke hostile reactions from others which might cause public disturbance or "breach of the peace." Then it is that the cry is raised that the speaker, demonstrator, or other "unseemly" noncomformist should be prevented from upsetting the comfortable routine and perhaps that he should be punished for his challenge to the well-ordered society.

Alternatively, it may be urged, in seeming friendliness, that the dissident few should be "protected" against acts of community hostility. The result of such friendly interruption is, however, no different; the person unlucky enough to speak out in opposition to the dominant community sentiment is at least silenced and perhaps taken into "protective" custody.

If the lot of those who speak in protest, picket with signs, or assemble to demonstrate is thus made difficult when the cause they support is out of the community mainstream, it is easy to understand how much more difficult is the role chosen by those who frankly set out to violate the law. We are all taught to obey proper authority, whether parent, teacher, police officer, or superior in employment; and we all recognize that sanctions may be imposed for disobedience. Accordingly, it is generally assumed that the person in authority need not, if he chooses, consider the justness of the rule whose breach is charged.

An ordered society which professes commitment to the rule of law need not be that inflexible in its demand for observance of the law. Obedience to the prescribed rules is of course the primary and proper mandate for all, regardless of agreement or disagreement with the particular rule. Yet surely one of the principal ways in which the democratic society is set apart from the authoritarian state is the differing attitude toward the finality of the state's command. Where the Soviet State, for example, allows judicial inquiry only to discover whether the letter of the law has been violated, the premise of United States constitutionalism is very different. It is undisputed that in the United States challenge is permitted to the validity of law itself on the theory that there is a higher law against which even statutory law, let alone commands of lesser force, must be tested. Until a law has been authoritatively held valid, as measured against that ultimate standard, the right to challenge its applicability to particular cases as well as its overall validity cannot be lightly denied.

Indeed, there is no way to secure authoritative interpretation of doubtful law or practice save by the test of an actual case involving violation of the law and imposition of some penalty. The American experience is that the merits of the opposing arguments are not likely to be presented adequately save in an actual controversy on the outcome of which freedom or other values will depend. Since the abstract ruling and the advisory opinion are not permitted, the person who raises a substantial challenge is serving a necessary function without which the system could not operate as it does. It is for this reason that the canons of professional ethics by which lawyers

278

are bound permit them sometimes to counsel disobedience to law. Canon 32 not only provides that clients must be advised to comply with written law and with "the strictest principles of moral law," but reminds as well that "until a statute shall have been construed and interpreted by competent adjudication," the lawyer "is free and is entitled to advise as to its validity and as to what he conscientiously believes to be its just meaning and extent."

From this perspective it can be seen that civil disobedience need not be an odious concept but, within proper limits, is an essential adjunct of the democratic process in a constitutional system. Father Robert F. Drinan, Dean of the Boston College Law School, has observed wisely that "civil disobedience to law arises not from contempt for the law but rather from a profound respect for the majesty of the moral law which the violated statute assertedly contravenes." Clearly, the idea and the practice of civil disobedience have been thoroughly Americanized. Exercise of the right of protest is as American an institution as the flight of the Pilgrims to the shores of Massachusetts in their search for religious liberty, as American as the Boston Tea Party, the American Revolution, the abolitionist and suffragist movements, and now the Negro protest against too-long continued discrimination.

The Founding Fathers of the Constitution believed in the right of protest for others in the future as they had practiced it themselves in the past. To make sure that the right of expression should be left unrestricted, permitting even complaints against the government, they added to the basic charter as the very first amendment the most explicit assurance of the right to freedom of expression and conscience that the wit of man could devise.

Then, as now, however, the hard philosophical question was the same: Under what circumstances should civil disobedience be tolerated—or even encouraged? The question has now taken on a new urgency as the Negro protest movement has gained a measure of success and a considerable degree of self-confidence. The pattern of protest has changed observably from the hesitant acts of individuals and small groups, seeking individual challenge to laws believed invalid, to massive group actions, such as the 1963 Freedom March on Washington and the growing array of school boycotts in the North in 1964.

As the protest movement grows in size and self-assurance, its momentum is hard to resist. The ever-mounting demand for action and the pressing necessity to find a means of continuing the support for the leadership of the movement leads to continuously enlarged demands. As is the case with any action group, achievement of the originally announced goals does not end the campaign. Modest victories prompt modest additions to the basic objectives, and major victories are likely to ignite demands for major additions to the scope of the action sought. In view of the long-withheld right to full equality, this cumulating pressure is understandable but is not without its elements of concern for the future. Dr. Martin Luther King, Jr., put it this way:

> Many Americans who consider themselves men of good will are asking: "What more will the Negro expect if he gains such rights as integrated schools, public facilities, voting rights, and progress in housing? Will he, like Oliver Twist, demand more?" What is implied is the amazing assumption that society has the right to bargain with the Negro for the freedom which inherently belongs to him.

As the ends sought tend always to advance to goals just beyond the immediately attainable, so also the means employed tend to change in character. When orderly picketing with placards becomes so commonplace that it goes almost unnoticed by those complained against, and when (possibly worse) the picketing fails to arouse enthusiastic support among members of the protesting group, the remedy is conceived to be bolder action—perhaps more singing of freedom songs, a little more interference with traffic, or a tolling of church bells at midnight. Usually in the South this is enough to provoke police action to break up the demonstration, to make mass arrests, or perhaps (if the police are unwise) to use police dogs or cattle prods. Such strong retaliation may even be desired by the protesters, knowing that strong reaction produces in turn strong support for the demonstrators. And so a collision course may be set for racial incidents, riots, or murder.

In the cities of the North where discrimination likewise begets protest, the matter is not so simple. It is harder to identify clearly the wrongdoer responsible for the obviously harsh facts of segregated life and employment discrimination, for there is no official command of segregation or other discrimination. Indeed, the law, government officials, and the courts appear to be on the side of the fight against discrimination. Peaceful protests and demonstrations are not only permitted, but also, if advance notice is given, police protection will be provided to protect the demonstrators against interference even if the protesters against the protesters represent majority sentiment in the community. This is scarcely a dramatic scenario in the name of protest when official policy supports, at least in principle, the demands made upon them and balks only at the practical problems said to lie in the way of effectuation.

It is scarcely surprising, then, that continuously more dramatic devices are sought with the twin goals of demanding faster action toward ending *de facto* discrimination and rallying greater support to the cause among members of the class discriminated against. Where orderly and peaceful protest produces no victories, the almost inevitable tendency is for the leadership to seek stronger methods looking more and more in the direction of civil disobedience, sometimes shading over into lawlessness. Thus it is that some propose, and others agree, to dump garbage on official premises; to bar entrance to board of education offices; to block the work at construction sites by lying in the paths of trucks and bulldozers (with sometimes unintentionally tragic results); or to embarrass officialdom by obstructing traffic or busy bridges or at a world's fair.

Defiance of law is undoubtedly heady stuff. In a curious way civil disobedience in a cause believed to be just has a compelling quality hard to resist. Leaders of civil rights groups may find that even tentatively raised objections to extension of the acts of disobedience may jeopardize their leadership, forcing retirement to the ranks of the "Uncle Toms"; and political leaders who must count on support from a racially disadvantaged group for success at the polls are scarcely well situated to defy even the most militant demands of such groups. Yet somehow the lines must be drawn between appropriate and improper challenge to ongoing law and order. Otherwise, the likelihood of violence is increased. Irresponsible leaders, emboldened by success, may, unless appropriately challenged, go on to ever bolder and more dangerous experiments, until lawlessness is substituted for civil disobedience.

Civil disobedience in the name of an aroused sense of injustice has assumed various forms in the protest against racial discrimination, but most frequently in the form of sit-ins, acts of trespass, parades without licenses, and picketing in defiance of prohibitions. The hard

281

question is how, if at all, to draw distinctions among these various classes of protest. Should the fact of violation of established law alone suffice to condemn any action unsupported by official permission? Surely an affirmative answer is not indicated. Equally, however, that is not to say that civil disobedience is always to be condoned so long as it can be described as a protest against some form of discrimination. No one suggests that individuals or groups should be allowed to take the law into their owns hands, no matter how worthy may sometimes seem their cause. Even as lynch law cannot be countenanced, neither should other infractions of the law be justified solely on the ground of disagreement with a law or a practice believed to be unjust.

Discrimination on grounds of race or color is today—as it has always been in the United States—very much a fact. The present is differentiated from the past principally because we are now more awake to that reality—in the North as in the South. It is important to recognize that this heightened awareness and this reinforced determination to strike out against discrimination find their root source in the strength of the protest movement. Witness four examples:

1. When the Civil Rights Act of 1963 was originally introduced by the Kennedy Administration, the objection most often heard was that the bill was too tough; and the compromise talk was accordingly in the direction of softening the "objectionable" features. It is noteworthy—and a tribute to the sustained vigor, enterprise, and compelling persuasiveness of the protest movement—that the Civil Rights Act of 1964, in its enacted form, is a substantially stronger bill than the one originally proposed. The new law is likely to prove the most effective civil rights legislation ever enacted in the United States. And it is certain that without the impetus provided by the protest movement the final legislation would have been delayed or less forceful, or both.

2. Much is heard now of preferential or compensatory treatment for Negroes and other long-disadvantaged classes. Time was— and not so long ago—that it was enough to say that the Constitution is color blind so that no demands were pressed except for equal treatment. But now all is different when, with not inconsiderable logic, a faster catch-up is demanded. Again the protest movement must be credited with the genius for recognizing the possibility of such a turn-around of theory and for devising effectively dramatic ways of making the point.

3. Similar is the change of operative theory in connection with the timetable of school desegregation. In 1955 such acknowledged legal spokesmen for the fight against racial discrimination as Thurgood Marshall and Robert Carter expressed reasonable satisfaction with the Supreme Court's mandate that desegregation of the public schools should proceed "with all deliberate speed." When that proved more a device for delay than a vehicle for movement, the impatience expressed in the protest movement found support in the Supreme Court. In 1963 Mr. Justice Goldberg warned in *Watson* v. *Memphis* that it had never been "contemplated that the concept of 'deliberate speed' would countenance indefinite delay in elimination of racial barriers in schools. . . ." (373 U. S. 526, 530). And in 1964, in *Griffin* v. *County School Board of Prince Edward County,* Mr. Justice Black stated bluntly that "there has been entirely too much deliberation and not enough speed in enforcing the constitutional rights which we held in *Brown* v. *Board of Education* had been denied Prince Edward County Negro children" (377 U. S. 218, 229).

4. School boards in Northern cities, New York, Philadelphia, Chicago, and elsewhere, are suggesting in 1964 far bolder plans to eliminate *de facto* school segregation than would have seemed possible (or even constitutional) only a few years before. Once more, the unrelenting demands of politically potent minority groups, often aligned with important elements of the white majority, have made it necessary for school boards to rethink their answers to these protests.

The problems are not easy, and no one any longer expects them to be so. The central difficulty for concerned members of the citizenry lies in the fact that each citizen is committed to a dual role which presents seeming conflicts. On the one hand, educated members of society cannot escape involvement in the critical issues here presented. The fair-minded citizen should be especially sensitive to injustice perpetrated by, or at least condoned by, the law. Oliver Wendell Holmes once truly said that a man must "share the passion and action of his time at peril of being judged not to have lived." On the other hand, however, the law-abiding citizen is charged with responsibility for upholding the legal order, including laws with which the citizen may be in disagreement—ordinarily, even laws that he may believe unreasonable or unjust. Yet we cannot be let off so easily by saying that the law is sacrosanct; for there is sometimes an obligation to a law that is higher than the unjust law.

Because there are several somewhat distinct questions presented, which are not all of the same order of difficulty, it may be well to dispose first of one relatively simple issue. The right of peaceful protest by way of picketing or other orderly demonstration is protected so long as it does not interfere with the rights of others in any major way. Moreover, it is important to remember that the opposing private rights must be very substantial before they can overcome the First Amendment-protected right of free expression. The interests that have been determined substantial enough to justify interference with freedom of expression include only such limited categories as the right to be free of defamation, obscenity (narrowly defined), or so-called "fighting words." And the state may protect itself against speech that has the quality of action, such as incitement to overthrow the government.

Everything not within these restricted exceptions is protected as a First Amendment right of free expression, thus necessarily including the right to speak; to picket, parade, or demonstrate; to assemble; and to associate with others to discuss common causes or even to plan protests. Indeed, the speaker is ordinarily entitled to police protection to assure his opportunity to express opinions, even those likely to upset the very persons whom he addresses. Mr. Justice Douglas, speaking for the Court in 1949, explained the reasons for the preservation of the right to expression of dissenting views. "A function of free speech under our system of government is to invite dispute. It may indeed best serve its high purpose when it induces a condition of unrest, creates dissatisfaction with conditions as they are, or even stirs people to anger. Speech is often provocative and challenging" (*Terminiello* v. *Chicago,* 337 U. S. 1, 4).

This has always been the theory of the First Amendment, indeed the genius of the democratic principle itself. As Mr. Justice Brandeis noted in 1927, those who won our independence "recognized the risks to which all human institutions are subject. But they knew that order cannot be secured merely through fear of punishment for its infraction; that it is hazardous to discourage thought, hope and imagination; that fear breeds repression; that repression breeds hate; that hate menaces stable government; that the path of safety lies in the opportunity to discuss freely supposed grievances and proposed remedies; and that the fitting remedy for evil counsels is good ones" (*Whitney* v. *California,* 274 U. S. 357, 375).

The Supreme Court has recognized the constitutional obligation of public officials to protect the right of peaceful demonstrations, even when noisy, against breach of the peace convictions. In 1963 Mr. Justice Stewart spoke for the Court in upsetting the conviction of 187 Negroes who came to the grounds of the state capitol building in Columbia, South Carolina, to protest against state laws that discriminated against Negroes. "The circumstances in this case reflect an exercise of these basic constitutional rights in their most pristine and classic form. . . . There was no violence or threat of violence on their part, or on the part of any member of the crowd watching them" (*Edwards* v. *South Carolina,* 372 U. S. 229, 235-36).

But peaceful demonstrations which involve no direct challenge to existing discrimination—no violation of allegedly unjust law—may prove to be of limited effectiveness, at least from the standpoint of the complainants. It is all too easy for a majority committed by tradition to prejudice to learn to live with the minor inconvenience of occasional parades, pickets, and assemblies of demonstrators. Unhappily, there is much evidence that action to put an end to discrimination, public as well as private, results only from the more dramatic forms of protest which more directly challenge the complained-against practice.

At the first level there are the sit-ins and the school boycotts. Both are, at least on their face, in violation of law, whether criminal trespass statutes or school attendance laws. However, we should be very careful about condemning such actions as violative of law on the books. So long as a serious contention is made that the challenged statute, ordinance, or local practice is invalid when tested against some appropriate higher law, the "test case" is in the American tradition. True, the test should be made with the minimum force or disorder possible, and he who challenges the law must be prepared to pay the price in terms of imposed sanctions if he is finally found to be wrong. But where that risk is assumed, as it has been by thousands of Negroes and cooperating whites in recent years, the effort to put an end to allegedly unlawful discrimination through non-violent disobedience of the complained-against law need not be criticized.

In a significant proportion of such tests in recent years the complainants have won their point and thus enlarged the area of freedom from discrimination. For example, it was not clear before 1961 that conventional breach-of-peace statutes could not be validly applied against non-violent sit-in demonstrators. But in that year the Supreme Court expressly made that point in the first sit-in case to reach the Court (*Garner* v. *Louisiana,* 368 U. S. 157). Nor was it necessarily clear before 1963 that sit-in demonstrators could not be penalized under trespass statutes where local ordinances required segregation or where public officials had announced their intention to prosecute such attempts at desegregation. But that was the point of *Peterson* v. *Greenville,* 373 U. S. 244, and *Lombard* v. *Louisiana,* 373 U. S. 267.

Who can say with assurance what will be the final, or even the next, step as these matters are further tested? Cases from Florida, Maryland, and South Carolina, decided by the United States Supreme Court in June of 1964, involved segregation practices of restaurants and similar facilities where state participation was limited to the use of the state's criminal processes for trespass convictions. The Solicitor General of the United States urged on behalf of the United States that the state was nonetheless implicated in these cases, too. "Until time and events have attenuated the connection, the state continues to bear constitutional responsibility for the conditions it has shared in creating by branding Negroes as an inferior caste." The earlier state support of segregation had been "so massive and continued so long as to leave no doubt that the official policy still exerts substantial influence upon the customs of the community." Although the Supreme Court reversed the convictions on various grounds, the several opinions of the Justices revealed a split within the Court on the ultimate constitutional question, which was left for decision another day. Meanwhile, no fault can be found with the bringing of further cases to test the question whether the Constitution forbids state enforcement of private acts of discrimination at places of public accommodation. Although passage of the Civil Rights Act of 1964 answers the question in many instances, there are other cases not covered by that act that must still be tested in court.

The question is sometimes asked: How can the deliberate violation of law by sit-in demonstrators be differentiated from the actions of Governors Barnett and Wallace in their calculated defiance of court order? The difference is clear in that the demonstrators acted to challenge statutes and ordinances of doubtful validity, not yet tested in the courts on the constitutional issue. Governors Barnett and Wallace did just the opposite. They resisted court orders *after* the questions at issue had been fully litigated, at a time when the necessity of admitting Negroes to their respective state universities had been already decided. In short, the difference was one of good faith, an essential element that was lacking in the actions of the governors.

There are, however, hard questions in connection with the right of protest that still remain. Particularly in the North there have been a number of instances of violation of laws which are not themselves challenged as invalid, or even unjust, and which are at best tangentially related to the complaint sought to be registered. Once again some differentiation is necessary.

School boycotts ordinarily involve violation of compulsory attendance laws which permit nonattending public school pupils to be punished as truants and parents who keep their children out of school without cause to be penalized for that act. Those responsible for planning a boycott are arguably guilty of a conspiracy to violate the school laws. However, it is not easy to describe as lawless a boycott that, as in New York, brought response from several hundred thousand parents and children as a means of dramatizing what they believed to be the wrongful *de facto* segregation of many New York City school districts.

Several factors should be taken into account. In the first place, it is not entirely clear that the school attendance pattern in New York might not be upset some day by judicial action. Several courts have already held that school boards have an affirmative obligation, not only to avoid intentional discrimination, but as well to promote integration or what is sometimes described as racial balance. In the second place, the individual parental act of keeping a child out of school for a single day is scarcely an important act of lawlessness nor one calculated to lead the child to disrespect for law in general. Finally, the boycott is closely related to the complaint against discrimination in the school system. Where there is no other effective way to raise the issue in a dramatic fashion, condemnation cannot be too quickly forthcoming.

There are, however, dangers. If one boycott is well received and apparently successful, the temptation is to mount others to the point of serious interference with the educational process of those who do not participate in the boycott as well as those who do participate. It is important that the rights of the nonparticipants not be jeopardized either by undue pressures to secure their participation

287

or by weakening the educational program to which they are entitled without dilution. The matter is difficult, but seems to be more a question of degree and of wisdom than one of lawless protest.

Quite different are some unlawful actions deliberately undertaken to dramatize complaints that are unrelated to the action taken. Where the complaint is against a board of education, it is one thing to picket with placards stating the grievance; it is quite another to block the entrance so that official business is made difficult or impossible. Where the complaint is against discrimination in hiring practices, largely as a result of union policies, it is one thing to test the validity of the grievance through the courts (as is being done in New York); but it is quite another to chain protesters together or to pillars as a means of blocking all construction (as has also been done in New York).

Finally, it should be reported that a further serious difficulty with the more or less justified violations of law just described may impose serious limitations on the effectiveness of the protest movement where the justification for protest is great. If otherwise friendly forces—legislatures, public officials, courts, and individual supporters—are alienated by too-extreme efforts to bring quick realization of the dream of equality, perhaps the price is too great. On the other hand, hasty retreat from protest in the face of even formidable community opposition is not by any means indicated. Seeking to strike a proper balance in each case, we should remember the telling words of André Gide: "The world will be saved only by the unsubmissive."

Appendix B

COMMONWEALTH OF PENNSYLVANIA
PENNSYLVANIA HUMAN RELATIONS
COMMISSION

Pennsylvania Human Relations Commission,
Complainant

v.

Chester School District,
Respondent

Docket No. S-10

OPINION, INCLUDING FINDINGS OF FACT,
CONCLUSIONS OF LAW,
COMMISSION'S DECISION AND FINAL ORDER

For many months beginning with the fall of 1963 and ending only when public hearings were instituted in the instant case on May 4, 1964, the city of Chester was the scene of repeated and uninterrupted civil rights rallies and demonstrations because of alleged de facto segregation in Chester's public schools.

Efforts to resolve differences between the Chester School Board and the civil rights groups were futile on the part of the local Chester Commission on Human Relations. Similar efforts were attempted by the Pennsylvania Human Relations Commission on April 20, 1964, but without success.

By the end of April, 1964, it became apparent that a crisis existed in the city of Chester when street battles between demonstrators and police resulted in mass arrests and imprisonment of hundreds of individuals, white and Negro. Elected officials, businessmen's associations, civic leaders, clergymen and educators in Chester and elsewhere appealed to Governor William W. Scranton for help in bringing to an end a rapidly approaching emergency situation.

Thus, on April 26, 1964, the Governor and Attorney General requested this Commission to institute proceedings immediately in

289

Chester, to hold public hearings, determine all facts concerning alleged de facto segregation in Chester's public schools, attempt in every way possible to resolve amicably differences among all parties, but failing in this, to issue an appropriate order.

The first day of public hearings was set by the Commission for Monday morning, May 4, 1964. At that time, attorneys for the National Office and the Chester Branch of the National Association for the Advancement of Colored People (NAACP) and for the Chester Committee for Freedom Now (CCFN), the two civil rights groups which led the protests and demonstrations, refused to act as complainants, claiming that the Commission might not have the legal authority to issue a binding order, and that it might preclude them from instituting a future court proceeding. The Commission, after discussion, unanimously agreed to act as complainant and filed a complaint against the Chester School District, setting forth therein verbatim the same nine averments of alleged discrimination as had theretofore been charged by the civil rights groups:

1. Respondent maintains all-one-color schools within the school system.

2. Textbooks authorized for use in the public schools by the respondent do not treat adequately or ignore entirely the contributions of the Negro in American life.

3. Negro teachers are assigned to all-Negro schools only.

4. Negro secretaries, clerks and telephone operators engaged by the respondent are assigned to all-Negro schools or substantially all-Negro schools only, and none is assigned to Administration offices.

5. The physical condition of all-Negro schools and substantially all-Negro schools is noticeably inferior to that of the substantially all-white schools.

6. The educational standards in all-Negro schools are inferior to those in substantially all-white schools; especially in that the Chester School Board has failed to provide for the highest possible educational standards in all-Negro schools, as, for example, by smaller classes, better counseling services and a program of motivation.

7. Respondent has failed to appoint qualified Negroes to supervisory and administrative positions or to encourage Negro personnel to apply for such positions.

8. Boundary lines defining school zones have been maintained and gerrymandered by school authorities in order to perpetuate all-Negro schools and in order to permit white pupils to attend substantially all-white schools.

9. Respondent has failed to adopt and make public an affirmative program and acceptable plan to desegregate the public schools and provide a timetable for implementation.

The respondent School District, by its attorney, Guy G. deFuria, Esq., waived all technicalities dealing with ten days' notice of public hearing provided by the Commission's Regulations, secured an extension of time within which to file an Answer to the Complaint, and expressed its willingness to have the controversy aired publicly and expeditiously.

An Answer to the Complaint was filed by respondent on May 5, 1964, denying all of the averments of the Complaint.

Eight days of public hearings were conducted before the whole Commission on May 4, 5, 6, 14 and 15, June 11, and September 17 and 29, 1964. In addition, a full evening was devoted by the Commission on July 15, 1964, in a final unsuccessful effort with the respondent to conciliate all issues raised by the Complaint, so that a Final Order might be entered by the Commission with the approval of all interested groups. The July 15th meeting and all hearings were held at the Pennsylvania Military College, 15th and Chestnut Streets, Chester, Pennsylvania.

The case in support of the Complaint was presented by Nathan Agran, Esq., General Counsel for the Commission and Arthur C. Thomas, Esq., Deputy Attorney General, and the respondent was represented by Guy G. deFuria, Esq. Harold J. Hughes, Esq., Attorney for Chester Parents Association, although not a party to the proceedings, was allowed to participate.

At the conclusion of the sixth day of hearings, on June 11, 1964, a Motion to Dismiss was filed by counsel for the Chester School District, alleging essentially that

(1) the Commission does not have jurisdiction of the matters set forth in the Complaint;

(2) the Commission may act only to redress grievances of specific individuals who claim violation of individual civil rights;

(3) the Commission may not supersede a school board in the performance of its duties (referring to matters raised by the Complaint); and

(4) the Commission may not act as complainant, prosecutor and judge.

Counsel for the respondent and General Counsel for the Commission filed briefs of law relating to evidence produced at the hearings and to allegations of respondent's Motion to Dismiss, but waived oral arguments at the conclusion of all testimony.

The Commission has carefully considered the legal briefs and all of the testimony given at the public hearings, has made findings of fact and conclusions of law which are set forth later in this Opinion, and has entered a Final Order against the Chester School District consistent with its said findings of fact and conclusions of law.

The Motion to Dismiss filed by respondent in this proceeding is hereby denied for the following reasons:

1. The Commission has jurisdiction under the fair employment practices provisions and under the public accommodations provisions of the Pennsylvania Human Relations Act.

2. Aggrieved individuals are not the only parties who may file complaints with the Commission alleging unlawful discriminatory practices. The Act, in Section 9, specifically provides that, "The Commission upon its own initiative or the Attorney General may, in like manner, make, sign and file such complaint." In accordance with this power, the Commission has initiated hundreds of complaints in its own name.

3. The Commission is not attempting to supersede the Chester School Board in its duties, as alleged in the Motion to Dismiss. The same legislative body which granted certain duties and powers to respondent as a school district, likewise granted certain duties and powers to this Commission by more recent legislation. The

Commission is acting in accordance with its duties to determine whether respondent has violated the provisions of the Pennsylvania Human Relations Act. The Commission will not, for example, prescribe the method by which respondent shall desegregate its all-Negro schools because the Chester School Board alone must decide that important matter. But the Commission may order respondent to desegregate the all-Negro schools in an expeditious and satisfactory manner according to a definite timetable and retain jurisdiction until such affirmative actions are taken.

4. The Commission likewise is not acting as "complainant, prosecutor and judge" in this case. It is following its duties by procedures set forth in the Act itself, similar to the methods adopted by hundreds of other commissions in this Commonwealth, in other states and in the Federal Government. So long as an appeal may be taken from any decision of this Commission to the courts, the respondent should not be heard to complain that the proceeding is unconstitutional.

In another case in which this Commission issued an order against a public school district, we said:

"The practice of racial or religious discrimination is ugly in any of its forms. It is particularly reprehensible and inexcusable when practiced in the public schools of this Commonwealth. These schools are supported by public funds derived from taxpayers, regardless of their race, religion or national origin."

The public school is the very backbone of American democracy and has been referred to as "the great equalizer of the conditions of men . . . the balance wheel of the social machinery." The wheel is definitely out of balance when a public school district permits one of its four junior high schools to be all-Negro as to pupils, principal, teachers and other personnel, and permits four of its eleven elementary schools to be all-Negro and one other of its elementary schools to be almost all-Negro.

In 1954, the United States Supreme Court ruled that racial segregation in public schools, when required by state laws, was unconstitutional. This brought to an end the pernicious doctrine of "separate but equal" facilities.

293

This historic decision in 1954 stimulated many attacks against public school systems in Northern states where segregation existed in fact, though not by law. Courts have generally required the elimination of segregation where the facts indicated that the school boards were in any way responsible for the creation or the continued maintenance of the segregated schools.

In the instant case, the Chester School District has taken the position that residential patterns are responsible for Chester's segregated public schools and that therefore there is no legal duty on its part to attempt to desegregate the all-Negro schools.

The Pennsylvania Human Relations Commission does not agree with this position. If, as stated by the Supreme Court, "Separate educational facilities are inherently unequal", then it would not matter whether the Chester School District created this condition intentionally or not. The harmful effects of the all-Negro schools would be felt by Chester pupils in either event.

The Commission is of the opinion that segregation in fact (de facto segregation) must be dealt with by the Chester School District as an educational problem because the education offered in all-Negro schools is inherently unequal to that offered in desegregated schools.

The Commission is also of the opinion that the segregation of public schools in Chester is not entirely accidental. There is much evidence that Chester's segregated schools are at least partly the result of racial motivation on the part of the respondent:

1. For many years, until about 1954, Negro pupils were required to pass nearby schools and attended all-Negro schools farther away;

2. Several of the all-Negro elementary schools, notably Washington and Watts, and one of the junior high schools, Douglass Junior High School, have been racially segregated as to pupils, principal, staff and teachers for many decades;

3. Respondent has not in any way attempted to change boundary lines from year to year so as to prevent the perpetuation of three 100% all-Negro elementary schools and one 100% all-Negro junior high school, one elementary school in which 99% of the pupils are Negroes, and one elementary school in which 90% of the pupils are Negroes;

294

4. After the William Penn School was built, Negro pupils were permitted to cross the William Penn school zone boundary lines in order to attend the all-Negro Dewey-Mann School;

5. At least one white pupil living within the all-Negro Dewey-Mann school zone has been crossing the Dewey-Mann boundary lines and attending the William Penn School.

6. On May 4, 1964, respondent changed the school zone boundary lines of the all-Negro Dewey-Mann School by eliminating therefrom an all-white populated section of Chester and adding it to the William Penn boundary lines;

7. Only Negro teachers and only Negro clerks have been assigned to all-Negro schools;

8. There has never been a policy of open enrollment in Chester;

9. The 13 members of respondent's supervisory and administrative staff are all white;

10. Only Negro orthogenic backward pupils are assigned to the all-Negro Dewey-Mann School;

11. The all-Negro school buildings have been noticeably inferior to other school buildings in toilet facilities, bad lighting, lack of paint, broken plastering and generally poor maintenance;

12. Of all tuition paying pupils who attend Chester public schools from outlying school districts, only Negroes are assigned to the all-Negro Douglass Junior High School;

13. Of the five kindergartens in existence, only one is conducted at an all-Negro school, four being conducted at substantially all-white schools; and

14. Respondent has failed to adopt or approve any effective plan, with a timetable, to desegregate the all-Negro and substantially all-Negro public schools in Chester.

Throughout the hearings, respondent constantly referred to its inability to provide the funds necessary to replace obsolete school buildings, to pay the same teachers' salaries as are paid by surrounding school districts or to adopt an effective plan to desegregate its school system. It is clearly the duty and obligation of the Chester School Board to find the means of producing sufficient funds with which to provide each and every child attending public school with a good education. The Commission is not at all convinced that respondent is unable to raise the required funds or that it has exhausted all possible sources of revenue:

1. The school tax rate in the City of Chester is lower in relation to market value of real estate than that of nearby school districts;

2. The School Laws of Pennsylvania permit respondent to seek financial assistance from Delaware County and from the State to provide adequate attention for all of the orthogenic backward and other exceptional children in Chester's public schools;

3. Funds are available for school purposes under the provisions of the National Defense Education Act;

4. New and modern school buildings should be able to be located within the several new urban renewal projects now planned in Chester; and

5. The use of other State and Federal funds could and should be explored by the respondent. Particular attention is directed to the Federal Economic Opportunity Act.

During the hearings, the respondent announced it had requested from the Pennsylvania Department of Public Instruction a professional examination of its entire school system. It was agreed that any reports issued in connection with that survey should be made part of the record in this case. One of the two written reports submitted by the Department of Public Instruction sets forth recommendations for improving the quality of education in the Chester School District. Although these recommendations are silent on the crucial issue of racially segregated public schools, they generally agree with the findings of this Commission in other matters involved in this case, as follows:

1. Intergroup relations material should be included as part of the curriculum;

2. The physical condition and educational facilities at Douglass Junior High School, the only all-Negro junior high school, must be improved;

296

3. Old and inadequate elementary school buildings, nearly all of which are all-Negro or substantially all-Negro, should be eliminated;

4. Overcrowded conditions exist in six elementary schools, five of which are the all-Negro schools;

5. Educational facilities and programs should be provided for all of the orthogenic backward and other exceptional school children; and

6. Kindergartens and special services are urgently needed for the economically deprived school children.

In the famous school desegregation decision of May 17, 1954, the United States Supreme Court was partly influenced by the strong testimony of social scientists, sociologists and psychologists to the effect that segregation in public schools is harmful. There was abundant testimony in the instant case, too, to convince the Commission that the racially segregated public schools within the respondent School District, although using the same textbooks as other schools, and although staffed by Negro teachers certified by the State, nevertheless provide an inherently unequal education for Negro pupils:

1. Three experts testified in behalf of the complainant to the effect that the segregated public education in Chester is unequal and inferior, and that desegregated education will improve the quality of education in Chester. They were Dr. Seymour Leventman, sociologist at the University of Pennsylvania, Dr. Kenneth Smith of the Crozier Theological Seminary in Chester, and Dr. Max Wolff, noted community consultant in educational matters, prominent educator and expert in the field of public school desegregation problems.

2. The parents of *three* Negro pupils whose children once attended all-Negro elementary schools in Chester and elsewhere in Delaware County explained how there was a noticeable change for the better in attitude, motivation and desire to learn when their children transferred to desegregated schools.

3. James Long, a teacher at Pulaski Junior High School, experimented with Negro pupils of the same I.Q. in his school, *one* from the desegregated William Penn School and *the other*

297

from the segregated Dewey-Mann School. He testified that there was a noted difference in the achievement ability of the two pupils, the one from Dewey-Mann being at a disadvantage most of the time.

4. Two principals of all-Negro schools in Chester and two teachers in Chester's school system testified that *two* Negro children of average intelligence and similar socio-economic backgrounds, one attending an all-Negro school and the other a desegregated school in Chester, do not have equal chances to receive a full education, the child attending the desegregated school receiving a fuller education. Mrs. Bernice F. Powell, teacher at the all-Negro Watts School for more than two decades, thus explained that teaching children in an all-Negro school is "like teaching chemistry where you teach all theory without a laboratory."

5. Most of the respondent's witnesses, too, agreed with the basic proposition that education in Chester's segregated schools is inherently unequal to that in its desegregated schools. Mrs. Emma B. Brinckley, principal of Douglass Junior High School, thus said:

"... Students are a product of the learning experiences which are provided for them, their experiences of interacting with people of various backgrounds socially, economically and culturally. Just as you don't learn to swim by just looking at a swimming pool and without ever getting into it, you don't learn to understand people unless you associate with them. Learning is not confined to just the direction which is given in the four walls of a classroom. Children learn through their association with each other in the cafeteria, eating lunch together. They learn through going on class trips together, journeys and educational excursions. They learn in the way in which they appreciate programs. They learn in the way in which they work together on committees in preparing class projects. And there is no way that a teacher, no matter how excellent she is, there is no way that he or she can give a child this experience."

Aside from this strong testimony, the Commission is convinced that sound educational policy, events which have shaken this nation during the past decade, the provisions of the Pennsylvania Human Relations Act and the provisions, intent and meaning of the Governor's Code of Fair Practices in Pennsylvania, demand that school boards throughout Pennsylvania take affirmative action to desegregate all-Negro and substantially all-Negro public schools within their school districts. The close cooperation between this Commission and the Department of Public Instruction of the Commonwealth of Pennsylvania, in accordance with the provisions of Section 8 of the Pennsylvania Human Relations Act; the preparation and distribution in large quantities of Curriculum Development Series No. 6, Guide to Intergroup Education in Schools, entitled, "Our Greatest Challenge—Human Relations" by the Department of Public Instruction in cooperation with this Commission; and the issuance by this Commission in June, 1964, of an Affirmative Action Policy on Education, all bear witness to the fact that this Commission considers as a major goal in the field of public education the desegregation of schools.

The Commission, charged with the duty by law ". . . to prepare a comprehensive educational program, designed for the students of the schools in this Commonwealth and for all other residents thereof, in order to eliminate prejudice . . . and to further good will" sincerely believes that desegregation is as vital for the white pupil as for the Negro pupil. Children in a segregated school are not likely to become committed to the brotherhood of man or to acquire strong convictions concerning racial equality.

The Commission sat as a body during all hearings in this case and has the distinct impression that the respondent, while showing a willingness to eliminate all-Negro and all-white faculties, to bus Negro children in order to alleviate overcrowding, to supply remedial teachers for Negro pupils and to spend money to repair outmoded and old all-Negro school buildings, has consistently been unwilling and still appears to be unwilling to meet the main and crucial issue involved in this controversy, that of desegregating the all-Negro schools in Chester at the earliest possible and practicable time.

On March 9, 1964, the president of the Chester School Board issued a strong statement that the Board will continue to maintain its strict policy of neighborhood schools, announcing to all that it will refuse to budge from its then existing boundary lines and school zones.

Respondent announced at the conclusion of the fifth day of testimony on May 15, 1964, that it would engage educational experts to study the entire situation in Chester and to "tell us what we can do to relieve the problem of de facto segregation in Chester." On June 11, 1964, when Dr. William M. Polishook, the expert engaged by respondent, testified that it was impossible to desegregate Chester's public schools because Chester was rapidly becoming an all-Negro city, he also testified that he did not even attempt to seek a workable plan of desegregation, saying, at page 1052 of the notes of testimony:

> ". . . By the way, I'd like to make clear one point—that I was not brought into this picture in order to help the Chester schools desegregate itself. This was not my mission . . ."

Community tradition and indifference to racial problems have influenced the respondent to assume its attitude about the *sanctity of neighborhood schools,* about the alleged impropriety of taking tne matter of race into account in making assignments of students to public schools, and about the inability of the school board to find the necessary funds with which to effect desegregation. It should be pointed out, however, that a school district should not try to shift its responsibility to the community in which it is located—it is the school district's responsibility to do what needs to be done to eliminate a condition of segregation, illegal under the provisions of the Pennsylvania Human Relations Act.

Desegregation proposals were submitted as a matter of record by the eminent Dr. Max Wolff, expert witness for the complainant, a community consultant and educator who has helped many communities, school districts and civic groups throughout the country to effect workable plans of desegregation of public schools. Dr. Wolff's proposals were divided into two parts, short range and long range. Under the short range proposals, Dr. Wolff explained that it would be possible to desegregate Chester's schools in all grades past the 4th grade by the beginning of the new school term in September, 1964. He spent nine days in Chester working out his plan, part of which required every principal of the 16 schools in the Chester School District to answer a lengthy questionnaire, supplying Dr. Wolff with all data necessary for him to know. He also personally visited school authorities and school principals and examined school buildings.

Under his short range proposals, the School District would be required to reorganize its schools on a 4-2-3-3 basis whereby the senior high school would continue to function for pupils between grades 10 and 12 inclusive and the junior high schools would likewise continue to function for pupils between grades 7 and 9 inclusive; but instead of elementary schools serving pupils between grades 1 and 6 inclusive, as presently constituted, Dr. Wolff proposed the creation of intermediate schools, two in number, to serve all pupils of grades 5 and 6 in the City of Chester. The remaining schools would continue to function for pupils of kindergarten grade through the 4th grade, inclusive, and would be known as primary schools. Part of Dr. Wolff's proposals also permitted desegregation of the all-Negro Douglass Junior High School on a short term basis, by making a single junior high school complex in the center of Chester to which all junior high school students would go in the same manner as all senior high school students now attend one single senior high school composed of three buildings in different parts of the city.

The long range proposals offered by Dr. Wolff would have permitted desegregation of the remaining grades, kindergarten through the 4th grade, on a gradual basis over a period of years, by gradually adding one grade at a time to the said intermediate schools.

In this simple manner, at a minimum of cost and without disrupting affairs unduly, the respondent, if it desired to do so, could have desegregated all grades above the 4th grade in Chester by September of 1964. The Commission is convinced that Dr. Wolff's proposals, either in their entirety or in part, could have provided respondent with a sound, workable plan of desegregation had it earnestly desired to find a means of desegregating its all-Negro schools by September, 1964.

On July 13, 1964, the respondent, for the first time, submitted to the Commission an eleven-point proposal of it own. While it is to the credit of the respondent that it finally agreed to submit a formal plan of its intentions, it is unfortunate that the plan again evades and does not squarely meet and resolve the principal and crucial issue involved in these proceedings—the desegregation of Douglass Junior High School, Dewey-Mann, Franklin, Washington and Watts, the five all-Negro schools within the respondent School District. The School Board proposals do not attempt, other than by vague and indefinite language unsupported by any important details, to propose an effective method whereunder this Commission can be reasonably certain that the all-Negro schools in Chester will be entirely desegregated according to a definite timetable.

It is likewise significant that the respondent has not attempted to determine whether it may be possible to desegregate its schools or

301

some of them by the simple expediency of adopting new boundary lines defining new school zones.

While it is commendable that respondent has already taken steps to assign some Negro teachers to all-white faculties and vice versa, the faculties of several of the schools within the Chester School District still remain either all-white or all-Negro. Of more importance, the testimony of Superintendent Charles B. Long that the community's feelings for tradition prevent the assignment of white teachers to all-Negro faculties except where such white teachers request or agree to such assignment, indicates a violation of the fair employment practices provisions of the Pennsylvania Human Relations Act. This practice should be discontinued.

The Commission finds that the respondent is in violation of Section 5(i) of the Act in failing to provide kindergartens for most of the Negro children in Chester. Four of the five kindergartens are conducted at desegregated schools with school populations predominantly white and only one is conducted at the all-Negro Washington School. The respondent owes a duty to find the means of providing kindergartens for the accommodation and use of larger numbers of Negro children who have special need for this kind of pre-school training.

In August of 1964, the Greater Chester Movement was created, a united effort which promises to develop a modern, progressive and vibrant community, and which bodes well for the future of Chester. The Final Order of the Commission in this case is consistent with the aims and goals of the Greater Chester Movement. The desegregation of the public school system in Chester will inure to the benefit of all by raising the educational quality and standards of the Chester School District. It will create a holding power in Chester's public schools in which all its citizens will take pride.

Dr. John Fischer, President of Teachers College, Columbia University, in New York City, once said that a Negro child entering school "carries a burden no white child can ever know, no matter what handicaps or disabilities he may suffer." The Commission sincerely believes it is the duty of the Chester School District to lighten that burden by making an honest attempt to desegregate the all-Negro schools in Chester. It should not be said that this is too difficult a task—the Chester School District has never really tried.

FINDINGS OF FACT

1. The respondent, Chester School District, administers 17 public schools in the city of Chester, Delaware County, Pennsylvania, one of which, the Martin School, is a special school for orthogenic backward and exceptional children. The other 16 schools are composed of 11 elementary schools, grades 1 through 6 inclusive (five of which have kindergartens and one of which provides classes for orthogenic backward children); four junior high schools, grades 7 through 9 inclusive; and one senior high school, grades 10 through 12 inclusive.

2. The senior high school is composed of three separate buildings operated as a single high school. It is the only public senior high school in Chester and is therefore desegregated racially. As of May, 1964, 1958 pupils attended this high school, of whom 51% (1003) were white and 49% (955) were Negro.

3. The four junior high schools in the Chester School District are Douglass, Pulaski, Showalter and Smedley. The number and race of pupils attending therein as of May, 1964, are as follows:

School	White	Negro	Total
Douglass	1	527	528
Pulaski	311	208	519
Showalter	114	672	786
Smedley	570	164	734

4. The names of the 11 elementary schools administered by respondent and the number and race of pupils attending each in May, 1964, are as follows:

School	White	Negro	Total
Dewey-Mann	None	823	823
Franklin	10	1,018	1,028
Jefferis	385	105	490
Larkin	224	207	431
Lincoln	69	490	559
Morton	77	122	199
Stetser	252	152	404
Washington	None	782	782
Watts	None	344	344
Wetherill	399	37	436
William Penn	732	89	821

5. The pupils at the elementary schools of Dewey-Mann, Washington and Watts are 100% Negro; Franklin Elementary School is 99% Negro; Lincoln Elementary School is 87% Negro; and Douglass Junior High School, with only one white student, is practically 100% Negro. The said public schools are racially segregated.

6. The population of the City of Chester changed racially between 1950 and 1960. In that time, it decreased from 66,069 to 63,658 by losing approximately 10,000 whites and gaining approximately 7,000 Negroes.

7. The total number of pupils in the Chester School District as of May, 1964, was 10,842, of whom 38% (4,147) were white and 62% (6,695) were Negro. In the senior high school 51% were white and 49% Negro; in the four junior high schools 39% were white and 61% Negro; and in the 11 elementary schools 34% were white and 66% Negro.

8. The capacities of the junior high schools are as follows: Douglass—550; Pulaski—700; Showalter—700; and Smedley—750.

9. The capacities of the 11 elementary schools are as follows:

Dewey-Mann	758
Franklin	980
Jefferis	490
Larkin	479
Lincoln	525
Morton	210
Stetser	360
Washington	770
Watts	385
Wetherill	420
William Penn	690

10. The orthogenic backward children in elementary schools situated in the western part of Chester are placed in six classes situated within the Dewey-Mann School, accommodating 108 pupils; orthogenic backward children in elementary schools situated in the eastern part of Chester are placed in six classes at the Martin School, accommodating 87 pupils. Only two white orthogenic backward pupils have been assigned over the years to the all-Negro Dewey-Mann School.

304

In the school year 1963-1964, there were 498 orthogenic backward pupils in the western part of Chester, white and Negro but predominantly Negro, 390 of whom were absorbed into the regular school classes because there was no room to accommodate them at Dewey-Mann. In the same school year, there were 108 such students in the eastern part of Chester, white and Negro but predominantly white, 21 of whom were absorbed into the regular school classes because they could not be accommodated at Martin School.

11. The average size of classes at the 11 elementary schools on December 11, 1963, indicated that the all-Negro or nearly all-Negro schools were most overcrowded, as follows:

Dewey-Mann	37
Franklin	35
Jefferis	31
Larkin	36
Morton	33
Stetser	30
Washington	34
Watts	32
Wetherill	31
William Penn	33

12. Most of the Negro children in Chester do not receive any kindergarten training, there being only five kindergartens, at Jefferis, Stetser, Washington, Wetherill and William Penn schools. Only one of these kindergartens is conducted at an all-Negro school, Washington Elementary School.

13. High school and junior high school pupils are accepted by respondent on a tuition basis from surrounding school districts, particularly Chester Township and Upland Township. Junior high school tuition students are both white and Negro and are assigned to Douglass and Showalter in Chester. Only Negro tuition pupils are being assigned to the all-Negro Douglass Junior High School.

14. As early as 1934, Negro parents protested to the Chester School Board concerning the poor physical condition of the all-Negro schools. As of February, 1964, the physical condition of the all-Negro school buildings, particularly of Dewey-Mann, Washington, Watts and Douglass, was poor, especially in toilet facilities, painting, lighting,

305

plastering, cleanliness and general upkeep. Generally speaking, the physical condition of the all-Negro schools has been inferior to that of other schools in the Chester School District, with the exception of Morton and Larkin schools, both of which were built prior to 1900.

15. The respondent School District had at no time prior to September, 1964, employed special teachers to assist handicapped pupils in remedial reading or other subjects; nor have there been tutorial programs or cultural enrichment programs in Chester's schools for the culturally or motivationally deprived pupils.

16. The social studies, history and civics textbooks used in Chester's public schools do not adequately treat the contributions of the Negro to the American scene. There are no other textbooks yet available which do give adequate treatment to this subject. The Chester School District has made plans to purchase such books when they become available.

17. The respondent School District has at no time engaged a specially qualified human relations expert to assist principals and teachers to prepare supplementary material in intergroup and intercultural relations for the pupils of Chester's public schools. The Curriculum Development Series No. 6, Guide to Intergroup Education in Schools, entitled, "Our Greatest Challenge—Human Relations" has been made available by the Pennsylvania Department of Public Instruction to the Chester School District, but its use had not been implemented as of May, 1964.

18. The City of Chester is approximately three miles wide. Within the concept of the requirement of the Public School Code that elementary school children must be bused if they are assigned to schools more than one and one-half (1½) miles distant from their homes, there are two and no more than three neighborhood school areas in the City of Chester.

19. The Chester School Board has the sole authority to establish or change school boundary lines for the assignment of pupils to particular public schools in accordance with law. Such boundary lines have been established for both junior high schools and for elementary schools in Chester. The minutes of the Chester School Board meetings do not indicate when the elementary school boundary lines were first established; nor do they reflect all of the changes

effected in such boundary lines during the past ten years. Only boundary lines of August, 1954 and September, 1959 are referred to in the minutes of the School Board meetings.

20. Prior to 1954, Negro pupils were required by the Chester School District to pass all-white schools near their homes to attend more distant schools which were all-Negro.

21. During the past ten years, when boundary lines for the William Penn School were established, Negro pupils were permitted by respondent to cross such lines in order to attend the all-Negro Dewey-Mann School. As of May, 1964, such practice was not permitted.

22. Boundary lines for elementary schools are known to have been established by respondent in August, 1954 and are known to have been changed by respondent in September, 1959, on May 4, 1964 and on August 24, 1964. During the past ten years, however, other changes in boundary lines, not recorded in the Chester School Board's minutes, were made changing the western vertical boundary line defining the school zone for the all-Negro Dewey-Mann School.

23. The boundary lines established by respondent for Dewey-Mann, Washington and Watts Elementary Schools and for Douglass Junior High School define Negro residential areas in Chester and therefore have the effect of perpetuating racially segregated schools in Chester.

24. Prior to May 4, 1964, at least one white pupil, Jacqueline Kelly, 905 Palmer Street, Chester, Pennsylvania, had been crossing the boundary lines defining the all-Negro Dewey-Mann school zone and attending the substantially all-white William Penn School.

25. On May 4, 1964, the Chester School Board changed elementary school boundary lines and, among other changes, eliminated from the pre-existing boundary lines defining the school zone for the all-Negro Dewey-Mann School, an area located in the northwest portion of such zone, said area being composed of white residents only.

26. On August 24, 1964, the Chester School Board again changed boundary lines for elementary schools, eliminating all changes but one in boundary lines put into effect on May 4, 1964. The change not disturbed by the Board's action of August 24, 1964, was the elimination of the all-white residential area from the Dewey-Mann school zone.

307

27. The Chester School District has established the Chester Creek as the boundary line governing the assignment of orthogenic backward pupils. There are 3,990 pupils, predominantly Negro, in the elementary schools west of that boundary line and 1,923 pupils, predominantly white, in the elementary schools east of that boundary line. There are 108 seats reserved at Dewey-Mann School for orthogenic backward pupils west of said boundary line, and 87 seats reserved at Martin School for orthogenic backward pupils east of said boundary line. The white orthogenic backward pupil consequently has approximately five times as many chances of receiving the special treatment he requires than the Negro orthogenic backward pupil in Chester.

28. The Chester School Board engages teachers for the Chester School District and the Superintendent of the said District assigns teachers to particular schools. Promotions to supervisory and administrative positions within the Chester School District are likewise made by the Board on the basis of recommendations from the Superintendent.

29. The Superintendent of the Chester School District engages and assigns all employes other than teachers, including clerks, stenographers and bookkeepers.

30. There were a total of 438 teachers in the Chester School District as of May 14, 1964, of whom 67% (293) were white and 33% (145) were Negro. As of that date, there were 95% (94) white and 5% (5) Negro teachers in the senior high school; there were 66% (91) white and 34% (46) Negro teachers in the four junior high schools; and there were 53% (108) white and 47% (94) Negro teachers in the eleven elementary schools.

31. A white teacher is not assigned or transferred by respondent to any Chester public school having an all-Negro faculty unless said teacher is willing to be so assigned or transferred.

32. As of May 14, 1964, with the exception of one white music teacher at Douglass Junior High School, only Negro teachers were assigned to the all-Negro schools of Douglass Junior High School, Dewey-Mann, Washington and Watts. Only white teachers were assigned to Jefferis, Morton, Stetser, Wetherill and William Penn schools.

33. The number and race of teachers assigned to junior high schools and elementary schools as of May 14, 1964, are as follows:

School	White	Negro	Total
Douglass	1	32	33
Pulaski	23	5	28
Showalter	31	7	38
Smedley	36	2	38
Dewey-Mann	None	25	25
Franklin	8	20	28
Jefferis	16	None	16
Larkin	14	2	16
Lincoln	8	9	17
Morton	6	None	6
Stetser	15	None	15
Washington	None	25	25
Watts	None	13	13
Wetherill	15	None	15
William Penn	26	None	26

34. There are no Negro employes in the Chester School District holding any of the 13 supervisory or administrative positions above that of principal. However, with the exception of one known applicant, Negroes have not applied for promotions to such supervisory or administrative positions.

35. Among the 29 bookkeepers, stenographers and other clerks in the Chester School District, five are Negroes, one of whom is assigned to Chester Senior High School. The other four Negro employes are assigned to the all-Negro Dewey-Mann, Franklin, Washington and Watts schools. Just as no Negro clerk has been assigned to predominantly white schools, no white clerk has been assigned to any all-Negro school. No Negro clerk has been assigned to work in the Administration Building.

36. The faculties and student bodies of Douglass Junior High School, Washington and Watts have at all times relevant hereto been all-Negro, with the exception of the music teacher and one white student at Douglass; and the student body, principal, faculty and other employes of Watts Elementary School have been all-Negro since its origin 75 years ago.

309

37. The same textbooks, courses and curriculum are used in all schools within the Chester School District. All teachers employed by the respondent have the necessary State requirements for teacher certification.

38. Despite use of the same textbooks and curriculum, the education offered to pupils attending the all-Negro schools of Dewey-Mann, Douglass, Franklin, Washington and Watts in the Chester School District, is inherently unequal and inferior to that offered to pupils attending desegregated schools in the District.

39. Two Negro children in Chester of average intelligence and similar socio-economic background, one attending an all-Negro school and the other a desegregated school, would not have an equal chance of receiving a full education. The all-Negro school is inferior and the child who attends the desegregated school receives a fuller education.

40. There is a noted difference in the achievement ability of two Negro pupils of the same I.Q., one entering Pulaski Junior High School from the desegregated William Penn School, the other from the segregated Dewey-Mann School, the pupil from Dewey-Mann being at a disadvantage most of the time.

41. The separation of pupils by race in Chester's public schools prevents experiences which would promote understanding and serves to reinforce divisive prejudices among such pupils.

42. Desegregation of schools and faculties in Chester will improve the quality of education in the Chester School District.

43. In order to relieve overcrowding, the respondent, in November, 1963, began to transport two bus loads of Negro pupils out of Franklin Elementary School to Wetherill School and continued this practice to the end of the 1963-1964 school term at a cost of approximately $7,800.00. Negro pupils thus transported from the overcrowded, all-Negro Franklin School to the Wetherill School became better motivated in attitude, desire to learn and demeanor.

44. As of May 6, 1964, the respondent, acting through the Chester School Board, had not proposed any effective plan under which the all-Negro schools in Chester might be desegregated; nor discussed at any Board meeting the advisability or inadvisability of eliminating Chester's all-Negro schools.

310

45. The 1964-1965 Chester School District budget is based upon a 46½ mills tax on real estate having an assessed valuation of about $71,000,000.00. The tax rate was 44 mills in 1963-1964; 40 mills in 1962-1963; 37½ mills in 1961-1962; and 32 mills in 1960-1961. The tax rate by mills is 75 in adjoining Chester Township, and 80 in adjoining Upland Township. However, the ratio of the assessed real estate valuation to market value thereof is 22.7 in Chester Township, 24.9 in Upland Township and 31.3 in the City of Chester. The school tax rate in the City of Chester is lower in relation to market value of real estate than that of nearby school districts.

46. Proposals for desegregating Chester's public schools were submitted by a duly qualified educator and community consultant, Dr. Max Wolff, whereunder, with a minimum of busing, overcrowding in all of Chester's public schools would be eliminated immediately, space would become available for the establishment of kindergartens at all primary schools, all segregated classes past the 4th grade in all schools would be eliminated immediately, and grades below the 5th grade would be desegregated on a long range basis. Dr. Wolff proposed that the Chester School District:

(a) Combine Douglass, Showalter, Lincoln and Washington schools into one single junior high school complex for all junior high school pupils in Chester;

(b) Convert Pulaski and Smedley into intermediate schools to serve all 5th and 6th grade pupils of Chester, making Stetser an annex to Smedley;

(c) Retain all remaining elementary schools as primary schools for children of kindergarten through the 4th grade; and

(d) Re-assign pupils below the 5th grade now at Lincoln, Washington and Stetser to nearby primary schools.

47. On July 13, 1964, the respondent rejected the Wolff proposals and offered its own eleven-point proposal as follows:

(a) Emphasis on quality education in all schools with special emphasis in schools with special problems with expenditures of special funds for this purpose;

(b) Overcrowdedness to be alleviated by transferring pupils to less crowded facilities by busing if necessary;

311

(c) No radical change is to be made in present 6-3-3 school organization plan and the policy of neighborhood schools;

(d) A long-range plan to alleviate overcrowdedness and eliminate old schools by relocating them in more desirable locations is to be undertaken;

(e) Provision of more facilities for special education students is an item of high priority in planning;

(f) Enlargement and conversion of the Showalter Junior High School into a new high school complex and use of the Douglass facility for special education programs;

(g) Maintenance of a close relationship with community groups to encourage understanding and cooperation;

(h) Development of plans for a new elementary school in order to relieve overcrowding and provide space for kindergartens and special classes;

(i) Provision of kindergarten classes in culturally deprived areas as soon as possible;

(j) Integrate the non-white staffs by filling vacancies as they develop and by encouraging voluntary transfers; and

(k) Continuation and expansion of the pre-school program financed by the Chester School District and the Ford Foundation.

48. Beginning with September, 1964, the respondent School District began to implement its said eleven-point proposal, as follows:

(a) Overcrowding at the all-Negro Dewey-Mann and Franklin schools is being relieved by busing 240 Negro pupils from Franklin to Wetherill and 69 Negro pupils from Dewey-Mann to William Penn; also 41 additional Negro pupils at Franklin have been re-assigned to walk daily to nearby desegregated schools less crowded. Such busing will cost the respondent between $26,000.00 and $27,000.00 for the 1964-1965 school year;

(b) Respondent has made plans and expended money to repair and alter the all-Negro Dewey-Mann, Douglass, Franklin, Washington and Watts schools. In the summer months immediately preceding September, 1964, respondent expended the sum of $69,000.00 on such repairs and alterations;

312

(c) Respondent has assigned one Negro teacher to each of the previously all-white faculties of Jefferis, Morton and William Penn, leaving all-white faculties only at Stetser and Wetherill; respondent also assigned four white teachers to the previously all-Negro faculty of Dewey-Mann and one white teacher to the previously all-Negro faculty at Washington; and

(d) Respondent engaged three reading specialists to teach slow readers at the all-Negro elementary schools.

49. As of September, 1964, the total public school population had decreased by 36, there now being a total of 10,806 pupils in the Chester School District, of whom 36% (3,909) are white and 64% (6,987) are Negro.

50. The eleven-point proposal of the Chester School District does not adequately or satisfactorily provide with sufficient particularity or a reasonable timetable, for the desegregation of Chester's all-Negro and substantially all-Negro schools.

51. The Chester School District has at no time desired or attempted to desegregate Chester's public schools by the adoption of new school zones through the medium of new boundary lines for all schools.

52. Although the respondent was aware or should have been aware of the existence of segregated schools within its system, it did not at any time prior to July 13, 1964, attempt to correct this condition.

53. Chester's segregated public school system has not arisen by accident but, in large part, by the following actions and failures to act on the part of the respondent:

(a) Failure to adjust boundary lines from time to time so as to prevent six of the 16 schools in Chester from becoming racially segregated;

(b) Failure to take affirmative action over the years to eliminate its segregated school system which was originally created by the Chester School District's requirement that Negro pupils pass nearby schools to attend all-Negro schools much farther away from their homes;

313

(c) Failure to permit a policy of open enrollment;

(d) Manipulating boundary lines

(i) by eliminating a white residential area from the all-Negro Dewey-Mann school zone and making it part of the substantially all-white William Penn school zone; and

(ii) by permitting crossing of boundary lines by Negroes from the William Penn school zone to the Dewey-Mann school zone, and by at least one white pupil out of the Dewey-Mann zone into the William Penn zone;

(e) Permitting the physical condition of the all-Negro school buildings to be inferior to that of other schools;

(f) Assigning only Negro teachers and only Negro clerks to all-Negro schools;

(g) Assigning only Negro orthogenic backward pupils to the all-Negro Dewey-Mann School;

(h) Assigning only Negro tuition pupils from nearby school districts to the all-Negro Douglass Junior High School; and

(i) Failure to approve or adopt any effective plan of desegregation, with a timetable, refusing to give consideration to such possible plan through its School Board.

CONCLUSIONS OF LAW

Upon all the evidence at the public hearings and the foregoing findings of fact, the Pennsylvania Human Relations Commission makes the following conclusions of law:

1. The Pennsylvania Human Relations Commission may properly act as the complainant in this proceeding.

2. At all times herein mentioned, respondent was and still is a place of public accommodations within the meaning of Section 4(1) of the Pennsylvania Human Relations Act.

3. At all times herein mentioned, respondent was and still is an employer within the meaning of Section 4(b) of the Pennsylvania Human Relations Act.

4. At all times herein mentioned, the Pennsylvania Human Relations Commission had and still has jurisdiction over the respondent, Chester School District.

5. At all times herein mentioned, the Pennsylvania Human Relations Commission had and still has jurisdiction over the subject matter of this proceeding and over the instant complaint.

6. The unlawful discriminatory practices involved herein have occurred and still occur within the Commonwealth of Pennsylvania and have deprived Negroes, residents of the City of Chester, Delaware County, Pennsylvania, of their civil rights.

7. At all times herein mentioned, respondent has committed and continues to commit unlawful discriminatory practices in violation of Sections 4(g) and 5(a) of the Pennsylvania Human Relations Act, in that the respondent assigns only Negro teachers to all-Negro schools and only Negro clerks to all-Negro schools.

8. At all times herein mentioned, respondent has committed and continues to commit unlawful discriminatory practices in violation of Sections 4(g) and 5(i) of the Pennsylvania Human Relations Act, in that (1) respondent maintains segregated all-Negro and substantially all-Negro public schools within its school system, (2) respondent has established school zones which confine the Negro to all-Negro schools, (3) respondent has failed to make available kindergartens in sufficient number to accommodate the children of Negroes living in Chester, (4) respondent has permitted the physical condition of the all-Negro school buildings to be inferior to that of other school buildings in its system, and (5) respondent has failed to accept or adopt any affirmative program or plan whereunder the schools it administers will be effectively desegregated within a reasonable time.

COMMISSION'S DECISION

Upon all of the evidence at the public hearings of this case, and in consideration of the findings of fact and conclusions of law above set forth, the Pennsylvania Human Relations Commission finds and determines:

1. The Commission has jurisdiction over the respondent School District, the subject matter of this proceeding and the complaint, and the Motion to Dismiss is denied.

315

2. The respondent has committed and continues to commit unlawful discriminatory practices in violation of Sections 4(g), 5(a) and 5(i) of the Pennsylvania Human Relations Act, in that (1) respondent maintains segregated, all-Negro and substantially all-Negro public schools within its school system, (2) respondent has established public school zones which confine the Negro pupils to all-Negro schools, (3) respondent has failed to make available kindergartens in sufficient number to accommodate the children of Negroes living in Chester, (4) respondent assigns only Negro teachers and only Negro clerks to all-Negro public schools, (5) respondent has permitted the physical condition of the all-Negro school buildings to be inferior to that of other school buildings in its system, and (6) respondent has failed to accept or adopt any affirmative plan whereby the public schools it administers will be effectively desegregated within a reasonable time.

3. The charge in the Complaint which avers unlawful discriminatory practices by the respondent for using textbooks which do not treat adequately or ignore entirely the contributions of the Negro to the American scene is dismissed.

4. The charge in the Complaint which avers that the respondent has committed unlawful discriminatory practices by failing to appoint Negroes to supervisory and administrative positions is hereby dismissed.

5. The Pennsylvania Human Relations Commission will retain jurisdiction in the subject matter of this proceeding until such time as the respondent fully complies with the Commission's Final Order.

FINAL ORDER

AND NOW, November 20th, 1964, upon consideration of the foregoing Findings of Fact, Conclusions of Law and Commission's Decision, and pursuant to Section 9 of the Pennsylvania Human Relations Act and Sections 105.23 and 105.24 of the Regulations of the Commission, it is hereby

ORDERED, by the Pennsylvania Human Relations Commission

1. That the respondent, Chester School District, by and through the Chester School Board, its officers, agents and employes, shall cease and desist from assigning only Negro teachers to those public schools, the faculties of which are entirely Negro.

316

2. That the respondent, Chester School District, by and through the Chester School Board, its officers, agents and employes, shall cease and desist from refusing to assign or transfer a white teacher to a public school, the faculty of which is entirely Negro or almost entirely Negro, unless said white teacher gives prior consent to be so assigned or transferred.

3. That the respondent, Chester School District, by and through the Chester School Board, its officers, agents and employes shall cease and desist from assigning only white teachers to Stetser Elementary School and to Wetherill Elementary School.

4. That the respondent, Chester School District, by and through the Chester School Board, its officers, agents and employes, shall cease and desist from assigning only Negro bookkeepers, stenographers and clerks to the all-Negro Douglass Junior High School, Dewey-Mann Elementary School, Franklin Elementary School, Washington Elementary School and Watts Elementary School.

5. That the respondent, Chester School District, by and through the Chester School Board, its officers, agents and employes, shall take immediate steps to establish kindergartens at the following all-Negro elementary schools: Dewey-Mann, Franklin and Watts.

6. That the respondent, Chester School District, by and through the Chester School Board, its officers, agents and employes, shall take immediate steps to desegregate effectively the all-Negro Douglass Junior High School, and the following all-Negro or substantially all-Negro elementary schools: Dewey-Mann, Franklin, Lincoln, Washington and Watts.

7. That the respondent, Chester School District, by and through the Chester School Board, its officers, agents and employes, shall take the following affirmative action which, in the judgment of the Commission, will effectuate the purpose of the Pennsylvania Human Relations Act:

a. Advise and direct in writing all individual members of the Chester School Board, all of its agents, employes and interviewers having any duty or function with respect to the solicitation, recruitment, referral, selection, hiring, assignment or transfer of teachers and of bookkeepers, clerks and stenographers, that it is the policy and intent of the respondent to comply fully with the Pennsylvania Human Relations Act, and that in the assignment of teachers, bookkeepers, clerks and stenographers, respondent will assign solely on the basis of individual merit and that

(1) respondent will not assign only Negro teachers, bookkeepers, clerks and stenographers to the all-Negro Douglass Junior High School, Dewey-Mann Elementary School, Franklin Elementary School, Washington Elementary School and Watts Elementary School,

(2) respondent will not assign only white teachers to Stetser Elementary School and Wetherill Elementary School, and

(3) respondent will not require the consent of any white teacher, bookkeeper, clerk or stenographer before assigning or transferring said employe to any public school which it administers;

b. Furnish the Commission with copies of said directive signed by each recipient to indicate its receipt by each of them;

c. Formulate a Plan consistent with the principles and findings of this decision, to establish kindergartens at the following three all-Negro elementary schools: Dewey-Mann, Franklin and Watts, and submit such plan or plans for approval of this Commission on or before December 31, 1964, so that said plan or plans may be implemented beginning no later than February, 1965;

d. Formulate a Plan consistent with the principles and findings of this decision, to desegregate effectively the following schools: Douglass Junior High School, Dewey-Mann Elementary School, Franklin Elementary School, Lincoln Elementary School, Washington Elementary School and Watts Elementary School. In the formulation of such plan of desegregation, the Commission urges the respondent carefully and seriously to consider the following guidelines:

(1) The plan must state all details as to the school or schools to be replaced, converted or repaired, including but not limited to costs, proposed methods of obtaining

318

the required funds, and actual dates when the proposed construction or alterations will be commenced and completed;

(2) If the plan proposes conversion of a present school facility, it must also state with particularity the boundary lines which will define the school zone for such converted school, the number of children required to be bused to such school, and the cost of such busing;

(3) If the plan proposes construction of new school buildings, it must state specifically all details concerning the exact sites at which such buildings will be erected, the boundary lines which will define the school zones for each such new school, the number of children required to be bused to each such school, and the cost of such busing;

(4) For short range and immediate action, the plan could embody any or all of the following:

(a) The adoption of new boundary lines creating new zones which would desegregate some of the segregated schools;

(b) The creation of middle or intermediary schools for all 5th and 6th grade pupils, to desegregate such grades;

(c) The establishment of a single junior high school complex in the central part of Chester, similar to the present senior high school arrangement, which would desegregate the all-Negro Douglass Junior High School;

(d) The conversion of Chester High School into a junior high school to accommodate pupils now attending Douglass and Showalter Junior High Schools, and the conversion of Showalter Junior High School into a senior high school, to desegregate the all-Negro Douglass Junior High School;

e. Submit said Plan of Desegregation, with detailed information and stating a definite timetable, to this Commission for its approval, on or before January 31, 1965, so that said Plan or Plans, if approved by this Commission, may be implemented no later than the beginning of the 1965-1966 school year; and

319

f. Notify the Pennsylvania Human Relations Commission at its office at 1401 Labor and Industry Building, Harrisburg, Pennsylvania, 17120, in writing, within fifteen (15) days of the date of service of this Final Order, as to the steps the respondent has taken to comply with each ordered provision of this Final Order.

PENNSYLVANIA HUMAN RELATIONS COMMISSION*

---

* In February 1966 the Court of Common Pleas of Dauphin County, Pa. reversed the foregoing Commission determination, not on the merits but on the ground that the Commission was without jurisdiction. A further appeal to a higher court is pending.

Appendix C

LAWYERS' VIEW

CIVIL RIGHTS AND DISOBEDIENCE TO LAW*

by

Harrison Tweed,
Bernard G. Segal,
AND
Herbert L. Packer

One of the most troubling aspects of the current crisis in race relations is the frequency with which it seems the law is being violated by those active in the struggle on both sides.

This is a serious matter because no one can doubt that this country must solve the civil-rights problem not by a resort to lawlessness and disorder but by reliance upon the administration of the law through due process in the courts and fair enforcement by the appropriate authorities.

Thus the spectacle of repeated violations of law, actual or apparent, by those who are pressing the fight for civil rights is deeply troubling to many thoughtful persons who reject the notion that the end justifies the means and who insist that those who work for good ends must remain morally accountable for the methods they use to work toward those ends.

What is the difference, these people ask, between the Southern governor who violates the law by standing in the schoolhouse door to prevent the court-directed entry of Negro pupils, and the Negro demonstrator who violates the law by participating in a "sit-in" at a segregated lunch counter in a Southern city that has an ordinance making it illegal for him to do so? Is there a meaningful distinction between these two cases? And what can be said about the position of an eminent clergyman who attacks segregation by taking part in a demonstration that ends in his arrest on the charge of having wrongfully trespassed on another's property; or the people who delay construction of a hospital by physically obstructing the movement of men

---

* Copyright 1964 by Presbyterian Life, Inc. Reprinted by permission.

and materials at the construction site during a protest against dis- criminatory hiring practices by the builder of the hospital? These and many similar instances that continue to recur require careful thought if we are to be clear about the bounds within which the struggle for civil rights may legitimately proceed.

In this article we shall not venture into the deep waters of philo- sophic speculation about the moral justifiability of disobeying an unjust law. Our concern is with the legal issues involved, and our purpose is to call attention to some aspects of the legal system that are often overlooked in discussions of this subject, to the detriment of clear thinking about it.

Let us start with a relatively easy case. On the one hand we have Governor Wallace vowing to "stand in the schoolhouse door." On the other hand we have a Negro demonstrator who sits at a lunch counter in Greenville, South Carolina, that is required by local law to be segregated. We think that these two cases are easy to differentiate; but there are obviously erroneous answers to the problem. It is no answer to say that in one case the objective is "bad" and in the other it is "good." Orderly social living would be impossible if people only obeyed laws they happened to like. And it is not much more helpful to say that in the first case the law being disobeyed was con- stitutional, while in the second case it was not. Whether a law is constitutional involves a prediction as to how a court will decide the question. We know now that laws and ordinances directing racial segregation in places of public accommodation are unconstitutional. The Supreme Court, to whom belongs the power of final decision, has so held. But we did not know it before the Court so held, although it may not have required great learning in constitutional doctrine to enable one to guess the outcome. The point is that Negro demon- strators who staged sit-ins before those laws and ordinances were held unconstitutional appeared on the surface to be engaging in conduct just as defiant of law as that of Governor Wallace in Tusca- loosa and of Governor Barnett in Oxford. The distinction between the cases plainly involved something more than a difference in accuracy of predicting the course of judicial decision.

> *"A free society would be doomed unless it provided the citizen with means for asserting the invalidity of laws and other official acts as measured against the funda- mental law of the Constitution."*

The crucial difference lies in the fact that the Negro demonstrators were not violating any court order, but rather laws which had not been tested, which the Negro demonstrators *in good faith believed were invalid,* and which they were determined to challenge *through the processes of law.* Under our system a person is entitled to challenge the validity of a law being applied against him by resisting its enforcement *in court* on a plea of invalidity. That kind of lawful resistance to law is a cornerstone of our liberties. A free society would be doomed unless it provided the citizen with means for asserting the invalidity of laws and other official acts as measured against the fundamental law of the Constitution. When the law being challenged provides criminal penalties, as these segregation laws do, the challenger runs the risk of going to jail if his challenge is not ultimately upheld by the courts. In the face of that danger, it is a courageous and commendable act for a man to defy a law in order to attack its validity through the processes of law. That is what the Negro demonstrators against segregation laws have done, and we should honor them for it.

The conduct of Governor Wallace and of Governor Barnett stands in sharp contrast to this kind of lawful resistance to law. Both sought to resist the execution of Federal court decrees ordering their respective state universities to admit Negro students. We may assume that both of them believed that the Federal court decrees were unconstitutional, that desegregation by law is an invasion of the rightful sphere of the states. But that belief, if it existed, was not accompanied by a determination to challenge desegregation through the processes of law. Quite the contrary. Both Governor Wallace and Governor Barnett did everything they could to avoid submitting their dispute about the validity of the law they were resisting to the orderly and due processes of law. Instead, they did everything they could to delay and defeat the execution of the court orders without involving themselves in a legal contest; and they acted after the validity of the desegregation orders had been fully and unsuccessfully challenged in the courts.

> "... a statute or ordinance that is valid on its face may
> be administered in an unfair way and may consequently
> be invalid as applied."

Governor Wallace's brief show of defiance at Tuscaloosa was evidently calculated to avoid subjecting himself to being held in contempt of the Federal court's order. His evident purpose was to harass by diversionary tactics, not to contest by law. His conduct was, simply and literally, lawless. The Negro demonstrators, on the other hand, were disobeying laws they believed to be invalid in order to invite rather than to evade a lawful resolution of their contentions. There may have been no other way to contest the validity of segregation laws. Defiance of a court order, however, is both unnecessary (since other means are available to test its validity) and subversive of the orderly processes of government. Such conduct by one who is sworn to uphold the law is particularly deplorable.

It is of course true that it does not require a multiplicity of sit-in cases to establish the legal proposition that state and municipal segregation laws are invalid. In the case of many sit-ins, freedom rides, and other demonstrations against segregation laws and other forms of discrimination, a somewhat different issue is presented. The purpose of mass demonstrations such as those that took place in Birmingham, Alabama, last spring was not primarily to provide an opportunity for court attack on segregation but rather to dramatize the contentions of the Negro community, to focus public attention on the pattern of racial inequality, and to bring pressure on the white community to alter their ways. Inevitably, these demonstrations appeared to involve violations of laws other than the admittedly invalid segregation ordinances. Demonstrators were arrested for such offenses as holding a parade without a permit, disorderly conduct, and trespassing upon private property. The same pattern of demonstration, disorder, and resulting arrests has taken place in many Northern cities.

Now, of course, there is nothing invalid about a statute or ordinance that prohibits disorderly conduct, or trespass, or that imposes reasonable requirements on the holding of public meetings in the interest of maintaining order. That is to say, there is nothing invalid about such a statute or ordinance on its face, as lawyers say. Many people leap from that fact to the erroneous conclusion that conduct in violation of such an ordinance necessarily is unlawful and should therefore be condemned. That conclusion overlooks the well-established proposition of law that a statute or ordinance that is valid on its face may be administered in an unfair way and may consequently be invalid as applied. For example, let us assume that it is unobjectionable for a city to have an ordinance requiring persons wishing to use public thoroughfares or parks for a parade or a meeting to obtain a license to do so from the chief of police. Such an ordinance may be used so that traffic will not be disrupted at inconvenient hours, or so that there will not be a conflict between two or more groups seeking to use the same location for a meeting at the same time, or for some other valid and nondiscriminatory municipal purpose. Such an ordinance can be valid on its face: that is to say, in its normal application it presents no problems, as opposed to an ordinance that requires segregation of the races, which has no valid application at all and is therefore invalid on its face.

Now let us suppose that the chief of police uses the ordinance to deny access to public facilities to Negro groups but not to whites. There is no question but that the ordinance is then being applied in an invalid manner to deny to the Negro groups the rights of speech and assembly to which they are entitled under the Bill of Rights. They are caught in a familar dilemma. If they stand on their rights, they are disobeying the local law; if they obey the local law (and do not parade without the license that they cannot get), then they are deprived of rights to which they are constitutionally entitled. That dilemma is dissolved by decisions of the Supreme Court holding that people may not be punished for violating a local law which, however fair on its face, has been applied in a way that violates their constitutional rights.

"It is the duty of law-enforcement authorities to protect freedom of speech by making arrangements for the safety of those who urge unpopular causes."

Of course, it is not always easy to tell when people's constitutional rights are being violated by the application of local laws and when they are not. For example, suppose that it is perfectly clear that the holding of a public meeting on a controversial issue is going to provoke an outbreak of disorder, and the authorities therefore try to prevent the meeting from taking place. Are civil-rights demonstrators justified in going ahead with a meeting even though they know that the result is likely to be violence? Perhaps it would be more prudent for them to abstain, but our American tradition of protection for free speech suggests that they may assert their right to go ahead and hold the meeting despite the threat of violence. It is the duty of law-enforcement authorities to protect freedom of speech by making arrangements for the safety of those who urge unpopular causes. Needless to say, that ideal is often not realized in practice, and never more obviously than in the failure of law-enforcement authorities in the South to protect the rights of Negroes and others who demonstrate for civil rights. In an extremity, the police may stop a meeting in order to protect the participants from violence and to prevent a general eruption of disorder. But that reserve power should not be used as an excuse to do nothing in advance to protect the rights of the speakers or demonstrators. It would be a strange legal system that held those who violently interfere with the freedom of others equally accountable with those who are their hapless victims. And our system is not in any ultimate way open to that reproach, whatever the views to the contrary of state and local police, prosecutors, and judges.

One of the most difficult questions in the civil-rights area that the Supreme Court has to face is whether segregation by private owners of facilities open to the public-at-large may be enforced by criminal prosecutions for trespass in the absence of any state law or policy requiring or favoring segregation. The Court has on its current docket cases that may force it to deal with the question. And the question was put dramatically in July, 1963, when a group of Protestant clergymen, including Dr. Eugene Carson Blake of the United Presbyterian Church, were arrested for criminal trespass while accompanying a group of Negroes who sought admission to a segregated amusement park in Maryland. It seems to us that Dr. Blake and his colleagues were well within the justifying principles that we have been discussing in this article. It is perfectly true as a general proposition that you may be subjected to criminal prosecution for going upon another's property against his will. There is nothing illegal on their face about laws that protect private property rights by penalizing people who willfully violate those rights. But it is fairly open to question whether the state may back up a private preference for segregation, at least when the premises in question are normally open to the public-at-large, by lending the aid of its criminal process to enforce the will of the would-be segregator.

To put it another way, the state's criminal trespass law may be invalid as it is applied to the case of the public facility whose owner seeks state aid in enforcing segregation. Valid or invalid, it seems entirely appropriate, until the question is finally decided for those who have a *good faith belief* that the law is being invalidly applied in these circumstances, to challenge the law by acting as Dr. Blake and

326

his colleagues did. If the courts were finally and definitively to rule against the argument that the trespass laws were being invalidly applied in this situation, continued defiance of the law would not have the justification that can presently be made for it. Then Dr. Blake and Governor Wallace would indeed be in the same boat insofar as the lack of legal justification for their conduct is concerned. Continued resistance to law that has been fully and fairly settled, whatever the appeal to conscience or to history may produce in the way of an answer, is no part of the American tradition and is in the deepest sense subversive of the legal process. But as matters stand today, whatever judgment men of the world might reach on prudential grounds about this sort of social protest, it cannot be labeled as lawless.

> *"Primary reliance should be placed, we believe, upon quiet and orderly processes of conciliation and negotiation...."*

We do not want to leave the impression that the mere fact that demonstration is carried on in behalf of civil rights can serve as a legal justification for it. There is much civil-rights activity that merits the condemnation of all who prize the ideal of liberty under law. When valid laws are broken simply to create sympathy for the civil-rights position or, even less defensibly, simply to dramatize the contentions of the demonstrators, it seems clear that important values are being unjustifiably sacrificed. The demonstrators who were convicted of breach of the peace for camping in Governor Rockefeller's office could offer no justification of the kind we have been discussing for the violation of law. The law they violated was not invalid, either on its face or as applied to them. Other instances of civil-rights demonstrations that have involved totally unjustifiable violations of law come also to mind. Last summer's blockade of the approaches to Jones Beach in New York by demonstrators lying down in the road can hardly be condoned, even assuming the correctness of the demonstrators' view that Negroes were being discriminated against in employment there. The same is true of the demonstrations that led to a halt in construction work on the Downtown Medical Center in Brooklyn, New York. The distinction between peaceful picketing and interference with the rights of others is not always an easy one to draw, as the history of labor relations in this country demonstrates; but both of these incidents violated well-accepted standards of behavior in labor disputes.

Even when demonstrations may not in themselves involve illegal conduct, there is a question of judgment involved if they are used indiscriminately. Primary reliance should be placed, we believe, upon quiet and orderly processes of conciliation and negotiation to resolve specific civil-rights disputes. Demonstrations which expose their participants to situations that may involve violations of law should be a last resort.

Disobedience to law is always prima facie unjustifiable. It can be justified, as we have shown, particularly in situations in which obeying the law defeats the enjoyment of constitutionally guaranteed civil liberties. But the burden is always on the person who claims that this violation of law is legally justifiable. And that burden applies just as strongly in the court of public opinion as it does in a court of law, a fact that makes it incumbent on proponents of the great struggle for civil rights to go about their important task with a keen awareness of the value of preserving the respect for law upon which any social order must ultimately depend.

Appendix D

A SUMMARY OF THE CIVIL RIGHTS ACT OF 1964*

This summary of the 1964 Civil Rights Act was prepared in response to questions about the Act which have come to the Commission from citizens in every section of the country. It is designed to provide a clearer understanding of the major provisions of the new statute.

Some of the questions raised about any new law cannot be fully answered until the policies and programs necessary for carrying out the law have been developed by the appropriate Government agencies. Other questions will be further clarified as the courts deal with cases brought under the law.

This summary was prepared by the staff of the Commission and is available for distribution as a service under the national clearinghouse function assigned the Commission by the new Civil Rights Act.†

Title I
VOTING

The purpose of this section is to provide more effective enforcement of the right to vote in Federal elections (for President, Vice President, presidential electors or members of Congress) without regard to race or color. It also speeds up the procedure by which voting rights suits may be decided.

---

* Originally appeared as a special bulletin published by The U.S. Commission on Civil Rights, August 1964.

† The United States Commission on Civil Rights is a temporary, independent, bipartisan agency established by the Congress in 1957 to:
- Investigate complaints alleging that citizens are being deprived of their right to vote by reason of their race, color, religion, or national origin;
- Study and collect information concerning legal developments constituting a denial of equal protection of the laws under the Constitution;
- Appraise Federal laws and policies with respect to equal protection of the laws;
- Serve as a national clearinghouse for civil rights information;
- Investigate allegations of vote fraud; and
- Submit interim reports and a final and comprehensive report of its activities, findings, and recommendations to the President and the Congress.

The Act:

a. requires that the same standards be applied to all individuals seeking to register and vote;

b. forbids denial of the right to vote because of some minor mistake or omission;

c. requires that only literacy tests that are written may be used as a qualification for voting; and that the tests and answers be available on request;

d. establishes that in voting rights law suits the court must presume that anyone who completed the sixth grade is literate, unless the State can prove otherwise.

In any voting suit brought by the Government charging that there is a "pattern or practice" of voting discrimination, either the Attorney General or the defendant may ask that a three-judge Federal court be appointed to hear the case. Appeals from the decisions of such a court may be taken directly to the Supreme Court.

Title II

PUBLIC ACCOMMODATIONS

Discrimination on the basis of race, color, religion or national origin is specifically forbidden in the following places of public accommodation:

a. hotels and motels, restaurants, lunch counters, movie houses, gasoline stations, theaters and stadiums;

b. any other establishment which offers its services to patrons of the covered establishment; for example,

—a barbershop or tavern located in a hotel, or
—a department store in which there is a restaurant:

so long as the covered facilities either affect interstate commerce in their operations, or are supported in their discriminatory practices by State action.

In addition, discrimination is forbidden in any other place of public accommodation that is required to segregate by State or local laws.

330

If there are no State or local laws requiring segregation, the Federal law does not cover:

a. barbershops, beauty parlors and other service establishments unless they are located in a hotel and offer these services to hotel guests;

b. retail stores that do not serve food, or places of recreation (except as listed above) which do not serve food;

c. lodging houses, hotels or similar places which take temporary guests if they have fewer than six rooms for rent in a building occupied by the owner.

Places that are actually owned and operated as private clubs are exempted from coverage of this title except to the extent that they offer their facilities to patrons of a covered establishment, such as a country club that customarily allows guests of a hotel to use its golf course.

No person may intimidate, threaten or coerce anyone for the purpose of interfering with the rights created by this title.

The provisions of this title may be enforced in two ways:

1. By *individual action* in a civil suit filed by the persons discriminated against, or

2. By *Government action* in a civil suit filed by the Attorney General.

In public accommodations suits filed by individuals:

—the court hearing the suit may appoint a lawyer for the person bringing the complaint and exempt the complainant from the payment of certain costs;

—the court may permit the Attorney General to enter the case;

—if there is a State law or local ordinance that prohibits discrimination, the complaint must first be taken to the State or local authorities, allowing them 30 days to begin a proceeding before suit can be filed in a Federal court;

—once the case is in court, the court can postpone action until the State or local proceeding is completed;

—if there are no State or local anti-discrimination provisions, the court may refer the matter to the Community Relations Service (see Title X) so that it may seek to secure voluntary compliance within no more than 120 days.

The Attorney General may file a public accommodations suit when he believes there is a pattern or practice of resistance. As in Title I voting suits, he may request a three-judge court for this action.

In public accommodations suits brought either by individuals or the Attorney General, the court may issue temporary or permanent injunctions or restraining orders against those found to be violating the law. A person or persons failing to obey such court decrees may be punished by contempt proceedings under the jury trials provision of the law (see Title XI).

Title III

PUBLIC FACILITIES

The Attorney General is authorized to bring a civil suit to compel desegregation of any publicly-owned or operated facility whenever he receives a written complaint of discrimination. He must believe that the complaint merits action and must certify that the individual or individuals making the complaint are themselves unable to take the necessary legal action. State or municipally owned or operated parks, libraries and hospitals are among the facilities covered.

Title IV

PUBLIC EDUCATION

Under this title the U.S. Office of Education is authorized to:

a. conduct a national survey to determine the availability of equal educational opportunity;

b. provide technical assistance, upon request, to help States, political subdivisions or school districts carry out school desegregation plans;

c. arrange training institutes to prepare teachers and other school personnel to deal with desegregation problems;

d. make grants enabling school boards to employ specialists for in-service training programs.

332

In addition, the Attorney General is authorized to file civil suits seeking to compel desegregation of public schools, including public colleges.

Before filing such a suit the Attorney General must have received a signed complaint from a pupil or parent and must have determined that the complainant, according to standards set forth in the Act, is unable to bring the action. The Attorney General is also required to notify the school board and give it a reasonable period of time to correct the alleged condition before filing suit.

Title V

COMMISSION ON CIVIL RIGHTS

The life of the U.S. Commission on Civil Rights is extended until January 31, 1968. Since 1957 the Commission's functions have included investigating denials of the right to vote, studying legal developments and appraising Federal policies relating to equal protection of the laws, and making recommendations for corrective action to the President and the Congress.

Title V gives the Commission added authority to:

a. serve as a national clearinghouse for civil rights information;

b. investigate allegations of vote fraud.

Commission hearing procedures are amended to further protect the rights of individuals who may be affected by Commission proceedings.

As a national clearinghouse, the Commission will provide civil rights information in such areas as voting, housing, education, employment and the use of public facilities to Federal, State and local government agencies and officials, organizations and businesses, and the general public.

Title VI

FEDERALLY ASSISTED PROGRAMS

Under this title every Federal agency which provides financial assistance through grants, loans or contracts is required to eliminate discrimination on the grounds of race, color or national origin in these programs.

For example, this title would require the following:

a. hospitals constructed with Federal funds would have to serve all patients without regard to race, color or national origin;

b. elementary and secondary schools constructed, maintained and operated with Federal funds would have to admit children without regard to race, color or national origin;

c. State employment services financed by Federal funds would have to refer qualified job applicants for employment without discrimination;

d. schools for the deaf and the blind operated with Federal funds would have to serve the deaf and blind of any color;

e. colleges and universities receiving funds for their general operation or for the construction of special facilities, such as research centers, would have to admit students without discrimination;

f. construction contractors receiving funds under Federal public works program would have to hire employees without discrimination.

Action by a Federal agency to carry out the requirements of this title may include the terminating of programs where discrimination is taking place or refusal to grant assistance to such a program.

Each agency is required to publish rules or regulations to carry out the purposes of the title. These rules and regulations are subject to the approval of the President.

Compliance actions are subject to the following conditions:

a. notice must be given of alleged failure to comply and an opportunity for a hearing must be provided;

b. in the event assistance is to be cut off, a written report must be submitted to Congress 30 days before the cut-off date;

c. compliance action may be appealed to the courts.

Social security and veteran's benefits, and other Federal benefits distributed directly to individuals are not affected by this law.

Federal assistance in the form of insurance or guaranty—for example, FHA insured loans—are not covered by this title (however, the President's Executive Order prohibiting discrimination in Federally aided housing remains in effect).

Title VII

EQUAL EMPLOYMENT OPPORTUNITY

This title establishes a Federal right to equal opportunity in employment. It creates an Equal Employment Opportunity Commission to assist in implementing this right.

Employers, labor unions and employment agencies are required to treat all persons without regard to their race, color, religion, sex, or national origin. This treatment must be given in all phases of employment, including hiring, promotion, firing, apprenticeship and other training programs, and job assignments.

When this title goes into full effect employers will be subject to its provisions if they have 25 or more regular employees in an industry that affects interstate commerce. Generally speaking, labor unions will be subject to the Act, if they either operate a hiring hall for covered employers, or if they have 25 or more members who are employed by a covered employer. Employment agencies are also included if they regularly undertake to supply employees for a covered employer.

(Enforcement of the nondiscrimination requirements for employers and unions is postponed for one year. Employers and unions with 100 or more workers will be covered beginning July 2, 1965 and coverage will be extended each year until July 2, 1968, when employers and unions with 25 workers will be covered.)

Not covered by this title are (1) public employers, (2) bona fide private clubs, (3) educational institutions with regard to employees working in educational activities and all employment in religious educational institutions, (4) employers on or near an Indian reservation with regard to preferential treatment of Indians; and (5) religious corporations, institutions, etc., with regard to employees working in connection with religious activities.

When someone believes he has been discriminated against because of race, color, religion, sex, or national origin in any phase of job placement or employment, he may bring his complaint within 90 days to the Equal Employment Opportunity Commission or to the Attorney General.

The Commission will handle his complaint directly, unless the State or locality where the alleged discrimination occurred has fair employment laws. If so, the person complaining must allow the State or local officials no more than 120 days to resolve the matter. If there is no satisfactory conclusion within this time or if the State or locality rejects the complaint before the time is up, the complainant may then go to the Commission, which is authorized to settle valid complaints by conciliation and persuasion. Nothing said during the conciliation proceedings may be made public or used as evidence without the consent of the parties.

If the Commission fails to secure compliance within a period of no more than 60 days, the individual may take his case to a Federal court. This court may appoint an attorney and may exempt the complainant from payment of certain costs. The court, in its discretion, may allow the Attorney General to enter the case.

A worker who thinks he has been discriminated against may take his complaint directly to the Attorney General, who may bring the case before a three-judge court if he believes there is a pattern or practice of resistance to this title.

If the court in either action finds discrimination, it will order the employer, employment agency or union to take corrective action, which may include hiring or reinstating employees with or without back pay.

Title VIII

VOTING STATISTICS

The Secretary of Commerce is required to conduct a survey of persons of voting age by race, color, and national origin and to determine the extent to which such persons have registered and voted in such geographic areas as the Commission on Civil Rights recommends.

A similar survey must also be conducted on a nation-wide basis in connection with the 1970 Census. No person questioned during such surveys may be compelled to disclose his race, color, religion or national origin and everyone must be advised of his right to refuse to give this information.

336

Title IX

INTERVENTION AND REMOVAL IN CIVIL RIGHTS CASES

The Attorney General is authorized to intervene in any Federal court action seeking relief from the denial of equal protection of the laws on account of race, color, religion or national origin. If a Federal court refuses to accept a civil rights case and sends it back to a State court, this action may be reviewed on appeal.

Title X

COMMUNITY RELATIONS SERVICE

A Community Relations Service is established in the Department of Commerce to provide assistance to persons or communities requiring help with civil rights problems where discriminatory practices impair constitutional rights or affect interstate commerce. The Service is authorized to cooperate with both public and private agencies, either on its own initiative or upon request from local officials or interested persons in situations where disputes threaten peaceful relations among the citizens of a community.

In addition, the Service is authorized to seek a voluntary settlement of public accommodation complaints which may be referred to it by a Federal Court. The Act directs that all activities of the Service in providing conciliation assistance shall be conducted in confidence and without publicity.

Title XI

MISCELLANEOUS

This title gives a right to jury trial in criminal contempt cases arising out of Titles II, III, IV, V, VI and VII. Title I retains the more limited jury trial provisions of the 1957 Civil Rights Act.

Appropriations are authorized to carry out the Act, and a separability clause provides that the rest of the Act will be unaffected if any portion is invalidated. Another section preserves existing remedies under Federal law. This title also preserves the rights of the States to legislate in the same areas covered by this Act, so long as such legislation is not inconsistent with the purposes of the Act.

APPENDIX E

SUMMARY OF RIGHTS GUARANTEED BY TITLE VI OF THE 1964 ACT*

All persons in the United States shall have the right to receive any service, financial aid or other benefit under the federally-aided program regardless of their race, color or national origin.

Specific discriminatory practices prohibited include:

- *Any difference in quality, quantity or the manner in which the benefit is provided*

- *Segregation or separate treatment in any part of the program*

- *Restriction in the enjoyment of any advantages, privileges or other benefits provided to others*

- *Different standards or requirements for participation*

- *Methods of administration which would defeat or substantially impair the accomplishment of the program objectives*

- *Discrimination in any activity conducted in a facility built in whole or part with Federal funds*

- *Discrimination in any employment resulting from a program established primarily to provide employment*

All Federal offices responsible for federally-assisted programs must implement Title VI by issuing regulations approved by the President.

Any persons who believe discrimination because of race, color or national origin exists in a federally-aided program have the right to challenge such discrimination by making a complaint to the officials responsible for that program.

- *Prompt investigations will be made of complaints received.*

- *If discrimination is found, negotiation and persuasion will first be used in an effort to eliminate the prohibited practices.*

* From CIVIL RIGHTS UNDER FEDERAL PROGRAMS, originally published by the U.S. Commission on Civil Rights, CCR Special Publication Number 1, January, 1965.

- *Should these efforts fail, Federal assistance may be terminated or discontinued after a fair hearing.*

- *Other means authorized by law, including court action, may also be used to enforce nondiscrimination.*

". . . SIMPLE JUSTICE . . ."

President Lyndon B. Johnson, explaining the basic reasons underlying the principle of equality under Federal programs, stated on December 10, 1964:

> "It is simple justice that all should share in programs financed by all, and directed by the government of all the people."

Simple justice has not always governed the operation of Federal aid programs. As has been amply documented by the U.S. Commission on Civil Rights, many of our citizens, because of their race, color, or national origin, have not been free to participate equally in programs supported by Federal funds. For example, the Commission has found that in some circumstances:

- *Libraries receiving Federal aid either have not allowed Negroes to use the facilities or have subjected them to segregation or discrimination.*

- *Elementary schools built and operated with Federal aid have discriminated in the admission and treatment of students.*

- *Hospitals constructed with Federal funds either have refused to admit patients because of their race or have discriminated in their placement after admission; they also have refused to allow Negro physicians to practice there.*

- *Vocational training programs established with Federal funds have not been available to all students.*

- *Employment offices financed entirely by Federal funds have refused to refer all job applicants to available openings on a nondiscriminatory basis.*

- *Agricultural Extension Service offices operating with Federal funds have been established on a segregated basis and have provided unequal service to Negroes.*

- *Dormitories have been built with Federal grants in colleges that have discriminatory admission policies.*

- *Employers receiving business loans from the Federal Government, designed to increase employment opportunities, have discriminated in their hiring policies.*

In addition to the legal and moral grounds for correcting such discriminatory practices, there are very practical reasons for moving promptly to eliminate them from Federal programs.

A Federal grant program which is enacted for the general welfare fails in its objectives if some citizens are intentionally excluded or provided inferior service. If a program is designed to promote better health standards, it will not achieve its purpose by allowing only white persons to benefit while Negro families are denied needed medical services.

In addition to frustrating the basic objectives of a given program, discrimination denies to those who are excluded an opportunity to improve themselves. For instance, both the Negro family and the economy suffer when the family's breadwinner is denied equal opportunity to participate in a federally supported job training program.

Federal payments to State and local governments, to private institutions and businesses play an important role in financing the many educational, health, welfare and economic programs required for our continued growth and development. When any person is denied the benefits of these programs because of race, color, or national origin, the fabric of our democratic society is weakened and our progress as a Nation is retarded.

EVOLUTION OF FEDERAL POLICY

The principle of equality under Federal programs was reflected in presidential actions long before the Civil Rights Act of 1964 became law. In the past twenty years, every President of the United States has directed the elimination of discrimination in a number of Federal programs and activities. Areas covered by presidential orders include: equality of treatment in the Armed Forces; employment by the Federal Government, by Government contractors and on construction projects financed with Federal funds; and equality of opportunity in federally-aided housing.

Other actions taken through departmental regulations have prohibited discrimination in particular programs. These include the Manpower Development Training activities, teacher-training institutes, mental health and mental retardation projects, apprenticeship programs, and employment in State agencies administering certain Federal programs.

Prior to the passage of the Civil Rights Act of 1964, all of these orders and regulations depended on executive initiative which was supported by a growing body of judicial decisions. These court rulings, based on constitutional requirements, held that no person, because of race or color, could be denied the benefits of a program receiving Federal assistance. However, these presidential orders, departmental regulations, and court rulings were limited to particular Federal activities or to only parts of Federal programs. In addition, in recent years attempts made in Congress to amend specific Federal aid proposals in order to prohibit discrimination have been unsuccessful.

By adopting Title VI of the Civil Rights Act, Congress has now written into law the right of all persons to participate in and receive the benefits of *any* federally-aided program or activity without dis‹ crimination on account of race, color, or national origin. The application of Title VI to federally-assisted programs is uniform and all-inclusive.

SCOPE OF FEDERAL ASSISTANCE

Congress has enacted many programs providing Federal funds to support public and private activities in such areas as health, education, employment, individual welfare, and the economic well-being of the general society.

Many citizens are not fully aware of the nature or extent of Federal assistance provided State and local governments, private institutions, businesses and individuals. The average citizen is likely to know about Social Security, veteran's benefits, and a few other programs involving direct Federal administration. However, many significant Federal aid programs are administered at the local level by the States, localities and private institutions which share in their costs. As a result the degree of Federal support is not usually apparent.

Federal financial assistance includes grants and loans of Federal funds, donations of equipment and property, detail of Federal personnel, proceeds from Federal property, and any other arrangement by which Federal benefits are provided.

341

In all, more than 190 aid programs are sponsored in whole or in part by the Federal Government and there are many 'sub-programs' within these. Major areas of Federal involvement include:

Aids to Education
    College Facilities Construction
    College Dormitory Construction
    Research Grants and Equipment
    Surplus Materials Distribution
    National Defense Education Activities
    Impacted Areas School Construction and Assistance
    School Lunch and School Milk Programs
    Vocational Education Activities
    Economic Opportunity (Anti-Poverty) Programs
    Loans to College Students

Aids to Communities
    Accelerated Public Works
    Urban Renewal Projects
    Public Housing Projects
    Airport Construction
    Library Services and Construction
    Economic Opportunity (Anti-Poverty) Programs

Aids to Health
    Vocational Rehabilitation Grants
    Hill-Burton Hospital Construction
    Research Grants
    Nurses Training Programs
    Loans to Medical Students
    Mental Health and Retardation Programs
    Public Health Programs

Aids to Employment
    State Employment Offices
    Manpower Training Activities
    Area Redevelopment Grants and Training
    Loans to Small Businessmen
    Highway Construction Projects
    Public Works Acceleration Projects
    Other Construction (Schools, Hospitals, etc.)
    Economic Opportunity (Anti-Poverty) Programs

Aids to Welfare
Old-age Assistance Programs
Services to the Blind and Permanently Disabled
Maternity and Infant Care Projects
Child Welfare Services
Other Public Welfare Programs
Economic Opportunity (Anti-Poverty) Programs

Aids to Agriculture
Extension Services
Watershed/Flood Control
Conservation Projects
Rural Electrification
Forest Protection

In short, citizens in all walks of life derive benefits directly or indirectly, from the services and assistance provided by the Federal Government.

During the fiscal year 1963, payments by the Federal Government to public and private recipients totaled nearly $11 billion or ten percent of all Federal expenditures. Federal payments average 14% of the total revenues collected by States and localities; in some States these payments reach as high as 32% of all revenues.

TYPES OF DISCRIMINATION PROHIBITED BY TITLE VI

The effective administration of Federal programs depends on the cooperative efforts of both the Federal Government and the recipients of Federal aid. The aims of these programs cannot be fully achieved until they are equally available to all citizens. Thus it is vitally important that aid recipients and the Federal Government work closely together to eliminate segregation and discrimination in the programs for which they share responsibility.

In drafting the Civil Rights Act of 1964, Congress attempted to provide every possible means for voluntary compliance with the Act. Regulations, issued pursuant to Title VI, reflect this congressional intent by directing Federal officials to seek the cooperation of recipients and to provide guidance and assistance to help them comply voluntarily with the Act.

343

As a first step in the process of voluntary implementation of Title VI, all concerned should fully understand the types of discrimination which must now be eliminated.

In order to be eligible for assistance under Federal programs, a recipient must give assurances that NO PERSON SHALL BE EXCLUDED FROM PARTICIPATION, DENIED ANY BENEFITS, OR SUBJECTED TO DISCRIMINATION ON THE BASIS OF RACE, COLOR, OR NATIONAL ORIGIN.

Types of discrimination prohibited by Title VI are best illustrated by specific examples.

A recipient of Federal financial assistance violates his assurance to comply with Title VI if, *because of race, color, or national origin,* the recipient:

(1) denies an individual any service, financial aid or other benefit under the program;

EXAMPLES: A federally-supported State Employment Office refuses to place a qualified job applicant because of his race.

A redeveloper of land in an urban renewal project area denies an apartment or office space to an applicant because of his race, color or national origin.

A National Guard Unit refuses to accept a volunteer because of his race, color, or national origin.

(2) provides an individual with a service, financial aid or other benefit which is different, or is provided in a different manner from that which is provided to others under the program;

EXAMPLES: An Agricultural Extension Agent encourages and teaches white farmers, but not Negro farmers, to grow a variety of crops to increase their income.

A library receiving Federal aid requires some readers, because of race, to request books through a branch librarian rather than allowing the direct access available to others.

(3) subjects an individual to segregation or separate treatment in any matter related to his receipt of any service, financial aid, or other benefit under the program;

344

EXAMPLES: A federally-aided State Employment Office, Agricultural Extension Service Office, or airport maintains racially separate waiting rooms.

The aided program assigns employees of a certain race or color to serve only persons of the same race or color or to process job applications only from such persons.

(4) restricts an individual in any way in the enjoyment of services, facilities, or any other advantage, privilege, or benefit provided to others under the program;

EXAMPLES: A federally-aided college admits students of a particular race but discourages their attendance at sports events and other college gatherings.

An aided hospital admits all patients but discourages use of the recreation room or specifies certain hours for use to patients of one race.

(5) treats an individual differently in determining whether he satisfies any admission, enrollment, quota, eligibility, membership, or other requirement or condition which is a prerequisite to the service, financial aid or other benefit provided under the program;

EXAMPLES: A federally-aided hospital refuses to permit doctors of a particular race to practice in the hospital because such doctors are not members of a medical association which discriminates.

A State Employment Office refuses to send a Negro applicant to fill a job request because he is not enrolled in an apprenticeship program which discriminates against Negroes.

(6) uses any criteria or methods of administration which would defeat or substantially impair accomplishment of the program's objectives for individuals of a particular race, color, or national origin, or which would subject such individuals to discrimination;

EXAMPLES: In selecting or approving projects or sites for the construction of public libraries which will receive Federal assistance, a State agency uses standards which will have the effect of limiting use of the facilities by members of a particular race.

345

In a district where students are assigned to schools on the basis of their race, free and reduced-price lunches are not provided on an equitable basis.

(7) discriminates against an individual in any program or activity which is conducted in a facility constructed in whole or in part with Federal funds;

EXAMPLES: A hospital constructed or improved with Federal funds segregates patients by race or discriminates in the selection of interns or student nurses. A hospital caring for indigent patients under contract with a welfare agency that receives Federal funds discriminates in like manner.

A federally-aided public housing authority either excludes tenants from a project or segregates them within a project because of their race, color, or national origin.

(8) subjects an individual to discriminatory employment practices under any Federal program or activity whose primary objective is to provide employment;

EXAMPLE: Employers receiving Area Redevelopment loans hire on a discriminatory basis.

The above illustrations do not reflect the full scope of possible discriminatory practices. Nor do they include all the programs which are subject to Title VI. Whatever the federally-aided programs may be and whatever form the discrimination may take, the language of Title VI and the intent of Congress is to assure to every individual equal opportunity and access to Federal benefits.

It should be noted that if the *final* Federal payment for a project was made to a recipient *before* applicable Title VI regulations went into effect, the recipient is not covered by Title VI for that particular project. On the other hand, *after* applicable Title VI regulations went into effect, all Federal aid recipients had to agree to comply with these regulations in order to receive or to continue to receive Federal assistance.

EXAMPLE: A hospital received approval in 1963 for Federal funds to pay part of the cost of a new addition and Federal installment payments were still forthcoming when Title VI regulations became effective. As a condition to receipt of

346

these additional installment payments, the hospital must agree to administer the entire facility in accordance with Title VI nondiscriminatory requirements.

COMPLIANCE UNDER TITLE VI

Title VI regulations provide the necessary framework for protecting the rights guaranteed to the recipients and to the ultimate beneficiaries under federally-aided programs. Compliance will first be sought by affirmative and voluntary means whenever possible. But in addition, provision is made for complaints, field reviews, investigations, informal adjustments, and, when necessary, more formal proceedings.

1. AFFIRMATIVE MEASURES

Recipients of Federal aid are to be given guidance and assistance to help them comply voluntarily with Title VI regulations. In public and private meetings and in instructions which accompany required nondiscrimination agreements, Federal aid recipients are to be assisted in making the changes necessary to bring their operations into compliance with Title VI.

2. COMPLIANCE REPORTS

Records and other information designed to show the extent of compliance with Title VI agreements must be maintained by recipients and reports sent to program administrators on a regular basis. A recipient is also required to inform the ultimate beneficiaries, participants and other interested persons of the provisions of Title VI regulations and of their applicability to the aid program.

3. PERIODIC FIELD REVIEWS

Reviews by designated officials are to be conducted on a scheduled basis to ensure compliance by aid recipients. Compliance reports, books, and other records may be reviewed during these regular field visits.

4. COMPLAINTS

An individual or organization may challenge any unlawful discriminatory practice in a Federal program or activity. All complaints must be filed with the appropriate Federal agency and should include sufficient information to serve as the basis for an investigation.

5. INVESTIGATION AND ADJUSTMENT

When a field review, complaint, or any other information indicates a possible violation of Title VI, an investigation is ordered. If any violation of the regulations is found, informal persuasion and conciliation will be used to secure the elimination of the prohibited discriminatory practices. During this entire process, names of complainants will be kept confidential to the extent possible.

No recipient or other person may intimidate, threaten, coerce, or discriminate against any individual because he has made a complaint, testified, or assisted in a Title VI investigation, proceeding or hearing.

6. FORMAL ENFORCEMENT PROCEEDINGS

If informal efforts at persuasion have failed to correct the situation, formal means for resolving violations of Title VI regulations are available.

a. Termination of Funds

Title VI authorizes "the termination of or refusal to grant or continue assistance" under any Federal program in which there has been a violation of nondiscrimination requirements. This action may be taken only after:

> (1) the recipient has been given an opportunity for a fair hearing and a finding is made that Title VI has been violated, and

> (2) appropriate congressional committees have been notified 30 days before any termination of assistance.

A recipient may seek judicial review of the final order issued by the agency.

b. Other Formal Actions Authorized by Law

Rather than follow internal administrative proceedings, an agency may take other formal actions authorized by law, including:

> (1) Referral to the Department of Justice for appropriate legal action.

> If there is a formal contract with a nondiscrimination agreement between the Government and the recipient, the appro-

348

priate legal action may be a civil suit to enforce the agreement or to invoke any other contractual remedies.

If the recipient is a public institution, such as a public hospital or a public school, the appropriate legal action may be a civil rights suit to secure a court order barring the unlawful practices under Title III or IV, respectively, of the 1964 Civil Rights Act.

(2) Referral to State or local authorities responsible for enforcing similar nondiscrimination standards.

When a recipient's violation of Title VI involves discriminatory employment practices, the case may be referred to a State or local Fair Employment Practices Commission or comparable body.

7. LIMITATIONS ON COMPLIANCE PROCEEDINGS

Compliance proceedings may only be directed against 'recipients' of Federal aid who are conducting a program for the benefit of others. A 'recipient' does not include the individual who ultimately receives the service, financial aid or other benefit under the program.

A farmer receiving Federal aid is not required to adopt nondiscriminatory policies in the operation of his farm.

An individual receiving unemployment insurance is likewise not a recipient. However, the State unemployment insurance office is a 'recipient' of Federal aid and must not discriminate against applicants for assistance.

In addition, any compliance activities must be limited to:

a. the particular recipient found to be in violation of Title VI; and

b. the particular program or activity in which noncompliance is found.

WHEN TITLE VI DOES NOT APPLY

The statutory language in Title VI specifically excludes programs involving "a contract of insurance or guaranty." Activities such as the FHA home mortgage insurance program are thereby excluded. However, Executive Order 11063, which prohibits discrimination in all Federal housing programs, continues in full force and effect.

CONCLUSION

The administration of Federal grant-in-aid programs over the years has been marked by a high degree of cooperation among the Federal, State and local agencies and private institutions involved.

Title VI of the Civil Rights Act of 1964 affords an additional opportunity for these agencies and institutions to improve the administration and efficiency of cooperative programs. The President expressed confidence in the future when he signed the first set of Title VI regulations on December 4, 1964:

> "The broad and encouraging compliance with the Public Accommodations Title of the Civil Rights Act has demonstrated the overwhelming desire of the people of this Nation to accept and to comply with the law of the land. I am confident that the provisions of the Civil Rights Act to be implemented by these regulations will be received in the same spirit of acceptance and cooperation."

TITLE VI—NONDISCRIMINATION IN FEDERALLY-ASSISTED PROGRAMS

Sec. 601. No person in the United States shall, on the ground of race, color, or national origin, be excluded from participation in, be denied the benefits of, or be subjected to discrimination under any program or activity receiving Federal financial assistance.

Sec. 602. Each Federal department and agency which is empowered to extend Federal financial assistance to any program or activity, by way of grant, loan, or contract other than a contract of insurance or guaranty, is authorized and directed to effectuate the provisions of section 601 with respect to such program or activity by issuing rules, regulations, or orders of general applicability which shall be consistent with achievement of the objectives of the statute authorizing the financial assistance in connection with which the action is taken. No such rule, regulation, or order shall become effective unless and until approved by the President. Compliance with any requirement adopted pursuant to this section may be effected (1) by the termination of or refusal to grant or to continue assistance under such program or activity to any recipient as to whom there has been

350

an express finding on the record, after opportunity for hearing, of a failure to comply with such requirement, but such termination or refusal shall be limited to the particular political entity, or part thereof, or other recipient as to whom such a finding has been made and, shall be limited in its effect to the particular program, or part thereof, in which such noncompliance has been so found, or (2) by any other means authorized by law: Provided, however, That no such action shall be taken until the department or agency concerned has advised the appropriate person or persons of the failure to comply with the requirement and has determined that compliance cannot be secured by voluntary means. In the case of any action terminating, or refusing to grant or continue, assistance because of failure to comply with a requirement imposed pursuant to this section, the head of the Federal department or agency shall file with the committees of the House and Senate having legislative jurisdiction over the program or activity involved a full written report of the circumstances and the grounds for such action. No such action shall become effective until thirty days have elapsed after the filing of such report.

Sec. 603. Any department or agency action taken pursuant to section 602 shall be subject to such judicial review as may otherwise be provided by law for similar action taken by such department or agency on other grounds. In the case of action, not otherwise subject to judicial review, terminating or refusing to grant or to continue financial assistance upon a finding of failure to comply with any requirement imposed pursuant to section 602, any person aggrieved (including any State or political subdivision thereof and any agency of either) may obtain judicial review of such action in accordance with section 10 of the Administrative Procedure Act, and such action shall not be deemed committed to unreviewable agency discretion within the meaning of that section.

Sec. 604. Nothing contained in this title shall be construed to authorize action under this title by any department or agency with respect to any employment practice of any employer, employment agency, or labor organization except where a primary objective of the Federal financial assistance is to provide employment.

Sec. 605. Nothing in this title shall add to or detract from any existing authority with respect to any program or activity under which Federal financial assistance is extended by way of a contract of insurance or guaranty.

APPENDIX F

Summary of

THE VOTING RIGHTS ACT OF 1965*

VOTING RIGHTS ACT OF 1965

signed by the
President of the United States
on August 6, 1965

- Suspends literacy tests and other devices (found to be discriminatory) as qualifications for voting in any Federal, State, local, general or primary election in the States of Alabama, Alaska, Georgia, Louisiana, Mississippi, South Carolina, Virginia and at least 26 counties in North Carolina.**

- Provides for the assignment of Federal examiners to conduct registration and observe voting in States and/or counties covered by the Act.

- Directs the U.S. Attorney General to initiate suits immediately to test the constitutionality of poll taxes because the U.S. Congress found that the payment of such tax has been used in some areas to abridge the right to vote.

- Extends civil and criminal protection to qualified persons seeking to vote and to those who urge or aid others to vote.

The Voting Rights Act of 1965 is the fourth bill to be enacted by the U.S. Congress since 1957 that attempts to safeguard the right of every citizen to vote, regardless of his race or color. The previous three legislative measures attempted to secure the right to vote through court cases initiated largely on a case-by-case, county-by-county basis. These cases, brought either by the U.S. Attorney General or an individual, did not adequately meet the dimensions of the problems of racial discrimination in voting.

The 1965 Act provides new tools to assure the right to vote and supplements the previous authority granted by the Civil Rights Acts

---

* From CCR Special Publication Number 4, United States Commission on Civil Rights, August, 1965.

** ED. NOTE: This and other key portions of the Act have now been held constitutional by the Supreme Court. *State of South Carolina* v. *Katzenbach*, 86 S. Ct. 803 (1966).

of 1957, 1960 and 1964. It is intended primarily to enforce the Fifteenth Amendment to the Constitution of the United States which provides in Section 1:

> "The right of citizens of the United States to vote shall not be denied or abridged by the United States or by any State on account of race, color, or previous condition of servitude."

The law has two central features:

1. Provision for suspending a variety of tests and devices that have been used to deny citizens the right to vote because of their race or color.

2. Provision for the appointment of Federal examiners to list voters in those areas where tests and devices have been suspended.

In this Act, the term "voting" includes all action necessary—from the time of registration to the actual counting of the votes—to make a vote for public or party office effective.

VOTER REQUIREMENTS OUTLAWED BY THIS ACT

No State or political subdivision (counties, municipalities and parishes) covered by the Voting Rights Act may require the use of any test or device as a prerequisite for registration or voting.

Tests or devices included in this Act are those which require:

1. A demonstration of the ability to read, write, understand or interpret any given material.

2. A demonstration of any educational achievement or knowledge of any particular subject.

3. Proof of good moral character.

4. Proof of qualifications through a procedure in which another person (such as an individual already registered) must vouch for the prospective voter.

353

COVERAGE

The Voting Rights Act of 1965 states that no person shall be denied the right to vote in any Federal, State or local election (including primaries) for failure to pass a test if he lives in a State or political subdivision which:

1. Maintained a test or device as a prerequisite to registration or voting as of November 1, 1964

and

2. Had a total voting age population of which less than 50 percent were registered or actually voted in the 1964 Presidential election.

If the above two factors are present, the State or political subdivision is automatically covered by the 1965 Act. If an entire State meets these qualifications, all of its counties come under the provisions of the Act. If only one county in a State meets them, the single county is subject to the requirements of the law.

States covered by the Act include Alabama, Alaska, Georgia, Louisiana, Mississippi, South Carolina, Virginia, and approximately 26 counties in North Carolina.

CESSATION OF COVERAGE

A State or political subdivision may be removed from coverage by filing a suit in a three-judge District Court for the District of Columbia. The State or political subdivision must convince the court that no test or device has been used for the purpose or with the effect of denying the right to vote because of race or color during the five years preceding the filing of the suit.

However, if there has been a previous court judgment against a State or political subdivision determining that tests or devices have been used to deny the right to vote, the State or political subdivision must wait five years before it can obtain an order from the District Court for the District of Columbia removing it from the coverage of the Act.

A judgment may be obtained more quickly if the Attorney General advises the court that he believes that the tests have not been used to discriminate on the basis of race or color during the five years preceding the filing of the action. He may also ask the court to reconsider its decision anytime within five years after judgment.

CHANGES IN VOTING LAWS

When a State or political subdivision covered by the Act seeks to change its voting qualifications or procedures from those in effect on November 1, 1964, it must either obtain the approval of the U.S. Attorney General or initiate a Federal Court suit. If the Attorney General objects to these changes, or if they have not been submitted to him for his approval, the new laws may not be enforced until the District Court for the District of Columbia rules that the changes will not have the purpose or the effect of denying the right to vote because of the race or color of any person.

FEDERAL EXAMINERS

Once it is determined that a political subdivision is covered by the Act, the U.S. Attorney General may direct the U.S. Civil Service Commission to appoint Federal examiners to list voters if:

1. He has received twenty meritorious written complaints alleging voter discrimination, *or*
2. He believes that the appointment of examiners is necessary to enforce the guarantees of the Fifteenth Amendment.

The times, places and procedures for listing will be established by the Civil Service Commission.

AUTHORITY OF THE EXAMINERS

The Federal examiners will list (that is, declare eligible and entitled to vote) those who satisfy state qualifications that have not been suspended by the Voting Rights Act. Examples of valid qualifications would be those of age and residence.

The examiners will prepare a list of qualified voters and send the list each month to State authorities who must register them—that is, place their names in the official voting records. This list must be available for public inspection. Each person on the examiner's list will be issued a certificate by the examiners as evidence of eligibility to vote in any Federal, State or local election.

No person listed by the examiner will be entitled to vote in any election unless his name has been sent to local election officials at least 45 days before that election thereby allowing the State election machinery to run without complication.

ENFORCEMENT OF ACTION BY FEDERAL EXAMINERS

At the request of the Attorney General the Civil Service Commission may appoint poll watchers in counties where Federal Examiners are already serving to observe whether all eligible persons are allowed to vote and whether all ballots are accurately tabulated.

If anyone who is properly listed or registered is not permitted to vote in any political subdivision where examiners are serving, a complaint may be made to the examiners of this denial within 48 hours after the polls close. If the examiner believes that the complaint has merit, he must inform the Attorney General immediately. The Attorney General may seek a district court order that provides for the casting of the ballot and suspends the election results until the vote is included in the final count.

CHALLENGE OF LISTED PERSONS

A formal objection challenging the qualifications of a person listed by the Federal examiner may be filed (at a place to be designated by the Civil Service Commission) within ten days after the list of qualified voters has been made public and must be supported by at least two affidavits. The validity of the challenge will be determined within fifteen days after filing by a hearing officer appointed by the Civil Service Commission. The U.S. Court of Appeals may review decisions of the hearing officer.

Until the final court review is completed, any person listed by the examiner is still eligible and must be permitted to vote. If a challenge is successful, the name of the registrant will be removed from the examiner's list.

WITHDRAWAL OF FEDERAL EXAMINERS

Examiners may be withdrawn from a political subdivision when the names of all persons listed by the examiners have been placed in the official records and when there is no reason to believe that persons in the subdivision will be prevented from voting.

The removal may be accomplished by action of:

1. The Civil Service Commission after it receives notification from the U.S. Attorney General, or

2. The District Court for the District of Columbia in a suit brought by a political subdivision after the Director of the Census has determined that more than 50 percent of the nonwhite voting age population in the subdivision is registered to vote.

A political subdivision may petition the U.S. Attorney General to end listing procedures and to request that the Director of the Census conduct a survey to determine whether more than 50 percent of the nonwhite voting age population is registered.

POLL TAXES

The Act contains a Congressional finding that the right to vote has been denied or abridged by the requirement of the payment of a poll tax as a condition to voting.

The U.S. Attorney General is directed to institute suits against Alabama, Mississippi, Texas and Virginia which require the payment of poll taxes in order to determine if such taxes violate the Constitution.* While a suit is pending, or upon a finding that the poll tax is constitutional, persons registered or listed for the first time in areas covered by the Act need only pay the tax for the current year. The poll tax may be paid up to 45 days prior to an election regardless of the timeliness of the payment under State law.

VOTING SUITS

The Voting Rights Act of 1965 gives new enforcement powers to the courts in voting cases. When the court finds that there has been a denial of the right to vote in a suit brought by the U.S. Attorney General, the court must:

1. Authorize the appointment of examiners by the Civil Service Commission unless denials of the right to vote have been few in number, they have been corrected by State or local action, and there is no probability that they will reoccur.

---

* ED. NOTE: At the suit of Virginia residents, the Supreme Court subsequently held Virginia's poll tax unconstitutional. *Harper* v. *Virginia State Board of Elections,* 86 S. Ct. 1079 (1966).

2. Suspend the use of tests or devices in an area where it has been proved that at least one such requirement has been utilized to deny the right to vote because of race or color.

When examiners have been authorized by court order, they may be removed by an order of the authorizing court.

LANGUAGE LITERACY

If a person residing in a State where tests or devices have not been suspended has completed at least six grades in an "American-flag" school (a school in the United States or its territories), his inability to speak the English language shall not be the basis for denying him the right to vote. For example, a person who completed six grades of school in the Commonwealth of Puerto Rico but who now resides on the mainland of the United States would satisfy literacy requirements.

CRIMINAL AND CIVIL PENALTIES

Public officials or private individuals who deny persons the right to vote guaranteed by the Voting Rights Act of 1965 or anyone who attempts to or intimidates, threatens, or coerces a person from voting are subject to criminal penalties. It is also made a crime to attempt to or to intimidate, threaten or coerce anyone who urges or aids any person to vote. Criminal penalties are provided for applicants who give false information about their eligibility to vote or who accept payment to register or vote in a Federal election. The U.S. Attorney General is also authorized to bring action for injunctive relief to restrain violations of the Act.

APPENDIX G

SUMMING-UP OF McCONE COMMISSION REPORT ON THE LOS ANGELES (WATTS) RIOTS OF AUGUST 1965*

The study of the Los Angeles riots which we have now completed brought us face to face with the deepening problems that confront America. They are the problems of transition created by three decades of change during which the historical pattern of urban and rural life—which for decades before existed side by side, each complementing and supporting the other—has been violently and irreversibly altered. Modern methods and mechanization of the farm have dramatically, and, in some regards, sadly reduced the need for the farm hand. With this, a drift to the city was the inevitable and necessary result. With respect to the Negro, the drift was first to the urban centers of the South and then, because scanty means of livelihood existed there, on northward and westward to the larger metropolitan centers. It was not the Negro alone who drifted; a substantial part of the entire farm labor force, white and Negro alike, was forced to move and did.

World War II and, to a lesser extent, the Korean War of the early '50's, tended to accelerate the movement, particularly the drift of the Negro from the south to the north. Because job opportunities existed in the war plants located in our cities, the deep and provocative problem created by the movement was not at first appreciated by society. Since then, caught up in almost a decade of struggle with civil rights and its related problems, most of America focused its attention upon the problem of the South—and only a few turned their attention and thoughts to the explosive situation of our cities.

But the conditions of life in the urban north and west were sadly disappointing to the rural newcomer, particularly the Negro. Totally untrained, he was qualified only for jobs calling for the lesser skills and these he secured and held onto with great difficulty. Even the

---

* The report, entitled "Violence in The City—An End or a Beginning", was submitted December 2, 1965. We reproduce here its final section, "A Summing Up—The Need For Leadership". The Commission, appointed by California Governor Edmund G. Brown, was headed by John A. McCone, former Director of the Central Intelligence Agency, Chairman. Its other members were Judge Earl S. Broady, Asa V. Call, Very Rev. Charles S. Cassasa, Warren M. Christopher, (Vice Chairman), Rev. James Edward Jones, Dr. Sherman M. Mellinkoff, and Mrs. Robert G. Neumann.

jobs he found in the city soon began to disappear as the mechanization of industry took over, as it has since the war, and wiped out one task after another—the only tasks the untrained Negro was equipped to fill.

Hence, equality of opportunity, a privilege he sought and expected, proved more of an illusion than a fact. The Negro found that he entered the competitive life of the city with very real handicaps: he lacked education, training, and experience, and his handicaps were aggravated by racial barriers which were more traditional than legal. He found himself, for reasons for which he had no responsibility and over which he had no control, in a situation in which providing a livelihood for himself and his family was most difficult and at times desperate. Thus, with the passage of time, altogether too often the rural Negro who has come to the city sinks into despair. And many of the younger generation, coming on in great numbers, inherit this feeling but seek release, not in apathy, but in ways which, if allowed to run unchecked, offer nothing but tragedy to America.

Realizing this, our Commission has made, in this report, many costly and extreme recommendations. We make them because we are convinced the Negro can no longer exist, as he has, with the disadvantages which separate him from the rest of society, deprive him of employment, and cause him to drift aimlessly through life.

This, we feel, represents a crisis in our country. In this report, we describe the reasons and recommend remedies, such as establishment of a special school program, creation of training courses, and correction of misunderstandings involving law enforcement. Yet to do all of these things and spend the sums involved will all be for naught unless the conscience of the community, the white and the Negro community together, directs a new and, we believe, revolutionary attitude towards the problems of our city.

This demands a form of leadership that we have not found. The time for bitter recriminations is past. It must be replaced by thoughtful efforts on the part of all to solve the deepening problems that threaten the foundations of our society.

Government. Government authorities have done much and have been generous in their efforts to help the Negro find his place in our society and in our economy. But what has been done is but a beginning and sadly has not always reached those for whom it was intended in time and in a meaningful way. Programs must not be oversold and exaggerated, on the one hand, or unnecessarily delayed on the other. What we urge is a submersion of personal ambition either political or bureaucratic, in the interest of doing the most good and creating the best results from each and every dollar spent in existing programs.

With particular respect to the City of Los Angeles, we urge the immediate creation of a City Human Relations Commission, endowed with clear-cut responsibility, properly staffed and adequately funded. We envisage a commission composed of a chairman and six members with special competence in the fields of research, employment, housing, education, law, youth problems and community organizations. This City Commission should develop comprehensive educational programs designed to enlist the cooperation of all groups, both public and private, in eliminating prejudice and discrimination in employment, housing, education, and public accommodations.

Business and Labor. Business leaders have their indispensable role. No longer can the leaders of business discharge their responsibility by merely approving a broadly worded executive order establishing a policy of non-discrimination and equality of opportunity as a basic directive to their managers and personnel departments. They must insist that these policies are carried out and they must keep records to see that they are. Also, they must authorize the necessary facilities for employment and training, properly designed to encourage the employment of Negroes and Mexican-Americans, rather than follow a course which all too often appears to place almost insurmountable hurdles in the path of the Negro or Mexican-American seeking a job. Directly and through the Chamber of Commerce, the Merchants and Manufacturers Association, and other associations, the business leader can play a most important role in helping to solve the crisis in our cities.

Labor unions have their very vital role. Union leaders must be resolute in their determination to eliminate discrimination and provide equality of opportunity for all within spheres of their jurisdiction and influence. For one reason or another, the records of the ethnic mix of the membership of many unions have not been furnished despite our repeated requests. In labor, as in business, pronouncements of policy, however well intended, are not enough. Unless a union conducts its affairs on a basis of absolute equality of opportunity and non-discrimination, we believe there is reason to question its eligibility to represent employees at the bargaining table.

News Media. The press, television, and radio can play their part. Good reporting of constructive efforts in the field of race relations will be a major service to the community. We urge all media to report equally the good and the bad—the accomplishments of Negroes as well as the failures; the assistance offered to Negroes by the public and private sectors as well as the rejections.

In our study of the chronology of the riots, we gave considerable attention to the reporting of inflammatory incidents which occurred in the initial stage of the Los Angeles riots. It is understandably easy to report the dramatic and ignore the constructive; yet the highest traditions of a free press involve responsibility as well as drama. We urge that members of all media meet and consider whether there might be wisdom in the establishment of guide lines, completely voluntary on their part, for reporting of such disasters. Without restricting their essential role of carrying the news to the public fairly and accurately, we believe news media may be able to find a voluntary basis for exercising restraint and prudence in reporting inflammatory incidents. This has been done successfully elsewhere.

The Negro and the Leader. Finally, we come to the role of the Negro leader and his responsibility to his own people and to the community in which he lives. The signing of the Voting Rights Act by President Johnson in the spring of 1965 climaxed a long and bitter fight over civil rights. To be sure, the civil rights controversy has never been the issue in our community that it has been in the South. However, the accusations of the leaders of the national movement have been picked up by many local voices and have been echoed throughout the Negro community here. As we have said in the opening chapter of this report, the angry exhortations and the resulting disobedience to law in many parts of our nation appear to have contributed importantly to the feeling of rage which made the Los Angeles riots possible. Although the Commission received much thoughtful and constructive testimony from Negro witnesses, we also heard statements of the most extreme and emotional nature. For the most part, our study fails to support—indeed the evidence disproves—

362

most of the statements made by the extremists. We firmly believe that progress towards ameliorating the current wrongs is difficult in an atmosphere pervaded by these extreme statements.

If the recommendations we make are to succeed, the constructive assistance of all Negro leaders is absolutely essential. No amount of money, no amount of effort, no amount of training will raise the disadvantaged Negro to the position he seeks and should have within this community—a position of equality—unless he himself shoulders a full share of the responsibility for his own well-being. The efforts of the Negro leaders, and there are many able and dedicated ones among us, should be directed toward urging and exhorting their followers to this end.*

The Commission recognizes that much of what it has to say about causes and remedies is not new, although it is backed by fresh additional evidence coming out of the investigation of the Los Angeles riots. At the same time, the Commission believes that there is an urgency in solving the problems, old or new, and that all Americans, whatever their color, must become aware of this urgency. Among the many steps which should be taken to improve the present situation, the Commission affirms again that the three fundamental issues in the urban problems of disadvantaged minorities are: employment, education and police-community relations. Accordingly, the Commission looks upon its recommendations in these three areas as the heart of its plea and the City's best hope.

As we have said earlier in this report, there is no immediate remedy for the problems of the Negro and other disadvantaged in our community. The problems are deep and the remedies are costly and will take time. However, through the implementation of the programs we propose, with the dedication we discuss, and with the leadership we call for from all, our Commission states without dissent, that the tragic violence that occurred during the six days of August will not be repeated.

Comments of The Rev. James Edward Jones

1. There is the observation at the top of page 71† that the generosity of California welfare programs encourage heavy immigration

---

* A comment regarding this by the Rev. James Edward Jones is set forth *infra.*
† In the full report, not here reproduced [ED. NOTE].

of disadvantaged peoples to the Los Angeles area. I have been unable to find statistics to justify this statement and violently disagree with this unjustifiable projection. The report has also stated that Negroes like other disadvantaged peoples have come to Los Angeles to seek the better opportunities offered in an urban area. Welfare programs discourage immigration to receive public assistance because new arrivals cannot qualify for aid with less than one year of residence. Have other immigrants come to Los Angeles to get on welfare rolls or rather to find job opportunities? I am sure that statistics bear out my observation rather than that which appears in the report.

2. I do not believe it is the function of this Commission to put a lid on protest registered by those sweltering in ghettos of the urban areas of our country. We speak of the malaise in our cities and in our society in general. We also recognize in our report that "The Negro found that he entered the competitive life of the city with very real handicaps: he lacked education, training, and experience, and his handicaps were aggravated by racial barriers which were more traditional than legal. He found himself, for reasons for which he had no responsibility and over which he had no control, in a situation in which providing a livelihood for himself and his family was most difficult and at times desperate. Thus, with the passage of time, altogether too often the rural Negro who has come to the city sinks into despair." Yet the report concludes that all of the ameliorating efforts—such as education and other governmental programs—will be of no avail unless he helps himself. It is true that you cannot make a musician out of a child who is unwilling to learn, even though you provide the best teachers and the best instruments. But it must be remembered in dealing with the member of a disadvantaged minority who has never heard music or seen a musical instrument that he must be motivated to help himself. Therefore, he has a right to protest when circumstances do not allow him to participate in the mainstream of American society. Protest against forces which reduce individuals to second-class citizens, political, cultural, and psychological nonentities, are part of the celebrated American tradition. As long as an individual "stands outside looking in" he is not part of that society; that society cannot say that he does not have a right to protest, nor can it say that he must shoulder a responsibility which he has never been given an opportunity to assume.

Practising Law Institute acknowledges with thanks the co-operation of Sorg Printing Company in setting the type for this volume.